Moral Development and the Social Environment

PRECEDENT STUDIES IN ETHICS AND THE MORAL SCIENCES

Moral Development and the Social Environment

Studies in the Philosophy
and Psychology of Moral Judgment and Education

Edited by

Georg Lind, Hans A. Hartmann, and Roland Wakenhut

General Editor and Translator
Thomas E. Wren

Precedent Publishing, Inc.
Chicago, Illinois

Precedent Publishing, Inc.
737 North LaSalle Street
Chicago, Illinois 60610
Copyright © 1985 by Precedent Publishing, Inc.
Printed in the United States of America
All Rights Reserved
Distributed by Transaction Books, New Brunswick (USA) and
    Oxford (UK)

Library of Congress Cataloging in Publication Data

Main entry under title:

Moralisches Urteilen und soziale Umwelt. English
    Moral Development and the Social Environment.

    Rev. translation of: Moralisches Urteilen und soziale Umwelt.
    Bibliography: p.
    Includes index.
    1. Ethics – Addresses, essays, lectures. 2. Moral develop-
ment – Addresses, essays, lectures. I. Lind, Georg, 1947– . II. Hartmann, Hans A. III. Wakenhut, Roland.
BJ1114.M6613 1985   153.46   85-19293

ISBN 0-913750-27-1

Precedent Studies in Ethics and the Moral Sciences

The term "moral sciences," which is the rubric for the present series, originated with John Stuart Mill, who used it to cover what are now called the social and behavioral sciences. Accordingly, the Precedent Studies in Ethics and the Moral Sciences have as a general subject matter the rich and problematic interspace between philosophical ethics and such empirical but person- and society-oriented disciplines as developmental psychology, sociology, and anthropology, to cite a few of the more salient "moral sciences."

The present volume is about moral judgment, especially its exercise in selected social settings such as the university. Because of this focus, as well as its simultaneous deployment of empiricial techniques and philosophical arguments, it vividly instantiates the term "moral sciences" as well as the term *Geisteswissenschaften*, which was coined in Germany as a counterpart to Mill's term. The contributors to this volume are all German or German-speaking psychologists, sociologists, and philosophers of morality, most of whom have collaborated on long-ranged research projects in Europe involving university socialization. Taken singly as well as in combination, their essays make it clear that the study of morality is an empirical as well as a conceptual task, one that involves data collection, statistical analysis, and the formulation and testing of hypotheses. It may be unreasonable to expect moral philosophers to assume the responsibility for such empirical inquiries in addition to their own theoretical pursuits, but it is not unreasonable to expect them to take a keen interest in the outcomes. For instance, the very question of whether moral cognition admits of *measurement* is a philosophical as well as scientific issue, the answer to which is to a large extent dependent on the de facto success or failure of the methodologies described in the following pages. Whether moral reasoning has a content-specific domain, whether its structures transcend specific issues of justice, obedience, etc. – these and similar questions suggest that moral philosophers and "moral scientists" have much to say to each other. This volume not only exemplifies that conversation but also makes an important contribution to it.

Thomas E. Wren
General Editor

Contents

Theory and Methods

Moral Judgment and Its Social Milieu

Philosophical Epilogue: Phylogeny and Ontogeny

Preface to the English Edition

The contributors to this volume represent diverse disciplines, but they have as their common concern the topic announced in the book's title: the relation and the interaction of individual or group-specific *moral development* on the one hand, and the *social milieu* on the other. Although deeply involved in empirical research, the authors maintain that research on moral development can be pursued properly only in conjunction with a well-formulated theory of the relationship between society, cognition, and behavior.

Readers not familiar with recent developments in the German-language literature on social philosophy and psychology, both its theoretical side and its application to educational contexts, will find this book a useful introduction to the increasingly important scene of German social theory as well as a stimulating discussion of the issues themselves. Its original impetus was a series of extensive and still on-going research projects in West Germany and Switzerland, concerning the process of moral development in social institutions such as schools, universities, and the military. In their various essays the authors all return to the same theme: the ability to formulate genuine and coherent moral judgments reflects social conditions at two levels, that of individual socialization and that of the historical development of the social system.

The book's fusion of developmental psychology, sociology, and social psychology is a distinctly German phenomenon, which in the present volume is related directly to the work of Jean Piaget of Switzerland and, more recently, Lawrence Kohlberg of the United States, who has written the foreword to the much-revised English edition of the book. The authors are not uncritical of these two figures, and are especially concerned to correct the imbalances which they perceive in Kohlberg's work between cognition and affect, as well as between the structures and contents of moral judgment. They are all deeply influenced by the cognitive-developmental tradition.

The first of the three major sections of the book deals explicitly with theoretical and methodological questions. *Jürgen Habermas,* who is one of Kohlberg's most important dialogue partners in Europe, comments on the theory of cognitive moral development from the viewpoint of his own theory of communicative action. His essay (ch. 1), which is part of a larger work on moral psychology, focuses on four questions that are central for the present discussion of Kohlberg's theory: (1) the question about the status of the postconventional stages, (2) doubts about the adequacy of a normative reference point in the face of the empirical regression phenomenon, (3) the problem of fitting relativists and value skeptics into the stage model, and (4) the necessity of including psychodynamic aspects of judgment formation within the structural theory of moral development. *Georg Lind* (ch. 2) attempts to assess Kohlberg's theory from a socio-psychologial perspective. Regarding the history of psychology, he says that cognitive developmental theory meant a shift from the "external effect" to the "internal structure" model of psychological functioning. From a review of the literature and from his own research he concludes that Kohlberg's theory of moral cognitive development has enriched social psychology with new and psychologically meaningful data and, at the same time, with empirical hypotheses that are *gehaltvoll* (informative) and empirically valid. However, Lind proposes three broad revisions in the theory: (1) it should be made clear that affect and cognition are analytically clearly distinct but ontologically inseparable aspects of moral judgment behavior; (2) accordingly, moral development should be viewed as a "two-sided" process of change in affects and in the structure of judgment, considered in a more formal sense than Kohlberg has suggested; and (3) the assumption of "structural wholeness" should be regarded not as an empirical hypothesis but rather as a methodological criterion that serves to measure the cognitive aspect of moral development. Finally, he discusses the relation of individual moral judgment and the social environment, including the issue of personalism versus situationism, the impact of what Max Weber called "positional fragmentation" on the mode of moral judgment, and the role of social selection in regard to moral development.

Although they are trained in quite different fields, *Georg Lind, Johann-Ulrich Sandberger*, and *Tino Bargel* have collaborated on a cross-national longitudinal research about university socialization. In their joint essay (ch. 3) they investigate the notion of a democratic personality from three theoretical points of view, the cognitive-developmental (Piaget, Kohlberg), the attitude-structural (Converse, A. Campbell), and the psychodynamic (Freud, Adorno) viewpoints. In the theoretical part of their paper, Lind, Sandberger, and Bargel argue that between the models of these different approaches there are some intriguing similarities which suggest a common conceptual basis for research. In the empirical part of their essay, they present evidence in support of a rather close relationship between moral judgment competence, ego-strength, and democratic orientations. In studies of the social ecology of moral behavior and thought, the research designs usually become quite complex and thus require rather large samples and easy-to-use questionnaires. *Georg Lind* and *Roland Wakenhut* (ch. 4) present a new method of assessing affective and cognitive aspects of moral judgment behavior, that of what they call "Experimental Questionnaires." These tests combine the transparency and economy of classical attitude questionnaires with the methodological postulates of cognitive developmental theory. To illustrate the methodology which they are proposing, they describe the construction of the *Moralisches Urteil Test* (MUT) by Lind and the *Moralisches Urteils Fragebogen* (MUF) by Wakenhut, both of which have been widely used in moral judgment research in Europe. Both instruments have proved especially useful for research on moral development in differential social milieus.

The second and longest section of the book focuses on the social context of moral judgment, with studies of specific social milieus such as the family, the professions, the university, the military, the scientific world, and political subcultures. The authors' major interest was in studying particular facets and levels of the relation between the individual's moral behavior on the one hand and roles, norms, and institutions on the other. Rather than merely trying to quantify the impact of the social environment on the development of moral competence, the essays deal with the quality of this relationship. In the first essay in this section, *Hans Bertram* (ch. 5) suggests a multi-level model of social reproduction. He presents empirical findings which show a significant impact of social class and the structure of work-organization (level one), mediated by parents' values, personalities, and forms of interaction between the parents (level two), on the moral cognitive development of children (level three). Bertram concludes that in spite of the increasingly greater importance of formalized processes of education, the family still plays an outstanding role in the individual's cognitive-moral socialization. *Rainer Döbert* and *Gertrud Nunner-Winkler* (ch. 6), propose the thesis that, contrary to Ronald Inglehart's now widely-accepted theory, value change cannot be reduced to an essentially non-cognitive substitution of one value content for another but, following Max Weber as well as Kohlberg, instead should be regarded as a cognitive process in which traditions are dissolved. They point out that there are three ways of describing the validity of norms, corresponding to

(1) their substantive validity, which refers to the existence or non-existence of norms and their relative place in a value hierarchy; (2) their social validity, which refers to the degree to which small or large groups or the whole society hold such norms; and finally (3) their validity mode, which refers to the legitimacy and justifiability of social norms from the individual's point of view. Döbert and Nunner-Winkler argue that the third of these dimensions of validity is, in spite of frequent neglect, as least as important as the others. They illustrate and support this claim through the analysis of public debates and the interview-based study of male and female adolescents on the issues of abortion and conscientious objection to military service.

Fritz Oser and *André Schläfli* (ch. 7) inquire about conditions and ways of fostering cognitive-moral development during professional training, which in Switzerland as well as in Germany is provided for adolescents in a secondary school curriculum that is an alternative to the college-bound *Gymnasium*. They show that, contrary to common beliefs, the trainees welcome the opportunity to discuss moral dilemmas and experience an increase of maturity in regard to their values, socio-political attitudes, and moral judgment behavior. Using interview and questionnaire data, Oser and Schläfli argue that moral education is enhanced by the tension and conflict produced by considering real life dilemmas and by walking the "thin line" between milieu and the individual's needs, duties, and rights. *Georg Lind* (ch. 8) tries to answer the question of why so many studies concerning the impact of schools and colleges on the individual's socio-affective development produce inconsistent if not negative findings. He hypothesizes that this finding does not reflect the actual effects of education but rather a methodological bias. Because classical research methods (e.g., attitude tests) rest on a simplistic model of man, they fail to assess the cognitive aspects of social, political, or moral attitudes. By reanalyzing findings of classical attitude research as well as data from his own moral judgment studies, Lind shows that higher education consistently stimulates the integration and differentiation of attitudes. *Gerhard Portele* (ch. 9) analyzes the views of natural and social scientists concerning the aims and means of scientific research and concerning morality. He comes to a conclusion which confirms the fears of those who regard the ever growing industrialization of our modern times as presaged by the famous Chaplin film of that title. Portele shows that natural scientists and technologists are inclined, much more than are their humanistic and social science counterparts, toward a segmentation between the world of research and everyday life, as well as toward political alienation and conventional or even preconventional moral perspectives in scientific and non-scientific issues. The differential moral thinking of individuals in contrasting social environments is also the topic of the study by *Thomas Krämer-Badoni* and *Roland Wakenhut* (ch. 10) of soldiers and reservists of the German Armed Forces, conscientious objectors, and others. They have investigated the effect of the objective and subjective conditions of military life on the moral judgment pattern of its members, concluding that the German Armed Forces are still morally cut off or "segmented" from the civilian part of society. This phenomenon of moral segmentation is studied more extensively by *Rainer Senger* (ch. 11), who discusses the educational ideal of the "citizen in uniform," which aims at the integration of the military and the democratic society. On the grounds of a critical discussion of Charles Levine's theory of inconsistency of moral judgment, Senger develops the outlines of his own theory of segmentation, which he illustrates with his interviews with officers and soldiers.

Michael Schenk and *Gerhard Bohm* (ch. 12) employ the cognitive developmental theory of moral judgment to study two political groups, each of which were involved in single-issue movements but in pursuit of quite different aims. Although the two groups differed less in regard to their mean judgment competence than the authors had expected, Schenk and Bohm's data show characteristic differences regarding the distribution of the moral reasoning within each group. While all moral levels were equally present in the group with "egocentric" political aims, in the group with the altruist goals the postconventional reasoning dominated and preconventional thought was more frequent than conventional ones, a difference which resembles Norma Haan's well-known findings concerning ego development and moral reasoning. *Horst Heidbrink* (ch. 13) argues that the moral domain and the political domain cannot be reduced on one another and that it is necessary to keep them distinct. Political judgments usually involve processing concrete information and hence require complex cognitive operations, whereas moral judgments can be fruitfully studied even with fictitious and abstract situations. Nevertheless, from his own experimental work Heidbrink concludes that moral judgment competence facilitates political learning. He favors a curriculum for social and political studies which makes use of Kohlberg's moral pedagogy but resists the temptation to consider itself as apolitical.

In the epilogue to the book, *Hans A. Hartmann* (ch. 14) describes the history of morality as a socio-cultural phenomenon and as inter-woven with the development of moral philosophy and socio-psychological research on morality. Hartmann puts the research presented in the other essays into historical and philosophical perspective by sket philosophy: the formalist ethics of Kant, French positivism (Comte, Durkheim), genetic epistemology (Piaget), and the cognitive development theory by Kohlberg as well as the theory of sociocultural evolution developed by Habermas and his colleagues.

Most of the essays originally appeared in this book's German counterpart, *Moralisches Urteilen und soziale Umwelt* (1983), but they have been expanded and substantially revised for their appearance in English as part of the Precedent Studies in Ethics and the Moral Sciences. The editors wish to thank all those who have helped in various ways to make this publication possible. Above all, we thank the authors for their great patience and willingness to revise their original manuscripts and to provide supplementary information for the English-speaking reader. We also wish to thank the Universities of Augsburg and Konstanz as well as the Hochschulsozialisation research project, which in various ways have supported the preparation of this book, as well as the following individuals. For their assistance, in several cases very extensive, in translating the German essays or preparing them for translation, we wish to thank Christian Lenhardt, Denise F. Deissenberg, Naomi Knapp, James Fearns, Raoul Eshelman, and Professor Bernard Mausner. We wish to thank Doris Lang and Karin Gauggel for keying the manuscripts into the word processor, Leonore Link, Mary D. Hawley, and Sheila Nolan Whalen for their editorial assistance, and Bruce Uttley, Director of the Department of Computer Services at the University of Waterloo, for his patient help in converting our computer files into a format suitable for typesetting. Last but not least we wish to express our gratitude to Thomas Wren, the general editor and translator, for his encouragement and his extensive advice, the outcome of which is not only a translation from the original German but also a substantially revised edition, updated and rendered more suitable to an English-speaking audience.

Georg Lind
Hans A. Hartmann
Roland Wakenhut

Foreword

Lawrence Kohlberg

This volume presents a body of recent research and theorizing done in Germany, providing the English-speaking reader with a very valuable addition to the research on stages of moral judgment and reasoning carried out in America and England. It is unique, and differs from the American work in three regards. The first is in its methodology, which relies on the stage measurement instruments developed by Georg Lind and his colleagues in order to systematically differentiate and integrate the assessment of the cognitive structure or stage of moral judgment and its content, that is, the attitudinal, affective, or normative content of moral judgment. Second, it focuses on the moral development and functioning of both adolescents and adults in a variety of educational and work settings, a topic on which relatively little research has been done in the English-speaking world. Third, it explicitly addresses the socio-political dimensions of moral judgment and functioning.

The basic research instruments of the contributors to this volume are psychological tests and interviews. However, their perspective is primarily sociological, directed toward the moral socialization resulting from institutional memberships and the effects of such socialization on sociopolitical attitudes and behavior.

For those unfamiliar with the theory and research developed in America by myself and my colleagues, I would especially recommend Hans Hartmann's concluding historical review of philosophic theory as well as Georg Lind's chapter on psychological theory, which provide excellent introductions to the cognitive developmental theory of moral judgment. Jürgen Habermas's provocative chapter on the theory is part of an ongoing dialogue between us, raising a number of sympathetic but important and pressing questions about the relation in my theory between moral stages and political ideologies. (Rather than responding here to his questions, I refer the reader to my other responses [Kohlberg, 1984, chs. 3 and 4; 1985]).

Placing this book in context, we may note that the American research on moral stages has centered on a complex structural and hermeneutic analysis of longitudinal data in the U.S., Israel, and

Turkey, including interviewing subjects from age 10 through the 30s (the 20s in Turkey and Israel). The method and quantitative data are published in Colby et al. (in press), the theoretical assumptions and interpretations in Kohlberg (1984). Core American research studies are published in Kohlberg and Candee (in press).

As an alternative methodology for assessing moral stages to the qualitative moral judgment interview, James Rest (1979a) developed and validated a multiple choice measure of moral judgment preference, the *Defining Issues Test.* This test evolved from his dissertation (see Rest, 1973), recently replicated more clearly by L. J. Walker (1983, in press). Rest and Walker have each found that comprehension of stages other than one's own forms a hierarchical Guttman scale, with no comprehension of stages more than one stage above one's own and with comprehension of all stages below one's own. Walker has found that subjects prefer the highest stage they comprehend, with no preference for higher stages than the subject can comprehend (unless a subject exhibits a general preference for abstract or flowery language). Based on these findings, Rest developed the *Defining Issues Test* based on rating of stage-prototypical statements as most important. This test correlated well with age and education but is not simply a measure of verbal intelligence or achievement, since it correlates with other moral experiences and attitudes when IQ and level of education are controlled.

However, based as they are on my early stage definition and scoring system (Kohlberg, 1958), the Rest statements confound stage structure with a focused content issue or norm; for instance, Stage 4 social system reasoning is confounded with a concern for law and order. In our current scoring system (Colby et al., in press), the norm of law is found to be used at every stage and clarification by content (law) precedes clarification by stage. In a roughly similar way, the methodology of Lind and his colleagues gets preference scores or content (pro and con), as well as a stage. Since preference is determined by both content and structure, a scoring algorithm can be arrived at for assigning a pure stage structure score for an individual. Some subjects are more consistent in preferring stage structure than content, a factor considered in the tests of Lind and his colleagues. Thus, individual preferences are factored into stage, content, dilemma, and interactive components in the procedure. I believe this to be a highly promising approach, and look forward to future research from Lind and his colleagues. In particular, I look forward to efforts on their parts to establish the correlation or concurrent validity of Lind's measure with our moral judgment interview, since it is the results of longitudinal work with the moral judgment interview which have established the validity of the moral stage construct and its assessment. This has been established (Colby et al., in press) by the threefold stage criteria of (1) step by step sequence, (2) structural wholeness or cross-dilemma consistency (represented by a single general stage factor), and (3) hierarchical integration established by Walker's study of comprehension and preference.

Turning from this book's methods to its findings, I am impressed by the various chapters showing the relation of moral judgment to the "life-worlds," or situations in the military and in the university. In our American research we also have constructed special dilemma situations directly relevant to "life-worlds" including those of schools and correctional settings (Power et al., in press). Our studies examine the "moral culture" or moral atmosphere of these institutions, assessing the strength (degree of collectiveness and phase) of collective norms as well as their stage. While using interviews and questionnaires, our approach is more ethnographic than those reported in this volume, in that they assess shared norms instead of aggregating individual scores. They confirm such sensible findings as those reported here, e.g., that an ideologically "democratic" army life-world is reasoned about largely in terms of obedience and discipline. Both the theory presented in this book and many of its findings indicate the serious concern on the part of contemporary German social scholarship and policy to create educational institutions which will produce a "democratic character" and democratic citizens, a concern shared by myself and other American authors (see Power et al., in press) who are working in the tradition of John Dewey (1916). It is encouraging to read the findings of Döbert and Nunner-Winkler, Portele, Schenk and Bohm, and Lind on university students' judgments, all of which indicate greater political participation or actions in higher stage subjects, as well as more democratic, liberal, flexible, and progressive attitudes and content in this participation. Equally encouraging are Oser and Schläfli's findings of increased social commitment and democratic attitudes developed through Socratic moral discussion, a procedure roughly similar to that used by my colleagues and myself in the United States.

In sum, this book raises issues of the philosophic justification of the adequacy of the higher moral stages on the one hand, and of democratic or liberal ideologies on the other. It is, therefore, useful not only as a window into contemporary German social thought but also as a contribution in its own right to the ongoing and now international discussion.

PART ONE

Theory and Methods

Philosophical Notes on Moral Judgment Theory

Jürgen Habermas

At present, the debates surrounding Kohlberg's approach revolve around essentially *four problems*. First, in view of the failure to prove experimentally the existence of Stage 6 of moral judgment, the question arises whether we can speak of *natural* stages at the level of postconventional morality. Second, the discovery that regression occurs in postadolescent life casts doubt upon the *normative point of reference of moral development*. Has it been chosen correctly? Can the ability to judge and act in morally mature ways be adequately conceptualized in terms of cognitivistic and formalistic theories? Third, the question of accommodating *relativists* or *value skeptics* as a group in Kohlberg's stage model remains problematic. Fourth, there is the question of whether his structuralist theory can be joined with ego psychology in ways that would give greater scope to the *psychodynamic aspects of judging*.

The nature of these problems will become clearer if we take a look at the adolescent's transition from norm-regulated action to discourse, focusing on the issue of how much freedom he gains as he leaves the social world of naturalness and embeddedness behind. This will be the subject of Section 1 below. Section 2 deals with the problem of mediating between morality and *Sittlichkeit*, which crops up when the social world is being moralized and cut off from the certitude the life-world provides. In Section 3 I will turn to the adolescent's way of dealing with the problem of partial maturation where he learns to distance himself from the world of traditional norms, which have lost their significance for him, without at the same time being able to reorganize the socio-cognitive content of the conventional stage as a whole. Finally, Section 4 will address discrepancies between moral judgment and moral action to the extent that they derive from an inability to separate success orientation from the orientation to reach understanding.

1.

Over several decades Kohlberg has repeatedly revised his scoring schema. The most recent one is described in the Standard Form Scoring Manual (Colby et al., in press). Is the latest version an unqualified improvement? I think not. Theories in the Piagetian tradition are best served by a type of response-coding that is informed by hermeneutic interpretation and the theory behind it. This interpretation is far from foolproof. It cannot take an operational form. If it did, highly complex pre-understandings would be neutralized and destroyed. Be that as it may, with the present research methods the scoring of interview material has forced Kohlberg to delete Stage 6 after longitudinal studies in the United States, Israel, and Turkey showed there was no evidence for its existence. Today he is reluctant to answer the question of whether Stage 6 is a psychologically distinct natural stage or a philosophical construct.[1] Whatever shape the revision will ultimately take (and I am assuming Kohlberg's problems cannot be sorted out in the area of measurement alone), it should be clear that the status of Stage 5 is at issue along with that of Stage 6. As soon as you give up the attempt to differentiate stages at the postconventional level, you face the question of whether principled moral judgments represent a natural stage *in the same sense* as judgments classified as preconventional and conventional.

From the standpoint of discourse ethics, I tacitly suggested a *different interpretation* of Stages 5 and 6 by distinguishing the orientation to general principles from the orientation to procedures allowing for the justification of principles. In so doing I have steered clear of the idea of differentiating stages according to the kind of principle involved (utilitarian vs. natural-rights vs. Kantian). The differentiation is conceived solely in terms of *stages of reflection.* At Stage 5, principles are viewed as being absolute and beyond the need for justification. At Stage 6, they are not only handled more flexibly but also made relative to explicit procedures of justification. Differentiating stages of reflection in this way is intimately tied into the larger framework of a specific normative theory and has to prove its mettle there. One must be able to show that a person relying not on the self-evident nature of universal principles but on the legitimating power of justificational procedures is in fact better equipped to oppose skeptical objections and to judge consistently. There are of course ethical positions that reject proceduralism as a concept, claiming that a procedure for moral justification is in no way different from, and cannot achieve more than, a universal moral principle itself. As long as this philosophical controversy is not settled, it is necessary to defend the premises of discourse ethics in the arena where they clash directly with other philosophical views, that is, ethical theory proper. To view them naturalistically as propositions about natural stages of moral consciousness is to misconstrue their intent. Discourse ethics itself offers no reasons for such a (reifying?) interpretation, which claims that *stages of reflection* have the same status as natural intrapsychic *stages of development.*

If there is no empirical evidence to suggest that we are dealing with several postconventional stages, then Kohlberg's description of Stage 5 becomes problematic as well. We may suspect that ideas such as the social contract and the greatest happiness of the greatest number are confined to traditions that hold sway in England and America. They represent a culturally specific, substantive manifestation of principled moral judgment and are not universal.

Along with John Gibbs, Thomas C. McCarthy (1982) points out that the relation between a psychologist who is knowledgeable about moral theory and his subject changes in a methodologically significant way as the subject moves toward the postconventional level, taking a hypothetical attitude to his social world.

> The suggestion I should like to advance is that Kohlberg's account places the higher-stage moral subject, at least in point of competence, at the same reflective or discursive level as the moral psychologist. The subject's thought is now marked by the decentration, differentiation and reflexivity which are the conditions of entrance into the moral theorist's sphere of argumentation. Thus the asymmetry between the pre-reflective and the reflective, between theories-in-action and explication, which underlies the model of reconstruction begins to break down. The subject is now in a position to argue with the theorist about questions of morality. (p. 74)

In the same essay McCarthy draws a useful parallel between sociomoral and cognitive development:

> Piaget views the underlying functioning of intelligence as unknown to the individual at lower stages of cognition. At superior levels, however, the subject may reflect on previously tacit thought operations and the implicit cognitive achievements of earlier stages; that is, he or she may engage in epistemological reflection. And this places the subject, at least in point of competence, at the same discursive level as the cognitive psychologist. Here, too, asymmetry between the subject's pre-reflective know-how and the investigator's reflective know-that begins to break down. The subject

is now in a position to argue with the theorist about the structure and conditions of knowledge. (p. 74)

Through formal operations the adult reflectively appropriates the knowledge he uses intuitively in problem-solving. That means he has acquired the ability to carry on constructive learning processes by means of reconstruction. In principle he has broadened his competence, which now includes the reconstructive sciences.

This acquisition has an important implication for the methodology of the reconstructive sciences. A psychologist trying to test his hypotheses about the formal-operational stage is dependent on his subjects; hence, he must deal with them as in principle *equal* partners in the business of scientific reconstruction. His own theory will convince him that at this stage the asymmetry existing at all earlier stages between pre-reflective mental functioning and reflective comprehension disappears. To the extent to which the reconstructive scientist views himself as standing within the open horizon of a research process whose results he cannot foresee, he must accord that *same standpoint* to his experimental subjects, provided they have reached the highest stage of competence.

The same holds for respondents who handle moral dilemmas from the standpoint of a postconventional participant in discourse. To the extent that they basically share the perspective of the interviewer, who is a moral psychologist, their moral judgments no longer have the form of utterances which are naively generated with the help of an intuitive understanding of rules. Postconventional experimental subjects are drawn into the business of moral psychology–that is, the reconstruction of the underlying moral intuitions of everyday life–to the point where their moral reasoning no longer *mirrors* a pretheoretical knowledge that is unreflectively expressed, but *explicates* potentially theoretical knowledge. Principled moral judgments are impossible to make unless the person in question has taken a step or two toward the reconstruction of his moral intuitions. In short, principled moral reasoning *in nuce* has the signification of moral-theoretical reasoning. As postconventional thought leaves the world of traditional norms behind, it operates in the same arena in which moral theorists debate their issues. This debate is fueled by historical experience and, for the time being, it is the exclusive preserve of philosophy. The psychologist's job is to identify developmental patterns; he cannot settle philosophical disputes.

2.

A second cluster of problems has sparked a wide-ranging discussion in the last few years. This cluster is difficult to disentangle. The studies by N. Haan (1978) and C. Gilligan (1977) marked the beginning of this particular debate. Its immediate cause was the suspicion that Kohlberg's schema might, in some crucial instances of classifying moral judgment, lead too far away from the intuitive understanding of a morally sensitive scorer. The two instances in question are: first, female respondents whose utterances put them at Stage 3 even though one would expect them to have greater moral maturity; and, second, experimental subjects classified as relativistic value skeptics belonging to Stage 4½ (see section 3 below), although their utterances generally seem more mature than post-conventional judgments. Gilligan and Murphy make the point that Kohlberg's criteria would peg more than half of the US population at some level below the postconventional in terms of moral consciousness. In addition they show that a majority in a sample of 26 subjects who were first classified as postconventional later regressed to relativistic positions (Stage 4½) (Gilligan & Murphy, 1980).[2]

Kohlberg (1982) claims his critics got the facts wrong, that there are no disproportionate numbers of female subjects at lower stages. He also denies the existence of regression to earlier stages. This controversy has drawn attention to problems which, in philosophical parlance, pertain to the relation of morality to *Sittlichkeit*.[3]

Gilligan and Murphy (1980) envisage a postconventional path of development leading from Kohlberg's Stages 5/6 (postconventional formal: PCF) to a stage they call contextual relativism (postconventional contextual: PCC). This notion is based on W. B. Perry's work on the overcoming of absolutist thought in late adolescence (1968) and K. Riegel's (1973) analysis of postformal operations. At the postconventional contextual stage, we are told, the experience of moral conflict teaches the adult to overcome the abstractions of an absolute, strictly deontological, Kantian type of justice morality. This *relativistic ethics of responsibility* supposedly represents a superior stage because it can handle real moral dilemmas rather than fictitious, hypothetical ones; it takes the complexity of lived situations into account; it joins justice with solicitude and responsibility for persons under one's care. In short, it presupposes a more inclusive concept of a mature personality than does the abstract notion of moral autonomy:

> While the logical concepts of equality and reciprocity can support a prin-
> cipled morality of universal rights and respect, experiences of moral
> conflict and choice seem to point rather to special obligations and
> responsibility for consequences that can be anticipated and understood
> only within a more contextual frame of reference. The balancing of these
> two points of view appeared to us to be the key to understanding adult
> moral development. In our view, this would require a restructuring of
> moral thought which would include but supersede the principled under-
> standing of Kohlberg's highest stages. (Gilligan & Murphy, 1980, pp.
> 159ff.)

This analysis distinguishes between the position of an ethics of
responsibility and that of value skepticism (in the transitional Stage
4½). Both have relativism in common. But only contextual relativism
is based on ethical formalism while at the same time superseding it.

From the standpoint of discourse ethics, this situation takes on a
somewhat different cast. Gilligan and Murphy do zero in on something important, namely the repercussions or consequent problems
of a successful transition to principled morality. The latter, we saw,
derives from a peculiar abstractive achievement that jettisons the
natural stability of the social world with its legitimately ordered
interpersonal relations, compelling it to justify itself. Initially the
social world owes its unshakable facticity to our embeddedness in
habitual, concrete forms of life where unreflective subjects act
against a background of unquestioned givenness. By contrast,
communicative actors have an explicit knowledge of given institutional orders. These they address in speech acts. However, at the
conventional stage their explicit knowledge is intimately tied up with
the implicit background knowledge of a particular form of life that
the intersubjectively accepted norms are valid absolutely. As the
social world becomes more and more moralized by the hypothetical
orientation of a participant in discourse, and as it begins to stand
over against the totality of the life-world, the erstwhile congruence
of validity *(Gültigkeit)* and what is merely accepted in society *(Geltung)*
is being eroded. The monolithic practice of everyday communication
splits up into two parts, norms and values. The first part is suscep-
tible to moral justification and to assessment in terms of its deontological validity, whereas the second is not, since it comprises value
configurations belonging to collective and individual modes of life.

Cultural values, embodied in total life-forms or total life-histories,
pervade the fabric of communicative everyday life so thoroughly and
are so important in shaping a person's life and in securing his identity as to make it impossible for him as an acting subject to distance

himself from them. He can distance himself from institutions of his social world but not from values, at least not in the same way. Cultural values do transcend the factual processes of action. As they congeal into historical and biographical syndromes of value orientations, they enable individuals to distinguish the reproduction of "mere life" from ideas of the "good life." An idea of the good life, rather than being a concept we posit abstractly as an ought, is something that shapes the identity of groups and individuals, making them integral parts of their culture and personality. Whoever questions a form of life in which his identity has been shaped questions his very existence. There is a specific mode of distancing involved when someone goes through such a personal crisis, a distancing that is different in kind from the one the norm-testing participant in discourse attains when he questions the facticity of existing institutions.

We can therefore conceive the emergence of a moral point of view as going hand in hand with a differentiation within the practical: between *moral issues*–which can in principle be decided rationally in terms of criteria of *justice* or universalizability–and *evaluative issues*–which are issues of the *good life* and which do not lend themselves to rational discussion except *within* the parameters of a historically concrete form of life or individual life style. The concrete *Sittlichkeit* of a habitual, naively accepted life-world is characterized by the fusion of moral and evaluative issues. Only in a rationalized life-world do moral issues and issues of the good life take on separate identities. It is only now that moral issues can and must be treated autonomously, i.e., as issues of justice, at least initially. (The word "initially" points to the problem of an ethics of responsibility.)

Isolating issues of justice leads to increased rationality, but this increase has a price. Issues of the good life have the advantage of allowing us to answer them within the secure horizon of a life-world. They are inherently contextual, hence *concrete*. The answers we give retain the *action-motivating* potential of a form of life that is presupposed. In a framework of concrete *Sittlichkeit* which harbors conventional morality, moral judgments derive their concreteness and action-motivating force from the intrinsic nexus between themselves and ideas of the good life as well as institutionalized *Sittlichkeit*. At this stage the tendency to question things has not yet reached the degree of development at which the advantages of an existing life-world are frittered away. This occurs only with the transition to postconventional morality when the social world is being moralized and thus divorced from its background, the life-world. This process of abstraction has a double effect: under a strictly deontological point of view moral issues become separated from their context, leaving room for moral solutions which have a rationally motivating force only as insights.

Moral issues are never issues for their own sake. Rather, people raise them to guide their actions. It makes sense therefore to *reinsert* the demotivated solutions postconventional morality finds for decontextualized issues *into practical life*. Morality has to make up for the loss of concrete *Sittlichkeit* it incurred when it pursued a cognitive advantage. This compensation is necessary if morality is to become practical. Demotivated solutions to decontextualized issues can become practical only if two problems are solved: the abstraction from contexts of action and the separation of rationally motivating insights from empirical attitudes must both be undone. Every cognitivistic morality confronts the actor with questions concerning both the *situational applications* and the *motivational anchorage* of moral insights.[4] These problems cannot be solved unless moral judgment is *supplemented* by something else: hermeneutic work and internalization of authority.

The notion of contextual relativism as a separate "stage" can be traced to a misconception of the basic problem, namely, how *Sittlichkeit* and morality are related. For one thing, C. Gilligan fails to distinguish clearly between the *cognitive problem* of application and the *motivational problem* of the anchorage of moral insights. Thus she tends to make the dubious distinction between postconventional formalism (PCF) and postconventional contextualism (PCC) in reference to hypothetical vs. actual situations. She ignores the fact that the question of whether what I ought to do is the same as what I would do concerns only the motivational side of the problem of mediation. The other side is the cognitive one: How am I to interpret a universal command (which merely says what I ought to do) in a given situation in order to be able to act accordingly?

In addition, C. Gilligan does not seem to realize that the two problems crop up only after morality has been abstracted from *Sittlichkeit* and after the basic question of ethical theory concerning the justifiability of norms has been given a cognitivistic answer. We must not confuse the question of context-specific application of universal norms with the question of grounding or justification. Since moral norms do not contain their own rules of application, to act on the basis of moral insight means to have an additional competence that one might call hermeneutic prudence or, in Kantian terminology, reflective judgment. It would incidentally be wrong to suppose that the adoption of prudence in this limited form weakens in any way the universalistic position one takes (Kuhlmann, 1975, pp. 483ff.; Habermas, 1984, pp. 134ff.).

Thirdly, C. Gilligan's contextual relativism is designed to offset certain deficiencies at the postconventional level of moral judgment which crop up when the two above-mentioned consequent problems are not dealt with. *Moral rigorism* is one such deficiency. It occurs when the hermeneutic sensitivity to the problem of application is impaired or lacking and when abstract moral insights are mechanically applied to concrete situations, in line with the adage *fiat justitia, pereat mundus.* It has always been popular to criticize Kant in this way. Max Weber's dichotomy between an ethics of absolute ends and an ethics of responsibility is one of the more illustrious examples. *Intellectualization* is another such deficiency. It covers phenomena in which moral abstraction serves as a defense against moral action. Now, Gilligan tends to misconstrue *deficiencies* like these as characteristics of a *normal* state of things at the stage of postconventional formalism.

Finally, she sets up parallels between PCF and justice orientation on one hand, and PCC and a caring and response orientation on the other, arguing that there is a gender-specific distribution of these orientations.

If one keeps in mind
- that the "moral point of view," strictly speaking, emerges only with the transition from the second to the third stage of interaction;
- that this moral point of view comes about when the social world is moralized from the hypothetical position of a participant in discourse and divorced from the life-world;
- that deontological abstraction separates justice issues from issues of the good life;
- that in the process moral issues are uncoupled from their context (decontextualized), whereas moral solutions are dissociated from empirical motives (demotivated);
- and that these dissociations create a need for contextual application and motivational anchorage of moral insights,

then the solution to these problems calls for a mediation between morality and *Sittlichkeit* that goes beyond what moral judgments, in the view of deontological ethics, can accomplish. That is why attempts to supplement or revise the Kohlbergian stage model of moral consciousness are useless. The two consequent problems I discussed operate on a different level of theorizing than does moral judgment. They require a different order of achievement, to wit, contextual sensitivity and prudence on the one hand, and autonomy and self-governance on the other.

I will summarize the discussion (cf. Kohlberg & Candee, 1983; Habermas, 1981; Nunner-Winkler, 1983) surrounding Gilligan's work under the following headings.

The cognitive problem of application

(a) Those who seek to complement Kohlberg's stage sequence, either by adding another postconventional stage (C. Gilligan) or by introducing a parallel stage hierarchy (N. Haan), fail to distinguish sufficiently between moral and evaluative issues, between issues of justice and issues of the good life. This difference corresponds to the one between self-determination and self-actualization at the level of individual life-styles (Habermas, 1981). Typically, the question of how to evaluate forms of life or purposes of life (ego ideals) or even personality types and modes of action arises only after moral issues, narrowly understood, have been resolved.[5] If you define the moral point of view in terms of discourse ethics, you rule out competition on equal terms by viewpoints other than justice or normative rightness orientation. Since valid norms cannot but embody generalizable interests, it follows that a principle of welfare (Frankena's [1973] principle of beneficence, for example) or a principle of caring and responsibility–as long as these expressions denote *moral* principles–is already contained in the meaning of the term "normative validity."

(b) Moreover, the type of moral principle I call discourse ethics rules out the constraint of moral judgment wrought by an ethics of ultimate ends. Again, the concern for the effects and side-effects which presumably flow from the general application of a contested norm to specific contexts is part and parcel of discourse ethics. It need not be brought in as an *adjunct,* i.e., as a separate ethics of responsibility. Interpreted from the perspective of discourse ethics, practical reason certainly requires practical prudence when applying rules. But when it makes use of this faculty, practical reason is not limited to the parameters of a certain culture or historical period. Even in the field of application learning processes are possible which are governed by the universal nature of the norm that is being applied.

(c) In moral psychology, ideal role-taking has come to mean a procedural type of justification. The cognitive operations involved are demanding. They in turn are linked with motives and feeling states like empathy. Where conditions of socio-cultural distance prevail, compassion for "thy neighbor"–who more often than not is anything but close by–is a necessary emotional prerequisite for cognitive operations we expect to find in participants in discourse. Similar amalgams of cognition, empathy, and agape can be drawn upon to explain the hermeneutic process of applying universal norms in a manner that is mindful of the context of application. This sort of integration of cognitive operations and emotional states typifies *mature* moral judgment both in its justificational function and when it applies norms. It is only when we conceptualize maturity in this way that moral rigorism can be seen for what it is: an inhibition of the faculty of judgment. It hardly serves any purpose to make this point by talking about the difference between a morality of love and one of law and justice. To do so represents an *extraneous* critique of postconventional morality. Rather, this criticism should flow directly from an adequate description of the highest moral stage itself.[6]

The motivational problem of anchorage

(a) Those who would complement Kohlberg's moral stages in one of the ways mentioned above do not distinguish clearly between moral and ego development. In the personality system, what correspond to moral judgments are behavior controls or structures of the superego. At higher stages they result from a distancing from, and conflict with, the social world understood as a matrix of relations that is integrated through norms. These structures of the superego can be analyzed in terms of the basic socio-cognitive concepts of norm-regulated action. The formation of ego identity, on the other hand, occurs in the more complex totality I call communicative action. More specifically, ego identity results from the interplay between an individual and the structures of objective, social, and subjective worlds, once these have been differentiated from a homogeneous life-world.[7]

(b) The postconventional disengagement of morality from *Sittlichkeit* signifies a loss of congruence between moral convictions and cultural taken-for-grantedness or any certainty of the life-world whatever. Moral insights and habitual, empirical motives are no longer one and the same. The resulting disproportion between moral judgments and moral actions needs to be leveled. This is achieved by a system of internal behavior controls which is triggered by principled moral judgment, that is, by motive-forming convictions, and which makes *self-governance* possible. This system must function autonomously. It must be independent of the external pressure of a factually recognized, legitimate order, no matter how small that pressure may be. Only the complete internalization of a few highly abstract and universal principles meets this prerequisite, principles which follow logically from the procedure of norm justification as seen by discourse ethics. The postconventional structures of the superego can be *tested* by, among other things, checking the standard type of question "What ought I to do?" by another type, "What would I do?" Kohlberg calls responses to these questions responsibility judgments. They are indicators of the respondent's *intention* or *confidence* to act on his moral judgments. Significantly, such responsibility judgments are at the same cognitive level as moral judgments. Although they can be construed as expressing a frame of mind *(Gesinnung)*, they cannot, as judgments, in any way vouchsafe the correspondence of judgments and actions. It is possible to derive the *type* of motivational anchorage, without which no postconventional morality can be translated into action, from the structure of our ability to act, that is, from the socio-cognitive endowment at the post-conventional stage. However, if we want to know whether the psychodynamic processes will live up to the standards of that structure, there is no point in looking for verbal *answers* to questions of the "Why me?" type. Only actual practice can give an answer here.[8]

(c) The successful passage to a postconventional stage of moral judgment can appear in combination with insufficient motivational anchorage. This will restrict the ability to act autonomously. One especially striking manifestation of such a discrepancy between judgment and action is the intellectualization of moral issues. It represents a misuse of elaborate moral judgment about manifest conflicts of action, because moral judgment is subordinated to the defense of latent instinctual conflicts.

3.

Let me turn to the complications Kohlberg faced when he dealt with that group of hybrid moral judgments which forced him to introduce a mixed Stage 4½. At issue are relativistic statements that tend to be made from a strategic rather than a moral point of view. Initially, Kohlberg and his collaborators were tempted to stress the affinities these relativistic statements have with the instrumental hedonism of Stage 2. But they soon realized they could not classify them as preconventional since the general level of reasoning was too high among these respondents. Also, while the respondents did not moralize the social world, they did take a hypothetical attitude toward it. Both facts argued for an affinity with postconventional judgments. In view of these ambiguous findings, Kohlberg decided to situate relativistic judgments between the conventional and post-conventional levels, assigning them to a transitional stage of their own. This stage, Kohlberg argues, calls less for structural description than for psychodynamic explanation, and the explanation he offers makes use of the idea of an unresolved crisis of adolescence (Döbert & Nunner-Winkler, 1975). This interpretation leaves something to be desired, for it cannot explain the fact that this level of judgment can become stable rather than being merely transitional. This stabilization can be variously proved. One index is the emergence in philosophy of value-skepticism, a Stage 4½-like position that is being seriously advocated by a school of thought beginning with Weber and stretching down to Popper and beyond.

Common to subjectivistic approaches in ethics is a value-skepticism that is grounded in empiricist assumptions. They all reject the rationalistic premises which underlie Kohlberg's theory of moral development. Modern value-skepticism holds that moral issues cannot be settled with good reasons, that is, with reasons that are intersubjectively binding. Instead it busies itself with metaethical investigations that are supposed to explain how language occasions the rationalistic illusions of everyday moral intuitions. In carrying on the dispute between skepticism and cognitivism, proponents on either side cannot appeal to psychology as a tribunal or forum. The issues between them brook no authority except philosophical argument. Moral psychology knows and accepts that. What it can and should do in this connection is explain why value-skepticism–for all its incongruity with the logic of moral development–seems to be a natural stage in that development. Kohlberg should not rest content with inserting a transitional stage in his overall scheme and with providing a psychodynamic explanation of it. By opting for classification, he commits himself to *locating Stage 4½ in terms of the logic of development.* In other words he should give a structural description of Stage 4½, as he has done with the other stages. The description offered so far does not meet this demand. It reads:

Level B/C. Transitional Level. This level is postconventional but not yet principled.

Content of transition:
At stage 4½, choice is personal and subjective. It is based on emotions;

conscience is seen as arbitrary and relative, as are ideas such as "duty" and "morally right."

Transitional social perspective:
At this stage, the perspective is that of an individual standing outside of his own society and considering himself as an individual making decisions without a generalized commitment or contract with society. One can pick and choose obligations, which are defined by particular societies, but one has no principles for such choice.(Kohlberg, 1981, p. 411)

My own explanation of the troubling phenomenon of a transitional stage goes something like this. The respondents in question have only partly completed the transition to the postconventional level. The integration of speaker perspective and world perspective partially fails, leaving out the social world and the attitudes that insure conformity to norms. This necessarily implies the failure to coordinate the success-orientation of the strategic actor with the communicative actor's orientation to seek understanding. Now, this integration–a fundamental prerequisite of discourse–fails to occur in exactly those cases in which *normative claims to validity* are being focused upon because they have become problematic. The socio-cognitive equipment of the conventional stage of interaction can be said to have been only partly reorganized. While the adolescent has learned how to reason theoretically, he stops short of moral reasoning.

I have dwelled on this hypothesis elsewhere (Habermas, 1982, pp. 260ff.). Hence a brief summary will suffice here. By acquiring the ability to think hypothetically about moral-practical issues, the adolescent fulfills a necessary and sufficient condition for *extricating himself from conventional modes of thought.* But in taking this step he does not yet make a decision as to which of two different developmental paths he is going to take. At this point these options are still open. There are different ways in which an adolescent can use this newly acquired distance from conventions which have lost the naive force of social currency and acceptance *(Geltung)* by being hypothetically transformed into just one among many possibilities, and which thus become invalidated by reflection. Given his new level of reflection, he can try to preserve something from that lost world, namely what it *means* for norms and prescriptive statements to have currency or be accepted. If he does that, he must reconstruct the basic concepts of morality without giving up the ethical perspective. He must relativize the de facto currency that norms have in society by comparing them to valid norms that satisfy criteria of rational justification. By clinging to a reconstruction of what it means for norms to be accepted, the adolescent fulfills a necessary condition for a *successful passage to postconventional thought.* This is one path he can take.

The other path is one whereby the adolescent extricates himself from conventional thought without being able to pass to postconventional thought. Here he views the collapse of conventions as an exercise in debunking false cognitive claims adhering to conventional norms and prescriptions. This alternative path has him looking for a retrospective explanation of the basic moral concepts once they have been discredited. The adolescent's job is to come to terms with the dissonance between his moral intuitions–which *continue* to determine his unreflective knowledge of everyday life and actions–and the (presumed) insight into the illusory nature of conventional moral consciousness–which reflection has discredited but not eliminated. For the second developmental path, the metaethical debunking of moral illusions is what the renewal of ethical consciousness is for the first. These cases of dissonance can be dealt with effectively by those demystifying metaethical explanations, provided there is a way to reconcile theoretical skepticism with the unchallenged sway moral intuitions have in one's everyday life. In this regard Weber's ethical skepticism, for example, has greater efficacy than Stevenson's emotivism. The former leaves untouched the existential nature of value bonds, whereas the latter explains away moral intuitions, reducing them to feelings. From the point of view of Kohlberg's theory, one is entitled to rank metaethical approaches like these *below* cognitivistic ethics. This subordination is backed by developmental logic.

4.

The last problem is one that Kohlberg's theory has in common with any approach that distinguishes competence from performance. Whenever this distinction is made, theories face specific measurement problems because competence by itself cannot be shown to exist except in its concrete manifestations, that is, through phenomena of performance. Only when these measurement problems are solved will it be possible to isolate factors determining performance from theoretically postulated competences. It may help to differentiate factors determining performance in the following way: those that *must* supplement an acquired competence (by acting as catalysts); those that *can* supplement it (by acting as stimulators or accelerators); and those that act as *inhibitors,* brakes or filters.

To consider, as is frequently done, moral judgment as an indicator of competence and moral action or behavior as an indicator of performance, strikes me as crude and simplistic. On the other hand, the motivational anchorage of postconventional judgment in homologous superego structures does represent an example of *supplementary,* performance-determining factors without which moral judgments at this stage could not become effective in practice (Döbert & Nunner-Winkler, 1978). As a rule, discrepancies between judgment and action can probably be accounted for in terms of the selective effect of *inhibiting* factors. A number of interesting studies point in this direction (Edelstein & Keller, 1982, pp. 22ff.; Döbert & Nunner-Winkler, 1983). Among the performance-determining factors that act as inhibitors, some serve to explain motivational deficits. Of particular interest are the defense mechanisms which Anna Freud was the first to study systematically. They interfere with the formation of motives which are structurally necessary, which is why they can be analyzed from a *structural perspective.*

Identification and projection are the two fundamental mechanisms of defense against conflict. The individual acquires them in early childhood. Only later, at the postconventional stage of interaction, do they seem to develop into what is known as a system of defense mechanism (Haan, 1969, pp. 14-29). Defense mechanisms differ in terms of the way in which they *counteract* the postconventional differentiation between success-oriented action and action aimed at reaching understanding. Generally, the way defense works is that barriers to communication are set up in the psyche, separating the (unconscious) strategic aspect of action (which serves the gratification of unconscious desires) from the manifest, intentional aspect (which aims at reaching understanding). This explains why the defensive individual fails to see his violation of shared presuppositions of communication for what it is. Unconsciously motivated actions can be explained as a reversal of differentiation. This process is latent and hidden from the actor and from others. The self-deceptive component of defense can be interpreted as an intrapsychic disturbance of communication. This interpretation makes use of the concept of systematically distorted communication, which manifests itself in similar ways on two different levels: the interpersonal and the intrapsychic. It is a concept that requires independent discussion in the framework of communication theory.[9]

NOTES

1. Kohlberg (1980) has emphasized that the construction of Stage 6 resulted from material obtained from a small élite sample, and that it included statements by Martin Luther King. "Such élite figures do not establish Stage 6 as a natural stage of development."

2. C. Gilligan's *In a Different Voice* (1982) appeared in book form after I had finished this manuscript.

3. [Editor's note: This term, which in the 19th century was proposed as a technical term by Fichte and developed further by Hegel, is probably untranslatable. Like the Greek word *ethos* from which its German parent *Sitten* (custom) derives, *Sittlichkeit* refers to what is customary, in this case to social norms, values, and ideals which collectively define the "good life" and which have a moral or near-moral status even though they are usually taken for granted by those concerned. Thus the demands of *Sittlichkeit* are more weighty than those of, say, etiquette, not cut and dried like those of positive law, and–most important here–less open to rational, transcultural discussion than the normative conclusions of that branch of philosophy which is sometimes called "ethics." They are culturally-bound in the sense that they are constitutive of a society's form of life as well as derived from it, functioning to integrate society by providing a network of tacit assumptions of decency, promise-keeping, etc. The translator's decision to leave the term in its original German reflects a growing reluctance in the English-speaking world to translate this term, which is less misleadingly explained by a gloss or paraphrase. Thus Bernard Williams (1985, p. 104) clarifies his mention of *Sittlichkeit* by explaining that it refers to "a concretely determined ethical existence that was expressed in the local folkways, a form of life that made particular sense to the people living in it."]

4. The general problem of applying norms to situations of action first arises at the preconventional stage of moral judgment and interaction. In our context the focus is on the particular aggravation this problem undergoes when a complex totality is being destroyed, wherein norms and situations of action are parts of one and the same unproblematic form of life, *referring to each other* because of their prior coordination. Cf. H. G. Gadamer (1957).

5. This is the case with the decisions about abortion studied by Gilligan: Possible repercussions–for the relation to friend/husband, for the occupational careers of man and woman, for a different family life– can be considered important only when abortion itself has been accepted as morally licit. The same goes for problems of divorce and adultery. This is confirmed by the two cases Gilligan and Murphy (1981) refer to. Only when extramarital sex is morally unobjectionable can the problem arise under what conditions it might be better to cover up the facts or to let the concerned party know immediately.

6. In terms of his moral theory, the young Hegel was still a Kantian when he worked out that historical dichotomy between a Christian ethics of love and a Jewish ethics of law and justice.
7. On the concept of ego development, see Habermas (1975; 1976) and Döbert, Habermas and Nunner-Winkler (1977).
8. To that extent Kohlberg and Candee (1983) assign too great a burden of proof to "responsibility judgments."
9. An interesting model for understanding "false self-perception" has been proposed by M. Löw-Beer (1982).

This paper originally appeared in Habermas, *Moralbewusstsein und kommunikatives Handeln* (Suhrkamp, 1983). We wish to thank Christian Lenhardt for his translation and MIT Press for their permission to use this part of their forthcoming American publication of the book. Title and incidental matters such as style of citation have been adapted to the format of the present volume.

The Theory of Moral-Cognitive Development
A Socio-Psychological Assessment

Georg Lind

For some decades in psychology, morality has been understood either as the individual's behavior evaluated on the basis of given socio-moral norms, or as any behavior which is determined by morally good motives and affects. Behavioristic psychology has focused primarily on the question of whether individuals comply with given rules of conduct, whereas affect psychology has regarded this behavior as determined exclusively by inner dispositions, that is, by motives, drives, or the like, which in their turn have been traced to a wide array of causes, including human genes, nursing behavior, and environmental pressures. Accordingly, intervention strategies for education and therapy treatments have been designed, in the first case, to weaken conditioned links between stimuli and socially disapproved responses, or, in the second case, to lessen "negative" affects (hate, envy, aggression) and to strengthen "positive" affects (love, justice, guilt, shame).

Both the behavioristic and the affect perspectives on moral behavior have recently been challenged by the cognitive-developmental approach, which postulates that moral behavior cannot be truly understood unless we also examine the cognitive-structural aspect of human behavior. This approach does not lose sight of the fact that human behavior is continually evaluated on the grounds of socio-moral rules, norms, laws, etc., nor does it deny that affective components are involved in every human behavior. But it points out that moral behavior also depends on the individual's ability to see the moral implications of a situation and to organize and consistently apply moral rules and principles to concrete situations. Concrete situations usually imply more than one rule to be observed, and these multiple demands are likely to conflict with one another. Moreover, social evaluations of a person's behavior may deviate considerably from each other and may themselves have to be critically evaluated on ethical grounds. To cope with such situations the individual must be endowed not only with moral affects but also with *moral judgment competence,* that is, with the ability for reflective thinking and rational discourse. Hence, psychological intervention must also—or even primarily—be concerned with the cognitive aspects of moral behavior as well as with the instilling of moral affects.

Cognitive-developmental extensions of these once important models of moral conduct have been suggested by a number of psychologists since the turn of the century, e.g., by Levy-Suhl (1912), Moers (1930), Hetzer (1931), and Piaget (1977/1932). Piaget was one of the first to develop systematically a theory of moral-cognitive development. His research concentrated on children's development of autonomous moral judgment in the ages 5 to 12, particularly in regard to rules of children's games. More than twenty years later, Kohlberg took up and considerably furthered this approach to the study of morality. On the basis of longitudinal research of adolescents' and young adults' moral judgment, he suggested an elaborate set of hypotheses about the nature and course of moral-cognitive development (for instance, see Kohlberg, 1958, 1969, 1979, 1984). Especially through Kohlberg's work, the cognitive-developmental theory of moral judgment has attracted much attention from academics as well as from practitioners. In the field of psychology it has stimulated an immense amount of empirical research, not only in the United States and Canada but, since the seventies, also in Europe, particularly in Great Britain (cf. Weinreich-Haste & Locke, 1983) and in West Germany and Switzerland (for example, cf. Döbert & Nunner-Winkler, 1975; Habermas, 1976a; Portele, 1978; Bertram, 1978; Lind, 1978a; Eckensberger, 1983; Oser, 1984).

In this essay I shall discuss the concepts and assumptions of cognitive-developmental theory as it has been formulated by Kohlberg, and, on the basis of my own research, suggest some modifications and extensions to improve the consistency, the scope, and the empirical validity of the theory. Above all, I shall offer two suggestions: first, that "structural wholeness" is a methodological criterion and not an empirical hypothesis, and second, that Kohlberg's stage model is truly supplementary to Piaget's phases from heteronomy to autonomy and is not a substitute for them. Finally, I shall discuss some implications of cognitive-developmental theory for the relation of individual moral development to the social environment, concerning, for instance, the concept of interaction of person and social environment, the relation of individual moral judgment competence and social position, and the role of selection mechanisms in socio-moral development.

FROM "EXTERNAL EFFECT"
TO "INTERNAL STRUCTURE"

Although the study of moral behavior has a long tradition, there is still much debate about its concepts and its methods. Psychological studies of moral behavior were already part of the "empirical study of the soul" *(Erfahrungsseelenkunde)* of the 18th century and the flourishing of "moral statistics" in the 19th century (Laplace, Ouetelet, Dufau, Drobisch). As early as the first half of this century, a number of psychological experiments were made concerning the conditions for and the development of morality (surveyed in Neumann, 1931; Pittel & Mendelsohn, 1966).

Many of these studies made a careful differentiation between physical behavior considered merely as localized in space and time, social behavior that is evaluated in regard to external standards, and moral behavior considered as possessing socio-psychological meaning. However, in most of these studies a "behavioristic" point of view prevailed. In these studies–more often in their research methods than in their theoretical premises–the social-evaluative and psychological-cognitive aspects of moral behavior were excluded from consideration. This research perspective is well represented by the studies by Hartshorne, May, and their collaborators under the supervision of the learning theorist Thorndike. As do many of their heirs, Hartshorne and May (1928-30) assessed moral behavior as a physical phenomenon without reference to socio-psychological categories. They argued that

> No progress can be made . . . unless the overt act can be observed and, if possible, measured *without* reference, for the moment, to its motives or its rightness or wrongness. (p. 10, italics added)

The rationale behind this "pragmatic orientation" (Burton, 1978) was that psychology could acquire a scientific reputation only if it focused its research on purely methodological considerations. Measurement should be as "objective" and free of "subjective" elements as it is, for example, in physics, and this could be achieved only if a physical conceptualization of behavior was adopted. However, this *physicalistic behaviorism* confused concept with methods: to use the words of Adorno (1980, p. 84), it turned the objectivity of the behavioral concept into the subjectivity of the research method. In attempting to avoid value judgments, psychologists actually stripped behavior of any socio-psychological meaning. In impinging upon the measurement of the physical aspects of behavior, it failed to assess what it intended to study. The morality or immorality of human acts cannot be adequately described without recourse to socio-psychological properties of behavior, that is, external social norms or individual motives and thoughts. *Moral actions,* as Blasi (1983) explains, "are responses to situations, as defined by and interpreted according to moral reasoning structures, that is, to a set of criteria determining the morally good" (p. 196).[1]

Although today there seems to be little disagreement over the fact that any research concerning moral behavior needs to take reasoning structures or moral criteria into account, the question remains as to which ones we should choose "to determine the morally good." Basically, there are two perspectives of research: one, already mentioned, conceives of moral behavior almost exclusively from the social-evaluative perspective, and the other does so from the point of view of the individual's motives. Allport (1961) has aptly labeled these two perspectives the *external effect approach* and the *internal structure approach,* respectively.

The external effect approach categorizes an individual's behavior according to socially given norms, laws, or regulations. This implies that behavior is categorized according to traits which are common to all individuals of a group or sample of persons (*common trait* approach). Though often the rationale of the measurement process is not made explicit but is hidden behind the implicit assumptions of the research method, in this approach behavior is judged according to whether it conforms to, or deviates from, social norms and expectations, that is, whether social rules and laws are transgressed or obeyed. In a typical research design the psychologist assesses a subject's behavior according to external social categories like deceiving/not deceiving, stealing/not stealing, killing/not killing. Pittel and Mendelsohn (1966) have shown in their review of half a century of psychological research on moral behavior that most methods of assessing moral behavior are indeed based

on normative or other evaluative standards of "correctness" determined by societally defined criteria. Thus, responses in agreement with norms established by the investigators are scored as moral, while those not in agreement lower the overall measure of strength of moral attitude or conscience . . . Even when scoring criteria are not explicitly linked to normative or societal standards, subjective scoring procedures and ratings . . . frequently rely on the same sort of external standards of evaluation. (p. 33)

The external effect approach to moral psychology can be criticized on several accounts. But, as Pittel and Mendelsohn (1966) noted, "perhaps the greatest single shortcoming underlying each of the specific criticisms discussed is the failure to view evaluative attitudes as subjective phenomena whose measurement is best achieved independently of a concern with the relationship of those attitudes to conventional and normative standards of moral valuation" (p. 34).[2] Because it is confined to the tacit evaluation of behavior according to the socially given norms, the external effect approach fails to assess the cognitive and affective aspects of individual behavior. When studying moral behavior from an external point of view, one must assume that the system of norms is monolithic, and that these norms have an immediate effect upon behavior, that is, that there is no need to assume mediating processes on the side of the individual. This view overlooks the fact that only when the individual accepts moral principles and orients his behavior to them do these principles become *actual*. Therefore, we may dismiss the external effect point of view as too narrow.

In opposition to the prevailing view, Allport (1961) has already demanded that psychological analysis of the individual personality should focus on the *internal structure* of human behavior. Similarly, Pittel and Mendelsohn (1966) have called for a change in the approach to moral behavior; for them "it is important to assess at an individual level the content, strength, and patterning of the subjective attitude of evaluation *per se*" (p. 34). Modern psychology seems to be ready for a psychological interpretation of the term "behavior," which "includes much of that which in other places is designated as thoughts, feelings, or ideas" (Cohen, 1984, p. 3).

It seems that the cognitive-developmental theory of human behavior has indeed succeeded in working out a research program on the basis of the internal structure point of view. The change in the research paradigm is marked by the change of terms from "moral behavior" to "moral judgment" or "moral judgment competence." But the concept of behavior or performance has not been completely abandoned because, as Habermas (in this volume) has succinctly noted, "competence by itself cannot be shown to exist except in its concrete manifestation, that is, through phenomena of performance." As an empirical science psychology is closely linked to the observation of behavior, because every empirical hypothesis concerning the content, structure, and development of moral reasoning must be verifiable or falsifiable by referring to a manifest pattern of judgment behavior (cf. Kohlberg, 1979). Nevertheless, we usually prefer to speak of "moral judgment" rather than "moral behavior" because the reference of the former term is more obviously restricted to behavior that can be related to the individual's own moral categories.

The differences in outcomes of the external effect and the internal structure points of view are marked if one considers, for example, the moral behavior of children. Children are often seen as lacking morality. But this is true only if morality is defined with regard to the norms of adults. For example, it is true that "honest" behavior becomes more frequent as children grow older, as does "dishonest" behavior in some children (Hartshorne et al., 1928-30; Block, 1977, p. 40). However, if one considers the reasons for behavior beyond particular social norms and the point to which the cognitive aspect of moral behavior has developed, it becomes clear that even in young children behavior is consistently organized according to rules, although these may be individual rules, that is, widely varying and not socially approved. Moreover, moral behavior becomes not only more consistent and integrated with age but also more differentiated. Thus a child who has attained significant autonomy regarding the moral principle "Thou shalt not lie!" will no longer judge a violation of this rule as always wrong. Rather, the child will also consider the circumstances, in consequence judging, "It depends." For example, children who at first consider lying to be generally prohibited later consider it to be all right if they can keep a friend out of trouble by lying (Bull, 1969, p. 210). Similarly, in the course of the child's cognitive-moral development, the rule of "returning like for like" is differentiated by the idea of mitigating circumstances (Piaget, 1977, pp. 321ff.). To the casual observer, those cases may appear to be morally regressive, whereas a cognitive-developmental psychologist would recognize in them progress in the child's development.

The fact that the terms "moral behavior" and "moral judgment" often indicate two fundamentally different ways of viewing morality in psychology rather than two different types of human behavior renders the study of their interrelation particularly difficult (Blasi, 1980; Eckensberger, 1983; Kohlberg & Candee, 1984). This has been aptly pointed out by Don Locke (1983a, 1983b, 1983c), who described the basic difference between the external and the internal approaches as the choice between an "evaluative" and a "neutral" definition of moral action: "We can either define moral action with reference to our own attitudes about what is right or wrong, good or bad . . . ; or we can define it by reference to the attitudes and beliefs of the agent" (1983a, pp. 112-113). He convincingly demonstrates that the evaluative definition of morality cannot provide a satisfactory basis for psychological research (nor for educational practice). Therefore, he proposes "to work towards a neutral definition, always bearing in mind that moral action in this sense will not necessarily be action that we would ourselves regard as good or bad, right or wrong" (p. 113).

Thus, if we want to understand the individual, two extremes must be avoided: that of defining personality structure solely from the "outside," and, at the other extreme, giving a purely idiosyncratic definition in which people are considered totally unique and therefore ineligible for comparison. People are bound to society, without which they would become "total abstractions" (Adorno, 1980, p. 197). However, they are also capable of assuming responsibility and exercising critical judgment on the basis of moral principles. We may therefore assume that, beyond the particular characteristics demanded by the situation, there are general personality characteristics on the basis of which people can be meaningfully compared without restriction to conventions. In this interactionist conception, "personality" is neither a purely external nor a purely internal category; rather it is that which is characteristic of the *relationship* between the individual and the social environment (see below). This relationship is twofold. On the one hand, moral behavior presupposes a cognitive structure: moral principles, norms, and values have to be balanced off against each other and in light of the specific circumstances of a decision situation. On the other hand, competence in moral judgment, that is, the ability to integrate and differentiate moral principles and apply them to everyday decisions, has a developmental character and so must be placed in reference to the individual's life experience (ontogenesis) and to the state of the socially developed strategies for solving problems (phylogenesis).[3]

ASSESSMENT OF THE THEORY

There is no theory of morality, moral behavior, and moral development that is fully elaborated and empirically proven. As Lakatos (1978) has shown, there can be only preliminary theories which are subject to alteration and error. Nevertheless, we can identify and deal in a critically constructive manner with a number of core concepts and assumptions, which have been empirically well supported and which we may provisionally call the *theory of moral-cognitive development*. This theory arose out of the tradition of Kant,

Baldwin, Janet, and Dewey, and has been elaborated upon extensively by Piaget and expanded and repeatedly varied by Kohlberg, on the basis of numerous creative as well as critical studies.[4]

Although like Kohlberg we will use the terms "theory" and "approach" interchangeably, we prefer to speak of an approach rather than a theory to make clear that our concern is not only with empirical hypotheses but also with the conceptual framework which provides the "positive heuristics" (Lakatos). The concepts and the hypotheses of any theory have to be analyzed in different ways and must not be confused. Concepts provide the basis for measurement and empirical testing, but they cannot themselves be empirically tested in a meaningful manner. Thus concepts may be assessed as to their usefulness in enlarging our intellectual capacity and discovering new facts and in regard to their internal consistency and absence of contradictions. Hypotheses in which these concepts are used to make statements about (causal) relations in the empirical world can be analyzed in two ways. First, they can be assessed with respect to their *information content* or *Gehalt*, that is, the degree of their unforeseeability and a priori unlikeliness (cf. Popper, 1968; Lind, 1978b, 1985d). As we shall see below, hypotheses with high a priori probability are–even if empirically true–of little theoretical and practical interest because they are likely to be supported by chance, and provide no information which deserves to be empirically tested and conserved in a scientific theory. Second, informative hypotheses can be assessed in regard to their empirical validity. Critics as well as defenders of cognitive-developmental theory have not always been aware of this distinction, a fact which has caused some confusion in the recent discussion about the value of this theory (cf. Kohlberg, 1976; Phillips & Nicolayev, 1978; Lapsley & Serlin, 1984).

In this presentation we want first of all to examine the central concepts and schema of cognitive-developmental theory and then to consider the extent to which the fundamental hypotheses of this approach have proven to be empirically valid–or may have to be treated as concepts which cannot be empirically tested. In particular, we want to make four points. The first is that, as has already been indicated above, the cognitive-developmental theory has provided very useful concepts for the study of moral behavior and thus has enabled us to make new discoveries in the field of moral psychology. The second point is that, in comparison to other psychological approaches, the empirical hypotheses (e.g., about the invariant sequence of moral-cognitive development, preference order of moral stage-types, and moral-cognitive parallelism) are both highly informative and well supported by empirical data. The third point is that the central concept of structural wholeness should not be construed as implying empirical predictions, but should be set up as the criterion against which the theoretical validity of the measurement of moral competence can be evaluated. Our fourth, and perhaps most important, point is that Kohlberg's stage schema of moral development does not include and replace that of Piaget, but rather succeeds in supplementing and extending it in regard to the social dimension of individual development.[5]

CONCEPTUAL FRAMEWORK: STRUCTURES AND STAGES

In cognitive-developmental theory, the cognitive-structural aspect of moral judgment and the stage scheme of moral development assume the position of core concepts. Sometimes they have been treated as empirical hypotheses which they certainly are not. Although their meaning has not yet been completely clarified, these concepts obviously cannot be dismissed without giving up the cognitive-developmental approach altogether. When we discuss them, we must keep in mind the fact that both concepts are frequently used in many different ways and have quite different connotations outside this approach (cf. Boesch, 1984; Entwistle, 1979; Glaserfield & Kelley, 1982).

Structures

In cognitive-developmental theory the concept of cognitive structure is usually juxtaposed with the concept of affective content (cf. Kohlberg, 1958, 1969; Lind, 1985d, 1985e). Kohlberg claims that, whereas traditional psychology has focused mainly on the content of moral behavior, his theory is dealing with its structure. It is often considered one of the major tasks, if not achievements, of this approach to distinguish both components and to devise an instrument which makes it possible to measure the structural aspect of moral judgment competence in addition to, and apart from, its content aspect. Although this topic has already been discussed, one can still reasonably ask, "Exactly what is structure and what is content?" (Lickona, 1976, p. 13). Is it the difference between opinions about concrete action dilemmas and the moral reasons given for them? Is it the difference between moral beliefs and moral attitudes? Or does content denote observable behavior, whereas structure is something "behind" behavior and therefore unobservable?

For cognitive-developmental theory the *structure* of moral judgment behavior reflects the organization and process of moral thinking, the way in which and the degree to which moral maxims or principles are brought to bear in specific situations. The concept of cognitive structure refers to Kant's concept of *Urteilskraft* (power of judgment) which is required

> partly in order to decide in what cases [moral maxims] apply and partly to produce for them an access to man's will and an impetus to their practice. For man is affected by so many inclinations that, though he is capable of the idea of a practical pure reason, he is not so easily able to make it concretely effective in the conduct of his life. (Kant, 1949/1788, p. 52)

This implies that moral action requires both "power of judgment" and real acceptance of moral maxims, that is, the cognitive ability to understand how a rule is to be applied in concrete situations *and* the motivation or will to base one's action on rational insights (Habermas, in this volume). Accordingly, Kohlberg defined moral competence as "the capacity to make decisions and judgments which are moral (i.e., based on internal principles) and to act in accordance with such judgments" (Kohlberg, 1964, p. 425); he defined the otherwise neglected cognitive and structural aspect of moral behavior as "the degree to which any of an individual's judgments approximate the criteria of a moral judgment" (Kohlberg, 1958, p. 7). Furthermore, the criteria which suffice for the categorical imperative are "impersonality, ideality, universalizability, pre-emptiveness, etc." (Kohlberg, 1971b, p. 215).

Thus, the organization of a person's moral judgment behavior is not characterized solely by the moral norms it serves (or fails to serve), which we may call the affective content of behavior, nor solely by the formal properties of the individual's reasoning, that is, the consistency or structure of reasoning. In other words, it is only by referring to content that one speaks meaningfully of behavioral *consistency.* There is no consistency of behavior as such; it is always consistency *in relation to* a criterion or principle. Consistency is a bivalent relation concept. Whereas purely formal structures, as found in physical and chemical nature, are arrangements of elements without dynamic-affective meaning, *dynamic* structures refer to human actions which possess a meaning, e.g., to behavioral elements which are characterized through a teleological, affective content and their relationship to this and other affective contents (Figure 1). For this reason we cannot define moral behavior without reference to particular moral principles. Yet, following D. Locke's *neutral defini-*

tion of morality, we should refer to the subject's own moral principles rather than to those of an external judge.

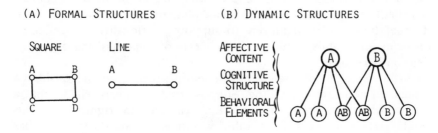

Figure 1. Purely Formal vs. Dynamic Structures

Some psychologists–even cognitive-developmentalists–tend to view these two aspects as separate faculties of the mind, a tendency which is evident not so much in theory as in concrete research methods. If we define the formal structure merely as a "system of inner relationships," these relationships are themselves purely formal and so lack an affective, dynamic dimension. Formal structures suffice for a mechanistic image of humans taken from associationist psychology, but a psychological definition of cognitive structures requires a teleological content (cf. Reese & Overton, 1970).

According to our model, affect is provided in a supplementary fashion by the moral contents–moral norms, issues, principles. These moral contents render a *behavioral* structure "comprehensible" by scientific analysis (Kohlberg, 1979, p. 14). Moreover, they direct and motivate the development of the cognitive aspect of moral judgment (Weinreich-Haste, 1975, p. 208). Therefore, Kohlberg's occasional insistence that cognitive-moral stages are, or are to be, defined solely by formal aspects deserves to be criticized, as we shall see below.

Does this imply, as Glaserfield and Kelley (1982, p. 157) and others have maintained, that structures are merely heuristic devices in the head of the observer but are not themselves observable? I do not think it does. There are examples, even in psychology, of conceptualizing a behavioral structure as an observable entity and measuring it directly. Of course, a single act, such as expressing an opinion on a particular dilemma, cannot be used by an observer as a basis for relational inferences. At least two acts are needed to suggest a relationship. Moreover, a single act is usually the result of an individual's reaction to the multiple demands of a complex situation. Hence, to make valid inferences on the content and structure of moral behavior, we have to make use of relational information and observe a whole pattern of acts in a particular behavior context and the reasons that justify them. To adequately understand which moral attitudes a person has and to what degree his or her behavior is actually determined by such principles, or, alternatively, to what degree these are used merely to support ("rationalize") unreflected opinions and habits, a hermeneutic circle of hypothesizing and verification is required.

As an example of such a hermeneutic process, let us consider a discussion about mercy killing. Suppose that a woman tells us that a doctor who committed mercy killing was morally right. From this single statement we cannot infer whether or not the woman has based her judgment on moral concern, and so we must ask for reasons. In the ensuing discussion, she expresses a high acceptance for a Stage 5 argument. We now know a little more, but we still cannot be sure that she actually reasons at Stage 5. Her acceptance of the argument may be determined by several considerations, of which the moral quality of the argument is only one among many. For instance, she may accept it because the argument is presented by an authority such as a doctor or a psychologist, or she may accept it because the argument supports her independently established opinion on euthanasia. We would be more confident of the latter interpretation if it turned out that she did not accept at least some of the other arguments presented in the discussion (especially those below Stage 5), and if she accepted the same moral reason even on occasions when it was at variance with her intuitively based opinion. If this were not the case, we would be inclined to say that her judgment was not determined by the moral principle on which the argument was based. In basically the same manner, this everyday process of probing to advance and eliminate competing explanations for a person's action is also employed in tests of moral judgment competence (cf. Colby, Kohlberg, et al., in press; Lind & Wakenhut, in this volume).

We may summarize so far by saying, first of all, that the two aspects of moral behavior, namely, cognition and affect, are both attributes of the same behavior. They can be differentiated only analytically and cannot be regarded as two ontologically separate entities. We shall refer to this basic claim as the *Non-Separability Axiom*, whose corollary is that the cognitive aspect which refers to the structure of judgment behavior must always be determined in relation to moral content (see also Lind, 1985a, 1985e). Secondly, both aspects, affective content as well as cognitive structure, are observable in principle; in cases in which this is not possible in practice we have to refrain from making an assessment. Thirdly, if acting according to principles involves equilibration, rationality, freedom from contradiction, and suitability, then structural wholeness of reasoning cannot mean a simple consistency or rigidity; concrete behavior which truly reflects the multitude of moral implications of a situation for an individual's value system necessitates integrated and differential judgments (Kohlberg, 1958, pp. 8-9; 1969, p. 348). Fourthly, the cognitive-developmental concept of cognition is at odds with those treatments which discuss cognition not as a set of general structures and processes, but rather as particular contents, such as beliefs or mental achievements. Fifthly, the notion of structural transformation as distinguished from merely attitudinal change improves our understanding of the development of moral behavior; it is the cognitive rather than the affective aspect of moral behavior which develops sequentially and invariantly (cf. Lind, ch. 8, in this volume).

Stages

To provide a conceptual framework for analyzing moral-cognitive development, Kohlberg has constructed six stages, and three levels each of which includes two stages of development. These are well known and need only be briefly summarized here.

Each of the Kohlberg levels of moral-cognitive development is primarily defined by the "socio-moral perspective" which the actor takes in making decisions on socio-moral problems (cf. Kohlberg, 1976). On Level I, the individual assesses a situation from the "concrete individual perspective." The morally right or wrong is determined by the material consequences of an act; the guiding principle is to avoid punishment and to satisfy one's needs. On Level II the person takes over the "member of society perspective" from which the maintenance of social relations and order becomes an important principle for assessing a dilemma situation. On Level III the actor makes judgments from a "prior to society perspective," that is, on the basis of general principles which are not tied to a particular social group or society but to humanity and human life as a whole. These three levels are further subdivided by Kohlberg into two stages, yielding the six stages of moral-cognitive development which are reproduced in Table 1. We have adopted the description of the six stages from Kohlberg and Turiel (1971, pp. 415-416) because these seem to be among the clearest of the many formulations given (cf. Lind, 1976, p. 125; Krämer-Badoni & Wakenhut, 1978a, p. 218; Montada, 1983, p. 7).

Table 1

Stages of Cognitive-Moral Development

PREMORAL LEVEL

Stage 0. Subject neither understands rules nor judges good or bad in terms of rules and authority. Good is what is pleasant or exciting; bad is what is painful or fearful. Has no idea of obligation, should, or have to, even in terms of external authority, but is guided only by can do and want to do.

I. PRECONVENTIONAL LEVEL

At this level the child is responsive to cultural rules and labels of good and bad, right and wrong, but interprets these labels in terms of either the physical or the hedonistic consequences of action (punishment, reward, exchange of favors) or in terms of the physical power of those who enunciate the rules and labels.

Stage 1. The punishment and obedience orientation. The physical consequences of action determine its goodness or badness, regardless of the human meaning or value of these consequences. Avoidance of punishment and unquestioning deference to power are valued in their own right, not in terms of respect for an underlying moral order supported by punishment and authority (the latter being Stage 4).
Stage 2. The instrumental relativist orientation. Right action consists of that which instrumentally satisfies one's own needs and occasionally the needs of others. Human relationships are viewed in terms similar to those of the market place. Elements of fairness, reciprocity, and equal sharing are present, but they are always interpreted in a physical or pragmatic way. Reciprocity is a matter of "You scratch my back and I'll scratch yours," not of loyalty, gratitude, or justice.

II. CONVENTIONAL LEVEL

At this level, maintaining the expectations of the individual's family, group, or nation is perceived as valuable in its own right, regardless of immediate and obvious consequences. The attitude is not only one of conformity to personal expectations and social order, but of loyalty, of actively maintaining, supporting, and justifying the order and of identifying with the persons or group involved in it.

Table 1 (Continued)

Stage 3. The interpersonal concordance or "good boy–nice girl" orientation. Good behavior is that which pleases or helps others and is approved by them. There is much conformity to stereotypical images of what the majority perceives as "natural" behavior. Behavior is frequently judged by intention: "He means well" becomes important for the first time. One earns approval by being "nice."

Stage 4. The law and order orientation. There is orientation toward authority, fixed rules, and the maintenance of the social order. Right behavior consists of doing one's duty, showing respect for authority, and maintaining the given social order for its own sake.

III. POSTCONVENTIONAL, AUTONOMOUS, OR PRINCIPLED LEVEL

At this level, there is a clear effort to define moral values and principles which have validity and application apart from the authority of the groups or persons holding these principles and apart from the individual's own identification with these groups.

Stage 5. The social-contract legalistic orientation. Right action tends to be defined in terms of general individual rights and of utilitarian standards which have been critically examined and agreed upon by the whole society. There is a clear awareness of the relativism of personal values and opinions and a corresponding emphasis upon procedural rules for reaching consensus. Aside from what is constitutionally and democratically agreed upon, the right is a matter of personal values and opinion. The result is an emphasis upon the legal point of view, but with further emphasis upon the possibility of changing the law by appeal to rational considerations of social utility, (rather than on rigidly maintaining it in terms of Stage 4 conceptions of law and order). Outside the legal realm, free agreement and contract are the binding elements of obligation. This is the acknowledged morality of democratic government and constitution.

Stage 6. The universal ethical principle orientation. Right is defined by the decision of conscience in accord with self-chosen ethical principles appealing to logical comprehensiveness, universality, and consistency. These principles are abstract and ethical (the Golden Rule, the categorical imperative) and are not concrete moral rules like the Ten Commandments. At heart, these are universal principles of justice, of the reciprocity and equality of human rights, and of respect for the dignity of human beings as individual persons.

Despite numerous variations in publications by Kohlberg and others over the last two decades, the stage schema has remained the same in its essential components (cf. Bergling, 1981; Kohlberg, 1983). Among the changes was the introduction of a so-called Stage 4½, so as to incorporate unexpected regressions in passing from Stage 4 to Stage 5 (this modification was subsequently abandoned in large part; today Kohlberg regards this problem as a coding error), and the attempt to expand the model to include a seventh stage (Kohlberg, 1973; Habermas, 1976a), which was set aside when Kohlberg, in response to academic criticism, omitted Stage 6 from his research program (but cf. Kohlberg, 1984, 1985, for his subsequent rethinking of Stage 6). In addition to these changes in the basic stage concept, the problem of assigning persons to stages on the basis of complex responses, the need for a more finely graded scale of moral-cognitive development, and the problem of relating moral thought to action have led Kohlberg and his associates to add a number of mixed stages and substages whose theoretical meaning is mostly unclear and which seem to contradict the central assumption of "structural wholeness" (which is true if this assumption is understood to be an empirical hypothesis; I will return to this point below). I believe that the differentiation into A and B substages is one of most important changes in the stage model (for an extensive account see Kohlberg, 1984).

However, this differentation necessitates a revision of our view of the relation between the models proposed by Kohlberg and Piaget. Kohlberg had postulated that his schema of moral-cognitive development substitutes for Piaget's model and extends it upwards (Kohlberg, 1958, pp. 151-228; Weinreich-Haste, 1975, p. 206), by which he means that Piaget's phases of heteronomy and autonomy are equivalent to his Stages 1 and 2 respectively. Stages 3 to 6, he supposed, extend beyond Piaget's developmental scale. This position can be justified only if (1) it is true that the moral judgment competency of a person manifests itself simultaneously in all areas of life, and (2) the age grouping in Piaget's two phases and Kohlberg's Stages 1 and 2 are indeed the same (cf. Kohlberg, 1958, pp. 70, 377-383; Kohlberg 1969; Bergling, 1981).

But both assumptions are questionable. First, "structural whole" does not in the least have to mean that moral autonomy is acquired all at once in all areas of life in relation to all moral issues. Even if his notion of "horizontal décalage" seems to imply the opposite, Piaget stated clearly that "there are no global stages that would characterize the complete psychological life of a subject at a particular time in development" (1973, p. 91). Second, I do not believe that it is permissible to set Piaget's phase of moral autonomy as equivalent to Kohlberg's Stages 2 ("hedonistic instrumentalism") or 3 ("group conformity"). We need not invoke Piaget's concept of logical development to see that the phase of moral autonomy more closely resembles Kohlberg's stage of principled morality and postconventionalism, even though they appear in completely different age groups because of the different issues and norm contents involved. Kohlberg seems to have been aware of this ambiguity when he once equated the phase of moral autonomy with both Stage 2 and Stage 6 (Kohlberg, 1969, Table 6.3, p. 377).

Therefore, I suspect that, as Weinreich-Haste (1975) has suggested, the two concepts do not substitute for but instead supplement each other. Exactly how they relate to one another may become clear if one analyzes the way in which the affective and the cognitive aspects of moral judgment are connected.

Cognitive and Affective Aspects of Moral Stages

In his dissertation, Kohlberg considered two dimensions of moral-cognitive development, the cognitive-structural dimension represented by the three levels, and the affective dimension represented by the six stages. In fact, in the newer versions of his model, he still defines the "structural" stages by moral content rather than by formal categories (cf. Kohlberg, 1976; also Table 1, above). Even abstract moral principles such as equality, justice, and universality are not in themselves structural but are contents if they are conceived of merely as deontic principles to which a subject *refers* in his or her argument. These criteria can be called "formal" only if the subject's judgment actually *matches* the principles of justice and universalizability. This fine, yet important, distinction seems to be taken up by Kohlberg through the introduction of *A*- and *B*-substages. The *B*-substages assume characteristics very similar to the main Stages 5 and 6, the level of principled morality and moral autonomy, and both criteria are indeed highly correlated in the examples provided by the Kohlberg interview manual (Rest, 1979a, p. 43; Eckensberger, 1984; Lind, 1985e). Moreover, the correlation shows also in the Milgram experiment on obedience, in which for 6 out of the 8 subjects who could be unambiguously assigned to stages, the two classifications coincided (Kohlberg & Candee, 1984, p. 69). Interestingly, this study also shows that the *A/B* distinction helps us better than does the stage distinction to understand the behavior of the subjects in Milgram's experiment on obedience. Whereas only 2 out of 7 substage *B* persons executed the order to torture another person in spite of his screams of pain (which they did not know were faked), all 9 subjects on substage *A* obeyed this inhuman order.

In accordance with our two-aspect model of moral behavior, and to account for the inadequacies of Kohlberg's stage model, I have suggested two distinguishable, albeit not ontologically separable, dimensions of moral-cognitive development (Lind, 1978b, 1984e; see also ch. 8, in this volume). Accordingly, moral-cognitive development may be understood as a two-dimensional process, in which Piaget's phases describe a recurring sequence of cognitive transformations on each of Kohlberg's stages. Whereas Piaget focused on conflicting norms of children's games, Kohlberg concentrates on norms of secondary groups and on universal moral principles and values of human life, replacing the child society studied in Piaget's work with the adult society. Hence, with his six types of moral issues, which are related to social institutions such as market rules, family and friendship norms, law, and moral principles, a completely new dimension of development has emerged: the differentiation of the affective aspect of moral judgment according to six types of socio-moral perspectives (see Figure 1).

In his recent writings, Kohlberg acknowledges the *A*- and *B*-substages as theoretically equivalent to Piaget's phases of heteronomy and autonomy (Kohlberg, 1984, pp. 652-683), though he interprets these substages in a somewhat different manner than I do. When he says that this distinction lies "midway between form and content" (Kohlberg & Candee, 1984, p. 44), he apparently views it as a new entity which is separable from both moral content and structure. This multiplication of psychological entities is, in my view, not necessary, and could be taken as a degenerating problem shift. As I have noted above, cognition and affect are distinguishable aspects of moral behavior but are not separable. The theory of an integral moral-cognitive development is distinct from approaches which either presuppose that the two developmental dimensions cannot be distinguished at all, or attempt to conceptualize two or more ontologically separate components or factors of development.[6]

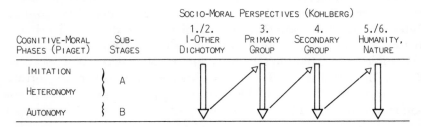

Figure 2. An Integration of Piaget's and Kohlberg's Models of Moral Development

EMPIRICAL VALIDITY AND INFORMATION
VALUE OF THE THEORY

The fruitfulness of Kohlberg's cognitive-developmental theory is documented through the wide array of new empirical hypotheses which could be formulated within this conceptual framework. Four hypotheses are especially noteworthy here, concerning as they do (1) the invariant succession of the developmental stages, (2) the structural whole, or organization, of moral judgment, (3) the hierarchical order or preference order of moral reasoning types, and (4) the parallelism between the development of the cognitive and the affective aspects of moral judgment. In the following I want to analyze what these hypotheses imply, whether they can be confirmed empirically, and to what extent they have been empirically validated.

Invariant Sequence

The most central hypothesis of cognitive-developmental theory is that there are qualitatively different stages of moral development which form an *invariant sequence;* social factors can accelerate or slow down the development but cannot change its sequential order (Kohlberg, 1969, p. 352; 1971b, p. 181; Colby et al., 1983, p. 1). This implies that "a single case of longitudinal inversion of sequence disproves the stage theory, if it is not a manifest case of measurement error" (Kohlberg, 1973a, p. 182).

This hypothesis is highly informative or testable, a fact which is not adequately reflected in the usually reported percentages, correlations, and tests of statistical significance, because these figures do not take into account the *Gehalt* (information content) of a hypothesis (cf. Popper, 1968; Meehl, 1978). A high *Gehalt (G)* means that there is a high a priori probability that the hypothesis is *not* confirmed by pure chance. For example, the a priori probability that an individual person will pass through the six stages in exactly the sequence prescribed by the theory is only $p = 0.0014$ and thus the *Gehalt* and information content of such a hypothesis is $G_1 = 1 - p = 1 - 0.0014 = 0.9986$ (maximum: 1.0).

The *Gehalt* of the hypothesis that, for example, 50 persons will develop as the theory states thus is extremely high; it is very close to 1; it is $G_{50} = 1 - 0.0014^{50}$ (power of fifty).

In comparison, the *Gehalt* of a vague but very common hypothesis like "variable x somehow influences variable y" is close to zero. For further details on this method of evaluating scientific hypotheses, and for an exact definition of p and G, see Lind (1984a). A similar method has recently been suggest by Turner (1980). However, his index is based on a mixture of a priori probability and empirical frequency. It is important to note that G is based purely on a priori or logical probability implied by the hypothesis.

Although the hypothesis of invariant moral-cognitive development is so highly informative and easily falsified by empirical data, it has by and large been corroborated by longitudinal studies. Infrequent deviations from this hypothesis were mostly found in short-term studies and in studies using special kinds of measurement. In the most important study by Kohlberg and his collaborators, which lasted more than twenty years, the developmental sequences anticipated have occurred with only a very few exceptions. Of the 58 persons interviewed every three to four years, only 14 out of 193 passages (7%) were reversed (when measured on a scale divided into 13 interval substages; cf. Kohlberg, 1979; Colby et al., 1983). The invariant sequence hypothesis could also be supported in studies measuring somewhat different aspects of moral judgment. In studies with Rest's *Defining Issues Test*, it has been shown that for persons between 13 and 22 years of age the consistency with which postconventional arguments are preferred to other kinds increases considerably (about 20 percentage points; see Rest, 1979a, p. 140). In our ongoing longitudinal study we found that the consistency of evaluating arguments with regard to moral principles grows with increasing age and educational experience, and the tendency to rationalize one's opinion by reference to moral reasons decreases (cf. Lind, 1985a, 1985d).

The small number of regressions, as well as the fact that only a few Stage 5 subjects and virtually no Stage 6 reasoners could be found, has stirred up a debate over how these anomalies should be dealt with. Following simple falsificationism, some tend to regard cognitive-developmental theory as falsified by these anomalies and thus argue for an enlargement or fundamental change of the theory. But following Lakatos (1978), I prefer to search first for methodological imperfections which can be remedied on the basis of an unchanged theory before inventing auxiliary hypotheses and thus reducing the *Gehalt* of cognitive-developmental theory. Besides, we should not give up a good theory before we have a better one at hand (cf. Lakatos, 1978; Kohlberg, 1979; Lapsley & Serlin, 1984).

The observed cases of regression may indeed be cases of measurement error which, however, can be determined in different ways. A classical psychometric way is to select a particular sample of people and assess their stage scores twice within a time span to calculate the correlation between these assessments (the so-called test-retest reliability), which provides an estimate for short-term variations (standard error of measurement). On the basis of this criterion, Colby et al. (1983) could show that in their longitudinal sample the number of downward movements over a three-to-four-year interval (approx. 7%) was clearly lower than the number of changes within one month. This is undoubtedly an impressive result. Nevertheless, I would like to question the adequacy of such psychometric criteria. The size of the standard error of measurement depends very much on the distribution of the stages in the sample (Colby et al., 1983, p. 26, report the standard deviation was here as small as 7/10 of a stage), and from a structural point of view one may rightly question the basic assumptions of classical psychometric theory (cf. Kohlberg, 1976, 1979; Lind, 1982b).

For this reason, we have pursued another way of determining possible sources of measurement error in moral judgment research. Kohlberg and his colleagues have taken great pains to improve the scoring method, but little attention has yet been paid to the design of the instrument itself. There are in particular three indications that the design of the assessment method could indeed be improved in regard to its theoretical validity. First, if one reviews the original Kohlberg and Kramer (1969) cases of regression, one finds that these cases are almost exclusively confined to the initially higher stage subjects, which indicates, as already noted above, that there may be a deficiency of the method in dealing with high stage reasoning. Second, as Broughton has found in an unpublished analysis of a severe case of regression, some regressions may reflect a lack of probing in the interview. Third, if one analyzes not only the number of times in which a subject reasons on each stage but also which (relative) weights he or she attaches to these reasons, as is done, for example, through the *Moralisches Urteil Test* (cf. Lind & Wakenhut, in this volume), then we find that persons with an initially high judgment competence accept Stage 5 and 6 reasoning slightly less after one year, but this decrease is relative only to the person's own initial acceptance; his or her absolute preference for high stages of moral reasoning remains much higher than that of the subjects with lower judgment competence (cf. Lind, 1985a); so here again the regression phenomenon seems to be caused by the developmental restrictions imposed upon the data by the research instrument.

As far as the lack of Stage 6 moral judgments and the infrequency of Stage 5 judgments in the research data are concerned, similar methodological considerations apply. To a certain extent, our present methods seem to be biased against moral reasoning at post-conventional stages. This may be due to a lack of probing, to the computation of average stage scores (favoring the scoring on Stages 3 and 4), or to the kind of moral issues involved in the research instruments.

In sum, our analysis shows that we can consider the invariant sequence hypothesis as empirically valid. True, there are some data which are apparently at variance with this statement, but there is no compelling reason to give up the core hypothesis of cognitive-developmental theory or to narrow its range of applicability as some authors have suggested (cf. Bergling, 1981; Gibbs, 1977; Kohlberg & Kramer, 1969; Kohlberg et al., 1983; Rest, 1979a). Such alterations may considerably diminish the *Gehalt* (information value) of the theory and should be undertaken only after the above-mentioned possibilities of methodological improvement have proven unsuccessful.

Structural Wholeness

Cognitive-developmental theory states that each of the stages of moral judgment forms a structural whole that unifies an individual's judgment behavior. This assumption is usually taken to imply a consistency of answers over different aspects. Moral orientations should appear "as a logical and empirically related cluster of responses in development" (Kohlberg, 1969, p. 353). As a confirmation of this hypothesis, Kohlberg points to the fact that a person uses moral principles largely independently of the specific dilemma, and that, in regard to this, the differences between persons are highly stable.[7]

Although in most studies considerable variation in individual judgment–that is moderate consistency–has been found,[8] this finding could be greatly improved by introducing new concepts and structural criteria. "The basic developmental concept underlying the revised stage sequence is the level of socio-moral perspective, the characteristic point of view from which the individual formulates moral judgments" (Colby et al., 1983, p. 6). This means that one cannot expect all judgments relating to moral dilemmas to be alike but that, if one follows an individual's reasoning to its roots, one will eventually find that he or she argues from a unique socio-moral perspective which is characteristic of his or her moral-cognitive development.

However, this finding does not yet fully support the original claim of the cognitive developmental theory. The fact of mixed stages, of substages, and of the grading of stages into one hundred developmental points involved in Kohlberg's assessment method still contradicts the proposition of whole stages of judgment. The introduction of *A*- and *B*-substages partly accounts for this. Finally, the interpretation of structural wholeness as response consistency is too narrow. It disregards differentation, which is also an important outcome of moral-cognitive development. To overcome this problem, it has been suggested that the six-stage model be replaced by a "more complex stage model" which would do more justice to a specific data state. The "complexity" hypothesis, however, is too imprecise and has little *Gehalt*, since it cannot be disproved empirically.

Considering these problems, I suggest that this assumption involves—as Austin has called it—a *descriptive error*. Structural wholeness as the description of a state is misunderstood; it has to be understood as a norm for an approach to the subject and as a norm for the methods used in dealing with the subject (for a discussion of this problem in respect to psychology in general, see Hartnack, 1962, p. 91). If we regard structural wholeness as a methodological criterion of cognitive developmental theory, the degree and kind of consistency with which a person brings a moral rule to bear in his interaction with social situations will gain the status of manifestations of judgment competence (Beilin, 1971, p. 173; Lind & Wakenhut, in this volume). As Piaget and Kohlberg have noted, structures have not always been present in the individual and do not emerge all at once, but are constructed through the individual's interaction with his or her social environment.[9]

At this point a problem may arise because of the right interpretation of the terms "integration" and "differentiation." If, within the trait model of personality, we translate integration with increasing and differentiation with decreasing consistency of judgment, two mutually exclusive assumptions result, namely that in the course of development, judgment becomes consistent and inconsistent at the same time. This contradiction is resolved only when "consistency of judgment" is defined explicitly in relation to the orientation to which judgment is consistent or inconsistent. If one analyzes the context that defines the consistency of judgment, then it appears that the consistency *decreases* in relation to "opinion conformity" (see Lind & Wakenhut, in this volume), so that judgment becomes more *differen-*

tiated. In contrast, consistency increases in relation to the moral quality of the arguments (the "Stage factor") so that it is simultaneously *integrated.* Earlier orientations are seldom abandoned; rather they are differentiated according to a new priority rule. It all depends on not losing the ability to make decisions while developing the capacity for moral reflection. One continues to form opinions about concrete moral dilemmas, but these opinions are reflective commitments, which are open to modification through arguments.

Thus both conditions must be met for a moral judgment to be called mature: it must be made on the basis of universally valid moral principles (integrated judgment) and, at the same time, it must attend to the particularities of the circumstances of each dilemma and to their specific moral implications (differentiated judgment).

Preference Order

The stages of moral development are not ordered only on the basis of their philosophical adequacy; in fact people intuitively prefer them in this order (Kohlberg, 1969). This hypothesis has been unanimously supported by a high number of studies in various cultural contexts. Because of this the hypothesis of a universally valid order of preferences for the stages of moral reasoning may seem to be a trivial one, but it is not. First, I think this coincidence of philosophical reasoning and "everyday" moral philosophy is most remarkable. If empirically warranted, it would provide the best and possibly the only constructive way to enter a moral discourse with another person–which is especially important for parents and teachers who are concerned with moral education. Second, this assumption, like the first hypothesis, has a comparatively high information content. If the order of preference is determined randomly, the six types of moral rules may be ordered in 720 different ways. Hence the information content of the prediction that a person or a group of persons will prefer the six types in the theoretically expected order is as high as $G = 1 - 0.0014 = 0.9986$. Third, the hypothesis of preference order may explain why the invariant stage-wise development of moral competence is found universally. The affective component of moral judgment may be considered a pacer for the development of the cognitive aspect of judgment: "The disposition to prefer a solution of a problem at the higher level available to the individual partially accounts for the consistency postulated as our third (structural whole) criterion" (Kohlberg, 1969, p. 353). It has been found in many studies that the preference for the morally highest stages is indeed much sooner developed than the ability to use these stages in an everyday argument in a consistent and differentiated manner (Rest, 1979; see also Lind, 1985d).

Moral-Cognitive Parallelism

Now that we have identified the cognitive and affective aspects of moral judgment, we must ask how closely the two aspects are related. Cognitive-developmental theory hypothesizes that "affective development and functions and cognitive functioning are not distinct realms. 'Affective' and 'cognitive' development are *parallel*" (Kohlberg, 1969, p. 349).[10] This hypothesis is at the heart of cognitive-developmental theory, though still not at the heart of research practice (Lind, 1985e). Its meaning has remained rather obscure, in spite of its very different interpretations. The interpretation most important for the theory of cognitive development goes back to Kohlberg's postulate that "a moral act or attitude cannot be *defined* either by purely 'cognitive' or by purely 'motivational' criteria" (1958, p. 16; my italics). In a similar vein, Piaget had already stated that "*every* form of behavior has an energy or affective aspect and a structural or cognitive aspect" (1976, pp. 7-8; my italics). Because this hypothesis had not been dealt with adequately in the design of research methods, it had not yet been submitted to empirical investigation (disregarding attempts in which the cognitive aspect has been operationalized as a separate mental faculty). To render it possible to test empirically the hypothesis of parallelism, a new research design was needed. We have suggested such a design with the *Moralisches Urteil Test* (MUT; cf. Lind & Wakenhut, in this volume). Through measuring simultaneously the affective and the cognitive functions as aspects of a particular pattern of judgment behavior, we are now in a position to test the hypothesis of affective-cognitive parallelism directly and non-tautologically.

Indeed, all studies with the experimentally designed MUT have shown a clear parallelism between the affective and the cognitive aspects, that is, between the content and the structure of moral judgment. The greater consistency is in relation to moral categories, the stronger the acceptance of the "higher" stages of moral argumentation and the rejection of the "lower" stages. In all studies, the pattern of correlations between the two aspects is surprisingly consistent with the theory of moral-cognitive development (Figure 3; see also Lind, 1985e).

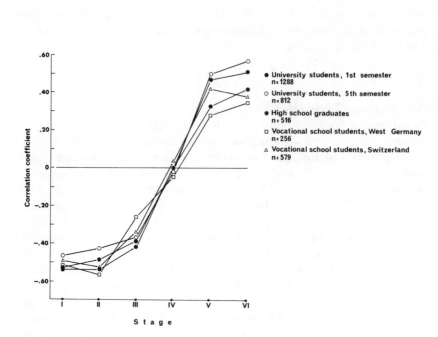

Sources. University students: "University Socialization," a research project conducted at the University of Konstanz. German vocational students: H. Heidbrink (personal communication, see this volume). Swiss vocational students: HASMU, a research project of F. Oser and his collaborators (cf. Lind, 1985c).

Figure 3. Affective-Cognitive Parallelism: Pattern of Correlations Between the Preferences for the Six Stages and the Response Determination by Stage

MORAL JUDGMENT AND SOCIAL CONTEXT

Turning to educational practice, we see that the theory of cognitive development has been increasingly confronted with the problem of the relationship between individual moral judgment and the social environment. As we have seen, this problem has always assumed a prominent place in the work of Piaget and Kohlberg. However, as Bertram (1980) has noted, the working-out of precise hypotheses and the incorporation of them into practical research plans has been incomplete and unsystematic. One exception is the domain of pedagogical intervention, which has already been frequently discussed (see Higgins, 1980; Leming, 1981; Scharf, 1978; Oser, 1981b). But until now other important fields have been largely neglected, for example, the relationship between the individual and the environment from the angle of the interaction of the person with the environment, the cognitive-moral import of positional differentiation in social institutions, and the role that social selection plays in moral development.

Interaction of Person and Social Environment

Hartshorne and May's *Studies in the Nature of Character* (1928-30) is still the best-known attempt to settle the controversy between personalism and situationism. These broadly planned studies were supposed to answer the question of whether people are really guided in their behavior by stable character traits or whether situational factors can be held responsible for "immoral" behavior, such as lies or deceit. In order to deal with the character trait of "honesty," children were brought into "natural" performance situations and their behavior was observed.

What were the results of these studies? There were few children who were honest or dishonest in all classes of situations, and few situations in which all children reacted in the same way. From this the authors of the studies concluded that the position of personalism is untenable, because human behavior is not determined by inner motives or attitudes but rather by the specific situation in which it appears. This conclusion has evoked a lively and long-lasting debate (see e.g., Allport, 1929-30; Asch, 1952; Bem & Allen, 1974). From an interactionist point of view, the results actually call both positions into question.

It has been attempted post hoc to save the (external) trait model of personalism by the hypothesis of measurement error. Thus, Burton (1963) tried, adhering entirely to psychological conventions, to explain the deviations by arguing that some of the situations in which the children were studied had led to "unreliable" measurements and that these situations ought in consequence to be eliminated from the analysis. But little is gained by this argument, since the alternative approach of situationism can also be verified by such a post hoc "explanation." The measurement error hypothesis can also be evoked for this position, if, following Burton's own procedure, one eliminates the "unreliable" persons from the analysis, that is, if one eliminates those cases which call the situationist approach into question and thus confirm this position "empirically."

Schematically simplified, the results of the Hartshorne and May study indicate the following pattern. In several situations there are no differences in moral behavior among the persons (in the matrix below: Situation A and B), whereas in others the person's behavior is differentiated (Situation C and D). Some children are honest (or dishonest) in all situations (Person 1 and 2), others vary in this respect from situation to situation (Person 3 and 4). Thus, without Situations A and B–between which there is no correlation (due to the lack of variance) and which, by convention, are labeled "unreliable"–there remains in the findings a pattern that confirms the position of personalism. Without Persons 1 and 2, between whom, likewise, no correlation exists, there remains in the results a pattern that confirms the opposite position of situationism.

	Situations				
	A	B	C	D	
Persons					
1	h	h	h	h	Behavior:
2	h	h	h	h	h = honest
3	h	h	d	d	d = dishonest
4	h	h	d	d	

Thus, a purely statistical treatment can support either position and, therefore, is unsatisfactory (cf. Olweus, 1976). The number of correlations and the proportion of variance accounted for by the person, the situation, or the interaction of both in a statistical sense cannot be a criterion for the model with which we try to understand moral behavior. The question is whether person and situation lend themselves at all to being contrasted in this way. In behavior, obviously, both person and situation are always involved. The individual and his environment can be clearly distinguished, but neither can be conceived of without reference to the other. The German term for behavior, *Verhalten*, indicates this, as it refers intrinsically to behavior which is not a solitary event but rather is part of the relation *(Verhältnis)* of persons to their environment. Accordingly, from the viewpoint of cognitive interactionism, as Kohlberg (1971b) has succinctly pointed out, "moral judgments and norms are to be understood ultimately as universal constructions of human actors . . . rather than as passive reflections of either external facts . . . or internal emotions" (p. 184).

Positional Fragmentation

The universality of the stages of sociomoral perspective may be due in part to transcultural commonalities of social institutions and positions therein. "All societies have many of the same basic institutions of family, economy, social stratification, law, and government. In spite of great diversity in the detailed definition of these institutions, they retain certain transcultural functional meanings" (Kohlberg, 1969, p. 397). The institutions of society furnish definitions of situation that constitute the life-world of the individual (cf. Krämer-Badoni & Wakenhut, in this volume). Since, however, social institutions are finite, historical, and thus incomplete, they intrude at the time of moral development as requesting and supporting obstacles. Freud calls them the third element, the source of social suffering from which the "discontents of civilization" are derived. Obviously, it is possible and even probable that the real moral atmosphere of a social institution will deviate from the idea upon which it is based (Piaget, 1977). Consequently some authors de-emphasize the educational significance of the ideas on which such institutions are based, or dismiss them as "unreal" ideology. Nevertheless, the moral ideology of social institutions is real and, therefore, can provide an opportunity for criticism and renewal of these institutions in that it makes possible an appeal to moral ideas even if, or just because, they are not fully realized in institutions (cf. Habermas, 1976a).

In modern bureaucratic systems, the relationship between the individual and society is characterized by social positions and memberships in social institutions. Max Weber assumes that the understanding of society by its members is "fragmented" accordingly (1968, pp. 472-473). Weber distinguishes between the understanding of a "client," who regularly obeys because of rewards and punishments; that of a "profiteer," who conforms by being reliable in the eyes of his superiors in order to gain recognition and social advancement; that of an "administrator," who enacts procedural rules and regulations in order to ensure institutional stability and smooth operation; and, finally, that of an "initiator," who chooses ethical principles, goals, or values freely so as to apply them universally and consistently in existing and future social institutions. The concept of positional fragmentation implies a developmental sequence analogous to cognitive-developmental theory. The individual's sociomoral perspective may be seen to develop through the perspectives of the client (Kohlberg's Stages 1-2), the profiteer (Stages 3-4), the administrator (Stage 5), and the initiator (Stage 6). Note that in this developmental scheme the phases of "institutionalization" and "complete approval of collective norms" are understood as leading to greater moral autonomy on the part of given institutional groups and thus are closer to Piaget's view than to Durkheim's. For a further discussion of the relationship between individuals and institutions see also Lavoi and Culbert (1978), Spence (1981), as well as several chapters in this volume.

Social Selection

A number of results from research in moral psychology allow the interpretation that the development of moral judgment is also bound up with processes of social selection, and that the environment determines through selection which forms of judgment are to be found within it. Kohlberg (1958) showed that children with a higher level of moral judgment were preferred by their friends (p. 75). Findings such as these are considered, for the most part, as proof of the causal significance of social participation in the process of moral development. This relationship, however, can also indicate the opposite causal relationship, that is, that the possibility for participation depends on the moral development. If this holds true, the selection (other or self) organized according to the individual state of development has far-reaching consequences for the constitution of society and changes within it.

Selection processes apparently play a remarkable role–be it a positive or negative one–in individual as well as social development. Studies have shown that the state of a child's moral development has little influence on mere participation in social activities. But its significance is related to social prestige in the eyes of classmates and teachers (Keasey, 1971). Furthermore, teachers are quite capable of estimating the moral level of their pupils (Kohlberg, 1969, p. 394; Peck & Havighurst, 1962, p. 183). What consequences this has for the person upon whom judgment has been passed is difficult to tell. Some studies show that children tend to choose as their leaders persons showing a comparatively high moral stage (Keasey, 1971; Peck & Havighurst, 1962, p. 198). This finding coincides with the idea that "leader positions require . . . 'rules and justice' forms of role-taking" (Kohlberg, 1969, p. 399). The higher the social position of an individual, the more he is objectively responsible for decisions in society and "the more he must take the roles of others in it" (p. 399).

Social selection along moral lines seems also to be involved in admission policy at the level of large social institutions. Portele (in this volume) has found that there is a close relationship between the standardization of fields of study and the moral consciousness of academics. In our studies we found that this relation is not due only to university socialization; these differences exist in part even before people enter the university. Likewise, the differences in moral judgment competence among soldiers, officers, and conscientious objectors seem to be linked only partly to the effects of their social environment. In part the differences exist even before they enter into these environments (Lind, 1984a; see also Lippert, 1981). In any case, important questions are hinted at that concern the working together of socialization and selection processes.

CONCLUSIONS

After enjoying a euphoric and uncritical initial reception, the theory of cognitive development, as formulated by Jean Piaget and Lawrence Kohlberg, has in recent years come up against opposition of an often undifferentiated and irrational nature. Especially in Kohlberg's work–typical of new, creative research paradigms–there are more than a few contradictions and inaccuracies that offer critics abundant points of attack.

The analysis presented here of the basic assumptions in cognitive-developmental theory and of the current findings to date show that we are concerned with an approach which should, in fact, be taken seriously. In several respects the tendency to immunize the theory has been rightly criticized. We do not, however, see any scientific reason that would justify referring to the cognitive-developmental approach as a "degenerating research program" or as a sterile approach. On the contrary, as the body of accumulated empirical research shows, the cognitive-developmental approach has very *informative* hypotheses at its center that are–with some exceptions– *verifiable* and *verified.* Therefore, we should regard the cognitive-developmental approach on the whole as a very "courageous speculation" which has proved to be of great significance for progress in moral psychology, even in the areas where it fails.

The most important innovation of the cognitive-developmental theory, in my view, is of a conceptual nature. It renders the concept of behavior more psychological by recourse to its affective and cognitive qualities, and it renders the cognitive aspect of moral judgment assessable in practice. I view as its core assumption a cognitive-affective parallelism in the development of moral thought and action, which presupposes a two-dimensional model of development. The differentiation of the developmental model into two dimensions or aspects should, however, be strictly distinguished from a bifurcation of cognitive-moral development, in which both aspects are conceived of (and operationalized) as separate faculties of mind. Moral content and moral structure are not composed of insulated behavioral acts which are accessible in an isolated state. Instead they are, as the concept of structural wholeness indicates, characteristics of a behavioral totality and thus have to be dealt with as an inseparable entity.

The methodological and pedagogical consequences of this theory have hitherto not received the attention they deserve. Two such consequences seem especially noteworthy. First, in the field of moral psychology we have to think about a new psychometrics which takes into account simultaneously both the affective and the cognitive aspects of behavior rather than interpreting cognitive characteristics as "errors" of the measurement instrument. We have dealt with this elsewhere in this volume, as well as in Lind (1982b; 1985e). Second, in the field of education, the distinction of the two aspects may help us better understand the cognitive nature of within-stage development and the best ways to foster this. Although modern pedagogy wants to refrain from the indoctrination of moral contents, it is seen to be responsible for stimulating the cognitive aspect of moral growth, that is, for the development of integrated and differentiated judgment.

NOTES

1. See also Moers (1930), who stated that behavior "becomes good or bad only through its motivation" (p. 441), because "the act that is without real insight and conforms to ethical norms only because of chance events in one's education or adaptation is not yet a truly good act" (p. 440). Similarly, Hartshorne and May (1928) postulated that "the essence of an act is its pretense" (p. 101), though this remained a play on words which had no real consequences for their research methods.
2. Piaget is exempted from this critique by Pittel and Mendelsohn (1966). Kohlberg's work was not included.
3. See Habermas, 1976a; Schluchter, 1979; Hartmann, in this volume.
4. For an overview and critical evaluation of recent moral judgment research we refer primarily to Bergling, 1981; Bertram, 1980; Blasi, 1983; Broughton, 1978; Colby et al., 1983; Eckensberger, 1983; Habermas, in this volume; Kohlberg et al., 1983; Lempert, 1982; Portele, 1978; Rest, 1979a.
5. Piaget's approach to the relationship of morality and environment has been revived by Bertram, in this volume, and Oser, 1981b.

6. See, above all, the complex "spiral model" by Eckensberger (1984; also Eckensberger & Reinshagen, 1980), the "two-factor model" by Nisan (1984), and the two-component model by Lempert (1982). I cannot discuss these sophisticated models as extensively as they deserve, but I should mention my concern that they also tend to multiply entities and thus to view content and structure–affect and cognition–as separate things rather than as two aspects of one and the same behavior (see also Lind, 1985e).

7. "Factor analysis indicates a single 'stage' factor cutting across all moral situations and all aspects of morality on which the individual is assessed" (Kohlberg, 1971b, p. 177). See also Kohlberg, 1958, pp. 11, 338; 1969, pp. 368, 389; 1976, p. 47; 1979, p. 21; Rest, 1979a, pp. 50-51.

8. Kohlberg, 1958, p. 104; 1969, p. 387; 1979, p. 21; Turiel, 1969; Rest, 1973.

9. Piaget, 1976, pp. 69-76, 1977; Kohlberg, 1969, p. 348.

10. See also Kohlberg, 1969, p. 434; 1971b, p. 186; Piaget, 1977; Lind, 1985e.

Moral Competence and Democratic Personality

Georg Lind, Johann-Ulrich Sandberger, and Tino Bargel

THREE THEORETICAL APPROACHES

Cognitive-developmental theory has been credited with a notable contribution to the study of the development of the democratic personality. In a review of "political socialization and models of moral development," Friedman (1977, p. 361) asserts that "the Kohlberg model of man, that is, the last stages toward which his system is directed, is a model which is democratic in process and goal." In this article we shall outline this conception together with two other "models of man" to demonstrate that, in spite of its great utility, the cognitive-developmental theory and methodology may be improved upon by taking into account aspects found in other approaches to political psychology, especially the neo-Freudian (psychodynamic) and the attitude-structural approaches. All three approaches have been utilized to describe and explain the nature and development of the political competences, and, as we argue below, their contributions to the theory of democratic personality may be integrated into a unifying model. Whether this is a fruitful endeavor should become clear when the empirical hypotheses derived from it are tested.

The Psychoanalytic Approach

In the 1930s and 1940s, political psychologists were concerned mainly about the rise of fascism and other totalitarian ideologies. Explanations were given in terms of psychoanalytic theory. The psychoanalytic approach was prominently adhered to by the Berkeley Group (Adorno et al., 1969), which in its study of the authoritarian personality assumed a high degree of coherence between personality and political orientation. For instance, Adorno and his colleagues believed that, if the personality structure lacked "the integration between the moral agencies by which the subject lives," authoritarian submission, conventionalism, and authoritarian aggression would result and would clear a path for the spread of Fascism (p. 234).

Such a "weakness in the ego is expressed in the inability to build up a consistent and enduring set of moral values within the personality, and it is this state of affairs, apparently, that makes it necessary for the individual to seek some organizing agency outside himself" (p. 234). Moreover, there seemed to be a close relationship between authoritarian "adherence to substitutes and crutches of this kind" and immature cognitive organization. The results of their empirical investigations showed that reliance on an "agency outside" relates to "a simple, firm, often stereotypical structure. There is no place for ambivalence and ambiguities" (1969, p. 480).

Though the significance of these findings has been widely acknowledged, the research of the Berkeley Group provoked criticism because of its methodological and theoretical shortcomings. Thus Selznick and Steinberg (1969) argued that a false conception of the role of cognitive factors in political socialization had led Adorno and his associates to an erroneous assumption about the direction of causality in the functioning of personality. Selznick and Steinberg pointed out that fascist attitudes are a result, not a cause, of cognitive structure. Sanford (1973, p. 167), reviewing the critique of research on the authoritarian personality, conceded that the "personality syndromes most useful in understanding political behavior will surely embrace both cognitive and psychodynamic factors."

Such an understanding does indeed seem necessary. More recent psychoanalytic research suggests that neurotic symptoms, which may in part be responsible for the democratically immature personality, are due to a lack of coping ability in the ego rather than, as Freud believed, to an overdeveloped superego (Mowrer, 1972, p. 350). Intolerance of ambiguity, fear of failure, and the feeling of being controlled by external forces may be "Type-2 symptoms" (Mowrer), that is, defensive reactions to an overwhelmingly difficult life situation when the individual lacks the competence to integrate different demands.

One might hypothesize that the development of an authoritarian character can be meaningfully described in terms of cognitive-moral development. Kohlberg (1964, p. 422) reported that authoritarianism, as measured by the F-scale of Adorno and his colleagues, correlated negatively ($r = -.52$) with cognitive-moral development. Whereas Kohlberg (1964, p. 422) is reluctant "to offer a view of moral ideology which combines personality type and developmental considerations within a single framework," other researchers have attempted to do just this (Habermas, 1976a; Loevinger, 1976;

Döbert and Nunner-Winkler, 1975). For Habermas (1976a), Kohlberg's and Loevinger's theories have provided a basis for positive definition of the properties of a democratic personality, an endeavor that Adorno had deliberately eschewed for fear of "false positivism."

One might conclude that, in order to become a democratic personality, one must have a strong ego—involving among other things tolerance of ambiguity, hope for success, and a capacity for internal control cognition (Lane, 1962, pp. 400-412). Yet this description remains incomplete, if for no other reason than that it could also fit the outline of a narcissistic personality who plays "hardball politics" (Etheredge, 1979). To define democratic personality, we need to take into account both political and moral orientations.

Attitude Structure Theory

Within the last decade a second major stream of theorizing has merged with the cognitive-developmental approach, resulting in a more paradigm of research into political socialization. The object of this research could be labeled "attitude structure" although several other, apparently interchangeable, labels are also in use, e.g., "focus of concern" (Campbell et al., 1960, p. 188), "ideology" (McClosky, 1964, p. 362), "belief system constraints" (Converse, 1964, p. 207), and "levels of conceptualization" (Converse, 1964, p. 215).

The application of the concept of attitude structure to socialization research has corroborated some straightforward hypotheses. As a major result of their study of pupils from grades two to eight, Hess and Torney (1967) found that at an early age children acquire some vague "ideal standards" with which they, like adults, evaluate political objects. However, children lack many of the logical, conceptual, and sensory links that make up an integrated self–be they links between these ideal standards and other standards, or between ideal standards and specific beliefs ("issue beliefs"). Many empirical findings show that the process of attitude formation continues beyond childhood and that many adults may never reach the more sophisticated levels of conceptualization, ideology, attitude structure, or belief system constraint (Campbell et al., 1960; Converse, 1964, 1970; McClosky, 1964). Only a small proportion of the population has organized the world of political problems into systems of values and attitudes.

These findings have not been uncriticized. In some studies, belief system constraint is operationalized as "level of verbal conceptualization" (Campbell et al., 1960; Converse, 1964), measuring to a large extent the level of verbal articulateness. This approach may largely underestimate the basic citizen's political competence (Brown, 1970). On methodological grounds, furthermore, there has been objection to the use of (synchronic or diachronic) interindividual correlations as indicators of the degree of individual attitude structure.

On theoretical grounds it has been argued that mainstream attitude structure research has been biased toward the specific "political logic" of political élites, who are found to be more consistent in applying general principles to specific issues (McClosky, 1964, p. 366). This argument neglects the possiblity that the man in the street may use different dimensions and ways of organizing attitudes and beliefs. Indeed, Lane (1962) found that the ordinary man also links events and beliefs to form an ideological system, even though this system may be different from the ideology of those who are politically active.

The implicit assumption that the organization of attitudes along a single universal dimension can be regarded as superior to other types of political consciousness now seems doubtful on normative grounds (Lane, 1973; Bennett, 1975). The public may have stable opinions on various matters without holding to an encompassing ideology. It appears problematic to infer an ill-structured consciousness from a lack of constraint in political attitudes, since a low degree of constraint may indicate a highly structured, highly differentiated consciousness. Even among the political élite, the priority and the sufficiency of the liberal-conservative dimension are contested. Furthermore, it is also questionable whether a variety of socio-political value systems can be condensed into a single dimension (Rokeach, 1973; Sandberger, 1979).

To understand political consciousness, one must survey the structure of at least three fundamental value orientations. Ever since the French revolution, liberty, equality, and brotherhood or solidarity have been regarded as core democratic values. Tomkins (1965) asserts that a general humanistic orientation in particular provides the resonance basis for democratic personality structures. He sees the humanistic posture centering on the belief in human goodness, whereas distrust or sociophobia constitutes an ideo-affective posture to which anti-egalitarian and authoritarian ideologies tend to resonate. For a heterogeneous sample of respondents, Tomkins was able to demonstrate a consistent pattern of correlations between expressed empathetic affects and ideological beliefs with regard to a wide range of topics. Furthermore, it seems that a democratically mature value system cannot coexist with political apathy. As Durio (1976) has put it, "Democratic behavior is a conscious commitment to a value structure requiring individual action" (p. 212). The "New Left Ideology" strongly emphasized a more direct and more encompassing participation by ordinary people in political decision making. Thus, a democratic personality is not completely described by value concepts (see Döbert & Nunner-Winkler, in this volume). We have not yet touched upon the more specific behavioral implications of such ideals. Do values exert any influence on specific action decisions? The problem of relating abstract moral and political ideals to specific judgments has been most thoroughly studied by cognitive-developmentalists.

Cognitive-Moral Approach

Cognitive theory of moral development is concerned with ego development, a topic which has long been neglected by psychoanalytic theory and research. According to Kohlberg (1964) one has to interpret "moral character as ego rather than superego strength . . . This interpretation implies that the major consistency in moral conduct represents decision making capacities rather than fixed behavior traits" (p. 391). We have seen that this view extends psychodynamic theory. Moreover, the cognitive-developmental approach is concerned with the structural organization of affects which attitude research has usually bypassed for lack of appropriate models and methodological tools.

Kohlberg has described six types of moral judgment which are combined into three levels: preconventional, conventional, and post-conventional. On the grounds of moral-philosophical considerations and empirical findings, Kohlberg asserts that these types form an invariant sequence of stages of individual development. He conceives of them as stages of justice and social perspective taking. Moral reasoning is regarded as hierarchically organized into structural wholes. Invariant sequential order and structural wholeness are important assumptions of the cognitive-developmental approach (Colby et al., 1983; Kohlberg et al., 1983; for a discussion of Kohlberg's theory, see Lind, ch. 2 in this volume).

Theoretically, the degree and kind of structural integration of behavior are the core features of personality development (cf. Loevinger, 1976, pp. 54-67). Hence, we would not expect consistency of judgment to be invariant across situations and throughout individual development. Methodologically, the assumption of structural wholes implies that we may not infer the level of an individual's cognitive-moral development from a single behavioral event, such as a single answer to a questionnaire item. Multiple assessment of behavior is necessary, not to estimate a "true" attitude score, but to provide information about the structural properties of an individual's behavior. To assess unequivocally the meaning of behavior, we must examine a configuration of responses to a carefully selected pattern of stimuli (cf. Lind 1982b; 1985e).

Moreover, the concept of consistency itself carries an ambiguous meaning which must be explicated in every instance: *Behavior is not consistent per se, but always with regard to some value criterion.* Regarding judgment behavior in moral situations, such criteria may be acquiescence (agreement with any argument to avoid debating), opinion agreement (supporting arguments that are in line with a person's issue beliefs), or orientation toward the moral quality of the arguments. Empirical investigations have demonstrated that the degree to which moral principles are consistently applied to judgments and behavior decisions follows some developmental trends, and that this degree also relates to different degrees of political articulation. Conversely, research has indicated that acquiescence and opinion agreement are negatively related to moral development (cf. Fishkin et al., 1973; Keasey, 1974; Lind, 1978a). Only when the subjective validity of moral values becomes independent of egocentric motives, that is, when the individual is able to *decenter* (Piaget), is the individual's moral competence transformed into what Habermas (1973) calls communicative competence. Only then can individual actions be rationally justified and criticized in terms of principles. The subjective reasoning becomes objective and open to argument from others.

TOWARD AN INTEGRATION OF MODELS
OF DEMOCRATIC PERSONALITY

We have seen that all three of the above-mentioned approaches are structuralist, psychodynamic theory being the least explicit and cognitive-developmental theory the most explicit in this regard. All three approaches assert that individual behavior and thought are organized into structural wholes, which does not imply that people behave uniformly across situations. The decisive criterion of belonging to a structural unit is not phenomenal similarity but *functional correspondence:* any behavior that serves the same goal can be regarded as an element of the same structure.

Structural wholeness is no metapsychological dogma. It is not a question of "being there or not being there." Not every belief or action of an individual is integrated under a single system of orientations, since several reference systems can coexist within the same person without being interrelated. As Adelson and O'Neill (1966) have found, domains of structurally organized behavior in young children may be scattered like islands in the stream of action. Only to the extent that a person has developed consistent relations between various orientations, values, and goals, can he or she be considered to have an integrated personality.

In the process of development, people experience phases of crisis and phases of accelerated change of thought and behavior. From the structural point of view, one is led to believe that this phenomenon is caused by the integration of previously unrelated substructures of personality. In phases of crisis, especially when an individual's ecological context changes or enlarges, the individual becomes aware of conflicting values and intentions. New criteria have to be found for deciding value priorities, and new modes of behavior have to be acquired to cope with situations of conflict. Contrary to associationist positions,[1] all three approaches take into account both motivational and cognitive components of behavior, although it is not always obvious how these components relate to each other and to behavior. In the face of the widespread practice of treating motivational and intellectual functions separately, one might well ask, "One psychology or two?" (Kuhn, 1978). Though the necessity of combining "a developmental approach with simultaneous interest in motivational and cognitive aspects of personality" (Loevinger, 1976, p. 101) has long been felt, a truly integrated model is still absent (see Kuhn, 1978, p. 116).

In all three approaches, motivational and cognitive components may be conceived of as entities of the same type. Psychodynamic approaches tend to assume that id, ego, and superego are different faculties of the mind which contest with each other for power over behavior. In attitude theory, even approaches that consider the existence of more than one affective dimension conceive of these dimensions merely as juxtaposed to one another. In Lasswell's (1951) or Greenstein's (1968) conceptions of the democratic personality, the cognitive component is essentially restricted to a belief in the basic goodness of man, and hence lacks the structural feature under discussion here.

Even in cognitive-developmental theory, the genuine structural character of moral consciousness is missed when one assumes that the cognitive component can be validly measured solely through logical tasks, or that this component precedes moral reasoning (Kohlberg, 1976; Kuhn et al., 1977; Ijzendoorn, 1979). This conception is questioned by Kärn (1978, p. 98), who points out that "stages of logical thought and stages of moral thought may be models of the same theory," that is, that the two content areas may have common structural properties.[2] Such a conception was also proposed by Lee (1971, p. 101), in whose view the ability to see the weight of a body unchanged by the alteration of its shape seems structurally equivalent to the ability to abstract the validity of a democratic value from specific applications. Both abilities are said to be based on the common structural property of what Piaget has called "conservation."

Moral behavior always contains aspects of content *and* of structure which reflect the distinction between elements and their interrelations. In organismic structures (see Werner, 1957), elements must be further differentiated into means and ends, that is, into concrete moral judgment behavior and abstract value orientations (content). The structure is then characterized by its content, that is, the purpose it serves, and by the development of its system of "logical relations."[3] As a preliminary operational definition, any value is said to be cognitively organized if it exerts noticeable influence on the pattern of judgment behavior, that is, if the value orientation is conserved across a class of judgment situations. Above all, moral values should be generalized across the particular population of persons that support them. Each person should be able to take the value perspective of any other person, which means that the conservation of values is the core of role-taking ability.

The consistency or "conservation" of moral judgment is a prerequuisite for democratic discourse. An autocratic social system is characterized by the limits it puts on the universal application of values through social power differences. In autocratic societies, members of a particular social class are allowed and even encouraged to prevent the universal application of certain moral values in order to defend their particularized positions. In such societies, morality is segmented (for the concept of segmentation, see Senger, in this volume, and Döbert & Nunner-Winkler, 1975). Conversely, democratic society rests on the unconditional application of certain basic values. Only if conflicts do not involve disagreement with regard to basic values can they be solved by means of rational discourse. Democracy is achieved insofar as individual judgment behavior is moralized, that is, insofar as it reflects "all values involved" (Mead, 1967).

Certain forms of segmentation are, however, legitimate. Considering the availability of means and mitigating circumstances, as well as weighing the values against one another, may lead to differentiations in judgment which are compatible with a democratic personality. The alternative is a monomanic adherence to abstract values, which may lead to Jacobinism. Indeed, a "temporary Jacobinism" appears to be part of most individuals' adolescence (Lipset, 1965). Perry (1970) conceives of this phase as one of "basic duality," in which the world is seen in dualistic terms, right versus wrong. But this phase is eventually challenged by relativistic thinking, and finally is subdued by the achievement of "contextual relativism," on which adult "commitment" is based. This commitment brings back the capability of firm judgment, tempered now by full awareness of uncertainty and relativism; "it is an act in an examined, not in an unexamined, life" (Perry, 1970, p. 136). In short, abstract value orientations, like id-impulses and superego-controls, or like general affect-loaded attitudes and goals, are the leading elements of the complex cognitive structure that organizes concrete judgment behavior and issue beliefs. Besides the many things that distinguish the three theoretical "domains" discussed above, these contiguities constitute the identification of three defining aspects of personality structure: abstract (motivational) content, concrete (behavioral) elements, and relational (cognitive) structure.

Table 1

Structural Concepts in the Study of Personality Structure

Theoretical Domain	Abstract Content	Concrete Elements	Relational Structure
Psychoanalytic Theory	Id, Superego	Thoughts, Dreams	Ego
Attitude Structure Theory	Affective Component, Orientations	Behavioral Component, Issue Beliefs	Cognitive Component, Constraints
Cognitive-Developmental Theory	Moral Concern, Socio-moral Perspective	Moral Judgment, Evaluative Behavior	Justification, Consistency of Evaluation

Research Questions and Hypotheses

This attempt to provide an integrated structural approach to the study of democratic personality and the outline of a model of democratic personality raises several questions, some of which can be investigated empirically. For reasons of time and space, we shall concentrate here on those aspects that seem most fundamental in the sense that they prepare the ground for further research into the nature and development of the democratic personality.

Hypothesis I: Prevailing methods of personality and attitude assessment presuppose that people vary only by the amount or degree of a trait, not by its structure. Inconsistencies in judgment behavior are attributed solely to measurement error. This position of classical test theory (Spearman, Gulliksen) is incompatible with structural theories, which assume that judgment consistency regarding some organizing perspective depends on a person's cognitive development. We expect, therefore, that even within a developmentally homogeneous group individuals will vary markedly in judgment consistency with regard to particular moral orientations.

Hypothesis II: Judgmental consistency (as defined above) seems to signify moral competence; that is, we believe that it reflects a particular organization of moral values. This particular organization is primarily defined by the developmental order of moral orientations, as has been suggested by Kohlberg (1971) and Loevinger (1976, pp. 27-28). In operational terms, we expect that the more a person judges concrete statements by the value orientation the statements represent, the more he or she will evaluate them in accordance with a hierarchy of moral orientations as described by Kohlberg's (1969) stage model.

Hypothesis 3: Though the mechanisms are not yet known in detail, we deduce from psychodynamic theory and from cognitive-developmental theory that ego strength and moral competence are correlated. A mature hierarchy of goals and values and their efficient organization, which is reflected in high judgment consistency, should be negatively related to intolerance of ambiguity, fear of failure, and perception of one's fate as controlled by external forces. Since moral competence means the ability to cope with moral conflicts, it renders superfluous the defense mechanisms of a weak ego, of which those three reactions may be symptomatic.

Hypothesis IV: Finally, it is hypothesized that adherence to abstract democratic orientations relates both to the structure and to the content of concrete judgments. Since, as many writers contend, democratic values are among, or even identical with, the highest stages of moral orientation, we expect that explicit commitment to democracy is positively related to moral-cognitive development.

For the present study, we expect that these hypotheses will be empirically valid even when important variables like level of formal education and cohort membership are controlled, that is, when relationships are tested in a developmentally and socially homogeneous sample. Studies which use more heterogeneous samples will presumably produce even clearer confirmations of these hypotheses.

METHODS

Sample

The 708 subjects of this study are a sample taken from a cohort of graduates of German upper secondary schools in Baden-Württemberg, whose median age was 18.5.[4] Standardized questionnaires were administered during classroom hours in 48 classes shortly after the students had taken their final (written) examinations in the spring of 1976. This survey is part of a more comprehensive research project on university socialization.

Moral Judgment Competence

For measuring motivational (or evaluative) and cognitive components of moral judgment, a new instrument was developed which utilizes questionnaire techniques and an experimental, multifactorial design. It is called the *Moralisches Urteil Test* or the MUT (Moral Judgment Test; see Lind, 1978a, 1984, and Lind & Wakenhut, in this volume). Its purpose is to infer behavior-guiding orientations and thought organization from an individual's pattern of judgments concerning the acceptability of certain arguments which are presented in connection with a moral dilemma. The test consists of two subtests, each containing a story which presents a behavioral dilemma, followed by a set of questions pertaining to the subject's agreement/ disagreement with a suggested solution to the dilemma and to the acceptability of arguments speaking for and against this solution. The arguments were constructed to represent moral reasoning at each of the six stages described by Kohlberg (1969, p. 376). The respondent is asked to evaluate twelve reasons for each story–twenty-four altogether. Hence, by virtue of test construction, the MUT items constitute an "Experimental Questionnaire," a tool which has been discussed at length elsewhere (Lind, 1982b; see Lind & Wakenhut, in this volume).[5] The independent variables form a 2 x 2 x 6 factorial design. The three factors included are: Dilemma, Pro-Con, and Stage. Each item belongs to a particular story, represents a pro or a con position, and refers to one of the six Kohlbergian stages of moral reasoning. The dependent variable is represented by the respondents' judgment of the acceptability of the given reasons on a scale ranging from -4 to +4. Since neither self-description nor introspection is recorded but only individual patterns of *judgment behavior*, this questionnaire can be viewed as a behavioral test. The dilemma of the subtest entitled "Mercy Killing" is adapted from Kohlberg's Situation IV (Kohlberg, 1958, p. 366). It is assumed that the life-death issue requires the most unambiguously moral reasoning. As a contrast, we used a second dilemma, labeled "Theft," which concerned two workers who break into the main office of their factory in search of evidence to support the allegation that the management has "bugged" their work area (for more details on the MUT, see Lind & Wakenhut, in this volume).

In this paper the interstage structure is elicited by calculating the average acceptability of every four statements for each of the six stages, and by combining them into individual profiles of stage-ratings. This method is a convenient device for depicting simultaneously the motivational (content) and the cognitive (structural) aspects of moral reasoning (cf. Lind, 1985d). The content of the judgment is indicated by the acceptance or rejection of the stage of orientation which the argument represents. The degree of structural or cognitive organization of judgment behavior is indicated by two measures: the distance of the average acceptability of a stage from the theoretical scale mean (± 0) and the steepness of the profile of stage-ratings. The less consistently a respondent evaluates statements with regard to their stage-appropriateness, the more the profile flattens and approaches the zero-line.

Ego Strength

Three scales for measuring ego strength were included in our study. *Intolerance of ambiguity* was measured through the scale developed by Budner (1962), which seemed appropriate since it is explicitly related to psychoanalytic concepts. The scale contains 16 items which are to be rated from -3 ("I reject completely") to +3 ("I accept completely"). After a linear transformation, the total scale ranges from 0 to 96 with 96 signifying extreme intolerance of ambiguity. *Fear of failure,* which is considered either to result from ego-weakness or to contribute to it, was assessed using seven items adapted from a larger Fear of Failure scale developed by Fend et al. (1974). The respondent was to decide between pairs of statements, e.g., "When I am confronted with a new task . . . (a) I am rather sure that I shall succeed. (b) I am often afraid that I shall not succeed." The scale ranges from 1 to 7, with 7 indicating extreme fear of failure. Finally, *Locus of Control* was measured by a shortened version of Rotter's (1966) scale. Our selection of items represents the personal control factor (cf., Gurin et al., 1969; Lefcourt, 1976).

Democratic Orientation

For this study we selected four indicators of democratic orientation. The questions we chose for the present analysis pertain to the following issues. Respondents were asked to take a stand on two questions involving *egalitarian values.* First, "Would you be for or against a reduction of social inequalities?" and second, "Would you support an increase of social equality even at the cost of material wealth?" These items are part of a comprehensive instrument for the study of orientations toward social inequality (Sandberger, 1983). For assessing *Humanism* a somewhat shortened version of Tomkins's (1965) scale was used. The respondent was to choose between polar statements, e.g., "Human beings are basically good" versus "Human beings are basically bad," with the option available of indicating neutrality or indifference. *Democratization,* taken as an abstract ideal of political action, is described by an item of the "New Left Scale" developed by Christie et al.: "The democratization of all areas of life should be the basis of a new society" (cf. Gold, et al., 1976; Robinson & Shaver, 1973, p. 470). The respondent was to indicate his degree of agreement or disagreement on a scale ranging from -3 to +3. A *readiness to participate* in political affairs was seen as a prerequisite for democratic orientation. We took as an indicator of this orientation the respondents' reaction to the statement, "I will not engage in political activity under any circumstances."

Evaluation of Data

To gauge the degree to which the data support our hypothesis, we have used two complementary approaches. In the first approach, information content and conformity with theoretical prediction are tested, and in the second statistical significance is checked. Our hypothesis is that students high in ego strength and democratic orientation will discriminate more between stages of moral reasoning, rejecting lower-stage arguments and accepting higher stage arguments more markedly than do their counterparts who are not so high in those orientations. In technical terms this means that the former group should exhibit a steeper profile of median scores for the stages. A thought experiment reveals that, for this hypothesis, the a priori chance of confirmation is rather low. When the median scores of two groups–to be denoted here as A and B–are compared for each stage, and a dichotomous distinction is made between "A is smaller than or equal to B" and "A is greater than B," there are $2^6 = 64$ possible sequences or configurations across the six stages. Among these, six configurations are in line with the hypothesis; their graphic form corresponds to that of an X.[6] Hence, under the assumption of randomness and independence of trials (stages), the probability of obtaining a configuration that conforms to the hypothesis is no larger than 6/64 or about 9 percent. The reciprocal value of this number constitutes a measure of the information contained in the data (see Lind, 1985d).

For computing *statistical significance*, two-way analyses of variance were run, using ego strength and democratic orientation–taken one at a time–as independent variables, and using stage as a repeated measurement variable. To analyze the effects of each of these variables, orthogonal polynomials as proposed by Bock (1975, pp. 447-488) were used.[7] Our hypotheses focus interest on the interactions between the variables of ego strength and democratic orientation with stage, with special emphasis on the linear component of this interaction. To support the hypothesis of a differential steepness of stage-score profiles, the linear component should be significant and should account for a sizeable proportion of the variance.

EMPIRICAL FINDINGS

Hypothesis I: Variation in the Cognitive Aspect of Moral Judgment

Intra-individual analysis of components of variance calculated from the MUT reveals that individuals do indeed differ greatly with regard to response consistency or, more precisely, consistency with respect to moral criteria. When confronted with a behavioral dilemma, some persons employ moral reasoning to a high degree while others consider nonmoral criteria of judgment, e.g., whether the reasons which are advocated support or oppose the opinion to which the person is committed. The degree to which respondents use moral categories in their judgments is depicted in Figure 1. The abscissa represents the proportion of individual judgment variance accounted for by the Stage factor. This measure is simply the ratio of the sum of squares due to this factor to the total sum of squares. In Figure 1, the degree to which individual judgment behavior is determined by the opinion-agreement variable (Pro-Con) is depicted as well. As compared to younger subjects (cf. Keasey, 1974), the upper secondary school graduates in our sample are obviously less oriented toward the agreement/disagreement aspect of the arguments.

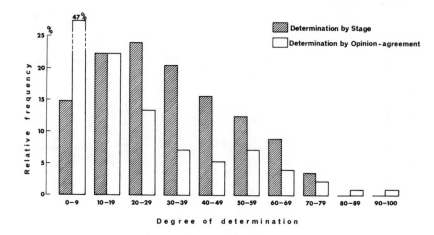

Figure 1. Distribution of the Degree of Judgment Consistency with Regard to Stage of Reasoning and Opinion-Agreement

Hypothesis II: Cognitive and Affective Aspects of Moral Judgment

If the preference for "high" levels of moral orientation is a pacer for a later form of cognitive organization, we are led to assume that the recognition of the moral priority of higher stage reasoning should go together with a more highly organized thought structure, that is, that motivational content and cognitive structure of moral judgment behavior should empirically correlate in a predictable way. The findings depicted in Figure 2 clearly corroborate this hypothesis. The more the "higher" moral orientations are accepted, and the more the "lower" stage reasons are rejected, the more the respondents evaluate the arguments morally, that is, with regard to the stages they represent. Configurations of intergroup median differences are all perfectly in line with the prediction.[8] Thus this finding supports the claim that even Stages 5 and 6 have a cognitive basis, a claim which has sometimes been questioned (cf. Gibbs, 1977, among others).

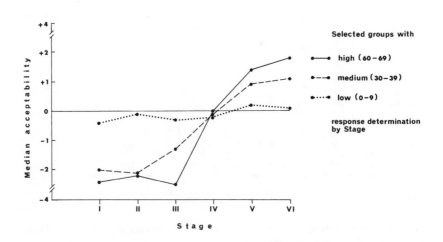

Figure 2. Correlation Between the Affective and Cognitive Aspects: Acceptability of Stages by Different Degrees of Judgment Consistency

Hypothesis III: Moral Competence and Ego Strength

A marked and well-structured value hierarchy coincides with high ego strength. Though the sample as a whole can be regarded as comparatively mature and as fairly homogeneous in its level of moral development, differences in ego strength correlate with differences in moral judgment structure. Although the orderings of moral orientations (stages) are similar, students of lower ego strength are obviously less consistent in the application of abstract orientations to concrete judgments. This is indicated by a less marked rejection of lower stage arguments. The pertinent data are presented in Table 2. High scores on intolerance of ambiguity turn out to be associated with relatively high endorsement of Stage 1 through Stage 3 reasoning. With regard to fear of failure and external control cognition, the findings are somewhat less articulate, yet they follow the same pattern. Those who fear failure, like those who feel they are externally controlled, exhibit a less consistent rejection of morally inferior orientations in their judgments. Except for the comparison of students who are medium and low in intolerance of ambiguity, all configurations of median differences between groups are fully congruent with the hypothesis. In each case the dependent analysis of variance yields a significant linear component of the Groups x Stages interaction; although, for intolerance of ambiguity, some higher order components also turn out to be significant, the bulk of the interaction variance is accounted for by the linear component, as shown in the last column of Table 2. This confirms the hypothesized differences in steepness of stage rating profiles.

These findings corroborate those of other studies. Sullivan and Quarter (1972, p. 156) report that Conventionals reveal a lower, "morally hybrid" and "pure" Postconventionals a higher, tolerance of ambiguity as measured by the Omnibus Personality Inventory. Haan et al. (1973) found a low but consistent correlation between tolerance of ambiguity and Kohlberg's moral maturity measure. Alker and Popper's (1973) study showed that moral development was negatively related to dogmatism. Correlations of moral development with the locus of control variable are only partially comparable, since in most cases the complete Rotter scale was used, which confounds several dimensions (Mirels, 1970, Gootnik, 1974). Nevertheless, (low)

Table 2

Moral Judgment and Ego Strength: Median Stage Acceptability by Students with Different Scores on Ego Strength Scales

Group	n^b	Acceptability^a of Stage 1	2	3	4	5	6	Testing of Hypotheses (c)	(d)	(e)
Intolerance of Ambiguity:										
low (0–27)	272	−2.1	−1.8	−1.7	−0.4	0.9	0.8	]		
medium (23–43)	411	−1.4	−1.4	−0.9	−0.1	0.7	0.8	]	1%	75%
high (46–96)	25	−1.1	−1.4	−0.3	0.3	0.6	0.6			
External Locus of Control:										
internal (6–11)	200	−1.9	−1.8	−1.4	−0.3	0.8	0.9	]	1%	94%
external (12–18)	431	−1.6	−1.4	−1.1	−0.2	0.8	0.8			
Fear of Failure:										
low (1–3)	230	−1.9	−1.8	−1.4	−0.2	0.8	0.9	]	1%	79%
high (5–7)	324	−1.5	−1.4	−1.2	0.2	0.8	0.8			

a From −4 (completely unacceptable) to +4 (completely acceptable).

b The n's usually do not add up to the sample size of 708 because of "don't know" answers.

c Configurations of median differences that are completely in line with the hypothesis are denoted by brackets.

d Statistical significance of the linear component of the Group x Stage interaction. Two-way analysis of variance with Stage as a repeated measurement variable, applying orthogonal polynomials according to Bock (1975, pp. 447–488).

e Proportion of the total interaction variance accounted for by the linear component.

Table 3

Moral Judgment and Democratic Orientations: Median Stage Acceptability by Students with Different Scores on Dimensions of Political Attitude

Group	n	Acceptability of Stage 1	2	3	4	5	6	Testing of Hypotheses (c)	(d)	(e)
Reduction of Social Inequality:										
For	563	−1.8	−1.6	−1.3	−0.3	0.8	0.8		5%	50%
Against	92	−1.4	−1.3	−0.6	+0.2	−0.8	0.9			
Increase of Equality:										
Support	391	−2.0	−1.6	−1.4	−0.3	0.8	0.8		5%	76%
Reject	126	−1.4	−1.3	−0.7	−0.0	0.9	1.0			
Humanism:										
High (28–36)	620	−1.7	−1.5	−1.2	−0.2	0.8	0.9	⎤	1%	74%
Low (18–27)	51	−1.1	−1.2	−0.5	−0.3	0.5	0.4	⎦		
Democratization:										
Agree (+1−+3)	437	−1.9	−1.6	−1.3	−0.2	0.9	0.9	⎤	1%	78%
Disagree (−1−−3)	46	−1.4	−1.1	−0.9	−0.2	0.4	0.6	⎦		
Participation in Politics:										
Yes	409	−1.9	−1.7	−1.4	−0.3	0.8	0.9	⎤	1%	71%
Not as all	72	−1.2	−1.1	−0.6	−0.1	0.8	0.9	⎦		

Note: For explanation see the notes of Table 2.

negative correlations between moral development and external control cognition have consistently been found (Alker & Popper, 1973; Bloomberg, 1974).

Hypothesis IV: Moral Judgment and Democratic Orientation

Finally, we hypothesized that conscious adherence to democratic values would correlate with moral-cognitive structure. The results shown in Table 3 are in line with this hypothesis. Though egalitarianism is only a prerequisite concept and not necessarily indicative of a fully developed democratic consciousness (Piaget, 1973; Rawls, 1971), students who support a reduction of social inequality–even at the cost of material wealth–show less preference for lower stage reasoning. This can be taken as an indicator of higher moral development. Humanistic values and the request for "democratization of all areas of life" seem to be at the heart of advanced moral development. This is indicated by the preference profiles of the "high" and "low" groups as presented in Table 3, and by their differences with respect to cognitive-moral consistency. In our sample, students with humanistic and democratic orientations show the clearest preference order of the six stages of moral orientation. The group of students disagreeing with democratization shows less discrimination between the stages of morality in evaluating arguments. In other words, this latter group possesses less decisional competence for making morally substantiated judgments. However, this is a small group. Except for egalitarian attitudes, the configurations of median differences conform perfectly to the hypotheses. Analyses of variance yield significant linear components for the Groups x Stages interactions for all the aspects of democratic orientation examined here. With respect to some of these variables, higher order components of the interaction also turn out to be significant, yet in all cases but one the linear component accounts for the greater part of the interaction variance.

CONCLUSION

A central prerequisite for a democratic society is the moral autonomy of its citizens. A person may be regarded as morally autonomous to the extent that he or she exhibits "general consistency of approach on principle to all situations" (Kohlberg, 1958, p. 131). This does not mean, of course, cross-situational rigidity. It means a greater awareness of the multiplicity of aspects of a situation, and a more general and more encompassing perspective on moral values. All three structural approaches discussed in this paper agree that a complex cognitive structure is needed to organize behavior in accord with such abstract ideals. As Nunner-Winkler (1980) has asserted, the stability and maintenance of democracy is intimately linked to the degree to which moral values are structurally anchored in the individual mind. It obviously does not suffice to reach consensus on the basic democratic values (Dahl, 1961, p. 325). Inability, or unwillingness, to apply these values in concrete situations renders the individual prey to autocratic submission.

Our integrated study of styles of reasoning, ego functioning, and values suggests that ego strength (tolerance of ambiguity, hope for success, internal control cognition), content and structure of moral judgment behavior, and positive valuing of democratic ideals are all interrelated. These findings, as well as those from other studies, provide insight into the importance of the cognitive component in democratic behavior. Hence, they clearly demonstrate that, as Binford (1983) has stated, "the tolerance of opposing viewpoints and the appreciation of the utility of such views for social change is an important organizing principle for the character-rooted democratic personality" (p. 678). Moreover, they suggest that the acquisition of abstract values may be considered a necessary, though not sufficient, condition for the development of democratic personality. Further studies are needed to clarify how value ideals function as pacers for cognitive development.

With the combination of survey research methods and sophisticated assessment techniques, we hope that new perspectives will open up for the study of processes of socialization and personality development. The new techniques for assessing moral judgment structure render cognitive-developmental theory, as well as other structural theories, testable through empirical research geared to using multiple measures with large samples of individuals. Moreover, it will be possible to systematically investigate processes of moral *décalage*, value conservation, cognitive anchoring, or–conversely–processes of moral segmentation, particularization, and isolation. This research will ultimately have to be directed at answering Allport's (1929-30) fundamental query of whether a fully developed democratic personality is merely a particular configuration of unrelated drives, attitudes, or traits which are accidentally juxtaposed by an individual's history of conditioning and shaping, or whether such a personality represents a more or less organized whole of thought and behavior which is continually striving for integrated ego identity.

NOTES

1. These are not identical with "behaviorist" psychology. Our cognitive-developmental approach is behavioristic in so far as it claims to be empirical. In contrast to the concepts of "latent traits" and "hypothetical constructs," the organization of cognitive structure requires that it be empirically verified by the structural assessment of patterns of judgment behavior. But cognitive-developmental theorizing is to be distinguished from atomistic behaviorism, which rules out a priori the possibility of measuring complex constructs by means of behavioral assessment. The position here may best be designated by Miller, Galanter, and Pribram's (1960) term "subjective behaviorism."

2. See Edelstein et al. (1980), who found that, contrary to Kohlberg's (1976) assertion, the hypothesis of a "general genetic primacy of logical, before social-cognitive, operations is not tenable" (p. 12).

3. By referring to "logical relations," we allude not only to propositional logic, on which Piaget has concentrated in his work, but also to the broad, yet not fully recognized, fields of modal and deontic logic. The insufficiency of Piaget's approach has, in the light of Hegel's dialectical logic, been thoroughly discussed by Broughton (1981).

4. This study was carried out by the Forschungsgruppe Hochschulsozialisation at the University of Konstanz, as part of an ongoing international longitudinal study. Besides the authors, Barbara Dippelhofer-Stiem, Gerhild Framhein, Hansgert Peisert (director), and Hans-Gerhard Walter have collaborated on the research. The cross-national FORM project is coordinated by the European Coordination Centre, Vienna, and comprises parallel research projects in Austria, the Federal Republic of Germany, the Netherlands, Poland, and Yugoslavia. The research design and questionnaire used with the graduates of West German upper secondary schools *(Abiturienten)* are fully described in two working documents, prepared by the Forschungsgruppe Hochschulsozialisation: *Wissenschaftlicher Bericht, 1976-1978* (Zentrum I Bildungsforschung, University of Konstanz, 1979); and *Anlage und Instrumente des Abiturienten–Follow-up, 1976/77* (Arbeitsunterlage 37, Zentrum 1 Bildungsforschung, University of Konstanz, 1981).

5. Note that these experiments are located on the level of the individual (idiographic experiment), and not on the level of an aggregate of individuals, as is the case in the correlational analysis below. Nor are these experiments conducted to assess the effect of an "independent" variable, but to measure individual structural dispositions (Lind, 1985d).

6. In formal terms, these configurations consisted of i times A smaller than or equal to B, followed by $(6 - i)$ times A greater than B, where A denotes the median scores of the group higher in ego strength or democratic orientation, and the range of the index i is between 1 and 6. In these configurations, scores A are at most equal to scores B for lower stages, and are larger than B for higher stages. By way of limiting cases, configurations with lower A scores for lower stages and equality of scores for higher stages are included in the conform subset, whereas, of course, the case in which $A = B$ for all stages is excluded.

7. The Box-Bartlett Test (Morrison, 1976, pp. 252-253) serves to check whether the assumption of homoscedasticity (equality of variance-covariance matrices for independent groups) is tenable. As revealed by the Huynh-Feldt pattern test (Morrison, 1976, pp. 214-215), the model that Bock (1975, pp. 459-460) presents as Assumption I proved too restrictive. The tests we applied (using term-by-term F statistics) are valid under Bock's most general Assumption III, which allows for heteroscedasticity as well as correlated polynomial error components.

8. Analysis of variance procedures cannot be meaningfully applied to these data, because the way the consistency measure was constructed implies that the homoscedasticity assumption is violated, that is, that the groups have different interstage covariance matrices.

A preliminary version of this chapter appeared in *Political Psychology* (Lind, Sandberger, & Bargel, 1981-82). We wish to thank the publisher of the journal for his kind permission to revise that article for the present volume.

Testing for Moral Judgment Competence

Georg Lind and Roland Wakenhut

Few if any psychological instruments have been based on such an intimate dialogue between theory formation and empirical research as has Kohlberg's well-known moral judgment interview, especially in its revised "issue scoring" version. The method embodied in this instrument has proven its worth in numerous studies since the first time it was used (see Kohlberg, 1958; 1984; Colby et al., 1983; in press), and by now belongs among the list of methods firmly established in psychological research. However, this method is not without controversy, which is hardly surprising in view of the conceptual complexity of many of its central terms, such as "morals" and "competence in moral judgment." It was, therefore, to be expected that alternative methods of investigation would arise, and with them instruments that would attempt to extend or even replace Kohlberg's moral judgment interview.

In this chapter we shall discuss some of the new methods of assessing competence in moral judgment. What information can be gained with them? What would be the most adequate design of the questionnaire and the best method of analysis? And finally, is it truly the case that the classical criteria of test construction can be applied–as seems generally assumed–to the evaluation of structural personality tests?

Cognitive-developmental theory does not always permit a conclusive decision in favor of one specific operational form in moral judgment research. To justify the development of a particular measuring instrument, further specification is necessary based on the specific scientific issue at stake. Thus the very process of constructing objective tests for psychological research (Loevinger, 1957) becomes an important means of increasing knowledge. Moreover, we believe there are some methodological postulates inherent in cognitive-developmental theory which also call for new decisions in psychometrics.

Like Kohlberg, we want to concentrate on concrete moral judgment behavior. In order to distinguish clearly between this approach and that of questionnaires in which persons have to report on how they "usually" behave or how they would "possibly" behave, we have designated the methods for assessing judgment behavior as "Experimental Questionnaires" (Lind, 1982b) or, less formally, simply as "tests." Following the cognitive developmental approach, the response behavior of the persons questioned is not considered a sign of a merely hypothetical moral disposition; rather, the pattern of judgment behavior is regarded as a manifestation of moral attitudes and cognitions, which are considered the two basic defining aspects of moral behavior (cf. Kohlberg, 1979; Lind, ch. 2 in this volume). In this way a number of problems involved with introspective, self-reporting questionnaires can be avoided–problems that result from the interference of the characteristic under study with the subject's state of being when answering the questionnaire (response set, etc.; see Eckensberger et al., 1980; Lempert, 1982).

INTERVIEWS AND TESTS

The instruments which we shall discuss under the rubric "tests" do not include those methods that attempt merely to approximate Kohlberg's interview method but thereby often ignore the central postulates of cognitive developmental theory. As Schuhler (1978) noted, those methods are inherently unable to account for the essential assumptions of assessing *competence* in moral judgment. Our point of departure is the still stronger claim that there are central statements in the cognitive theory of moral development which contradict the "hidden anthropological requirements" of the theoretical assumptions of classical tests and questionnaires.[1] Whereas the latter assume that the characteristics of personality can be separated like substances into isolated components, the cognitive developmental theory postulates that the affective and cognitive aspects of moral judgment competence are aspects of the same mental "substance" and thus must be be dealt with together.[2]

The best way to determine the differences between the Kohlbergian interview method and the tests of moral judgment competence described here is to examine the operations involved in interviewing and evaluating. Both methods have certain basic features in common. They involve systematically varied testing of moral judgment behavior and are standardized to a great extent in the way they are conducted and evaluated. In each, several dilemmas are presented as short stories and require that the respondent be able to judge the adequacy of moral reasons. The major difference is that interviews are production tasks, whereas the tests under discussion here ask for recognition. In the Kohlbergian interview, the subject has to answer a number of successive questions and account in his own words for his answers. (Did Person X act in the right way? Why do you think so? etc.) In the Experimental Questionnaires, answers and reasons are given to the subject, who must rank them on the basis of their acceptability. In the interview technique, the answers given by the subject are compared afterwards step by step with the exemplars or criterion answers provided in the coding manual. Thus for every issue, e.g., Life, a score is determined from which a total score is calculated in strict arithmetic fashion. In the tests, on the other hand, the "criterion answers" are presented directly to the subject, who then compares them with his or her own moral judgment. Regarded from a practical point of view, the two methods are not antagonistic: their differences reflect a difference of research interest. Both production and recognition are important expressions of moral judgments, which complement rather than substitute for each other. However, from a theoretical point of view the differences between Experimental Questionnaires and the Kohlbergian interview are more subtle.

These differences can be set forth in terms of the following four problems associated with the interview method. First, the statistical evaluation of the moral interviews is still virtually atomistic, despite great efforts to make it "more structural." The assignment of a response to a stage according to the coding manual still presupposes a classical theory of psychometrics in which each individual response is taken as a sign of a probable underlying trait. When variation of reasoning across dilemmas and issues occurs, the variation is not, as one would expect on the basis of the structural theory, taken as an important manifestation of organization of judgment but is viewed merely as an error in the assessment instrument (cf. Colby et al., 1978; 1983). Therefore, the calculation of the mean moral judgment scores neglects the structural or process-related information in manifest judgment behavior.

The second problem involved in the interview method has to do with differential motivation in judgment behavior. Interview scores reflect not only a person's ability to argue at particular stages, but also his or her motivation to exhibit "high-sounding" moral arguments in a relatively artificial situation such as an interview, in which there is no real or perceived need to reason at the highest stage. This can result in underestimating the stage of moral judgment competence.

Third, in the interview method the force or intensity of an individual's argument is not recorded. It is only inferred from the number of times it has been given in the course of the interview. The assumption of a close correlation between intensity and frequency is valid in many cases, but it is not always close enough to permit a reliable inference. In contrast, experimentally designed tests, which clearly differentiate between the intensity and the consistency of responses, provide direct information on the force of an argument without relying on unsecured inferences.

Fourth, if one is more interested in the moral arguments people perceive and prefer, and less in which moral arguments they themselves produce, the interview method would stand second to that of Experimental Questionnaires with regard to theoretical validity (Rest, 1975, p. 748).

In sum, tests–at least tests in the narrow sense of what we have called Experimental Questionnaires (see also Lind, 1982b)–have several advantages over interviews. They are more economical, a fact which permits their extensive use and the examination of hypotheses requiring great numbers of people; they are more transparent, a fact which promotes both a critical examination of their theoretical (content) validity and efforts to analyze moral judgment behavior and its determinants differentially; moreover, in such tests the intensity of preference for a particular moral orientation can be directly obtained by appropriate response scales. However, this does not mean that Experimental Questionnaires can completely replace the clinical interview method. Highly standardized and carefully designed interviews are, in many cases, indispensable for research as well as for praxis. The method of choice depends, above all, on the particular question one has in mind.

TESTS FOR MORAL JUDGMENT COMPETENCE

Because we wanted to construct not merely an economical replacement for the interview method, but rather a research instrument capable of answering particular theoretical questions in current moral psychology, we have created a new family of "Tests for Moral Judgment" (referred to collectively as TMJs), in which "moral judgment" means moral *competence* in the sense described above. Other questionnaire methods, such as the *Defining Issues Test* (DIT) developed by Rest (1979a) come close to our aims, but they fail to meet the special requirements which we believe characterize cognitive-developmental theory.

Regarding moral judgment, there are two kinds of test procedures, which vary according to the method's design and the strategy involved in evaluation: (1) classical tests of moral attitudes, and (2) new structural tests for both affective and cognitive aspects of moral judgment behavior. The DIT is the best example of the first type. It has proven its worth as a psychometric "technique" in Coombs's sense of the word (Coombs et al., 1975, p. 45); however, it is problematic as a "criterion" for cognitive developmental research. The DIT is based on Kohlberg's theory of moral development. At the same time, it complies with the rules of classical testing theory, rules whose basic assumptions seem incompatible with the cognitive theory of development. The variation of responses across more than one stage or level (i.e., the degree of inconsistency), is, on the one hand, used as a methodological concept to determine the state of development, and, on the other hand, employed as empirical evidence against the theory. But these two interpretations are mutually exclusive. Rest has resolved this dissonance between theory and method partly at the expense of the theory of cognitive development. Of the two components of moral judgment competence, the DIT deals explicitly with the content or affective aspect. However, the structural-cognitive component is expressed implicitly by the P score, which is a measure of response consistency in relation to postconventional morality.[3]

The second type of method pursues and seeks to extend this line of structural diagnostics. It refers to Rest's earlier research on the relationship between arguments produced on one's own and preferences for given arguments (Rest et al., 1969; Rest, 1973). In contrast to these pure preference tests, structural tests include the cognitive aspect of moral judgment behavior as well as the content-affective components of moral attitudes. Dealing with both components simultaneously seems indispensable, "because a moral act or attitude can be defined neither by purely 'cognitive' nor purely 'motivational' criteria" (Kohlberg, 1958, p. 16).

The attempt has been made to realize this new approach with two instruments developed for German-speaking subjects. The *Moralisches Urteil Test* (MUT; Moral Judgment Test), which requires a judgment of acceptability, was developed as part of the research project "University Socialization,"[4] which accounts for such features as its highly differentiated reasons scale and the selection of themes. The test has been used in studies of various groups of people in Germany, Austria, and Switzerland, and translated versions have also been employed in moral judgment research in the Netherlands, Poland, and Yugoslavia (Lind et al., 1976; Lind, 1978a; 1984a) A translation of the MUT is appended to this chapter.

The second test, the *Moralisches Urteil Fragebogen* (MUF; Moral Judgment Questionnaire) developed by Krämer-Badoni and Wakenhut (1978b; Wakenhut, 1982), constitutes a variation of the MUT and has been geared to the special goals of the study set by the authors; it was originally created for the research project "Socialization in the German Armed Forces,"[5] but in the meantime has also been used in a number of other studies, as has the MUT. New dilemmas, a modified response scheme, and special characteristic statistics were developed for the MUF–the least of these being especially important in view of the project's aim to measure the phenomenon of segmentation in moral consciousness (cf. the chapters by Krämer-Badoni & Wakenut, and by Senger, in this volume).[6]

The similarities and differences between these three types of methods for measuring moral judgment competence, i.e., the Kohlberg interview method, the DIT, and the MJTs discussed here for measuring moral judgment competence (viz., the MUT and MUF), are shown in Table 1.

DESIGN AND CONSTRUCTION

The construction of tests to measure competence in moral judgment presents four problems: systematics of test design, selection and construction of moral dilemmas, selection and construction of moral arguments and answers, and computation and interpretation of various indices from the individual's pattern of judgment behavior.

Experimental Design

Since we view tests of moral judgment competence as behavioral tests, which allows us to infer affective and cognitive dispositions of judgment behavior, the question of test design is of particular

Table 1

Structural Methods for Assessing Moral Judgment Competence

Method	Behavior	Dispositional Aspects Affective Content	Cognitive Structure
Kohlberg Interview	Production of moral arguments	Stage-typical orientations, concerns, norms, elements	Consistency of moral argumentation on systematic probing
Measure: The Moral Maturity Score (MMS), common to both aspects and based on frequency of moral arguments produced.			
Defining Issues Test (DIT)	Judgment of the importance of given moral arguments	Intensity of preference for stage-typical concerns	Consistency of judgments regarding postconventional reasoning stages
Measure: The proportion of postconventional preferences in the total of top-ranked arguments, P score, common for both aspects.			
Test for measuring Moral Judgment Competency	Judgment of the acceptability or legitimacy of given moral arguments	Direction and intensity of preferences for stage-typical concerns	Consistency of judgment behavior regarding one's concerns independent of their opinion-conformity
Measure: Different scores for the affective and the cognitive aspects of moral judgment, as well as common scores.			

importance. A person's ability to bring to bear in concrete acts of judgment moral attitudes which compete with other orientations that can potentially guide action, and to do so in an integrated and differentiated manner, cannot be measured by individual items, taken singly or in summation. It must be dealt with in terms of the *structural relationship between the pattern of questions and the pattern of answers.* In structural methods, systematic questioning facilitates the hermeneutic intention to create the possibility for testing competitive hypotheses about an individual's motive in judgment behavior (see Lind, 1982b; 1984b). This approach can be found in the intuitive assessments of other persons in daily life, and is made explicit by the scientific techniques of standardized interviews and experimental tests. The structure of a TMJ consists of elements (responses to items) and their relationships (factorial design). Whereas the items elicit individual behavioral acts, the factorial design is devised to reveal the hypothesized dispositions—if and when they really exist in an individual. Because a TMJ is designed to measure judgment behavior oriented to moral categories, the items given must represent moral concerns. The MUT and the MUF incorporate Kohlberg's (1969) six different moral stages as their main design factor. Each type or stage is represented by arguments which the subject has to evaluate. With this experimental design, one can determine whether moral dispositions are effective in an individual pattern of judgment behavior, in that one assesses the degree to which the person consistently rates arguments according to their moral differences.

The TMJs attempt to analyze the degree to which moral judgment is integrated and differentiated—a task for which a one-factorial construction and evaluation design is insufficient. Whereas in classically designed questionnaires, one is solely concerned with the degree of attitude consistency (integration), the use of multifactorially designed Experimental Questionnaires permits us also to investigate the degree of differentiation of a person's judgment. That is, TMJs are intended to assess properties of judgment behavior which, in the classical questionnaire construction, are covered by the concept of "measuring error." In the latter, error is equated with the total of unknown factors and thus has, to a great extent, removed these factors from the researcher's attention.[7] Some of these other factors, however, are familiar from cognitive developmental theory, though they have not been the subject of much if any empirical study. In the course of discussing a decision dilemma, agreement or disagreement with a line of argument may be supported not only by one's moral concerns, but also–or even exclusively–by other motives or combinations of motives. On the one hand, agreement can be simple *acquiescence,* resulting from the subject's respect for the psychological instrument or from a general tendency to agree with whatever arguments are given. On the other hand, agreement would be *opinion conformity* when it is post hoc, that is, the argument is accepted because of the action it advocates rather than the reasons it invokes.

Acquiescence and opinion conformity are the two most important orientations to be considered in addition to moral motive when studying a person's moral judgment competence, if one is to avoid false interpretations (Lind, 1978a, pp. 181-185). If we study only a person's evaluations of a particular stage of conforming moral reasoning, for example, the "law and order" reasons that support his or her opinion on a moral dilemma, we cannot unambiguously infer from these evaluations which of the three motives have determined them. In the TMJs, the moral motive is differentiated from acquiescence by examining the person's evaluations of qualitatively different arguments. (Following the terminology of analysis of variance, ANOVA, we call this the "Stage factor.") In order to differentiate moral concerns from a person's concern for supporting his or her intuitive opinion, the TMJs incorporate arguments based on both conforming and contrary opinions (the "Pro-Con factor"). In his interviews Kohlberg also uses this technique to test the "firmness of a person's 'structure'" (Eckensberger et al., 1980, p. 340; Kohlberg, 1958, pp. 12, 131).

A third dispositional factor to be considered when assessing moral judgment is the person's differential attention to the particular moral principles involved in the moral dilemma that is presented. As Kohlberg wrote in 1958, a morally adequate solution to a dilemma must "do justice to one's own conviction and the demands of the situation" (p. 128). To deal with situational differentiation and hierarchical integration of moral judgment in the total personality systems, the TMJs take the story or dilemma situation into account as an experimental factor (the "Dilemma factor"). By combining these three orientation factors, extensive models of the structure of judgment behavior can be tested empirically. We are thereby able to deal not only with the main effects but also with instances of personality integration that go beyond consistency in regard to single moral principles.

As behavioral tests, TMJs do not stop with the assumption of a hypothetical construct, but aim at moral dispositions which are actual–that is, dispositions which are manifested in the act of judgment. With TMJs based on the Experimental Questionnaire concept, the presumed (hypothetical) judgment dispositions are built into the questionnaire situation as "factors," so that they can be tested using the example of an interaction between the subject (person) and the questionnaire (situation). From the characteristics of the situation considered in conjunction with the response pattern, we can infer the extent to which the presumed dispositions have become effective in this interaction. TMJs do not demand extensive introspection and self-description and, therefore, are not troubled with the diagnostic distortions these demands create (Shweder, 1975).

The MUT consists of two sub-tests, and the MUF of six, in which conflicting decisions and lines of argument are presented. In each case the dilemma and a description of its solution is followed by the question: What does the subject think about it? Then come six arguments, and the subject is asked to indicate how acceptable or how valid the particular argument is for him or herself. Thus, each argument exists in three meaning-contexts accounted for in the tests; they build a three-factorial, completely crossed experimental design (Dilemma x Pro-Con x Stage) that can be extended according to the research interest. In longitudinal or experimental studies, the factors Time and (sometimes) Treatment and their combination with the foregoing factors are also introduced.

The "Moral" Dilemma

In test application practice, the subjects first note the description of the objectively given situational content, including the spatio-temporal background. This information is identical for all subjects but is open to subjective interpretation and definition by means of which the individual makes sense of the situation. Only if the situational definition proceeds according to ethical criteria does the situation become morally relevant, that is, it constitutes a moral dilemma (see Kohlberg, 1969, pp. 393-397; Krämer-Badoni & Wakenhut, in this volume). To suggest such a situational definition, or even to make one possible, several conditions have to be fulfilled. The situation should be constructed a priori as a moral dilemma in which two or more moral values are in conflict. Kohlberg (1976) names a total of eleven "moral issues": punishment, property, feeling, authority, right, life, freedom, equality, truth, conscience, and sexuality.

The subject should be able to put himself in the actor's place in the dilemma. As a rule, this condition can be satisfied by situations that relate to the subject's life-world and life-experience. These situations can involve dilemmas which the subject has experienced himself or dilemmas which the subject has observed or experienced vicariously through the descriptions of others. To empirically ensure the symbolic accessibility of a situation, the question to be posed at the conclusion of a dilemma is whether or not the subject can actually place himself in the dilemma. What is essential for the dilemma's effectiveness is not the frequency with which it is experienced in everyday life but the degree to which it presents a moral challenge.[8]

As we have seen, the level of moral reasoning is affected by the choice of the dilemma "issue(s)" (see Eckensberger & Reinshagen, 1980, p. 80). The preference hierarchy for the argumentation stages already points to the fact that not every dilemma must be solved at the highest stage, i.e., Stage 6. Whereas for some dilemmas (e.g., the Mercy Killing Dilemma) the arguments are most strongly accepted at Stage 6, in the case of the Worker Dilemma (see the translation of the MUT at the end of this chapter) reasoning at a lower stage, Stage 5, is more strongly accepted. The latter does not necessarily imply a lower stage of judgment competence since, from a moral point of view, the workers' dilemma may indeed be most adequately dealt with at Stage 5 rather than at Stage 6. This reminds us that not every dilemma is a Stage 6 dilemma, and that many dilemmas are not even moral dilemmas. Hence, a highly developed competence in moral judgment might in some instances lead one to prefer a stage of reasoning lower than Stage 6. This is not a paradox if one recognizes that dilemmas are not equal.

It is, therefore, important to choose at least some dilemmas that require a discussion at the postconventional stages. That is the case when the issue is human dignity or human life. Which other issues and situations are selected for the dilemmas depends also on the study's interest. If the dependency of moral judgment on specific areas of life, the so-called segmentation effect (Döbert & Nunner-Winkler, 1975), is to be studied, the areas of interest must be represented in the dilemmas; this was true in the MUF, in which some of the dilemmas were written for the military life-world of soldiers fulfilling their military obligations in the armed forces, while the other dilemmas were related to their civilian life-world.

The apparently plausible demand for ecologically valid situations (see Pawlik, 1976), that is the demand that the test statistically represent a particular environment, cannot be fulfilled, because the basic totality of morally relevant situations in the area of life under study cannot be determined. Rather, the dilemmas (like the arguments) must be representative of the research questions and the theory. This agrees well with the "moral definition" on which the dilemma's construction has been based. The subjects have less frequently used the term "moral," since in daily life this term often connotes "conventional" or "adhering to norms." Asked to define the kind of problem characteristic of this dilemma, first semester university students ($N = 538$) defined it predominantly as a "humanitarian" one (Table 2). In the case of TMJs, theoretical representativity can be secured in three ways: by basing the selection of dilemmas on moral philosophy, by submitting the dilemmas to experts' ratings, and by letting the subjects define the kind of problem at stake in a dilemma. TMJs are regularly validated in the first and second way.

Table 2

Definitions of the Mercy Killing Dilemma

As a humanitarian problem	51.3%
As a moral problem	25.8%
As a religious problem	10.6%
As a legal problem	6.5%
As a social problem	5.0%
As a scientific problem	0.7%

Source: University Socialization Research Project, University of Konstanz.

The Arguments of the TMJs

The arguments which serve as test items have been designed to meet two requirements in particular. (1) To constitute a theoretically valid instrument, every argument presented on the TMJ must represent one and only one of the six stages of moral reasoning. In any case, it is useful to double check, using an expert rating, or better, inter-expert comparisons, whether the arguments presented on the TMJ truly correspond to the Kohlbergian "criterion judgments" which they are supposed to represent. Of course, this requirement is itself constrained by the current state of cognitive developmental theory, which is still in the process of defining the stages more precisely (Colby et al. 1978; see also Eckensberger & Reinshagen, 1980; Oser, 1981a; Lempert, 1982). (2) The subject's selection of an argument should be made apart from the decision it leads to and independently of the stage of moral judgment to which it belongs. To this effect, for each of the directions a decision can take (pro and con) and for each of the six stages, at least one argument should be included in the questionnaire so that the stage of moral orientation can be logically determined independently of the subject's opinion concerning the outcome of the moral dilemma. As we will see below, this independence permits the analytical distinction between the structure and content of moral judgment and frees the hypothesis concerning the empirical correlation between these two aspects (Kohlberg's parallelism thesis) from the reproach of tautology (Phillips & Nicolayev, 1978; Eckensberger, 1984).

Sometimes it is difficult to formulate meaningful arguments for all six stages of moral judgment. "Meaningful" here means that the arguments should not seem ridiculous or artificial at any stage. The empirical findings indicate the success of such constructions. The pro arguments are ranked in the same order by the proponents of the action described as are the corresponding con arguments by the opponents. That does not deny the fact that certain opinions, e.g., those favoring racial discrimination, are inconceivable on principle at a postconventional level (Kohlberg, 1976). From our own experience we know the difficulty involved in formulating "good" reasons at Stage 1 or 2 for certain issues (e.g., for euthanasia). It is still an open question whether these difficulties are a matter of principle or could be resolved by someone thoroughly familiar with the methodology of the cognitive development theory.

Strength and Direction of Moral Attitudes

In the TMJs a numerical reaction scale is given for each of the arguments: in the MUT, the subjects state how acceptable the argument appears to them (from -4, completely unacceptable, to +4, completely acceptable); and in the MUF, they state how well one can justify or reject the action described in the argument. Allowing for the possibility of graded reactions permits the direct study of degrees of affective tendency, which in Kohlberg's interviews are only inferred from response frequency. The number of choices on the scale may be adjusted for the population being studied. For persons of a higher intellectual level, nine choices are provided, which lowers the chance of ties among the item ranks. For other persons, three to five reaction possibilities would be more appropriate (see Rohrmann, 1978). In any case, answering can be facilitated if reaction possibilities, or at least the extreme ones, are paraphrased from the numerical scale. Furthermore, it is important that there be an odd number of possibilities: subjects should not be forced in one judgment direction by even-numbered response scales in which the middle category is missing.

Finally, to deal with the outcome of a moral dilemma the so-called opinion question is posed after the dilemma but before the arguments. The subject's answer to this question determines whether the pro and con arguments are to be classified in his or her case as "conforming to opinion" or as "contrary to opinion."[9]

THREE-STEP STRATEGY FOR THE EVALUATION OF THE TESTS FOR MORAL JUDGMENT

Our experimental tests for moral judgment competence have been set up to allow for measurement of the two principal aspects of moral judgment behavior: the content-affective aspect and the structural-cognitive aspect. Classical attitude tests attend only to the first of these two related but by no means identical aspects. In the Kohlberg interview, the structural aspect is supposed to be dealt with apart from content, insofar as that is possible. Actually, in this case the measuring scores represent a mixture of the two aspects, namely the stage a person prefers in his or her reasoning *and* the consistency of this preference.

At first we also intended that our TMJs resemble Kohlberg's interview method, with a single stage score to be assigned each of the subject's responses. Corresponding evaluation strategies are presented below. Efforts in the last few years have shown not only that results comparable to those of the Kohlberg interview can be attained (see Krämer-Badoni & Wakenhut, in this volume), but also that the same problems will be encountered. In order to distinguish clearly the two above-mentioned aspects of moral judgment, we found it necessary to modify the methodology of the cognitive development theory. Instead of assigning only one stage to describe the cognitive-moral development of a person, we had to represent two developmental dimensions simultaneously, namely, (1) the stage of moral affects, i.e., the highest moral stage preferred, and (2) the level of moral cognition, i.e., the stage of morality which one *consistently* applies to one's judgment behavior in an integrated and differentiated manner. Neither dimension can be reduced to the other, nor can one be fully understood and valued without the other. Mere preference for moral maxims says nothing about competence in moral judgment, because the determination of that sort of ability cannot be specified until the subjective moral reference is taken into account and is put into the place of the alleged objectivity (on the problem of "objectivity," see Adorno, 1980, p. 84). Because it deals reciprocally with the content and structure of moral competence, this cognitive moral psychology is distinguished from approaches that deal with moral behavior by using the conventional definitions of what is moral.[10]

To avoid separating the two aspects of moral judgment, the methodology used in our TMJs is directed at the question of whether or not an individual is capable of making judgments based on his or her own maxims. Measurement in a TMJ makes assigning a score to the direction and intensity of a moral attitude dependent on the dispositions actually operating in a person's moral judgment behavior; furthermore, it makes recognizing cognitive (ability) components dependent on behavioral consistency relative to individually accepted categories.

Definition of Cognitive-Structural Scores

We view the relationship between moral maxims and behavior in the individual person as an important and extremely interesting object of psychological research. We cannot assume a priori that moral maxims have absolutely no influence on concrete judgment behavior, nor that they determine an individual's behavior in every case. Tests dealing with competence in moral judgment should be especially sensitive to this point. We have assumed that the question of whether, and to what extent, moral orientation is cognitively anchored is a serious question, and one which is capable of being answered. But the development of this question cannot be processed by the traditional methods involved in the construction and evaluation of questionnaires (cf. Lind, ch. 8 in this volume).

In this context it is important to remember that cognitive moral development is characterized not only by a greater cognitive anchoring of moral maxims in action, but also by the necessary process of breaking up old behavioral ties (differentiation) and taking situational circumstances and competitive values increasingly into account (hierarchical integration). Without referring definitely to contents in interpreting behavioral consistency, we can make no distinction between progressive integration and regressive rigidity, nor between a developed differentiation and a retarded lack of orientation. Research on "pure" cognitive structures and styles would not provide the means necessary to distinguish between these opposites. "Consistency" is a bivalent relation whose univalent counterpart ("consistency per se") is incomplete and leads necessarily to ambiguities in psychological measurement.

Defining response consistency in relation to motivational contents in the design of Experimental Questionnaires enables us to define various measures of cognitive structuredness unequivocally in relation to various action-guiding dispositions. Thus with the MUT or the MUF, degrees of orientation for a person's judgment behavior can be ascertained with regard to (1) one or several of the six moral types described by Kohlberg (we call this moral structuredness, or the Stage factor), (2) the subject's opinion about the solution for the particular dilemma, on which he or she has settled before the discussion of arguments (opinion conformity, or the Pro-Con factor), and (3) the specific dilemma context (the Dilemma or Dilemma-context factor, which includes issue differentiation and the interaction between Stage and Dilemma). By combining the orientations of (1), (2), and (3), one can formulate and empirically test a number of highly differentiated hypotheses concerning the formation and function of moral judgment competence and its development, as we shall see below by means of a concrete example.

Multivariate analysis of variances (or sum of squares) is the technique best suited to calculating the scores to be assigned to the structure of the subject's moral judgment. The design variables (dilemma, stage argumentation, opinion conformity), or more exactly the subject's representations of these variables, comprise the *hypothetical* determining factors of judgment; to the degree to which these account for variance in judgment behavior, they are considered the *manifest* determining factors. Thus, the dependent variable is the total pattern of an individual's acts of judgment.

Definition of Affective-Content Scores

Once it has been established that moral categories do play a role in individual judgment behavior, one can proceed to assess the *direction* and *intensity* of the subject's preference for any stage of moral argumentation. The dual-aspect concept in the Experimental Questionnaire method proves its worth here, because the ambiguity inherent in interpretations of the intensity index can be reduced–which is not possible in classical attitude measurements (Nunner-Winkler, 1978). Using the structural analysis in a TMJ, one can distinguish between the intensity and the consistency of an individual's judgment behavior. So, for example, a comparison of preferences for the six moral stages lets one decide between the two interpretations. If there is variation among an individual's judgments but no significant differentiation in regard to moral concerns, the degree of intensity must be interpreted as an expression of response behavior that is "inconsistent in relation to moral categories." Apart from this, behavior can indeed be consistent in relation to other orientation categories, e.g., the subject's attitude to the whole questionnaire (acquiescence) or the conformity between the argument and one's own opinion.

According to the usual standards, the influence of a variable on another variable is said to be "significant" if their correlation attains a certain magnitude, depending on the number of measurements. In the MUT, which contains 24 items, any correlation between the Stage factor and an individual's judgments that is larger than $r = .33$ (which is equivalent to 10 percent of the variance of judgment) is significant on a level of $p = 0.05$. In the MUF this requirement is fulfilled with five percent variance, since there are four dilemmas or 48 items. If one believes, as does Mischel (1968), that such low coefficients represent a "barrier" in personality research, this criterion might give rise to the fear that the effectiveness of a moral disposition can hardly be proven. Fortunately, this impression, which is derived from past personality research, is not supported by research with TMJs. The average range of common variance lies far above the 10 percent barrier. In the studies to date, the average acceptability of stages or levels, or their rank (modal stage or modal level), were meaningful in most cases and could be properly calculated.

As very different studies have shown, the rank order of stages, which is the main index of the affective-content aspect of moral judgment, differentiates only slightly between subjects. A preference for the higher stages of moral judgment can be found among young people and children; even across various cultures, there seems to be a consensus in regard to this rank order of moral stages (see Damon, 1977; Piaget, 1977/1932; Portele, 1980; Rest et al., 1969). For a differential psychologist to be concerned with this affective aspect seems inappropriate, in that his or her research is limited to differences among people. Psychology must not, however, neglect the intra-individual dimension, especially in its affective aspect. It is of great importance for (1) legitimizing the competence concept (in any case it relieves the psychometrician to know that his or her conception of progress in moral development is shared by the person affected), (2) clarifying the question of what initiates cognitive-moral development (moral affect represents, among other things, a fact to which the social agents can appeal in case of a controversy), and (3) analyzing situational differentiation and segmentation.

Definition of a "Stage" of Moral Development

Although the concept of stages of moral development is controversial, the simplicity of such a concept and its fruitfulness in the interview studies conducted by Kohlberg and others suggest that there might also be value in constructing appropriate indices for closed tests. Prerequisite to that, normatively and methodically, is the empirical establishment of a developmental order in the orientations to stages, that is, (1) that preferences for stages form the theoretically expected ranking, and (2) that this affective aspect parallels the cognitive-structural aspect.

Both assumptions can be empirically confirmed. (1) In all studies which have used the MUT and MUF, the theoretical preference ranking was confirmed. Even though single individuals and single sub-tests show deviations, on the average there emerges as a social fact a consistent pattern of preferences increasing from Stages 1 to 6 (see Lind, 1978a, 1984a, 1985c). (2) Correspondingly, we have found that the second assumption, that of parallelism, is empirically confirmed with similar clarity. In all studies, a pronounced pattern of correlations between the cognitive and the affective aspects of moral judgment emerged, which was in perfect conformity with the theory (Lind, 1985e, ch. 2 in this volume).

However, although there are a number of very suitable procedures for measuring the cognitive stages of moral development, the task of assessing them is not yet complete. These procedures share the common intention of dealing with the most highly preferred moral orientation that is cognitively anchored in an individual's acts and thoughts. This means that an individual's judgment is consistent in the area between Stage 1 and the highest cognitively established stage, and is inconsistent in the area that lies "above it." For groups that show a relatively homogeneous development, such a partial consistency among individuals is easily demonstrated. For German high-school graduates and beginning university students, three kinds of analysis (longitudinal, correlational, and factor analyses) point quite clearly to a shift in consistency that takes place between Stages 3 and 4; for university graduates the shift occurs between Stages 4 and 5 (Lind, 1980a). This finding points to the fact that moral judgment competence in the first group is cognitively established until Stage 3, and in the second group until Stage 4, a finding which is consistent with the more recent results by Kohlberg and his associates (Kohlberg, 1973, 1979).

The (intra-)individual analyses, for which the tests dealing with moral judgment competence are actually designed, use various measurements for individual response consistency in order to ascertain cognitive stage scores for single individuals. In the *Entwicklungslogische Skaliervektoren* method (stage vectors logical to development), ideal types of response patterns for each stage are compared with real ones (Lind et al., 1976). Wakenhut (1981a) has extended this method by utilizing the phenomenon of partial consistency for scaling an individual's moral judgment. His computer program MODI assigns a stage of cognitive-moral development on the basis of an empirical consistency test of preference values. Briechle (1981) has suggested a similar but simpler evaluation algorithm in which the cognitive stage attained in every dilemma is by definition the lowest of those stages at which the arguments presented are preferred "consistently" by the subject (i.e., none of the reasons proper to this stage are rejected).

Finally, there are other forms of combined analysis which, however, do not produce a stage score. Heidbrink (in this volume) has suggested measuring moral judgment ability by calculating intra-individual correlations of stage preferences with the theoretical stage sequence (from Stage 1 to 6), using Kendall's *tau*. The widely used individual preference profiles (Rest, 1979; Oser, 1981a) also permit simultaneous analysis of the preference for the stages (content) and their cognitive establishment (structure), and thus have proven their value to research (see Lind, Sandberger, & Bargel, in this volume).

Anatomy of a Sample Moral Judgment Behavior

The differences and similarities among the previously discussed measures of content and structure of individual moral judgment competence can be illustrated by the response patterns elicited by the MUF from a concrete, albeit hypothetical, male subject, as portrayed in Table 3. We will assume that our hypothetical subject is able to imagine himself equally well in all the dilemmas, so that no dilemma need be excluded from the evaluation.

(1) Using the individual analysis of variance, the analysis of this sample shows that in his judgment behavior the subject orients himself slightly, but noticeably, toward moral categories. The degree of determination by the Stage factor is 14.8%. What is especially noteworthy here, however, is that the subject's own opinion (34.5%) greatly outweighs his concern with moral stages in determining his

Table 3

Response Pattern of an Individual

Dilemma:	WORKERS Pro	WORKERS Con	LÜDDERSEN Pro	LÜDDERSEN Con	NEUMANN Pro	NEUMANN Con	SCHNEIDER Pro	SCHNEIDER Con	Mean (Total)
Stage 1	3	3	3	2	2	3	3	2	2.6
2	2	4	3	3	4	3	4	3	3.3
3	2	5	4	4	5	2	5	2	3.6
4	5	5	4	5	5	2	5	1	4.0
5	3	3	3	4	3	2	4	2	3.0
6	3	5	3	4	4	2	4	1	3.3
Opinion:	*"wrong"*		*"wrong"*		*"right"*		*"right"*		

Note: The cell entries are the individual's answer, ranging from "1" (not justified at all) to "5" (completely justified).

judgment behavior. Further analysis shows that the combination of Stage and Pro-Con factors, that is, the acceptance of reasons on grounds of both their moral quality and their opinion conformity, is also of great importance for this person.

(2) Analysis of the content aspect of judgment competence results in a modal preference for Stage 4, as portrayed in Table 3. In the present case this applies to the matrix of our subject's responses to reasons that conform with his opinion as well as to those responses that conflict with his opinion (Table 4). For a rougher characterization, it would suffice to calculate the modal level, which in the present example is the conventional level (B).

(3) A mere preference stage, as we have seen, is not sufficient to ascertain the subject's stage of morality, nor can one expect at the present stage of the inquiry that the various common procedures will converge on one value. In our example, the calculation of a stage score with the help of the MODI program shows Stage 4, and using Briechle's calculation, Stage 3.

Finally, out of the multitude of other, quite diverse topics of evaluation by TMJ (see Lind, 1978a; 1980b; 1985d; Wakenhut, 1982), the phenomenon of context-dependent segmentation should be mentioned here. As Table 4 shows, segmentation is apparent if the initial matrix (portrayed in Table 3) concerning the subject's opinion about the dilemma is broken down into an opinion-conforming and an opinion-opposing response matrix). As the varying mean values in the example indicate, it is generally more difficult for this subject to prefer arguments that are directed against his already established

Table 4

Opinion-Conforming and Opinion-Opposing Response Patterns

Dilemma:	Civilian		Military				
	WORKERS Con	LÜDDERSEN Con	SCHNEIDER Pro	NEUMANN Pro	Civilian Mean	Military Mean	Total Mean

(a) Opinion-Conforming Responses							
Stage 1	3	2	3	2	*2.5*	*2.5*	*2.50*
2	4	3	4	4	*3.5*	*4.0*	*3.75*
3	5	4	5	5	*4.5*	*5.0*	*4.75*
4	5	5	5	5	*5.0*	*5.0*	*5.00*
5	3	4	4	3	*3.5*	*3.5*	*3.50*
6	5	4	4	4	*4.5*	*4.0*	*4.25*

(b) Opinion-Opposing Responses							
Stage 1	3	3	2	3	*3.0*	*2.5*	*2.75*
2	2	3	3	3	*2.5*	*3.0*	*2.75*
3	2	4	2	2	*3.0*	*2.0*	*2.50*
4	5	4	1	2	*4.5*	*1.5*	*3.00*
5	3	3	2	2	*3.0*	*2.0*	*2.50*
6	3	3	1	2	*3.0*	*1.5*	*2.25*

opinion. If, following Heidbrink, one calculates separately the structure values for the opinion-conforming (*tau* = 0.46) and the opinion-opposing response profiles (*tau* = 0.55, both corrected for ties), then it becomes clear from the discrepancy that the latter in particular points to a low degree of cognitive establishment of moral maxims. Commitment to an opinion about a concrete dilemma before judging arguments represents an important "situational threshold" on which to test moral competence, as we saw earlier in this chapter.

In the response to opposing reasons, the arguments preferred for both dilemmas drawn from the military life-world–the Schneider and the Neumann dilemmas–are consistently lower after Stage 3, compared to the arguments preferred for the other two dilemmas, which are drawn from the civilian life-world. That is, contrary arguments at conventional and postconventional stages are less often preferred or allowed in a military context; military and non-military life-worlds may be evaluated morally in different ways by this person. This initial reference to the segmentation of one's moral judgment can be further pursued in a two-way analysis of variance of the responses to opposing reasons. The first factor is defined by the moral stages, the second factor by the dilemma included in the two contexts (military vs. non-military). The degree of determination of the individual judgments by the factors of Stage and Dilemma-context combined is, at 34.2%, in fact significantly higher than that by the Stage factor alone (7.0%).[11] That is, our hypothetical subject differentiates among moral reasons only if they conform with his opinion. Opposing reasons are differentiated to a lesser degree.

CONCLUDING REMARKS AND OPEN QUESTIONS

Structural tests dealing with moral judgment competence were designed to show that various possibilities for structural evaluation can be directly related to the cognitive theory of moral development. That is exactly what distinguishes this approach from other psychological conceptualizations; for example, in the deservedly criticized concept of attitude there is a gap, difficult if not impossible to close, between the theory and the empirical-operational access to it. Furthermore, the idionomic scaling method characteristic of our TMJs is *independent* of the distributions of traits found in particular samples. The test for consistency in moral reasoning is conducted on an *intra*-individual and not an *inter*-individual basis. In this way our approach takes into account the numerous and justified criticisms of classical attitude and personality measurement in general and of its application to moral psychology in particular (Kohlberg, 1958, 1979; Broughton, 1978; Eckensberger et al., 1980).

It would therefore be inappropriate to evaluate these methods using the criteria of classical test construction—reliability and validity—as is sometimes done in criticisms of research on the cognitive theory of development (see Kurtines & Greif, 1974; Eckensberger et al., 1980; Schmied, 1981). Thus, within the cognitive-structural paradigm—and perhaps even within that of classical psychometrics, as Lumsden (1976) argues—it is not meaningful to determine "reliability" for a TMJ in the classical manner. The hypothesis has often been proposed that a mediating random process takes place between "true" moral orientation and the measuring value, but it has seldom been tested empirically. It therefore seems reasonable, as Kohlberg (1979) has emphasized in his discussion of psychometric approaches, to start with a "manifest construct" model in which inconsistencies can be analyzed systematically. Structural wholeness cannot be equated with test reliability, but refers instead to "a developmental task that can only be completely carried out at the highest stage" (Lempert, 1982, p. 117).

The criterion of "validity" will be similarly treated. To speak of the validity of a test ("How well does this test measure that which it is supposed to measure?") assumes the existence of an elaborated theory upon which the test is based ("How well does the researcher know that which he wishes to measure?"). The tests presented here are, in regard to several central hypotheses, capable of demonstrating the *empirical validity* of the cognitive-developmental theory. That capability leads to the further conclusion that the tests themselves are to some extent *theoretically valid*. Nonetheless, it may well be that one should argue, as has Broughton (1978), in the following manner. On the one hand, to test theoretical positions one must first assume that the theoretically established test is valid and that it is the responsibility of the theory to account for its predictions. On the other hand, if the theory is considered sufficiently supported, one must question the way the theory has been operationalized. The two critiques cannot be carried out simultaneously, but they can be managed by means of an interactive procedure in research which Kohlberg and others have called "bootstrapping." In sum, the validity of measuring methods is embedded in the validity of the research processes in which they are used, and therefore the development of our instruments is closely bound up with progress in theory foundation.

The ideas discussed here can also be applied to approaches outside the tradition of cognitive-developmental theory. Potential areas of application include those of cognitive-social development (Selman, 1976; Edelstein & Keller, 1982), ego development (Loevinger, 1976), the development of interaction (Oser, 1981a), and other areas in which a comparable theoretical base has been formulated. The TMJs have already been used in a number of studies to examine the conditions, course, and results of socialization processes.[12] In those studies, not only was the cognitive theory of moral development confirmed on a far-reaching scale (convergent validation), but new insights were also made possible into the way the content and structure of moral competence are related (see Lind, 1985d, 1985e).

However, the discussion of these test methods continues. This is as it should be, since there are a number of open questions and problems of a methodological nature, not confined to the tests presented here, that confront the findings of this approach but at the same time confirm its fertility.

NOTES

1. See Bereiter, 1963; Holzkamp, 1972; Lumsden, 1976; Kempf, 1978.
2. The concept of "competence," which has many meanings, is chosen to emphasize the aspect of cognitive ability involved in every moral judgment. It is preferred to the concept of "consciousness" because we, like Habermas (1976a, p. 86), do not want to confine our analysis to conscious judgment behavior. Our use of the concept of competence differs from that of other authors, who equate competence with a value posture that is not yet translated into action (performance). On the contrary, competence here means precisely the ability to translate moral attitudes into specific judgment behavior.
3. For other methods of assessing moral attitudes without reference to cognitive aspects, see Pittel & Mendelsohn, 1966; see also Kuhmerker et al., 1981; Eckensberger et al., 1980; Rest, 1973.
4. This research is supported by the Deutsche Forschungsgemeinschaft (German Research Council). The MUT has been developed in close collaboration with the following members of the research group: Tino Bargel, Barbara Dippelhofer-Stiem, Gerhild Framhein, Hansgert Peisert (director), Johann-Ulrich Sandberger, and Hans Gerhard Walter.
5. The research has been conducted at the Sozialwissenschaftliche Institut der Bundeswehr (German Armed Forces Institute for Social Research), with Thomas Krämer-Badoni (now at the University of Bremen), Ekkehard Lippert, Paul Schneider (Staatsinstitut für Schulpädagogik, Munich), and Roland Wakenhut (University of Augsburg).
6. For further instruments developed on the basis of the MUT see Briechle, 1981; Hinder & Kanig, 1981.
7. It is easily overlooked that in mathematical statistics "error" is defined precisely as the result of a pure random process. This means that "error" is a particular fact which, like any fact, can be investigated empirically.
8. For a discussion of "hypothetical" versus "real" dilemmas, see Damon, 1977; see also Döbert & Nunner-Winkler as well as Oser & Schläfli, both in this volume.
9. Kohlberg and others sometimes call the opinion concerning the solution of dilemmas ("What should X do?") the "content" of moral judgment. But we have already used this term to designate the affective aspect of moral judgment, so in the present context we have decided to use the term "opinion" in order to avoid ambiguity.
10. Concerning the problem of "ideological bias" of moral psychology, see Pittel & Mendelsohn, 1966; Simpson, 1976; Hartmann, in this volume.
11. The Dilemma factor by itself does not indicate, as we once believed

(Lind & Wakenhut, 1980, p. 322), the phenomenon of "segmentation."

12. See Bald et al., 1981; Blass, 1982; Heidbrink, 1981; Krämer-Badoni & Wakenhut, 1979; Lind 1978a, 1980d, 1984b, and ch. 2 in this volume; Schmidt, 1981; Schmied, 1981; Schmitt, 1982; Wischka, 1982.

This chapter is a revised version of the original German chapter. It also contains, especially in the discussion of the evaluation of the TMJs, many alterations of our original statement (Lind & Wakenhut, 1980), made in the light of recent critical and constructive suggestions on the MUT and MUF (Eckensberger et al., 1980) as well as of the results of our recent research.

I. Due to a number of seemingly unfounded dismissals, some factory workers suspect the managers of eavesdropping on their employees through an intercom and using this information against them. The managers officially and emphatically deny this accusation. The union declares it will only take steps against the company when proof has been found that confirms these suspicions. The two workers then break into the administrative offices and take tape transcripts that prove the allegation of eavesdropping.

Do you tend to agree or disagree with the worker's behavior?

agree   disagree
−3 −2 −1 0 +1 +2 +3

How acceptable do you find the following arguments in favor of the two workers' behavior? Suppose someone argued...

I find the argument...
completely acceptable   completely unacceptable
−4 −3 −2 −1 0 +1 +2 +3 +4

1. that they didn't cause much damage to the company.

2. that due to the company's disregard for the law, the means used were permissible to restore law and order.

3. that most of the workers would approve of their action and many of them would be happy about it.

−4 −3 −2 −1 0 +1 +2 +3 +4

4. that trust among people and individual dignity of the employees count more than the firm's internal regulations.

5. that since the company had committed an injustice first, the workers were justified in breaking into the offices.

6. that the workers saw no legal means of revealing the company's misuse of confidence, and therefore chose what they considered the lesser evil.

How acceptable do you find the following arguments against the two workers' behavior? Suppose someone argued...

I find the argument...
completely acceptable   completely unacceptable
−4 −3 −2 −1 0 +1 +2 +3 +4

7. that law and order in society would be endangered if everyone acted as the two workers did.

8. that when no universally valid principles justify doing so, it is wrong to violate such a basic right as the right of property ownership and to take the law into their own hands.

−4 −3 −2 −1 0 +1 +2 +3 +4

9. that it is unwise to risk dismissal from the company because of other people.

10. that the workers didn't sufficiently exhaust the legal channels at their disposal and in their haste committed a serious violation of the law.

11. that one doesn't steal and commit burglary if one wants to be considered a decent and honest person.

12. that they weren't affected by the dismissals of the other employees and thus had no reason to steal the transcripts.

II. A woman had cancer and there was no hope of saving her. She was in terrible pain and so weakened that a large dose of a painkiller such as morphine would have brought about her death. During a temporary period of improvement, she begged the doctor to give her enough morphine to kill her. She said she could no longer endure the pain and would be dead in a few weeks anyway. The doctor complied with her wish.

Do you tend to agree or disagree with the doctor's behavior?

disagree   agree
-3 -2 -1 0 $+1$ $+2$ $+3$

How acceptable do you find the following arguments in favor of the doctor's behavior? Suppose someone said he acted rightly...

I find the argument...

completely   completely
acceptable   unacceptable
-4 -3 -2 -2 0 $+1$ $+2$ $+3$ $+4$

1. because the doctor had to act according to his conscience. The woman's condition justified an exception to the moral obligation to preserve life.

2. because the doctor was the only one who could fulfill the woman's wish; respect for her wish made him act as he did. ....

3. because the doctor only did what the woman talked him into doing. He needn't worry about unpleasant consequences because of it. ....

-4 -3 -2 -1 0 $+1$ $+2$ $+3$ $+4$

4. because the woman would have died anyway and it didn't take much effort for the doctor to give her an overdose of painkiller. ....

5. because the doctor didn't really break a law, since the woman couldn't have been saved and he only wanted to shorten her suffering. ....

6. because most of the fellow doctors would presumably have acted in the same way that he did..

How acceptable do you find the following arguments against the doctor's behavior? Suppose someone said the doctor acted wrongly...

I find the argument...

completely   completely
acceptable   unacceptable
-4 -3 -2 -1 0 $+1$ $+2$ $+3$ $+4$

7. because he acted contrary to his colleagues' convictions. If they are against death on demand (euthanasia), the doctor shouldn't do it ....

8. because one should have complete faith in a doctor's devotion to preserving life even if someone with great pain would rather die. ....

9. because the protection of life is everyone's highest moral obligation. Since we have no clear moral criteria for distinguishing between euthanasia and murder, no one should take the life of another into his own hands......

-4 -3 -2 -1 0 $+1$ $+2$ $+3$ $+4$

10. because the doctor could get himself into a lot of trouble. Others have already been severely punished for doing the same thing. ....

11. because he could have had it considerably easier if he had waited and not interfered with the woman's dying. ....

12. because the doctor broke the law. If one does not think that euthanasia is legal, then one should not comply with such requests. ....

MUT 77 © Georg Lind

PART TWO

Moral Judgment and Its Social Context

Social Inequality and Moral Development

Hans Bertram

A certain theoretical model is generally referred to in order to explain the barriers to vertical mobility between professional groups. Since it explains, from the viewpoint of socialization theory, how social inequality is reproduced from the parents' generation to that of the children, it is called the Reproduction Model. It relates the unequal distribution of social privileges such as education, income, prestige, and power to the professional position of the father, which usually determines the social position of the family and which influences both parents' views on education. Thus influenced by parental values, the socialization milieu of the family disposes the children to acquire attitudes and values which either help or hinder their success at school and their careers (see Aldous, Osmond, & Hicks, 1979, p. 239).

REPRODUCTION OF SOCIAL INEQUALITY THROUGH SOCIALIZATION

Many sociological mobility analyses have demonstrated the existence of probability barriers and, in this respect, can be cited in support of the Reproduction Model. However, the empirical results are less convincing in the case of socialization studies which have examined the relationship between parental values and class membership or the relationship among children's attitudes, parental orientations, and the system of social inequality (Bargel, 1973; Erlanger, 1974; Bertram, 1976; 1981; Zängle, 1978; Steinkamp, 1980).

Still, these criticisms need not be interpreted as a falsification of the Reproduction Model. Accordingly, in this chapter I shall use them as the basis for a critical discussion of four distinctive contributions to the development of the Reproduction Model.

Melvin Kohn (1969; 1973; 1977; 1981) has shown that the father's professional orientation is determined not only by professional position, income, and education but by his working conditions, such as the work's complexity level, the extent of control, and the extent of routinization, which are just as important for professional values and values in general. In contrast to most socialization studies, which have examined only class membership, or rather the unequal distribution of privileges, the Reproduction Model also takes into account the concrete working situation of the parents.

Lawrence Kohlberg (1969) has demonstrated that, in spite of the large number of naturalistic socialization studies that have been carried out, only small correlations between parents' and children's outlooks can be obtained. Kohlberg suspects that this low correlation is caused, on the one hand, by the failure of these studies to represent empirically and appropriately the considerable theoretical differences in the various models of family socialization and, on the other hand, by the prevalence of ad hoc theories. In the analysis of the Reproduction Model, the selection of the parent and child variables must, therefore, be founded on their relation to the "professional world" and must be plausible, so that the selected behavioral indicators are really those which influence the behavior of the adults concerned.

Urie Bronfenbrenner (1973) has indicated that family socialization can take place only in the framework of family interaction, i.e., in the context of the child's living environment. Until now, research in socialization has been largely confined to analysis of the mother-child relationship. However, in the framework of the Reproduction Model, the father plays a decisive role as the mediator of socio-cultural values. Consequently, the social inequality theory described above requires an analysis of the family triad of father-mother-child. The object of this analysis must not be limited to the investigation of individual outlooks but must include the family's relationship structure.

Finally, in my own work (Bertram, 1981) I have indicated that the Reproduction Model assumes that the socio-cultural values which arise from differing socio-structural living and working conditions are transmitted to the individual in the framework of family interactions. Empirical research concerning this hierarchical relationship among socio-structural working conditions, interaction-relationships, and individual action or personality is most adequately carried out within the framework of a multiple-level model, in which the different levels of socio-structural living and working conditions, family role-relationships, and individual action are integrated. For this research the structure of levels is the crucial part of the Reproduction Model. Moreover, one must not attempt to examine the indicators and variables of each level individually, but must instead reconstruct the relationship pattern of the variables on each level. Above all, the whole model, not only its parts, must be examined since a comprehensive examination of the model is needed for estimating its validity. In other words: "The object of research on the transmission of values in the family has generally not been to demonstrate a similarity that was assumed to exist" (Kohn, 1982, p. 1).

THE EMPIRICAL MODEL AND THE VARIABLES

With these multi-level features of the Reproduction Model in mind, we now turn to the two topics of social inequality and individual moral development. In what follows I shall differentiate among the individual level, the family interaction level, and the socio-structural level.

The Individual Level

The analysis of children's personalities measures cognitive variables, such as abstraction capabilities (Vygotski's concept formation test), role-taking (Flavell), intelligence (Raven), and moral orientations, with the aid of a questionnaire (Kemmler) about moral judgment. This questionnaire for 8- to 11-year-old children is comprised of twelve dilemma-stories with four alternative answers, each of which represents a specific level of moral judgment according to Jean Piaget's theory. In addition, a social attitude test (Joerger) has been applied to measure social maturity, also on the basis of Piaget's concept.

The relevant cognitive variables here are concept formation, intelligence, and role-taking, all of which are involved in work tasks whose complexity is an essential characteristic of working conditions and of professional position. The theoretical relevance of these variables and the consistency of these personality characteristics should be obvious (Jencks, 1979; Eysenck, 1980), but the selection of moral judgment preferences may at first be surprising. There seem to be several reasons for this selection. Since not only the political orders but also the economic and professional systems of society are subject to profound changes, concrete political views or concrete professional orientations can hardly be the basis for the thesis of the Reproduction Model.

The scope of the moral judgment concept is not concerned with whether someone prefers an authoritarian or a democratic social order; rather, it is concerned with why the individual attends to different structures of social order. Therefore, in considering social and economic changes, we can retain the Reproduction Model of social inequality, as long as it allows us to analyze the socio-cultural reproduction of heeding rules from the parents' generation to the children's. With Piaget's and Kohlberg's models of moral judgment levels, there is also the question of an integrative model, in which previously unrelated theoretical principals of respect for rules are brought together in a hierarchical order.

Piaget's and Kohlberg's attempts to logically systematize the several clearly distinguishable types of respect for rules is especially significant if one asks which specific types of respect for rules are typical of which socio-cultural and professional contexts. That is, we máy hypothesize that professions with complex working conditions, broad scope for decision-making, and few routine tasks contribute to individual self-direction and to moral autonomy as understood by Piaget (cf. Kohn, 1969, pp. 35-36). Should this hypothesis be empirically confirmed, then one might (using the cognitive-developmental model of moral judgment) relate the reproduction of social inequality to changes in society and its structure.

The Level of Interaction Relationships

Although there have been few previous attempts to analyze family triads from a socialization theory perspective, remedying this lack was not the central concern of the study, so we assessed the parents' personalities by using Cattell's 16 PF test. In doing so, we followed Cattell's assumption that individual personality factors demonstrate action-forming or situation-deciding interaction strategies. In addition, the concrete parental values were measured by Kohn's scales of self-direction versus conformity. Other variables were family size, living-space size, and other similar characteristics of family structure. With these variables, forty-five in all, we attempted to construct empirical, clearly-differentiated levels and theoretically profound relationship patterns.

The Levels of Social Structure

Owing to Kohn's broadly empirical orientation, the empirical analysis of socio-structural influence carried out within the framework of the Reproduction Model is relatively straightforward. Under the influence of Blauner's (1966) alienation theory, Kohn distinguishes among three essential aspects of working conditions: the extent of authority given to make independent decisions (control of other people's work); the amount of routine work entailed (frequency and repetition of completed work); the complexity of the work (dealing with data, things, or people). These are aspects which determine the extent of autonomy. Kohn himself has shown that aspects of work are themselves influenced by the structure of the working organization (bureaucratic vs. unbureaucratic).

Kohn merely examines whether the father's values, which correlate with his professional position as an indicator of a society's class structure, can be related to his concrete working conditions. However, the Reproduction Model requires a precise empirical analysis of the relationship between class (hierarchy of professional positions), working organization, and working conditions. The hitherto unsatisfactory correlations between class membership and children's or young people's values, which led until now to severe criticism of the Reproduction Model, can be caused by the fact that working conditions vary only partially with class membership, and the working organization does not vary with it at all. In such a case one could expect the validity of the Reproduction Model to be present only where class membership, working-organization, and working conditions converge in accordance with the Reproduction Model.

The Integrated Model

Figure 1 illustrates the integrated model with each of its three levels, along with the variables which represent them. This causal model of social reproduction is a further differentiation of the general Reproduction Model of social inequality through socialization. On the socio-structural level, it corresponds to Kohn's model and assumes that the socio-structural variables, transmitted by parental values and personality structures, influence the child's socio-moral development only indirectly.

In order to test the postulated hierarchical model structure, we must first examine the influence of the socio-structural variables on moral judgment. To ascertain the combined characteristics of the socio-structural variables which most influence the child's tendency toward an individual judgment style, the joint impact of parental values, attitudes, and personality traits will be examined. If the resulting profile of parental values and attitudes corresponds to Kohn's results and also to the conditions which Kohlberg, Hoffman, and Piaget have formulated in relation to parents' behavior, one should also be able to establish the corresponding behavioral pattern

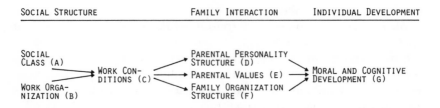

Testing instruments: (1) Income, professional position, professional training, and education. (2) Bureaucratic vs. non-bureaucratic organization. (3) Extent of control, work complexity, routinization, and intrinsic work orientation. (4) 16 PF Test (Cattell) of both father and mother. (5) Parental values with Kohn's scales, each from father and mother, each for oneself and for the child. (6) Family size, mother's employment, constellation of siblings. (7) "Piaget-histories," Raven's Progressive Matrices, Vygotski's Concept Formation Experiment, Flavell's Role-Taking Task.

Figure 1. Empirical Multiple-Level Model of Reproduction

of the parents by taking into account the socio-structural conditions in which children have developed one or the other type of judgment. However, this evidence does not confirm the hierarchical model. In order to prove the indirect influence of the socio-structural variables on moral judgment, which can first be regarded as confirmation of the multiple-level model, the influence of the family environment on moral judgment must be judged independently of socio-structural variables. Should covariances appear here, it will be necessary to check whether the covariances between the social structural variables and the moral judgment can be eliminated through partialization of the covariances between the family environment and the moral judgment. If any such covariances can be eliminated this way, the structure of the model is confirmed, or it is demonstrated that the socio-structural conditions which lead to a certain moral judgment type also promote, in both children and parents, the behavior necessary for this judgment type. Thus we shall have proven that these parental behavioral patterns intervene between the socio-structural conditions and the moral judgment.

The following findings are based on an investigation of 176 boys nine to ten years old and their parents, conducted in 1974. The data have been reanalyzed, taking into consideration certain suggestions made by Köckeis-Stangl (1980). Except for minor changes, the findings were not different from those of our former analysis (see Bertram, 1978).

FINDINGS

The Socio-Structural Conditions of Moral Judgment

There is no doubt that the types of moral judgment investigated here vary enormously from a socio-structural viewpoint. In Table 1 the judgment types "autonomous," "conventional," and "conformist" are represented according to their socio-structural distribution; accordingly, I have restricted myself to naming only the socio-structural conditions which most positively influence each type of judgment. Boys are especially likely to judge autonomously when their parents belong to the upper middle class and possess high autonomy at their place of work. Boys tend to judge conventionally when their fathers belong to the lower middle class and possess high autonomy at work within a medium-sized or large bureaucratic organization. Finally, boys usually judge in a conformist way when their fathers work in less bureaucratic organizations or in small firms, and belong to the lower classes. In such cases, autonomy at the place of work does not play a significant role, whereas in the lower and upper middle class the conformist type of judgment is dominant in small firms or in less bureaucratic organizations if the father has little autonomy at his workplace.

Table 1

Socio-Structural Constellations and Types of Moral Judgment

Autonomy at Workplace	Lower Class			Lower Middle Class			Upper Middle Class		
				Degree of Bureaucratization					
	low	medium	high	low	medium	high	low	medium	high
little	CF	–	–	CF	–	–	CF	–	–
medium	CF	–	–	–	–	–	–	–	–
much	CF	–	–	–	CV	CV	AU	AU	AU

Note: CF = Conformist, CV = Conventional, AU = Autonomous.

The socio-structural distribution of the three judgment types as depicted in Table 1 shows clearly that moral judgment does not vary according to class; instead, each judgment type can be assigned to specific constellations of class, workplace conditions, and workplace structure. Only when fathers in the upper middle class experience autonomy at work do their sons show corresponding judgment pref-erence, while fathers of the same class who work in small firms but have little autonomy, influence socialization at home in such a way that the boys are more likely to judge in conformist manner. Moreover, the significance of socio-structural factors for moral judg-ment also varies. Under reciprocal partialization the class member-ship, followed by autonomy in the workplace (*beta* = .18), most influ-ences the type of autonomous-flexible judgment (*beta* = .27). In comparison, the conformist judgment type is influenced by the father's membership in a bureaucratic or unbureaucratic organiza-tion (*beta* = .23) and by autonomy in the workplace (*beta* = .23). In regard to the conventional judgment type, all three socio-structural variables are equally meaningful.

The socio-structural variation of moral judgment, evoked through workplace conditions and the structure of the working organization, make it clear in the first place that the prevalent, class-specific inter-pretation of the Reproduction Model for social inequality is inappro-priate for explaining the influence of socio-structural variables on moral development. This is because the variation in judgment types is caused to at least the same extent by other socio-structurally meaningful variables. However, the consideration of these variables, which differentiate the individual class groups, does not lead to a leveling of attitudes and behavioral patterns, as is repeatedly asserted in class sociology. Rather, it leads to a constellation-specific differen-tiation, which presumably leads to a more appropriate description of the relationship between social structure and moral development than a global class model could provide.

The socio-structural variation of moral autonomy largely corre-sponds to Kohn's (1969) hypothesis that professional self-direction, which leads fathers to place great emphasis on personal indepen-dence and self-sufficiency, also stimulates children to develop similar values, whereas professional dependence (little autonomy) leads to conformist attitudes and values, which also promote similar attitudes in the children. Kohn (1981) assumes, of course, that the profes-sional working conditions merely intervene between class and indi-vidual values, whereas it has been demonstrated here that all socio-structural variables together form typical constellations and that the significance of individual variables varies among the judgment types. Thus the importance of the small bureaucratic working structure or of the small firm may be surprisingly important to the judgment preference, in view of the more common beliefs that conformist preference is found almost exclusively in lower classes or that conformism is generally produced by bureaucratic structures. For example, Miller and Swanson (1958) believed that they had documented a systematic variation between children's conformist judgment preferences and bureaucratic structures. On the other hand, Kohn (1973) argued that intellectual flexibility and orientation towards professional self-direction can be found particularly in bureaucratic organizations. This contradiction disappears if one compares Miller's and Swanson's ideas about conformity with those of Kohn and the others mentioned above. While conformity is traditionally understood to be less specific than obedience in regard to behavioral expectations, Kohn and I also assume, following Piaget, that obedience in relation to behavioral expectations results either from internalized rules or from subordination to authority out of fear of punishment. Obedience on the basis of internalized rules, described here as conventional morality, is certainly a characteristic typical of bureaucratic orientations, as displayed here in the lower middle classes; at the same time, subordination to personal authority is without doubt a typical characteristic of traditional worker relationships as displayed in small firms. Thus, the orientation to the principle of following rules and the differentiations in a conformist, conventional, and autonomous judgment allow a meaningful differentiation between the dominant types of "rule-following" in individual social institutions. The traditional approaches, which consider only the extent of compliance, or only one type of compliance, do not admit such a differentiation between traditional institutional structures and newly developing bureaucratic structures. Even if the three levels and six stages of Kohlberg's model should one day be replaced by an even better systematization of the rule-following principles, this model is already set up for tracing moral judgment preferences in different institutional contexts and for uncovering in these contexts those role patterns which stimulate the respective preferences or types of moral judgment.

Family Conditions of Moral Judgment

From a theoretical role-perspective one can agree with Kohlberg that the interaction structure of a child's total social environment ultimately influences his moral development, and that therefore the family has no special theoretical role in the stimulation of moral development. However, in western industrial societies the reality of the child's living world is very much shaped by the family, a fact the Reproduction Model emphasizes by underlining the family socializa-

tion influences. It is not the peer group which fundamentally determines the extent and opportunity of role-taking, but the parents who
do so through the openness or rigidity of family interactions.
Similarly, it is not the school which gives children their principle
opportunities to try out their behavior and to test the interpretation
of other people's behavior on the basis of mutual trust–in other
words, to practice role-playing. On the contrary, this happens primarily in the family, and not in the bureaucratic context of schools. In
addition, the duration and intensity of family togetherness far exceeds
the togetherness which children experience in other social institutions
(cf. Döbert & Nunner-Winkler, 1985).

The importance of family socialization conditions is also made
clear by the empirical data. The parental attitudes toward upbringing, the parental personality structures, and the aspects of family
organization (for a definition of the variables see Figure 1) can
jointly explain 48% of the variance in the autonomous moral judgment type with partialization of the class variables. In the case of
children who judge conventionally, it is 28%, and in the case of
those who judge in a conformist fashion, it is 33%. As Köckeis-Stangl
(1980) asserts, these unusually high covariances are in no way
dependent on the procedure, since they can be reproduced and
analyzed by contrast groups as well as by regression (Bertram, 1978,
p. 249). In fact, they are much more likely to be causally related to
two other factors: (1) In contrast to former socialization research,
these studies show that parental attitudes have little meaning,
whereas parental personality structures can explain the largest part
of the covariance (between 25% and 34%). (2) Moreover, the father's
personality plays a vast role, even if he works outside the home all
day. Norma Haan (1977, p. 194) reports similarly high covariances
in this regard.

Some findings about the three judgment types should be stressed
here, beginning with the findings about the parents of children with
relatively high *moral autonomy.* Those fathers who have considerable
autonomy at the workplace believe it important for their sons to be
interested in their environment, and to show consciousness of
responsibility but not social conformism. Moreover, the mothers
reject obedience and subordination. These attitudes toward child-
raising indicate that both parents try to give their children possibilities for development which are necessary for them to achieve independence. This attitude pattern is enhanced by their personality
structures, in that the parents, especially the father, are not preoc-
cupied with upholding norms and conventions. Both parents are in a

position to respond to their children's wishes and needs and to recognize their problems, since they are relatively sensitive socially. Also, on account of their intelligence, both provide the prerequisites for explaining the meaning of norms and rules in a differentiated way. The family climate comprises the three decisive characteristics of inductive control functions, namely "the predominance of warm affectionate sympathy and support for the child, a cognitive structuring of the context, and the opening of scope to make independent decisions" (Ceasar, 1972, pp. 62-63).

The constellation of parental personality factors within the socio-structural conditions, which tend to be associated with *conventional* boys, cannot be interpreted as clearly as in the case of youngsters with autonomous judgment. In respect to attitudes toward child-raising, these parents formulate prominent tendencies (Bertram, 1978). The child's interest in his environment is important for them, while obedience and subordination take less priority. Furthermore, the father considers successful action important, while the mother thinks it important that the child be well respected. In contrast to the child-raising values that emphasize independence, the parents' personality profiles show a rather dominant father and mother who in many respects seem overprotective. The father is dominant, i.e., independent, expressive, seizing the social initiative, nonconservative, and nonconventional. The mother shows a strong superego, is emotionally stable, warm-hearted, and, like the father, nonconventional, i.e., a little anxious but not nervous. At the same time, however, the mother is socially accomplished, a personality trait that she also formulates as an educational goal. This personality structure of the parents can be interpreted along with the educational values as constituting an open-minded, "modern," success-oriented family; these parents are able to make themselves heard and want to pass their experience on to their children. Although neither the parents nor their sons show any special intellectual capabilities, the sons of this sort of family have the best grades at school (cf. Bertram, 1976), a fact which implies that, somewhat paradoxically, this nonconformist family constellation promotes conformity to school rules and norms.

The family conditions which favor the *conformist* judging in children correspond to those found by Kohn. In such families, conformity, willingness, and obedience are important child-raising styles, whereas interest in the environment is less important. Parents display little intellectual flexibility. The mother is emotionally warm-hearted but evidences a weak superego; in addition she is somewhat

anxious. The father tends towards careful behavior and demonstrates social sensitivity. In such a home background, it is unlikely
that the children are taught an orientation to rules, since the parents
scarcely show rule-consciousness, nor possess intellectual strategies
for explaining rules. The lack of orientation to rules, in combination
with the emotionally warm-hearted context, could be interpreted as
an indication that conformism may be a result of positive, understanding parental sanctions, while in sociological literature (for
instance, Devereux, 1977) conformist behavior is generally traced to
parents' negative sanctions.

Examination of the Whole Model

Because parental attitudes and personality traits generally correspond
to the optimal conditions for moral development (Hoffman, 1970;
Bertram, 1978; 1981), it is reasonable to expect that the variance
between the social structure variables and moral judgment will be
considerably reduced by the partialization of family socialization
variables. This expectation, which seems fulfilled in the case of
autonomous judgment types, supports the multi-level Reproduction
Model of social inequality through socialization. However, the same
expectation does not hold for the conventional and the conformist
judgment types, because the personality profiles do not correspond
in every respect to the optimal family conditions. Table 2 confirms
this result, since the covariance between the socio-structural variables
and moral autonomy are reduced from 26% to 1%, in contrast to the
variance part of family variables which remains, with over 48%, the
most important variable group. Surprisingly, the variance between
the cognitive variables and the moral judgment is reduced to only
2%, so that the question arises of whether the frequently demonstrated covariance between cognitive and moral judgment variables is
caused by a third variable. Of course, reductions are evident in both
the other judgment types, although the remaining covariances of
about 8% show that in both cases the socio-structural variation of
moral judgment types is not related only to family socialization
conditions as described here, but also to other variables.

If one tries to draw some general conclusions from the previous
analysis, one can say that Kohn's assumptions regarding concrete
working conditions, as well as Bronfenbrenner's and Kohlberg's
assumptions regarding the analysis of complete interaction structures,
are confirmed by the results. Whereas the Reproduction Model of
social inequality through socialization is traditionally reduced to class

Table 2

The Multi-Level Model[a]

	Social Structure with / without Partialization[c]		Family[b]	Cognitive Structure	Explained Total Variance
Autonomous	26	1	48	2	51
Conventional	11	8	28	–	36
Conformistic	13	8	33	2	43

[a] The figures correspond to the (partialized) beta square coefficients of the regression analysis with the variable constructs, which represent the contextual effects of each level, and are to be interpreted in terms of percentage of the explained variance. The last column contains the multiple determination coefficient R^2_{REG}.

[b] This column contains the sum of the value and personality constellations and the family organizational structure (see Figure 1 above).

[c] Results of the three analyses with and without partialization of the family indicators.

dimensions (of education, prestige, and income), the additional considerations of workplace conditions and of the working organization demonstrate that the class dimensions promote the occurrence of certain types of moral judgment only in very specific constellations or combinations of workplace conditions and working organization factors. A class-specific model of the social reproduction of socialization only partially represents social reality, in comparison to a model of socio-structural constellations which can be justified in sociological differentiation theory (Lepsius, 1979). It appears more suitable to illuminate the socio-structural aspects of the Reproduction Model. All three things–the consideration of parental personality in addition to the most frequently used measurements of attitudes, the analysis of paternal personality, and the attempt to comprehend the familial interaction patterns in an appropriately methodical way– reveal that, as Norma Haan's findings suggest, the generally low covariances between aspects of familial socialization and children's personalities can be related to an inadequate operationalization of familial interaction. As Bronfenbrenner has suspected, only a comprehensive analysis of child-raising is able to show that the family indeed has a great influence on a child's development.

On the basis of the data at hand, we must reject the thesis that the father plays no great role in the socialization process of the contemporary family because of his frequent absence, as well as the thesis that the family has no special meaning in early childhood socialization. As assumed in the Reproduction Model, the family plays a prominent role in spite of today's more strongly bureaucratically oriented upbringing processes. This is because the family determines the children's social conditions, and because it is still the only institution in which children can develop self-respect on the basis of trust, free from social achievement pressures.

Our research focuses in a relatively empirical way on the analysis of the variation of types of moral judgment within a society due to certain societal conditions. The question follows of what the implications might be for the empirically founded relationship of theory construction, and which problems remain open for further empirical research. One may, for example, employ Durkheim's differentiation model, in the version developed by Pierre Bourdieu, to identify certain institutional constellations in which specific forms of moral judgment are more adequate than others. For the same purpose, we may use Wolfgang Schluchter's (1979) differentiating interpretation of Max Weber's model of the development of "occidental rationalism." With such concepts we may hope to learn more about the conditions for different types of moral judgment on both the societal and the institutional levels than traditional concepts have taught us.

Such theoretical concepts might also help to improve the developmental focus in the models of Piaget and Kohlberg. Considering the correspondence of social and institutional forms and stages of moral development, it must be possible to determine the relationship between the development of some types of institutional differentiation and the individual genesis of moral judgment. Those theoretical and empirical efforts may provide a better basis for the interpretation of the stability or change of social values than that provided by the Reproduction Model of social inequality through socialization.

I think that the constant realization of values and norms in spite of evident changes in the values and institutions of society can be adequately understood only if institutional conditions are analyzed with as much differentiation as are the individual's socio-moral orientations. One could speculate that stability in the realization of norms and values in changing political systems can be explained by the fact that conventional forms of consciousness provide an adequate frame for interpreting new values and attitudes which develop under changing political conditions. Most individuals act in a socially conforming way even under structurally changed conditions. In order to comprehend this, we must not merely postulate social change in general; rather, we need to reconstruct in detail the societal and institutional variations from a differentiation-theoretical perspective and put them together with the respective forms of moral consciousness. We may find that, in spite of the change in our society, the contexts of acting, i.e., the relevant institutional conditions, have remained largely stable.

To elaborate and substantiate these theoretical considerations, we plan to conduct a longitudinal study of the development of socio-moral orientations in children and juveniles. The focus of the analysis will be the development of rationality, especially Weberian-type rationality, and the development of patterns of socio-moral orientations. We will also use several indicators to describe the familial milieu. We want to investigate two age groups, children of 8-10 years and adolescents of 14-16 years, and follow them up for six years. This selection of age groups is not due only to developmental psychological considerations, but also to the fact that in the Federal Republic of Germany the first decision about an occupational career is made by selecting a certain type of school at the age of 10; the second decision follows at the age of 14. The subjects will also be selected with respect to the institutional contexts in which their parents work.

This research will enable us to demonstrate the relationship which has been postulated here between social differentiation and forms of socio-moral judgment, or valid forms of means-end action. Through the longitudinal design, we will be able to investigate the influence of the institutional contexts on the structures of rationality and socio-moral orientations of fathers, mothers, and children, as well as the consequences for the occupational decisions of the children and juveniles, since the moment of investigation and the moment of those decisions will coincide. In reconstructing the causal chain between social structure and individual personality, we hope finally to gain empirical support for our thesis that the transmission of bureaucratic institutional contexts is of greater importance to the further development of a society than are developments in the areas of politics, culture, and economics which we see at the surface.

Value Change and Morality

Rainer Döbert and Gertrud Nunner-Winkler

Social scientists are currently engaged in a lively debate about value change in modern industrial societies. Until now this discussion, which was kindled by Ronald Inglehart's *Silent Revolution* (1977), has been largely restricted to changes wrought in the content of value orientations due to socio-economic changes. That is, *post-materialist values* include knowledge and ideas as well as free speech and political participation, all of which are seen to supersede relatively materialist values such as those underlying appeals for "strong defense forces," "battle against crime," and "stable economy, economic growth," once the demands of safety and subsistence needs are satisfied. However, without denying the phenomena described by Inglehart,[1] we will show here that value change cannot be reduced to a mere substitution of one value content for another. Since the rationalization process, originally analyzed by Max Weber, concerns mainly the mode of validity of orientation systems, changes in this dimension are more appropriately described as the dissolution of traditions than as changes in values. We wish to discuss this process of the dissolution of traditions using two problematic examples: abortion and compulsory military service. In both cases a public discussion has taken place, and so the change has taken place more conspicuously than in Inglehart's description of changing value priorities. Even so, this process also has a less visible aspect: the public discussion must be received and assimilated by the population, and this reception and assimilation can proceed in different ways. The aim here is to investigate the reasons for differences in the reception. In doing so we refer to data from representative surveys on both topics, as well as to the results of our research on "identity-formation" in adolescence, in which attitudes toward abortion and toward conscientious objection were among the topics explored.

Since the examples chosen deal with moral questions (and not with values based more or less on ego-interests like those analyzed by Inglehart), it seems useful to examine those variables that generally influence the solution of moral dilemmas, so that the details of the reception process may be illuminated. Those variables are: personal interests, which can collide with moral decisions; the internalization of normative traditions, which provide for specific types of decisions; and finally, the structure of moral consciousness, which promotes a preference for certain types of argumentation.

VALUE CHANGE AS A SOCIETAL PROCESS

A widely different range of changes in the normative system can be implied by the title "value change." A norm traditionally valid for a particular area of life can be replaced altogether by new norms; it can assume a lower position in a new hierarchy of values; or it can lose its validity completely, so that an area of behavior which previously was normatively regulated falls prey to instrumentalization. All of these changes concern the *substantive validity* of norms. Furthermore, norms can be held by groups or subgroups of differing sizes or by the society as a whole; the variations in this dimension concern the *social validity* of norms. In the phenomenon considered by Inglehart, aspects of substantive and social validity are merged, in that an increasingly large part of the population of modern industrial societies is turning to post-materialist contents such as those mentioned above.

However, the *validity mode* of norms is at least as important as these other two dimensions. Undoubtedly, the justifiability and legitimacy of given traditions can be questioned. Thus, as Max Weber pointed out, traditional action is transformed into rational action based either on conceptions of absolute value *(wertrational)* or on the adequacy of means to ends *(zweckrational)*, that is, it is transformed into either the dissolution or the instrumentalization of tradition. Furthermore, norms can be propped up by sanctions of differing effectiveness (differentiation of law, morality, and convention). For the individual, then, it is always a question of how much he wants to conform to the ruling system of norms, and from which *motives*–out of his own interest, out of fear of sanctions, or on account of absolute values. Moreover every social ruling is embedded in a complex social network, and therefore, always has latent functions and unknown secondary consequences. Further information about actual costs and the secondary consequences of the observance of norms can effect each of the above-mentioned dimensions of value change. Conversely, the search for further information can itself be a consequence of value change: the dissolution of tradition, which leads to a rational coordination of actions, always increases the need for information. Thus, the expansion of the knowledge system and of the media, that is, of the main producers and distributors of information, is simultaneously cause and effect of value change.[2] These become more influential, of course, whenever a public discussion about a controversial topic arises in which all relevant aspects are brought up by different parties. When such a complex context of argumentation is publicly displayed, the question of selective reception processes becomes more relevant.

Taking as an example the controversy about abortion (i.e., about Art. 218 in the German legal code, which regulates abortion), we will briefly demonstrate what types of arguments have been used and what the abstract dimension of value change means as far as concrete issues are concerned. We will begin with changes in the *substantive validity of norms,* that is, the question of the complete or partial replacement of traditionally valid norms through new orientations.

In traditional church teachings, "abortion" falls exclusively under the value "preservation and protection of unborn life." Those on the other side of the issue set up the norm of "individual freedom to decide responsibly and ethically," which has been sharpened by certain parts of the women's emancipation movement to mean "the right to self-determination." Today the whole spectrum of possible points of view is represented by the positions of different institutions and associations. The Roman Catholic Church most uncompromisingly supports the protection of unborn life. Since according to its view "human life . . . [begins] with the fusion of the germ-cells, that is, at the moment of conception," it follows that "from this day on life is inviolable. The mother has no right to consider the unborn life her property, for the child in the womb is not part of the mother's body but is on the contrary its own independent life" (Heck, as cited in BMJFG, 1981b, Vol. 2, p. 68). An abortion can be justified only (and this is the single concession which the Catholic Church has made in the course of the controversy) if the mother's life is physically threatened by the bearing of the child. Examining unreasonable demands for the future life of the child (e.g., "an unloved child will only lead a life of misery") is not considered legitimate: the child's value consists "in that dignity which comes to him on account of his autonomy and uniqueness. It is this dignity which forbids any vicarious decisions about the reasonableness of this life" (Schäffler, as cited in BMJFG, 1981b, Vol. 2, p. 68).

Invoking competing values (a humane and dignified life for the mother and child), the Protestant Church tries to allow for exceptions to the norm of the protection of unborn life: "The aim of the preservation of future life must also incorporate the issue of the maintenance of bodily and psychic developmental chances for mother and child. The protection of life in the widest sense gives rise to the recognition that in particular cases the refusal to permit an abortion can also be a wrong. There is no 'clean hands' strategy for this difficult ethical problem . . . . Even refusing to love is a dimension of killing. After all, the fifth Commandment does not refer only to the preservation of life, but also to the creation of humane conditions for life." In view of this dilemma, the Protestant Church opts in favor "of helping the pregnant woman to make a responsible decision for her situation according to her own conscience, so that she does not overtax her vital strength, and so that she does not have to fear later psychic harm, either for herself or for her child" (BMJFG, 1981b, Vol. 1, p. 155). Thus one can justify an exception to the prohibition against killing not only if the physical survival of the mother is endangered, but also if one expects that future living conditions would psychically overburden the mother or the child. Whereas in the Catholic view the legitimacy of an exception can be established "objectively" (through the competent expert judgment of a doctor), in the Protestant view the final assessment of potential overstrain is allocated to the moral judgment capacity of the woman concerned. To be. sure, for both churches abortion falls under the prohibition against killing. Yet the more encompassing Protestant conception of "life" as psychological viability as well as physical survival requires a subjective decision, one which the Protestant Church leaves to the woman.

It does not, however, regard the decision as an arbitrary choice of whether or not to bear a child. Rather, the decision which is envisioned in this view is the "morally responsible" decision as to whether circumstances justify an exception to the prohibition against killing.

In contrast to this view, the secular agencies which offer abortion counseling deal with the conflict almost exclusively in relation to the norm of self-determination. Two examples may be cited here. First of all, the *Bremer Pro Familia* interprets the "social indication of severe hardship" so extensively that the woman is ultimately free to decide according to her own needs. "Everything which is directed against and endangers the woman's needs and life perspectives must be seen as a situation of severe hardship" (BMJFG, 1981b, Vol. 1. p. 180). Secondly, the *Arbeiterwohlfahrt* (Workers Welfare Institution) insists that women in hardship should be granted an abortion with impunity, for "only women are expected to ignore their needs and interests in favor of those of the child. Women with unwanted pregnancies are entitled to consider an abortion when they cannot reconcile their life situation and their professional and nonprofessional expectations with the birth and responsible upbringing of a child" (p. 139). Admittedly, the prohibition against killing is acknowledged in this official viewpoint: the abortion is formally termed an "exception." However, an analysis of the reasons which permit a justification of the "exception" shows that the value of self-determination has attained priority. The militant women's movement's slogan "My body belongs to me" contains no reference to the value of unborn life. While these women do support the prohibition against killing, they deny that it is applicable to abortion, on the grounds that the fetus is not a human life.

The above-quoted opinions of various associations and institutions exemplify the substantive validity of the competing norms at stake in abortion, namely the preservation of unborn life and the right to self-determination. We now come to the question of the *social validity* of these norms. An analysis of the attitudes toward abortion over the last 20 years in West Germany shows the following trends. The prohibition against killing is no longer acknowledged in its original strictness: more and more exceptions are being permitted, and the number of people rejecting abortion is continually decreasing. At the same time, the norm of unlimited self-responsibility is becoming predominant, so that the prohibition against killing is less often seen as relevant to abortion.

In 1953 44% of the population was anti-abortion, even in the case of rape (von Friedeburg, as cited in Hochheimer, 1963, p. 102). This figure fell in 1963 to 35%, in response to the criminal law bill of that year (*Der Spiegel*, 1963, No. 37, p. 16). In March, 1971, the number of opponents rose again to 39%, only to drop to 29% as early as September 1971 in response to a renewed debate on reform and to heavy protests by women's groups (*Der Stern*, 1971, No. 24, p. 260). This downward trend continued: 1973 only 15% were strictly against abortion (see IfD, 1973), a figure which appears to be stable at least until 1977, when it dropped to 14% (BMJFG, 1981a, p. 327). The results of our admittedly non-representative study in 1976 of 112 male and female adolescents between 14-22 years of age and of different SES backgrounds are compatible with these data: 8% were for an absolute no to abortion; 15% for a restrictive no (allowing for exceptions in cases of danger to the mother's life or rape); 35% for a broad exemption permit (grave hardship); 42% were for declaring abortion legal (either during the first weeks of pregnancy or at any time during pregnancy).

This change in attitude has obviously come about in conjunction with the public discussion which took place in the course of attempts at reforming Art. 218. Nor was this only a question of inherent values, rights and duties. After all, the whole discussion was sparked by information about the costs and consequences which different statutory rulings would entail for the whole of society (demographic considerations, i.e., problems of financing pensions or of overpopulation), as well as for certain subgroups of society (the higher classes being in a privileged position concerning contraception and the chances of evading the law), and for the individuals concerned, including the woman (her psychological burdens, curtailments of career prospects and life expectancy) and the child (failures in socialization like those resulting in juvenile delinquency).

Detailed information about concrete costs and consequential burdens does indeed seem to influence people's attitudes. A survey by Zundel et al. demonstrated that "subjects disregard the abstract norm and judge in a more differentiated and tolerant way when confronted with concrete situations" (BMJFG, 1981b, Vol. 3, p. 219). For example, when first questioned abstractly about their attitudes toward abortion, 28% of the subjects either did not want to permit abortion at all or would permit it only when the "mother's life and health is endangered." Two thirds of them became more tolerant, however, when they were given more concrete descriptions of situations: they would permit an abortion "if there was a danger that the child would be born mentally or physically defective, or if the pregnancy resulted from a physical assault" (p. 216). More detailed descriptions of situations lead to even greater liberality. For example, 83% spoke out against an abortion "if the parents have to give up certain things on account of a further child." This figure fell to 57% when a concrete case description was presented in which an added child forced a family to abandon a home already under construction, which was to have given the existing children more developmental possibilities. When such situational details are provided, costs or burdens which were at first not taken into account become visible, and the subjects appear more ready to make exceptions. In unstructured interviews it is the interviewer who by his questions often calls attention to aspects of the problem not originally considered by the subject. This may lead to a complete and sometimes abrupt change of mind, as the following conversation with one of our interviewees (Subject #16) shows:

S: Of course one should allow women to have abortions–that is a woman's affair. Why make a lot of rules?
I: Why do you think other people are against it?
S: They think that the children are simply killed off–and that isn't right either. Every living being has the right to life.

The extensive public debates must have worked along a similar pattern. Large sections of the population must have come to recognize that their attitudes have not done justice to the complexity of the problem and that more thought must be given to this issue. Such changes in attitude exemplify the above-postulated interaction between value change and access to information. A detailed investigation of such changes in attitude resulting from an awareness of the implications (costs) of social statutes, as well as from other types of learning experiences and motives, follows in the second part of the present essay.

The reform of Art. 218 was primarily a change in the criminal sanctions for abortion. Subsequently, abortion has become legalized under certain circumstances: the pregnant woman consents to it; she has undergone the legally prescribed advisory procedure; and the abortion is recommended by a medical authority as the only remaining measure reasonably expected to relieve the pregnant woman of "grave hardship"–taking the mother's present and future living conditions into consideration. Abortion would also be permitted for "medical or eugenic indications and if pregnancy resulted from a criminal assault" (*Drucksache des Deutschen Bundestages*, 1980, No. 8/3630, p. 19). The pregnant woman is also guaranteed immunity from prosecution if the abortion is undertaken on medical advice but without her having gone through the formal procedures with an advisory board, if she was in extreme distress at the time. These, however, are only personal reasons for exemption from punishment, which do not deny the unlawfulness of the act. The legislative authority quite explicitly does not intend this exemption from punishment to be understood as a change in norms: "The protection of the life of the fetus does on principle prevail over the right of the pregnant woman to self-determination" (p. 16).

The legislator's position is thus similar to that of the Protestant Church: The relevant norm is the "prohibition against killing," but extraordinary circumstances can justify exceptions. Yet the revised legislation does not leave the decision about the justifiability of such exceptions to the woman's capacity for moral judgment, but instead entrusts it to the alleged expertise of the doctor and of the advisory board. Nevertheless, these changes in the criminal penalties are often construed by the public as the state's acknowledgment as a woman's legal claim to abortion. Hence the Caritas Association, in its testimony concerning the reform, complained that "an increasingly negative development" is apparent. "Abortion is becoming normal; in part it is even interpreted as a legal claim for which it is sufficient if the pregnancy is 'undesired' and 'unplanned' without there being any objectively grave hardship" (BMJFG, 1981a, Vol. 1, pp. 141, 143). Insofar as this diagnosis is correct, it shows the effect criminal penalties have on the moral sensitivity of the public, who, if it suits their interests, give the legally conceded latitude a very wide interpretation. It is then easy, though fallacious, to draw the conclusion: That which is not legally punishable is morally permitted.

Regardless of which model predominates among the public, i.e., whether it is the legislator's "exception model" or the "self-determination model" as diagnosed and deplored by Caritas, the change in the legal sanctions has certainly had one effect: given the legalization of an exception clause and given the establishment of the advisory boards, abortion has become a real option for conduct. Whereas previously one had to bow to the exigencies of nature and to the regulations of religious tradition, the law now provides room for consciously-made decisions. Thus, one aspect of the global trend toward rationalization described by Max Weber asserts itself in the area of reproductive behavior and its corresponding value system. To the extent that the "self-determination model" wins acceptance, one can regard these changes in the value system as the introduction of a new value *content.* This is done in the discussions of value change that have been stimulated by Inglehart. On these terms–analogously to the transition from materialist to post-materialist orientations–the issue is simply one of a transition from the absolute value of unborn life to the value of the woman's free self-realization. Without doubt this is one aspect of this change process. However, the novel element is that a special type of value has for the first time gained relevance for this life sphere, a value which at the same time constitutes a *procedural* norm. This latter feature is emphasized clearly in the conception of the Protestant Church: the woman's right to self-determination here does not specify the substance of the decision which she should make, but only defines the procedure. Whatever decision each individual woman makes depends on her own value orientations, which are no longer imposed by society. In whichever way each woman uses her capacity for decision-making, the values on which she bases her decision and the reflections behind the decision have another mode of validity than that of purely tradition-oriented decisions. This is true even in cases in which people are indeed following tradition, for example, the doctrine of the Catholic Church. As the following excerpt from one of our interviews with a young girl (Subject #90) shows, even a traditional orientation can be held reflexively.

> Up until the third month everyone should decide for themselves. For me it's murder–I wouldn't do it. But for other people it's not murder.

It should also be obvious that this change in validity mode cannot easily be reversed by new cultural fashions, since these usually affect the content of orientation and not the modality of thought. For example, it seems that within the cultural subgroups who initially were in the vanguard for the legalization of abortion, antimodernistic counter-currents arise which tend to revalue the role of the mother. Should this tendency lead to a decrease in the number of abortions, it would not amount to a return to a purely traditional lifestyle, since the individual here is deciding freely and consciously to have the child. This involves only an exchange of value contents without affecting the validity mode of the orientations.

Let us now turn to the second example investigated: that of compulsory military service. Here we will discuss only the central dimension of value change, i.e., the dimension of the validity mode. Today carrying out one's military service is no longer a matter of fulfilling an unambiguous, obvious civic or moral duty, but rather–as is the case with carrying a child to full term–is only one of a number of options. Granting the individual the right to free decision is one aspect of the process of the dissolution of traditions (what Max Weber called *Enttraditionalisierung*). One of the causes of this development is the spreading awareness that an exception ruling, which was originally introduced for some well-defined special cases, is frequently invoked successfully: here we see the effectiveness of the "normative strength of the factual." Once a process of change in behavior has started for arbitrary external reasons, it will soon gain a self-intensifying force. The knowledge that many others make "discrepant" behavioral decisions has the consequence that even behavior conforming to traditional routine comes to be understood as the outcome of a conscious decision, because, obviously, one could have acted differently. So, what was so far taken for granted now needs to be justified.

This pattern is exemplified by the rise in the number of applications for recognition as a conscientious objector. Since the introduction of general conscription, it fluctuated between 2,500 and 5,500 applications from 1957 to 1966, only to climb dramatically in the following years, as Table 1 shows.

Table 1

Applications for Conscientious Objector Status (in thousands)

5.9	12.0	14.4	27.2	33.8	35.2	34.2	32.6	40.6
1967	1968	1969	1971	1972	1973	1974	1975	1976

Source: Hecker & Schusser, 1980, p. 189.

These figures are detailed in our 1976 study. Only 30% of the male interviewees were clearly set on completing their military service. 21% were still undecided; 48% did not want to complete military service. (These data refer to the attitudes of adolescents, that is, in many cases some years prior to the actual decision). In other words, over two-thirds of the population considered the completion of military service not a self-evident demand, but an open question for which reasons must be given and weighed.

THE DIFFERENTIAL RECEPTION OF VALUE CHANGE

If the dissolution of traditions is one central–albeit in Inglehart's discussion somewhat neglected–aspect of value change, the question of the differential reception of this change must be analyzed differently. In Inglehart's model value change is described primarily as the replacement (or at least the subordination) of materialist values with post-materialist values. This exchange of the contents of values is explained by socio-economic changes in society interacting with a universal human motive hierarchy. Following Maslow, Inglehart proposes a hierarchy of needs, in which the needs of physical safety and of material prosperity lie at the bottom, followed by the need for social recognition, and finally the need for self-realization and for the full realization of democratic basic rights. Only when the "lower" needs are satisfied are the higher needs articulated.

According to Inglehart's international comparative analyses of representative opinion polls, this supposition holds for those groups of the population who in their "formative" years (i.e., in the first years of their life) have experienced taken-for-granted prosperity, or even excessive wealth. In Inglehart's model an early experience of wealth imprints a motivationally based preference for a "new" type of value contents. Thus affinity to specific value contents is seen to be caused primarily by socio-economic conditions, and processes of reflection are not explicitly considered. Quite in contrast to this approach, we will make use of Weber's rationalization paradigm and emphasize conscious learning processes and a differential sensitivity to the immanent rationality of argumentations. In this way we can proceed to investigate causes of such learning reasons and their effects on a differential reception of value change.

Methods

The data to be analyzed originate from a 1976 study of 112 German male and female students between the ages of 14-22 from three types of high schools *(Hauptschule, Realschule, Gymnasium)*[3]. The students were interviewed in depth about a variety of problems (intrafamilial milieu, value attitudes, moral consciousness, defense mechanisms, political socialization). Among other questions about political socialization, we discussed the attitude toward the armed services, and the justifiability of laws and possible transgressions, taking as an example the recently reformed Art. 218 concerning abortion. The questions read as follows:

> There have recently been discussions about Art. 218. Which solution to the abortion problem do you believe to be right? Do you think that abortion should be allowed or not?

When the interviewee's viewpoint had been revealed, he or she was asked to name possible objections to his or her own position. If necessary, the interviewer confronted the subject with counterarguments such as:

> Is it not a question of murder or of killing (i.e., in the case of full legalization)? Should the woman bear the child if she has been raped; if her life is endangered; if the child is disabled; if the financial resources are inadequate?

Regarding military service the boys were asked:

> One day you will have to decide whether you want to do military service. Have you already thought about this? Can you see yourself refusing to do so? Would you try to get out of it with a medical certificate? Do you think it would have consequences for you if you conscientiously objected? Would you do military service voluntarily? It has been suggested that the

examination for conscientious objection should be abolished. What's your opinion?

For the girls the question was altered:

> In Israel women are conscripted into the army. If this were the case in Germany, what would you do?

The answers to these questions were coded as follows:

CONTENT OF THE DECISION
Concerning abortion: No abortion; restrictive exception ruling (mother's life endangered, rape, child with genetic defects); flexible exception ruling (indication of "grave hardship"); free decision (within the first 12 weeks of pregnancy or complete legalization).

Concerning military service: Do military service; still undecided with reasons for and against military service; do not do military service.

STRUCTURE OF THE REASONS
Complexity of arguments: The number of different arguments presented were assessed. In the case of consenting to abortion, considerations such as the following each counted as one argument: an unwanted child will suffer; the mother's life will be impaired; other countries legalize abortion; the state does not have the right to intervene in the private sphere.

Conviction versus instrumentalist arguments related to armed forces: Conviction arguments *against:* I don't want to kill; violence is no solution to conflicts; defense is no longer possible today; social work is more meaningful; *pro:* it is a duty. Instrumentalist arguments *against:* conscription means drill and subordination; waste of time; *pro:* the armed forces offer attractive educational opportunities; concrete advantages (compensation, driving license); community service is less pleasant.

In addition to pure social statistical information, the following variables were included in the analysis as independent variables:

> *Stage of moral development:* Classification on the basis of the answers to a hypothetical moral dilemma (euthanasia) drawing on Kohlberg's coding instructions.
>
> *Moral reliability:* The individual's tendency (not related to stage) to hold to his moral views in practice, that is, neither to consciously subordinate moral values to extra-moral objectives nor to defensively distort the perception of the situation, so that extra-moral interests would be satisfied under the guise of moral justifiability (e.g., through denial, rationalization, etc.). Three hypothetical action conflicts were presented to the interviewees in which the actor's interests collide with an acknowledged

norm (e.g., a hit-and-run offense). Subjects were classified on the basis of their answers to the question: "What would you do in this situation?" Interviewees who in all three situations proposed a moral way of acting were classified as "reliable"; interviewees who in all three situations offered an action decision that conforms to interests but is in conflict with norms were coded as "strategist" (see Döbert & Nunner-Winkler, 1985).

Intra-familial milieu: Parent-child relationships were classified on the basis of the description which the subjects gave to open-ended questions such as: "How do you get on with your parents in general? If conflicts arise what happens?" In addition, the interviewees were asked to indicate from a standardized list which styles of conflict resolution were typical of their parents. A cluster-analysis of these answers grouped parents according to the dimensions of frequency and intensity of conflicts, and power symmetry versus one-sided dominance.

RESULTS AND DISCUSSION

One of the most interesting results is our finding, reported above, that the majority of young people consider both dilemmas open to their own free decision. The traditional norms (in the case of a pregnancy, the bearing of a child; in the case of compulsory military service, the fulfilling of one's civic duty) are in fact supported by a relatively small minority (on abortion: 8% favor strict prohibition; on conscription: 21% view compliance as "self-evident"). Even when the individual regards traditional norms as binding, he will tend to justify them not merely by referring to "sacred traditions" (abortion is a sin), but by recognizing that possible opponents also have significant arguments. For example, Subject #1 argued for her rather restrictive attitude to abortion as follows:

> I don't find it correct that every woman should decide on her own whether she will have the child or not . . . This is something one should think about beforehand . . . I do believe that life starts with conception. Admittedly, this is a matter of belief . . . Scientifically one can neither prove it nor deny it . . . but somehow that is connected with the whole of our human development: the death penalty has always been the worst form of punishment right through history. And if we now say we can have abortions, then that is somehow a breach in the way things are done.

Now, what determines the restrictive or more liberal attitude to abortion, and what is behind a more supportive or more critical attitude to the armed forces? Without wanting to deny the importance of quasi-automatic learning processes, we are primarily interested in those learning experiences which provide rational reasons for convictions and which can thus be seen as part of the ubiquitous process of rationalization. An individual's convictions are a subset of all possible argumentations, a subset that he or she has specifically selected, weighed, and integrated, in order to come to a more or less clear-cut conclusion, i.e., an attitude that is pro or con. Which arguments are discerned and which arguments carry a special weight depends on different types of learning processes. There is a rather automatic "learning by content" resulting from socialization into given (dogmatic) traditions. Through internalization, institutionalized principles gain an almost indisputable status and the question of the truth of the orientation systems so transmitted is disregarded. Also, there is "learning by experience," which–independently of a person's cognitive developmental level–lends immediate evidence to such arguments as accord with his own life experiences. Finally, there is a differential sensitivity for types of arguments that is mediated by specific aspects of moral development. What is at issue in the learning process is essentially structural: as his moral development progresses, the individual becomes able to consider and integrate an increasing number of viewpoints, so as to see not only immediate consequences but also complex cause-effect chains on the system level. The extent to which competences generated by structural learning are made use of hinges in turn on "performance determining factors." These factors will be discussed below under two headings: (1) Haan's and Gilligan's thesis of sex-specific morality, according to which men focus more on abstract principles and women focus primarily on concrete circumstances; and (2) the variable "moral reliability," which indicates the relative weight accorded to moral and non-moral considerations.

Content-Based Learning

In our data the influence of learning by content is especially evident in the church and school environments. In the case of abortion, a clear picture arises which coincides closely with the results of other surveys. While even among Catholics the majority no longer votes for restrictive legislation,[4] nonetheless the more restrictive exception rulings are supported significantly more often by Catholics. Starting from a sample average of 70.6% Catholics (not unusual for the state of Bavaria), the proportion of Catholics rises to 100% in the group favoring "total prohibition," drops to 81% in the group favoring a "restrictive exception ruling," going to 73% among those in favor of a "flexible exception ruling," down to 55% among those for "free decision." This correlation is even higher if one includes as an intervening variable "religious upbringing" (cited almost exclusively by Catholics): only 14% of the group advocating "complete legalization of abortion" were religiously educated by their parents. This percentage increase to 24% and 53% in the groups supporting the flexible and the restrictive exception ruling respectively, and to 78% in the "total prohibition" group.

The connection between membership in the Catholic Church and choice of the more "traditional" solution is less direct in the question of military service than in that of abortion. Admittedly, among those unquestioningly accepting compulsory military service, the percentage of Catholics is somewhat higher (85%) than in the more critically minded groups who reported themselves "undecided" or "not going" (57% and 69% respectively).[5] This connection is, however, probably not–as in the case of abortion–a product of a specific learning-by-content process. After all, the Church does not advocate specific actions concerning military service. Rather, a more general, superficial conformity with ruling conventions may be reflected here. Including the variable "religious upbringing" actually reverses this connection: in the "not going" group 56%, and in the "going" group only 45%, have experienced a religious upbringing; the lowest percentage, 29%, is found in the "undecided" group. This may be taken to indicate that the undecided subjects in particular gear their decision less to convictions than to a strategic weighting of pros and cons (see also the discussion below under the heading "moral reliability").[6] In addition the higher quota of subjects with religious upbringing among the potential conscientious objectors suggests that a religious background may influence the decision, even when religious motives are no longer explicitly given as grounds (only one subject refers to an explicitly religious motive).[7] Here we are dealing with a kind of "secularized reverberation" of an upbringing guided by religious-ethical principles.

In our data we find that the *type of school* contributes very little to the explanation of the attitude towards abortion. Though students from *Hauptschule* are somewhat overrepresented in both restrictive groups, they are by no means underrepresented in the "complete legalization" group.[8] On the other hand, as in other representative surveys, the type of school proves to be an important factor in the question of conscientious objection. In our sample, 78% of the

Gymnasium students, as compared to only 44% of the *Hauptschule* and
Realschule students, thought about refusing to do military service.[9]
While this may be a consequence of "structural learning" (practice in
how to argue, to be discussed below), conformity with ruling norms,
that is, content-based learning, also plays a role. Usually in the
Gymnasium a pacifist orientation predominates: most "opinion
leaders" support a critical attitude toward the armed forces; conscientious objection is discussed more frequently than is military service
(see Warnke & Moosmann, cited in Hecker & Schusser, 1980, pp.
51ff); and conscientious objectors appear more frequently in the
circle of acquaintances of *Gymnasium* students.[10] The following
remark from one of our interviewees shows that individuals feel a
certain group pressure: "In our class it almost takes courage to be in
favor of the military."

Experience-based Learning

The affective climate in the family has some influence on the attitude toward abortion. Young people who have experienced rejection
or indifference from their parents advocate the more restrictive
solutions (no abortion: 0%; restrictive exception ruling: 7%) significantly less often than do children who feel accepted and loved at
home (no abortion: 11%; restrictive exception ruling: 15%). They
opt more often for the flexible exception ruling (60% versus 24% of
subjects with positive family experience), a ruling that specifies
future burdens of an unwanted pregnancy for mother or child as
permissible reasons for the termination of the pregnancy. As the
following remarks of Subject #3 vividly illustrate, the liberal attitude
of these young people toward abortion can be seen as a virtual
resumé of their own experience of life:

> One should have allowed it up to the third month . . . When one doesn't
> want a child then one should give it a miss . . . or when the people are
> too young, like my mother was when she got me.

At the objection of the interviewer:

> But if your mother had had an abortion, then you wouldn't be here now.

he replies:

Well . . . sometimes I'd be glad if I wasn't here. Living in a children's home is no fun; it's easy to get in, but getting out is more difficult . . . for me it's like this: my stepfather doesn't like me to visit my mother. (pp. 24-25)

The intra-familial milieu also influences attitudes toward military service. We find a higher percentage of adolescents with an unambiguously positive attitude toward military service in families in which the parent-child relationship and the relationship of the parents are harmonious and free of conflict.

In both problem contexts, the influence of the family constellation on the attitude of the adolescent can be regarded as experience-based learning. It is one's own experiences in life which lead to certain points of view or lend specific considerations direct plausibility and, therefore, particular weight. In the case of abortion, it is the argument that an unwanted child will suffer that carries a particular weight for young people who have had precisely this experience. Similarly, the argument commonly put forward as a reason for conscientious objection, namely that violence is not an appropriate solution to conflict, may be regarded as a resumé of the experience of conflicts which the adolescent has himself had with his parents or has observed between his parents. An argument against the armed forces that has this explicit form may, however, be only the tip of the iceberg of a critical attitude toward the armed forces, shaped through a familial experience rich in conflict. Studies in the field of political socialization have shown that an unquestioned basic loyalty to fundamental social institutions is a product of the generalization of a consistent trust in authority as experienced from early childhood: from the "good father" comes the "good, benevolent president" (cf. Greenberg, 1970). In the case of families rich in conflict, this basic loyalty was either backed up insufficiently from early childhood, or broken down and criticized in the course of a severe adolescent crisis. For the latter hypothesis we have presented evidence elsewhere (cf. Döbert & Nunner-Winkler, 1975; also Roeder, cited in Hecker & Schusser, 1980, pp. 196-197).

Structural Learning and Moral Performance

Haan's and Gilligan's thesis of two moralities. Starting with the observation that, according to Kohlberg's Scoring Manual, women are on the average assigned a lower moral stage (Stage 3) than are men (Stage 4), Haan and Gilligan postulate the existence of a second morality, which counters Kohlberg's Kantian view of a "rigorously universalistic principled morality." They object that Kohlberg's morality provides a "rational, autonomous decision-making model, independent of time and place" (Gilligan, 1980, p. 7); its "principles of justice [are] context-free and generate objectively correct solutions to moral problems" (Murphy & Gilligan, 1980, p. 83) whose justification must be "irrespective of personal social context" (Haan, 1978, p. 287). Central characteristics of the alternative which they propose, namely, the model of an "interpersonal morality" (Haan) or of an "ethic of care and responsibility" (Gilligan), are a focus on situational context and a desire to avoid harm. Specific details of the particular action situation or peculiarities of the individuals affected are taken into consideration in making moral judgments; the prime target is the minimization of harm done to individuals affected. Both authors claim that Kohlberg's rigid principled morality is typical of the male way of thinking and that the contrasting morality of a more flexible context orientation is typical of the female way of thinking.

In what follows, the conceptualization of two contrasting moralities will be criticized. Admittedly, this criticism is partially motivated by an extra-scientific prejudice on our parts: namely, that there is either *one* morality or *no* morality. Of course, relativism does have its place in certain well-defined areas, in which, legitimate zones of relativism can be delimited with *reasons*. What is presented as a "second morality" is, in our opinion, better conceptualized as the problem of the application of a universalistic morality, inasmuch as different strategies in the application of moral principles to concrete situations give rise to different moral decisions. But let us now turn to the criticism in detail.

The focus on the situational context is a necessary implication of an ethical conception which admits of exceptions. For Kant, negative duties (you should not kill, steal, lie, etc.) allow no exceptions under any circumstances and, therefore, can be applied irrespective of any contextual considerations. (Kant's dictum that a man may not tell a lie to a potential murderer, even if this lie could save the life of a friend, has become famous.) Kohlberg, on the other hand, holds the transgression of a negative duty (you should not steal) to be one's duty if this is the only way a life is to be saved (cf. the Heinz dilemma). To be sure, Kohlberg does not want the duty to save life to be understood as an *unconditional* duty–nor can it be so understood when it is formulated as a "positive" duty (cf. Nunner-Winkler, 1984).

True, some of Kohlberg's formulations and operationalizations occasionally sound like a rigid, principled morality, and in this respect the accusations of Haan and Gilligan are not completely unfounded. However, the allowance of exceptions is not only a logical implication of his conceptualization of "positive" duties; it is also an explicit component of his scoring procedure. To give an example: In the "Joe dilemma," a father, in spite of his promise to the contrary, asks his son to sacrifice going to a holiday camp and to let him have the money that has been saved for it. Answers were coded as postconventional by Kohlberg if they showed the following pattern of reasoning: "Joe might consider giving his father the money (even though his normal obligations to his father do not hold because of the father's unfairness) because the long-term consequences would be best for all concerned. He clearly considers consequences for both individuals" (Kohlberg, 1973b, p. 99). What constitutes the postconventionality of this answer is precisely that ability which is postulated by Haan and Gilligan as the heart of the "second morality." It is the ability to make *exceptions* appropriate to the situational circumstances (consequences for all involved), that is, not to insist that a promise must be kept. It is this ability to make appropriate exceptions that differentiates principled orientations based on structural learning from those which reflect mere content-learning. In contrast to learning theoretical explanations of "morality" as mere adoption of given norms, the cognitive approach conceives of moral development as "the progressive understanding of the purpose, function and nature of social arrangements" (Rest, 1983, p. 562). To master a moral principle means to be able to comprehend its interactive meaning, to be able to control its application according to its "meaning," and to be able to make appropriate exceptions. Anyone can master the mere parroting of principled phrases; therefore, in many cases it is only from the ability to make appropriate exceptions that a higher stage of moral thinking can be demonstrated. Situational differentiation is thus without doubt a constitutive factor in postconventional thinking. Conversely, it also holds that mere flexibility and minimization of costs–and these are the only characteristics which Haan and Gilligan mention as constitutive for their contrasting morality–cannot be distinguished from purely situational opportunism, unless they are based on general fundamental principles. It is only when principles are understood together with their flexible and situationally adequate application, that they can constitute a mature, moral judgment. Emphasizing either of these two aspects at the expense of the other produces only unnecessary mock controversies. Hare (1963), taking experience of life as the basis of moral development, argues in a similar vein:

> The thesis of universalizability does not require moral judgment to be made on the basis of highly general moral principles . . . Moral development . . . consists in the main in making our moral principles more and more specific, by writing into them exceptions and qualifications to cover kinds of cases for which we have had experiences. (p. 40)

So far we have argued that whenever exceptions to principles are seen as legitimate, the consideration of the concrete details of a situation is imperative for deciding whether an exception ruling is required, or even justifiable. It could be, however, that although the admissibility of exceptions *logically* requires a consideration of concrete circumstance, the sexes may nevertheless differ in their *actual* tendencies to consider contingent conditions and costs in reaching a judgment. The thesis of different moralities would then be refuted, but not the assumption of differences in "moral character": the female tendency to focus primarily on the costs to people involved when applying moral rules or principles contrasts with the male inclination to pay attention first of all to laws and duties–largely without considering consequences.

Now, is there any evidence for this somewhat more limited thesis? Gilligan herself quotes data from her research on women who are considering a termination of pregnancy. These data show convincingly that women do explicitly consider concrete consequences and situational circumstances. However, our analysis of male and female argumentation structures in the discussion of abortion and conscientious objection makes even the more limited thesis seem implausible. Instead, our data suggest an interpretation which can also explain Gilligan's results: it is not sex-membership but what we have called "affectedness" *(Betroffenheit)* that decides whether concrete situational circumstances are taken into account in the manner required by an ethics that admits of exceptions. Our interviews show that in the case of conscientious objection it is the boys, and in the case of abortion the girls, who more frequently include concrete costs and resulting burdens in their considerations. In the discussion of abortion, twice as many girls as boys (48% vs. 24%) refer to the costs the woman has to bear in the case of an unwanted pregnancy (e.g., the mother is too young, she can no longer continue with her education, her life could be impaired); also the consequences which await the unwanted child are considered far more frequently by girls than by boys (38% vs. 22%).

It should be noted that the concept of "affectedness" is understood here in a broad sense, namely as potential rather than immediate affectedness. The results of a representative survey by Zundel and his collaborators about attitudes to abortion agree quite well with this thesis of affectedness. They found that "women of child-bearing age, that is, those most affected by the problem, tend to have far more liberal views . . . than the average person in the population" (cited in BMJFG, 1981b, Vol. 3, p. 236). That we are not dealing here merely with extra-moral interests of the people affected is evident from another of their results. While the subjects, as reported above, allow more exceptions when more details are given, those whose own life situations are reflected in the case description (e.g., a divorced woman or a woman with many children, when confronted with a case description in which a divorced woman or a mother of many children considers a termination of pregnancy), do not tend towards a "more permissive" solution, but instead tend to react with greater uncertainty. The authors call this result surprising and offer no explanation. However, the "affectedness" thesis provides a way of explaining this finding: what is reflected in that uncertainty is an awareness of the fact that those affected are always in danger of granting themselves overly generous excuses. It is this leniency that they carefully try to avoid, even in situations where they would unhesitatingly grant others an exception ruling. Since those directly affected take great care not to allow their own interests to enter into their judgment, it seems less problematic to regard affectedness as a morally relevant dimension: anyone who is (potentially) affected is more sensitive about costs and consequences which an unbiased person might acknowledge as legitimate grounds for the justification of exceptions.[11]

Conversely, in the discussion about conscientious objection, it is mainly the girls who mention only abstract, moral considerations: e.g., "One should not kill," "Wars are senseless," "Defense is not possible," etc. (63% girls vs. 23% boys). On the other hand, more than half of the boys refer to the concrete costs of conscientious objection or of completion of military service (59% boys vs. 12% girls), either exclusively or in combination with principled moral considerations. Of course, in some cases it may well be that the decision is treated as belonging solely to the realm of instrumental action. That is, norms are simply disregarded and no attempt is made to specify legitimate exceptions. However, as the following passage from the interview with Subject #12 shows, cost-benefit calculations can be an integral component of moral reflection:

I: Would you refuse to do military service?
S: One has to take into consideration that the offer of an education in the armed forces is a good opportunity, and that attracts me. But I would

refuse to do military service with a weapon. I'd rather go into an old people's home and see what it's like there . . . I prefer that, I'd find more satisfaction there. I would also be seeing what I'm doing and would know that I'm really working productively.

I: On the other hand, you said that the offer of an education appeals to you. Could you imagine going voluntarily into the armed forces?

S: If I'm offered the opportunity of further education, then yes–but not to learn how to kill.

I: But you can't have the one without the other.

S: When you enter the armed forces, you get a normal education and maybe even go to university or college. To me that does seem like parasitism, but I'd still not refuse it. If I didn't see any other chance, then I'd still not refuse it. If I didn't see any other chance then I'd do it.

I: You said you didn't want to be taught how to kill. Why would you then consider it justifiable to accept this offer of an education?

S: I meant what I said without taking war into consideration. Of course, if I knew that there was the prospect of a war, then I wouldn't do it. But if I knew that there is no danger, then why not? I'd just hop around a bit with a rifle.

To summarize, it would appear that to some extent our findings point in the same direction as Gilligan's. They show that women do consider more often the costs incurred in concrete situations, at least in the abortion dilemma. However, the fact that in the case of conscientious objection the ratio of abstract principled arguments to concrete situational considerations between men and women is reversed shows that the determining factor *is not sex-membership but acute affectedness.* Gilligan has supported her thesis with a dilemma which affects women more strongly. If the dilemmas presented do not introduce any obviously feminine topics, then hardly any sex-specific differences result, as is also shown in the research by Haan (1978), who started from similar hypotheses. So what Haan and Gilligan want to treat as sex-specific types of morality becomes a matter of performance in the case of affectedness. Affectedness here means the anticipation of resulting hardships from a partial perspective. Thus, affectedness fulfills a function similar to that of learning by experience: costs of actions are taken seriously.

Stages of moral development. Stages in the socio-cognitive theory of development represent "structured wholes," which are generalized styles of thinking. Moral development is thus a kind of "master variable," because the acquisition of a particular moral stage presupposes that the corresponding cognitive and socio-cognitive developmental processes have been completed. Thus the notion that the level of moral development will influence the way a given realm of argumentation is employed, that is, which points of view will be perceived and coordinated, is almost a tautological expectation. On the other hand, in the given case, the extensive public discussion of these two problems has brought the essential aspects into general consciousness, weakening the correspondence between stages of moral development and individual arguments raised in this discussion, since at all stages the main arguments of the debate can be easily reproduced on the basis of learning by content. Thus we do not expect a complete correspondence between level of development and attitudes toward abortion or conscientious objection. But how close is the actual correspondence?

Let us begin with the problem of abortion: First, even a relatively rough and superficial measure of the complexity of the argumentation shows a difference in favor of the postconventional interviewees: on the average they use one argument more (4.0 arguments) in comparison to the preconventional interviewees (2.9 arguments) to justify their position (the conventionals are in the middle). Still more informative than this purely formal measure is a content analysis of the position adopted and the reasons given in its support. Postconventional subjects opt less frequently for the restrictive forms of Art. 218, advocating no abortion or only restrictive exceptions (11%), compared to conventional (30%) or preconventional subjects (26%). Most of them speak out for the flexible exception ruling, which relates abortion to the prohibition against killing but does admit of exceptions when there are good reasons. This agrees with the idea presented above that higher moral development means above all the competence to handle in a flexible manner previously rigidly-held norms and rules. Even where the postconventional subjects choose the most far-reaching solution, namely, complete legalization, they frequently do so with reasons which show that throughout they are aware of the problems of killing. They name only reasons which in the restrictive rulings are considered legitimate grounds for exceptions (many refer to the suffering of an unwanted child, but hardly any to the mother's distress). Or they demand legalization of abortion, arguing that the state has no right to decide and dictate a general prohibition, either because it is not clear whether abortion is killing (only postconventional interviewees state that it is scientifically undecided when human life can be said to begin), or because they believe that a universal consensus about the legitimacy of exceptions cannot be reached. Hence, Subject #57 argues in this fashion: "Abortion should be free. A prohibition by the state is an intervention in the individual's life, whereby the state acts according to a blueprint applied to everyone, although in each case different motives and viewpoints are involved." Only 27% of the postconventional interviewees (in contrast to 60% of the preconventionals in the group favoring complete legalization) believe that every woman should be free to do as she pleases. As stated by our preconventional Subject #48: "To have a child is a restriction for the woman. If she doesn't want to, it's her decision." It is important to note that a preference for the same rulings, even if backed by the same principle, does not have one single implication, for principles mean something very different at different stages of moral development. For example, the woman's right to self-determination at the postconventional level means that no one can stand proxy for the woman: she herself must *responsibly* weigh the various justificatory reasons. This is how Subject #4 argues: "The government cannot judge ·whether the woman has *justifiable* reasons or not." On the preconventional level, it is usually a matter of an unquestionable freedom "to do or not to do what one wants to do"; in the words of Subject #41: "It must be left to the woman herself to decide whether she wants it done or not. I mean, poking his nose into other people's affairs is not any goddamn government official's business." Thus postconventional subjects treat the issue as a moral question, while the preconventional subjects tend to shift it to the realm of extra-moral biographical decisions (such as entering a profession).

The same holds true for the issue of conscientious objection. The influence of moral development bears more on reasoning than on choice: irrespective of their stages, about half the interviewees had decided to refuse to do military service. The postconventional interviewees are, however, clearly underrepresented among those who have already made a clear decision for military service. That this is due partly to the fact that adolescents are not normally confronted with convincing principled reasoning in favor of military service is shown by the distribution of the considerations which they put forward. The arguments presented for conscientious objection are: ethical arguments, such as "not killing" (20 times); political arguments, such as: "war is senseless," "violence is not a means of solution of conflicts," and "defense is not possible" (25); pragmatic cost calculations, such as "conscription means subordination and drill" and "brings professional disadvantages" (29). The arguments put forward for the fulfilling of military service were: ethical arguments such as "duty" (3); "defense of our lifestyle" (1); pragmatic advantages, such as "opportunity for further education," "chance to make a lot of money," and "the satisfaction of technical interests" (23).

The interviewees were divided into four groups, according to the type of argumentation used:

- *Pure conviction: Only* ethical or political arguments
- *Balanced:* Conviction *and* pragmatic or instrumentalist considerations
- *Instrumentalists: Only* pragmatic considerations
- *Traditionalists:* Decision taken for granted, not needing justification.

This grouping correlates with the stages of moral development. Most of the instrumentalists are preconventional, most of the traditionalists are conventional, and most of the balanced type, integrating moral and instrumental considerations, are postconventional. This result corresponds quite well with the moral stage definitions, since we do not–as is often done–equate the concept of postconventionality with an ethical rigor that totally disregards personal needs.

Moral reliability. The influence of a further aspect of moral consciousness also arises, namely, moral reliability. By moral reliability we mean the tendency to keep to norms recognized as valid even if doing so runs counter to one's own interests. Subjects less consistent in their moral beliefs are termed "strategists," those who are consistent, "reliables." This variable has practically no bearing on the discussion about abortion; it does, however, bear on conscientious objection. This may be due to the fact that in discussing abortion we asked not for hypothetical action decisions, but for the most reasonable type of legal ruling. There the problem of consistency between judgment and action did not arise. Conversely, in discussing military service, concrete action decisions and their justifications were asked for. Hence, inconsistencies between judgment and action are likely to arise, so that the variable moral reliability becomes more relevant. It turned out that the majority of "reliable" subjects had definitely decided not to do military service: in fact, the figure was 67% in comparison to only 33% of the strategists. It is also worth noting that in the case of most "reliable" subjects (69%), convictions entered into the decision, while 67% of the strategists employed exclusively instrumental considerations. Thus, when convictions are brought to bear, the decision will most likely be against military service. This again confirms that the realm of argumentation confronting adolescents is more elaborated for one side of the picture: traditionally, fulfilling military service needed no justification, since it was a taken-for-granted civic duty. The mere fact, however, that a considerable number of young men obviously do not fulfill this "taken-for-granted duty" makes even the decision for military service appear as the result of one's own choice–a choice that needs justification, for which mainly instrumental considerations are available; consistently elaborated principled reflections are found only for conscientious objection. This explains why the reliable subjects–who in terms of our definition remain true to their convictions in their actions–are overrepresented on the side of the conscientious objectors.[12]

CONCLUSION

We have discussed two examples of value change, namely the attitudes toward abortion and toward military service. We chose both of these instances of value change because they do not–as do Inglehart's analyses–involve an underlying substitution of value contents. In both cases there has been a controversial public discussion which still continues. With this, one enters the sphere of normative change which Weber termed societal rationalization. This is the sphere of the conscious coordination of interests, the conscious guiding of actions by values, and of explicit decisions between competing values. Such processes of rationalization as are coupled with an increase in reflexivity always bear on the validity mode of normative systems, but also affect the substantive and social validity of norms. The value change discussed here centrally affects the status of self-determination in the normative system. Self-determination becomes prominent in action contexts, which so far have been governed mainly by tradition. Reducing this process to a mere exchange of value-contents does not do it justice, since self-determination is a procedural norm, compliance with which–quite unlike other value contents–does not determine the direction for action. Self-determination in each individual case demands a processing of the relevant information and a weighing of the pros and cons. This produces ambivalences which render improbable an unbroken transmission of cultural values to the individual. The process of reception of value orientations becomes tinged by subjective factors. We saw that in the process of content learning, the arguments raised in the public discussion are received differently by members of different subcultures. These arguments also meet with different family milieus and other biographic experiences, which lend them different degrees of plausibility. Furthermore, those affected by social rulings are more sensitive to the anticipated costs of these rulings. How the publicly discussed viewpoints and arguments are perceived and interpreted by individuals ultimately depends on one's level of ego development (here operationalized as moral development). This brings in structural learning, which focuses on the motivational force engendered by better arguments. The effectiveness of better moral arguments in a given situation hinges in turn on moral reliability. It is precisely these latter aspects of moral consciousness which point up the ambivalence of the transition to the "value" of self-determination. They determine whether the individual, set free from conventional constraints, will instrumentalize his whole life-sphere or, adopting a value-rational attitude, will make responsible ethical decisions. The dissolution of traditions has two faces, value rationality and instrumental rationality. Which form of rationality prevails depends, to a large and very interesting extent, on the individual.

NOTES

1. See Klages and Kmieciak (1979) for an overview of the state of the research.
2. In particular Meulemann (1981), in his secondary analysis of survey results, has worked out the causal significance of the expansion of educational systems and of mass communications for value change.
3. The terms *Hauptschule, Realschule,* and *Gymnasium* refer to the German tripartite secondary school system, the *Gymnasium* being required for university enrollment. Attendance at one of the three types of schools is correlated with socio-economic background.
4. 30% of the Roman Catholics in our sample approve of a restrictive exception ruling. This corresponds quite well with the results of a representative survey carried out at about the same time and reported by the Federal Ministry for Youth, Family and Health, which found that 32% of the Catholics questioned declared themselves in favor of a restrictive exception ruling (see BMJFG, 1981b, Vol. 3., p. 208).
5. A somewhat higher percentage of Catholics among those in military service and a distinctly lower percentage among those in community service, respectively, is also reported in other studies. An exact comparison is not possible due to the different group classifications. In our study the interviewees have, for the most part, merely considered conscientious objection, and have not yet applied for it as their official status.

6. This agrees with the result of a representative survey of draftees conducted by Infas in 1983: "Anyone who is undecided–in whatever context–seems to be processing the available information to a particularly high degree. But charity begins at home. That is to say, those undecided concerning military service are not typically ideologists. Cost-benefit calculations are certainly not unknown to them."

7. Hübner counts 6% "religious" reasons among the reasons given for conscientious objection). See also the survey by Kröll, who also establishes that the influence of religious motives has decreased greatly in the years 1968-1970. In the survey by Nagel and Starkulla, 18% of those in community service religiously justified their decision in favor of conscientious objection (Hecker & Schusser, 1980, pp. 202, 205).

8. This result contrasts to a certain extent with the clear difference in liberality between *Hauptschule* students and *Gymnasium* graduates, as reported in the representative survey (BMJFG, 1981b, Vol. 3, p. 219). One can perhaps assume that, in this discussion, the college or university plays the same role as the *Gymnasium* plays in the question of conscientious objection: subcultural patterns of interpretation and formal modes of thinking, simultaneously transmitted, allow and require a systematic justification of one's own position.

9. According to Korte et al. (see Hecker & Schusser, 1980, p. 193) the willingness of those with an *Abitur* (see n. 3) to enter military service is distinctly lower (45% in the 1973/74 age-groups) than of those with an *Hauptschule* diploma (1973: 51%; 1974: 56%) and of those with a *Realschule* diploma (1973: 50%; 1974: 54%).

10. In other studies, there are indications that the fathers of conscientious objectors and of those who enter military service of their own free will have a higher tendency to support the respective decisions of their sons. Thus, direct transmission of values also appears to be effective here (see Infas, 1977, pp. 23ff; also Kröll, cited in Hecker & Schusser, 1980, p. 195).

11. Kudera's (1982) critical discussion of the theory of value change can, we think, also be read from the "affectedness" point of view.

12. Such instrumentalist attitudes toward military service have probably spread recently, since the educational opportunities offered by the armed forces will seem more attractive as young people's situation in training and job markets becomes more difficult. True, the armed forces may in this way solve recruitment problems; it is doubtful, however, whether such a complex organization will function effectively when most of its members have merely an external-instrumental relationship to their roles. Especially at the middle and high levels of a hierarchy, "role expectations" are necessarily formu-

lated in a very general and abstract way, so that a meaningful interpretation and an appropriate fulfillment of such roles is possible only on the basis of an identification with an organization's aims and tasks. Yet an organization will have problems with recruiting intrinsically motivated persons when principled considerations and convincing arguments seem to be advanced only by the other side.

The Thin Line Phenomenon

Helping Bank Trainees Form
a Social and Moral Identity
in Their Work Place

Fritz Oser & André Schläfli

Occupational socialization can act as a catalyst in the process of moral identity formation in young people, especially adolescents such as the trainees discussed in this study. The latent patterns of interaction, the existing social rules and values, and the company's practical moral standards all constitute the framework in which a young person is able to fulfill not only the occupational role he or she has chosen but also many of the important social and moral competences that accompany them. As with any professional framework, the moral horizons of this work setting are specific and limiting, but the developmental process takes place within them nontheless.

THE THIN LINE PHENOMENON

Although many successful work training programs exist, most lack the moral expertise necessary to settle the many social and ethical conflicts that arise in the work place. They offer few opportunities for either organized or incidental learning. Instead, conflicts present in occupational interactions, value differences, and social and moral development are often regarded as impediments to the company's operations. Indeed, one of the expressed goals of many companies is the avoidance of all such differences in the interests of "frictionless" action. As a result, a young person in such a firm has no chance to test his or her limits, or to exceed them. The company's system of rules concerning interaction in social and moral matters precludes any such possibility. It follows that that which the young person in a firm regards as his or her moral self consists essentially in the ability to avoid conflicts. Those responsible for job training usually equate proper conduct with conformity to the company's norms, social rules, and corresponding moral standards, thus creating a setting in which genuine development is barely possible. No one would suggest that teaching professional skills can ensure that socio-moral competence will emerge spontaneously. Nevertheless, training personnel, vocational school teachers, and company management share the common desire that apprentices–or, as we shall call them here, trainees[1]–should develop a moral and social identity–a goal that is usually included under the general heading of "personality development."

In this essay we shall offer some thoughts on the possibility of stimulating the moral and social competences of trainees, and shall present a study which shows how this can be done. We shall discuss the division of opinion described above concerning educational and occupational goals, prevalent social rules, and moral standards. Anyone who wishes to investigate or intervene in existing training programs must walk a thin line between the moral domain and that of corporate functioning. The sources of this problem, which we have designated as the "thin line phenomenon," are twofold. On the one hand, an investigator or intervener who strays from the specific issues of the work place would render the trainees' moral discourse abstract and ineffective; on the other hand, if he dwells too much on the company's inner workings he risks being regarded as at best an interloper and, more likely, an *agent provocateur*. Our point can be illustrated with the following example: Should a bank official lend someone money when he knows that person cannot pay it back and will probably have to surrender cherished personal property to the bank in a foreclosure? In this example the system–the bank–is confronted with a client's personal needs and weaknesses. The bank says: Business is business. Moral decency says: Business must give those who are weaker a chance. The training instructor might say: That is not a matter for bank trainees, whose training should be restricted to business transactions and not be concerned with the moral problems involved. The moral teacher believes that such problems should be dealt with during the training period, since only by coming to terms with real, work-related moral situations can one achieve a higher competence: only in this way can the person's social role and moral position in the firm be made clear, and the practical judgment be tested. In other words, development is possible only if the social and structural conditions are examined and the "heat energy" produced by the friction of this confrontation is diverted and used for developmental purposes.

Thus, the existence of the thin line phenomenon suggests on the one hand that moral education can and should influence the real moral world of the trainee, but on the other hand that moral education is itself shaped and constrained by the structure of the work setting, that is, by the given patterns of interaction, social rules, and moral standards. The trainee is forced to test the boundary between the "artificial" world created by the educational curriculum and the "real," seemingly unchangeable world of work. The thin line phenomenon originates from the dilemma that, in order to change a cognitive moral structure, we must change the context (the latent pattern of interaction) in which the individual lives as well as the existing social rules and practical moral standards of the firm. The thin line phenomenon means that moral intervention has to take place within the work setting, but also that it has to begin with hypothetical dilemmas in order to protect the developing identity of the trainee. Thus, the border between these two worlds is being crossed one step at a time. The thin line phenomenon reflects the felt hiatus between social reality, which influences the cognitive moral structure of an individual, and the belief that this cognitive structure can be influenced without reference to this realism. It leads to the hypothesis that moral learning can be successful only insofar as it deals with the real life world of a trainee. Where this contact with real issues and not just artificial dilemmas is impossible, either because of explicit company policies or practices tacitly agreed to within the professional system, genuine moral development cannot take place.

Thus, in order to turn the thin line phenomenon into a growth-producing situation, we have tried to stimulate moral judgment competence in a work setting (a bank) by presenting behavioral conflicts taken from this social context, and also by involving–at least partly–those who hold positions of responsibility in this context.

DIRECTION AND LIMITS OF DEVELOPMENT

To begin with, we would like to explain what we mean by the change in social and moral growth. We assume there is a difference between "academic" and "social" intelligence (Ford & Tisak, 1983; Keating, 1978), and that both have an influence on identity formation in trainees. On the whole, a good deal is done by way of developing the "academic and occupational intelligence" of adolescents in the training program; there are highly structured programs and extremely efficient course material. In contrast, very often nothing more than lip service is given to the development of social and moral abilities. In the curricula of many, if not most, vocational schools there are only indefinite, general formulations. If one wants to change social competence, however, one has to know what it is and which direction it has to take. Above all, there must be instruments for measuring the improvement.

With this last point we come to Lawrence Kohlberg's theory of stages of moral development. Kohlberg's theory operationalizes development in the social and moral area, but it also goes beyond mere operationalization in that the stages serve as a clear measure of development. It can be shown that each stage is more adequate, better equilibrated, and more reversible (Kohlberg, 1971b; 1981), and that the effects of a moral and cognitive education can be measured by appropriate interviews and tests.

Intervention studies assume that every structural change in the social and moral realm comes about only through disequilibrium of the structures present up to that time or, in more general terms, through crises. We have brought together a series of such studies and analyzed the problems of higher development (see Oser, 1981b). More recent studies (Berkowitz, 1981; Walker, 1983; Kegan & Noam, 1982) confirm the importance of experiencing crises for moral and cognitive development. The realization of such crisis experience through discussion is not easy in a firm, because the creation of cognitive disequilibrium takes place not in a vacuum but in the course of struggling with real, non-hypothetical dilemmas, where varying norms, values, and interpretations come into existential conflict with each other.

One must recognize that the trainee is just beginning to see the banking system as a whole, to understand how it functions, and to comprehend the relationship of a bank to society. To see these relationships clearly one must have attained a moral competence which the trainee does not yet have. Bank secrets are not yet an immediate moral problem for bank trainees, who by and large are unaware of, for example, the bank's investment policies, or its dealing with third world countries. The relevant problems for trainees are matters such as cooperation in the firm, the loosening of their family ties, and relationships to their colleagues, friends, and instructors. In short, their thinking is at Kohlberg's Stage 3 (see Lempert, 1982). Educational intervention must relate to this context, at whose center are the internal structures of the firm, namely, the trainee's relationship to colleagues, training personnel, teachers, and counselors.

THE EDUCATIONAL INTERVENTION

Goals

In pilot studies (particularly with agricultural apprentices) we have found that outside the laboratory it is extremely difficult to stimulate advancement to the next higher stage.[2] Time and interest on the part of the subjects are often in short supply. Also, development has a cognitive ceiling: it cannot proceed indefinitely. A 6-year-old child cannot judge at Stage 4, a 17-year-old trainee presumably not at Stage 5. The strategy of educating-to-the-next-stage also becomes problematic if a person has not yet completely tested and consolidated the position just attained. Piaget strongly warned against such precipitousness when he was awarded the Erasmus prize in 1972: "I have often been asked whether or not one can accelerate the sequence of the stages that we have observed. That is obviously the case, but is it advisable?"

Our intervention study with bank trainees takes up the goals and methods of the theoretical cognitive and developmental approach by Kohlberg and his followers. It has been expanded, however, so that *not only development but also a change in the prerequisites to development is measured.* These prerequisites for moving to a higher Kohlbergian stage induce corresponding increases in the following capacities: more moral self-confidence, the ability to bring in a moral point of view, sensitivity to moral questions, social responsibility for oneself, and moral self-reflection (see also Lempert, 1982, p. 124).

In an attempt to differentiate between these several prerequisite moral capacities, as well as to create a positive learning climate, we have set up five specific goals in our intervention program. We consider and measure these goals independently of one another, although they are closely entwined in the course of the intervention. They are:
- Value awareness: recognizing and clarifying the personal value systems of other trainees
- The promotion of problem-solving ability in the social sphere
- Metacognition: reflection on what was learned, application of what was learned
- Promotion of tolerance, empathy, openness toward others
- Stimulation of competence in moral judgment.

The first four of these goals are conceived as closely related to the fostering of a higher moral judgment competence. For example,

Breslin (1981) showed that in Ireland it is often the case that the competence of a postconventional moral judgment is fully developed only when the person has high tolerance (Goal 4). People at Stage 5 have a certain tendency to stand up for minorities, and, in cases of injustice, to disassociate themselves from the majority. They are also more committed to equal rights, independently of which religious, political, or status group they belong to (see Kohlberg, 1976; Fenton, 1978).

Experimental and Control Group

The experimental group consisted of 45 bank trainees from the Schweizerische Kreditanstalt who participated in the intervention study as subjects. They were randomly divided into two course groups. A control group consisting of 20 trainees was studied at the same time, but there was no intervention made in that group. The results of another study on the moral-cognitive development showed that about 15% of the Swiss trainees are at Stage 2 on Kohlberg's scale, 25% at Stage 2½, and 50% at Stage 3. The same holds true for the groups studied here.

Procedure

The intervention lasted one week (40 hours) for each group. The methods and goals spoken about changed every day so that there was a well-balanced design. This design was planned in detail and structured according to a time plan. We carried out the intervention in the bank's main building (training rooms). The trainees worked with the intervention group leader. For certain purposes subgroups were formed (with specially trained group leaders). The first intervention took place with half of the trainees. In the second week the same program was conducted with the other half of the trainees. The control group had normal instruction during the time of the intervention. Although the program of intervention had been clearly defined in advance, it was possible for the leaders to deviate from the curriculum in response to the trainees' needs, desires, and special experiences.

The methods for reaching the goals of intervention were: discussion of the dilemmas, role playing, information giving, discussion strategies for increasing awareness, and practice in the rules of discourse. The contents included moral dilemmas taken from the trainees' private lives and from the work situation and those opinions and value hierarchies the trainees themselves brought up. In addition, information was provided concerning rules of communication and about Kohlberg's theory, as well as examples of moral action.

The course of the intervention can be shown with two examples, corresponding to the second and the fourth learning goal. The second goal, *value awareness,* includes: knowing what a value is, becoming aware of one's own individual values, being able to compare value systems, and comparing values in the occupational position, all of these being events that take place in the course of personal development at different stages. We have seen that the majority of the trainees are at Stage 3, with some still at Stage 2 or 2½, and hardly any at Stage 4. Thus, we set up Stage 4 as the most realistic developmental goal. It is expected that at this stage one gains insight into how rules, norms, and laws regulate our social life and why they should be adhered to. At Stage 4, however, the values can be weighed against each other; the choice of a certain rule, which is observed voluntarily because one has acquired enough self-knowledge, takes place through reflection and the balancing of this rule against other rules. On this subject Holstein (1976) ascertained that taking part in value discussions is the best way of advancing to a higher moral stage. To sensitize the trainees to normative matters and at the same time to stimulate them in the direction of Stage 4, we made them aware of their own value hierarchies and that of the firm; this led to lively and controversial discussions about values. The sensitization to values was also expected to help the trainees relate more consciously to values when involved in discussions that they perceive as meaningful and are able to account for. Furthermore, material and ideal values were contrasted with each other–as in the question: "What is more important: money or health?"–because arguments at Stage 4 and 5 are based on ideal rather than material values. We took special care to elaborate, with considerable detail, the value "fairness," since a sense of fairness is one of the main goals of moral development. But the implicit values had first to be ascertained and then analyzed. By playing the game "Starpower," in which an exchange was made between different groups (at the end of the game one group had everything and the other had nothing, and the group that had everything could make the rules for the rest of the game), we were able to precipitate a discussion about the nature of fair distribution.

The fourth goal of learning, namely, *promotion of empathy, tolerance, and openness toward others,* was an underlying motif throughout the week, with the discussion leaders instructed to be sure that certain rules of discussion were observed. Observance of these rules helped create a positive atmosphere for working. Roughly speaking, the rules concerned the following practices: standing up for one's own opinion, keeping to the subject, speaking in the first person if possible, giving "I" messages instead of "you" messages, listening actively and with concentration, respecting other opinions, and letting others talk without interruption, except to ask for clarification on points not understood.

These discussion rules helped create a constructive and relaxed atmosphere for talking, which is not surprising in view of studies (e.g., Johnson & Johnson, 1979) showing that destructive discussions impede a positive development. In our intervention, the discussion rules also led individual trainees to express their opinions no matter what the others thought about a particular topic. Being allowed to express one's opinion in front of a group leads to greater autonomy, a condition which, according to Kohlberg, is an absolute prerequisite to creating an atmosphere of fairness. A particularly important issue was tolerance for other opinions and persons. In complex questions concerning values, there were often differences of opinion remaining at the end of a discussion (e.g., which ideology, socialism or capitalism, is better). Social life, however, is made possible only by mutual acceptance. Observing the above-mentioned discussion and tolerance rules forced trainers and trainees to enter into a discourse in which not the social position but the human element of the interaction was placed in the foreground. The trainer learned that a genuine discussion did not lessen his authority, and the trainee learned that openness and trust cannot be misused without making the interaction suffer. A free and tolerant interaction was never fully assured. It had to be recreated every day. The danger that the interaction would fall apart due to unanticipated conflicts was never completely eliminated.

SOME IMPRESSIONS AND EXAMPLES

At the beginning the trainees were very skeptical about the course. Not until the second or third day was there a positive atmosphere. The increased mutual trust, the increasingly positive atmosphere, and the increased interest were illustrated in three episodes. At the end of the second day, two trainees said they had to speak to us. They asked whether all the teachers, trainers, and supervisors had reached the highest stage of moral judgment and whether we could talk more about the morals in the bank as a whole. On the third day a group of trainees wanted to talk to the training directors, because there was no time available to apply what they had learned and old conflicts had to be set aside. In the discussion, the rules of the transactive operational dialogue described by Berkowitz (1981) were applied, i.e., the trainees tried to repeat what was said, to reconstruct it, and to put themselves at the same time in the role of the other. At the end of the very positive discussion, one trainee saw the director for the first time as a person rather than as a teacher.

On the whole, the intervention was very well received by the trainees: 94% felt that courses like this should take place in a series on successive days; 98% thought that discussion rules were essential for an orderly group discussion; 98% said they actively participated and 98% felt they had expressed their opinions openly; 92% thought they had been emotionally engaged in the discussions, and 90% said they had made an effort to fill out the working sheets and tests. When we asked what they thought the effects of the courses were, they consistently gave positive answers (Table 1). It was striking, however, that the values noticeably diminished after half a year, which suggests that interventions should be repeated at regular intervals.

Our example of the thin line phenomenon is especially instructive. After having introduced Kohlberg's stages of moral development to all the bank trainers, we were told by one that he could not conceive how the system of the bank could be developed beyond Stage 2, and that therefore socialization of trainees could not go beyond Stage 2 socialization. This comment started a lively discussion among the trainers. Similarly, the trainees compared the hierarchical system of the bank with the actual competences of persons in this occupation, concluding that the gap between position and competence remained unbridged.

These impressions and episodes raise the question of whether the intervention may have "impaired" the functioning of the bank, in the sense of having called fixed positions into question. This question can be answered only in principle: latent social rules and moral standards can be accepted by the individual–without losing his identity– only if he or she can gain a meaningful relationship to them through practical reasoning. The adolescent is not simply to accept the present state of affairs, but is to develop further, and to gain insight into rules and the justifications behind them. The degree to which this can be done is, of course, limited by the individual's cognitive-moral development (Stages 2 and 3). Nevertheless, within these limits we aimed at fostering such development.

Table 1

Subjective Judgments about the Effects of the Course

In comparison to the time before the course, I think . . .	Percentage of Agreement	
	At the end	Six months later
1. I can discuss better.	96	82
2. I can listen to others better in a discussion.	96	82
3. I am more able to give reasons for my opinion in difficult situations.	96	75
4. I can think over my decisions in difficult situations more thoroughly.	96	60
5. I can better balance various arguments against each other.	96	60
6. I can express my views with less inhibitions.	96	69
7. I will reflect more intensively about my decisions and deeds.	94	82
8. I am better able to solve personal conflicts.	88	72
9. I can better take into consideration various interests and points of view.	98	82
10. I can empathize better with others.	94	69
11. I will reflect more about social problems.	92	53
12. I got to know my fellow trainees better.	100	91

EMPIRICAL FINDINGS

Enlarging the Scope of the Problem

We expected that the experimental groups would bring up a wider variety of moral topics in the discussion of social and moral dilemmas than would the other trainees, who were not exposed to the course. In the discussion of various dilemmas during the course, the most diverse topics were brought up. These topics were meant to influence the argumentation; however, the argumentation always led to a discussion of the company's norms and values so that more complex reasoning processes could develop. To test the thesis, data were used from Hinder's test for judgment consistency and from interviews, as discussed below.[3]

Table 2 shows that the experimental groups actually did discuss more topics. It is also true that the types of reasoning increased in the control group, but the increase in the course group was clearly greater. The mutual effect of group and treatment, which is the point here, is also statistically significant. It should be mentioned that this result cannot be attributed simply to speaking more, since the control group was no different from the experimental groups in the length and extent of its statements.

Table 2

Number of Moral Topics Mentioned in Reasoning Before and After Intervention: Means (x) and Standard Deviations (s)

	Intervention Group ($n = 38$)		Control Group ($n = 18$)	
	x	s	x	s
Before:	*9.4*	2.2	*9.8*	2.7
After:	*12.1*	3.2	*10.4*	2.7

Note: Test of group $\times$ time interaction: $t_{54} = 2.10, p = 0.05$.

Recognizing Conflicts

We expected that the trainees in the intervention group would be better able to determine the moral issues involved in dilemmas presented to them than would the trainees who had not participated in the courses. Through the course work, trainees were to be sensitized to the central values of a dilemma. We did not conduct special exercises in determining conflicting issues. We expected, however, that by discussing moral dilemmas (and particularly dilemmas which concerned the company) they would acquire the ability to recognize moral issues in a dilemma situation. To test the hypothesis, we counted the number of moral issues spontaneously named in the interview about Kohlberg's Heinz Dilemma and about the Bank Dilemma mentioned above.

The trainees in the experimental groups determined the conflicting issues significantly better than did the trainees in the control group (Table 3). The answers from the experimental group were clearer and referred more unequivocally to experience gained in the course. The trainees in the experimental group learned how to analyze a social and moral problem at their place of work. The open discussion about latent norms and norm conflicts seems to have created the friction and heat energy needed to set off learning processes.

Table 3

Number of Moral Issues Named Before and After Intervention: Means (x) and Standard Deviations (s)

	Intervention Group (*n* = 38)		Control Group (*n* = 18)	
	x	s	x	s
Before:	*1.6*	0.98	*1.8*	0.87
After:	*3.1*	0.75	*2.0*	0.99

Note: Group × time interaction: t_{54} = 5.1, p = 0.001.

Value Preferences

As we mentioned, one of the goals of our intervention was to make trainees more cognizant of ideal values, especially those relating to the firm. They made a list of the kinds of values that seemed important to them. A maximum of 17 items were named. On the average the intervention group listed 12 values, the control group 11. Later the trainees listed in order of importance the 5 values most important to them. As can be seen from Figure 1, several values are constantly rated high–above all, the values "love" and "friendship." Moreover, a number of interesting changes developed during the course. In the course group, several of the things which were rated high at the beginning, such as sport, friends, money, and leisure time, were eliminated by the end of the intervention; in their place appeared tolerance, health, self-confidence, and family.

In contrast, we did not find in the control group such important changes in individual value hierarchies, though there were some changes in the ranking order. It seems that the social intercourse, which was influenced by the discussion rules and the course instructor's behavior, had an influence on the trainee's value concepts. It is characteristic that the value "tolerance" was never spoken of explicitly. But the trainees apparently learned to appreciate the instructor's influence in getting them to accept the rules of discussion, to consider a wide variety of opinions, and to express their own opinions openly. It is gratifying that six months after the course, this

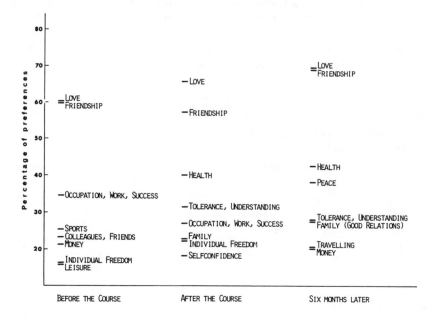

Figure 1. Value-Preferences: Percentages of Respondents Who Ranked the Value Among the Five Most Important Ones Before the Intervention, Immediately After, and Later

value was still esteemed. The value "health" also gained importance after the intervention and was still considered very important by the trainees six months after the end of the course. This value actually turned out to be very important in all the discussions about values. The value "peace" probably gained importance six months later under the influence of the demonstration for peace which took place during the experiment.

Further confirmation and clarification with regard to these socio-political values can be found in the three subtests of our questionnaire:[4]

- *Social Commitment.* The desire for changes in various social institutions to attain better social living conditions
- *Democratic Values.* Political values which are important in a democracy; values which are aspired to in a democracy
- *Tolerance and Understanding.* The willingness to accept and listen to contrary opinions.

According to our hypothesis, there should have been a greater increase in the preference for such items in the experimental group than in the control group. Indeed, we have found in all three subtests a significant increase in the intervention group as it is compared to the other group (Table 4).

Table 4

**Socio-Political Values Before and After Intervention:
Means (x) and Standard Deviation (s)**

	Intervention Group		Control Group		t-values
	x	s	x	s	
Social Commitment					
Before:	*29.2*	5.2	*31.0*	5.0	$t_{60} = 2.14^*$
After:	*30.5*	4.9	*29.0*	5.9	
Democratic Values					
Before:	*35.8*	5.2	*37.9*	5.6	$t_{59} = 2.50^{**}$
After:	*38.5*	4.2	*38.5*	4.0	
Tolerance and Understanding					
Before:	*10.6*	1.9	*11.2*	1.5	$t_{61} = 2.52^{**}$
After:	*11.6*	1.5	*11.1*	1.6	

Note: Group × time interaction effects: $^*p = 0.05$. $^{**}p = 0.01$.

Working Atmosphere

Another hypothesis of this study was that after an initial period an improvement in the working atmosphere will take place in the course groups. The discussion leaders and group leaders noticed this improvement daily. Their subjective impression was confirmed by empirical analysis. Every day the trainees filled out a daily evaluation form which contained the same questions each time. These questions referred to how they felt, the effectiveness of what they had learned, and their personal commitment. As Table 5 shows, the atmosphere clearly changed from day to day. It seems that the model problem-solving of real conflicts was highly appreciated and had a positive effect on the atmosphere. However, the good atmosphere did not come about by the course instructor's agreeing to the trainees' demands simply in order to please them. Conflicts that arose were discussed openly between instructors and trainees and a consensus was sought.

Table 5

Subjects' Daily Evaluations of the Two Courses:
Means (x) and Standard Deviations (s)

	Intervention Group		Control Group	
	x	s	x	s
Monday:	17.0	1.7	16.7	2.8
Tuesday:	19.2	3.0	16.7	2.1
Wednesday:	20.0	3.9	20.7	1.8
Thursday:	20.5	2.1	21.7	1.6

Note: Group × time interaction effects: $*p = 0.05. **p = 0.01$.

Moral-Cognitive Development

Our initial expectation was that the conditions of social interaction would improve after a week's intervention, but not in such a way as to affect the level of moral-cognitive development to any noticeable extent. However, we did employ three instruments to measure any such changes as might occur. These were the *Moralisches Urteil Test* (MUT; Moral Judgment Test) by Lind (see Lind & Wakenhut, in this volume), whose theoretical validity had already been demonstrated in several studies, and two newly developed instruments of our own, the *Urteilskonsistenz Test* (UKT; Judgment Consistency Test) by Hinder (see Hinder & Kanig, 1981), and a brief open interview procedure incorporating the Heinz Dilemma by Kohlberg and the Bank Dilemma. As it turned out, the results from the MUT and the UKT (but not those from the interview) show that the pedagogical intervention had a significant effect. The trainees learned from the course to think morally in a more differentiated way.

SUMMARY

Our basic concern was with the concept of development as the goal of education. Although the ultimate goal was to increase competence in moral judgment, the specific concern in the pedagogical experiment under consideration was to promote the conditions for it, i.e., to promote those particular abilities and attitudes of the trainees that may be essential to cognitive and moral development. The central point was to change the thin line between education and disruption from a threat to an opportunity. By deliberately including in the discussion the corporate structure, i.e., the bank, we provided the basic material for the intervention. Two aspects were of great importance. First, the intervention was set up so that the adolescents themselves were part of the intervening environment, a point that was explicitly stated in the courses (see Noack & Silbereisen, 1982, pp. 3ff). Second, the environment, i.e., the latent interaction structures, social rules, and usual standards were generally untouched. We wanted to use this environment and its conflicts as a means of improving learning. This implies problems. The term "thin line phenomenon" refers to the delicate balance that must be preserved in an intervention program such as ours, which involves an intrusion into the interior of the company and open discussion of impending conflicts. Therefore, our introduction of our project to those in charge aimed at lessening any fear on their part that we would disrupt the working climate without producing anything fruitful. They would have been happier if the content of the discussion had to do with issues arising from the outside and not from within the company itself. Consequently, it proved advantageous to start out by discussing "neutral" problems and to take up the social rules and moral standards of the company later.

The findings of our intervention experiment can be summarized in the following way. Discussion about the important values, role playing (trainer-trainee in various situations of conflict), and the analysis of values in various dilemmas which concern the company as well as other areas of life, all lead to more importance being placed on those values which stimulate responsibility to the company as well as to family and society. Thus, really to "take hold of" or "critically" analyze and illuminate the values of the bank, the family, and society does not serve to destroy them: rather it is a first step in the direction of assuming responsibility, having a sense of the whole, and bringing about an understanding of ideal values. All of these qualities are basically real features of Stage 4 of moral development.

Discussing "sacred" values and thereby getting a feel for their real function does not lead to the system's disruption, but rather to a larger overview and to the setting aside of one's own particular interests. Perhaps the thin line phenomenon is best expressed in a report by one of the group leaders (Karlen, 1981). She wrote:

> Without a doubt our course brought new experiences to most of the trainees, such as a non-hierarchical, partner-relationship to "persons of authority," minimal constraints, and the possibility of discussing personal problems and of getting to know fellow trainees better.
>
> The fact that we conducted the course in the bank's training center had advantages and disadvantages. I had the impression that a link with everyday life could be better assured there than elsewhere. On the other hand, a certain restriction of freedom of action was present, because trainees were in a marked dependency relationship to their work and training. The trainees were completely aware of that and let me feel a certain anxiety and distrust in several situations. (p. 15)

This study has strengthened our belief that adolescent development can be understood and promoted only in relation to the work world in which adolescents such as the bank trainees are socialized and grow into their occupation. It can be an advantage that the contents of the course are neutral at the beginning because the dilemmas are general, as compared to the occupational surroundings, and only gradually do the topics of conversation turn to those interactional patterns, social rules, and moral standards which are regarded as indigenous to the company. We do not believe it suffices to change the social and structural conditions of life, nor that moral education becomes unnecessary (see Simpson 1983, p. 209). But it would also be wrong to assume that development takes place on its own, by individual reasoning about socially sterile dilemmas. A dialectical link is necessary: interaction between the life-world and the individual must take place through discourse which recognizes the need for action, respects the seriousness of the situation, and implies understanding and change as its foremost goal.

NOTES

1. The term "apprentice" refers to a trainee who receives three or four years of occupational education in a company and trade school (*Berufsschule*).
2. The intervention was part of the HASMU research project, which was financially supported by the Schweizer Nationalfonds. In addition

to the authors, Guntram Kanig, Eugen Hinder, and Georg Lind have collaborated in this research project.

3. Some of the findings reported here have been published by Oser and Schläfli (1985).

4. The scales were derived through factor analysis from a longer questionnaire which we have developed, concerning diverse attitudinal domains.

An earlier version of this essay appeared as "Das moralische Grenzgänger-Syndrom," published in Oerter (1985). Permission by the Chemie Verlag, Weinheim, to revise that essay for the present volume is gratefully acknowledged.

Attitude Change or Cognitive-Moral Development?

How to Conceive of Socialization at the University

Georg Lind

There is a gap between the expectations concerning the socialization effects of the university and the empirical findings. On the basis of common sense, many people would expect education at a university or college (these terms are interchangeable in this essay) to "make a difference," not only in regard to specialized vocational skills but also generally, in regard to such supra-vocational "skills" as critical thinking, judgment ability, and social responsibility. Contrary to this normatively charged expectation, however, some researchers have concluded that university socialization has *no* effect on such skills, or at least no general and lasting effect.[1]

Two basically different explanations for this gap are suggested: Either university education actually fails to reach its proclaimed aims, or the "university-makes-no-difference" finding is due to our inability to actually "see" those supra-vocational effects, i.e., it results from shortcomings of the concepts and instruments employed in the studies on which that finding is based. The first explanation can be contested only indirectly, e.g., by providing a measurement methodology which improves our ability to assess the effects of socialization. If the results remain the same, we would then have to accept as a matter of fact that university education fails to achieve its aims. However, if we could demonstrate a general democratizing effect of university education by using better methods, we could refute the implicit assumptions of the research methods which have produced these "no-difference" findings.

In this paper I shall try to show that it is indeed the case that the concepts of *attitude* and *attitude change*, which were the core concepts of the impact-of-college research, have been defined too narrowly to permit an adequate assessment of such effects of university education. To be sure, the development of classical attitude tests represented a major step forward in social research (see, for example,

Feldman and Newcomb, 1970; Cloetta, 1975), primarily because, in comparison to case study methods, such tests are more transparent and more applicable to large scale surveys. This implies that they are objective and can easily be criticized and improved. However, the classical concepts of attitude and attitude change limit the possible outcomes of socialization in two ways: (1) in regard to the evaluative aspect of attitudes, and (2) in regard to those attitudes which differentiate among persons. In doing so, classical attitude research ignores a central aspect of educational outcomes, namely, the cognitive aspect of attitudes and its structural transformation. Consequently, this approach reduces the process of socialization to *changes* in affective magnitudes. This self-confinement also seems responsible for the fact that the process of socialization is often perceived only under the narrow categories of "adaptation" and "deviation."

The cognitive-developmental approach (cf. Kohlberg, 1973a; Perry, 1970) offers a conceptual and methodological alternative for higher education research. From this point of view, the general democratizing effect of university education is conceived of, and assessed as, the development of both affective *and* cognitive aspects of personality. Accordingly, the effects of socialization are not reduced to changes in affective magnitudes but are construed as more complex processes of integration and differentiation. By viewing the process of socialization through the wider conceptual lens of cognitive developmental theory, we are able to see effects of university education which have hitherto been invisible to the researcher. From this point of view, even using classical attitude research techniques, we have obtained indications of a sequential, irreversible development of supra-vocational competences in university students. These show that, contrary to the findings of most classical attitude research, university education in fact facilitates, or even stimulates, the development of moral and democratic competences among students in general.

SOCIALIZATION AS ATTITUDE CHANGE

Attitudes in Impact-of-College Research

Until recently, the concept of attitude has predominated in research on the effects of university socialization (cf. Jacob, 1957; Newcomb, 1957; Sanford, 1962; Feldman & Newcomb, 1970; Dressel &

Mayhew, 1971; Lenning et al., 1974; Cloetta, 1975; Dann et al., 1978; Huber & Vogel, 1984). This proposition is not invalidated by the fact that only a few studies contain an explicit definition of their research subject. The theoretical assumptions of these studies can be perceived in their concrete research methods, which define in operational terms the constructs being employed. There are many variants in research methods. However, there are some core features of attitude testing which are common to nearly all studies and which are based on classical testing theory. This makes it possible to speak of a unique paradigm: the "classical attitude concept" (cf. Scott, 1968; Fishbein & Ajzen, 1975). As we will see below, the concept and its measurement contain certain psychological assumptions about the nature of the human mind. Thus, the central question is whether these assumptions are compatible with the research hypotheses which they are being used to test.

Hypotheses of Attitude Research

One major focus of research into university socialization deals with its hypothesized democratizing effect, i.e., with the democratic personality it is supposed to shape. This includes attributes such as innovative competence (liberalism), critical judgment ability, moral autonomy, willingness to assume social responsibility, and general liberal attitudes. Of particular interest in research has been the dimension of "conservatism," which is considered a kind of antipode to the democratic attitudes (liberalism) expected of university and college graduates (cf. Newcomb, 1957; Cloetta, 1975). The hypothesis to be tested is: Is the university capable of instilling democratic attitudes in the student? Or is it appropriate to resign ourselves to the conclusion that the university has no, or no lasting, influence on attitude change?

Results of Attitude Research

Until now the research results have seemed surprisingly clear–and negative. When asked what college does for the individual, the college researcher Theodore Newcomb (1974) answered: "Frankly, very little that is demonstrable" (p. 73). The findings of impact-of-college research confirm this conclusion in that they are concerned with the prediction of the non-vocational effects of college education. With only a few exceptions, research either does not show any of the anticipated attitude changes, or it shows that such changes are revised at the end of college or in the initial phase of the individual's professional life. Even Jacob (1957), in his highly regarded summary of a quarter-century of attitude research, ascertained that college had *no* significant impact on attitude change. Feldman and Newcomb (1970), after studying extensive research, concluded that college effects very little change in attitudes and values, or if there is a change, it occurs in a very specific manner. They reported varying outcomes, depending on the college attended, subject of study, and student characteristics, but one can hardly speak of a general, encompassing effect produced by college education.

If one considers in particular the democratizing effect, some consistent changes were observed in the first years of study. According to Feldman and Newcomb (1970) and other surveys in this field, there is a slight but general turning away from conservative, authoritarian, nondemocratic attitudes during the college years.[2] This trend could also be shown in a longitudinal study carried out by the research project "Teachers' Attitudes" (Cloetta, 1975; Dann et al., 1978). In this excellently designed research, many new insights into the process and conditions of socialization could be gained, demonstrating that, at least in regard to profession-related attitudes, higher education has some general and stable effects. But in regard to more general conservative attitudes, the initial trend in the liberal direction is reversed. The democratizing effect abates again at the end of college and in the initial phase of work. The authors refer to a "practice shock," which cancels the effect of college.[3] This seems to prove that students' attitudes do not, as Newcomb (1974) had expected, stabilize, but instead adapt to the particular climate of opinion in the environment: that is, attitudes appear to be ephemeral, fleeting phenomena in the course of development.

Problems of Interpretation

Must we therefore repudiate the idea that college graduates gain supra-vocational abilities? Are the findings so evident that one can consider colleges and universities ineffective in fostering democratic competences? We will see that these questions cannot be answered with an unambiguous "yes." First of all, these findings are influenced by the methods used and hence are theory-impregnated interpretations which are debatable. Of course, these findings are not produced completely independent of reality, but are constrained by the methods of assessment and data evaluation. Therefore, the fact

that no effect of higher education was ascertained does not necessarily mean that no effect exists.

Indeed the findings of attitude research give rise to several problems of interpretation. Concept and measurement of attitudes have
long been criticized (cf. Converse, 1970; Deutscher, 1973; Meinefeld,
1977). There have been attempts to discover a satisfactory explanation for empirical findings by introducing auxiliary assumptions
without abandoning the classical attitude paradigm. As far as I can
see, however, most of these attempts have created new, unsolved
problems. For example, to solve the reliability-change dilemma, it
was suggested that we require not only the stability of attitude scores
(more exactly: their *rank order* for all persons in a group studied),
but also the stability of change rates (i.e., to determine "reliable"
types of changes). However, since these two demands contradict each
other, attitude scales that meet the new criterion would have to be
eliminated according to the old criterion, and vice versa. This
dilemma is especially evident in the conservatism scores which have a
comparatively high level of *rank reliability*, but whose *reliability of
change* is, on the average, close to zero (Hohner & Dann, 1978; see
Figure 3 below).[4]

Equally paradoxical are practical suggestions associated with this
interpretative framework. If we retains the attitude paradigm, we
have to demand that the socialisand adapt to democratic values *and*
at the same time resist them. Not surprisingly, many authors evade
normative questions and are reluctant to determine precisely the
direction and intensity of the attitudes most compatible with the goal
of socialization. To understand these paradoxes and ambiguities, it
seems necessary to revisit the classical concept and method of attitude research. (For a discussion of these problems of interpretation
and valuation, see Cloetta, 1975, pp. 180ff.; Dann et al., 1978, p. 90;
Fend, 1971).

Critique of Attitude Concept and Measurement

It is surprising that many authors neglect to define explicitly the
term "attitude" in order to go on to questions concerning the origin
of, and changes in, attitudes. Feldman and Newcomb (1970) discuss
the concept of attitude only tangentially, although their reports
contain almost exclusively studies based on the classical attitude
paradigm. Some, like the authors of the "Teachers' Attitudes" study
who refer to Kelman's (1974) definition of attitudes, outline a
complex conceptual framework which, however, may not be fully

compatible with the classical research methodology they actually use. The closest we have come to a definition has been in methodological treatments of attitude measurement (cf. Thurstone, 1931; Scott, 1968; Dawes, 1972). Of course, almost all the studies use the same kind of attitude tests and hence the same implicit definition of attitudes. This more or less implicit definition and its limitations–but not the intentions and allegations that accompany them–will be examined here.

An "attitude" is defined as the "degree of positive or negative affect associated with some psychological object" (Thurstone, 1931). This definition is the starting point and a basic part of most methods of attitude measurement (Scott, 1968), even if some researchers go beyond it to include purely descriptive statements, as well as affective ones, in their attitude scales.[5] Thus, in classical terms attitudes are distinguished solely by their direction and intensity. This creates a problem: if attitudes must be either positive or negative, no conceptual tool is available for distinguishing among average, neutral, or other cognitively differentiated attitudes. When a person gets a medium score on an attitude scale, its significance must remain ambiguous in that such a score can mean that he or she has either (1) no attitude, (2) a conflicting attitude, or (3) a highly differentiated attitude (cf. Shaw & Wright, 1967, pp. 7ff; Converse, 1970). Neutral answers are considered uninteresting[6] or expressive of a tendency on the part of the subject to hide his or her attitude. Hence, a researcher working within the framework of this paradigm must attempt to force the subjects to express an attitude through the use of "forced choice items."

Furthermore, in attitude testing it is assumed that the affective tendencies under investigation are in one way or another *characteristic of everyone*. Classical attitude measurement is based on tests of groups of people, not of individuals. A "reliable" and "valid" attitude measurement is spoken of only when the subjects of a particular group under study meet two requirements. First of all, the subjects must differ considerably from one another regarding the direction and intensity of this attitude: i.e., "the object of attitude must be controversial in the investigated group" (Cloetta, 1975, p. 37).[7] At the same time, however, the subjects must be similar to one another in regard to their attitude *structure*, i.e., the particular attitude must be present in all persons and must determine the same set of responses to the same degree. A violation of any of these assumptions leads to charges that the research instrument is "unreliable" and "invalid." Thus paradoxically, in the moment in which the group's attitudes become either similar in direction and intensity or structurally heterogeneous, the particular "attitude" disappears or becomes inaccessible. Attitudes common to all members of a group and attitudes associated with individually varying forms of cognitive structure are eliminated from the analysis, supposedly on the grounds of purely methodological criteria, even though these attitudes are essential to the socialization process (cf. Cloetta, 1975, p. 39; Geulen, 1975, p. 86; Portele, 1975b, p. 98).

However, in focusing on the affective components of attitudes–i.e., on their direction and intensity–psychology limits itself to cases in which the attitude in question is already completely integrated but is at the same time not yet differentiated according to higher values and ideas. This occurs rarely and is therefore of only limited interest. If taken seriously, these assumptions would prevent all attitudes from being tested, since there is virtually no instrument of attitude measurement that achieves "reliability" or "validity" indexes which agree with the basic model. Moreover, because they are restricted to affective aspects, the measured effects of socialization are limited to simple, one-dimensional changes in the affective components of attitudes. Even in multi-component theories of attitude (for example, see Rosenberg & Hovland, 1963), the structural aspect of the individual behavior is eliminated and only structural properties of the correlations *among* persons are considered. This elimination reduces the process of university socialization to a mere contrast between conformity with given norms and deviation from them. It conflicts with the notion of socialization as an

> active process, [which] differs from that widespread concept that uses as its basic terms the opposites "adaptation" and "deviation" . . . . Although it is stressed in the theoretical development of these terms, because its concern is with descriptive categories free of values "deviation" is regarded as socialization which has failed and thus is, subsequently, once again excluded from the concept. (Zentrum I, 1973, p. 852)

What can be done? If one keeps the attitude paradigm, one could simply "admit nonconformist behavior [as] a necessary element of socialization" (Zentrum I, 1973, p. 852). That would necessarily lead to successful socialization being defined both as adaptation and as deviation, and would thus broaden the realm of desirable educational effects so much that only trivial expectations could be derived from it, because they would be fulfilled from the outset. However, if one defines the area of desirable socialization results as the narrow, almost imaginary margin between conformity and autonomy, then as

Fend (1971, p. 39) has pointed out, this margin becomes "very narrow," possibly too narrow to be examined empirically at all.

The dilemma of socialization research is thus laid bare: things that we can study with the concept of attitude allow socialization theory to formulate only empirically empty hypotheses, and the things we really want to examine lie outside its conceptualization. Thus, the simplicity and explicitness of the attitude concept indeed "render its inadequacies obvious" (Scott, 1968, p. 208). Its major inadequacy is its failure to account for the structural aspect of attitudes in addition to the affective aspect. This should imply that neither the behavioral structure of a particular group of subjects nor a specific kind of behavioral content (so-called "cognitive beliefs") is separate from affective content. Rather, the structural aspect refers to the relational properties of an individual's responses, properties which are ontologically inseparable from the affective aspects (Lind, 1985e).

SOCIALIZATION AS MORAL-COGNITIVE DEVELOPMENT

With their methodical elaboration of the concept of cognitive-moral development, Kohlberg, Perry, and others have introduced a new approach to research on higher education, which has served as an alternative to the classical paradigm of attitude change. The volume *The Modern American College* that appeared in 1981 is centered on the concept of development since, in the words of its editor W. Chickering, the development concept should "offer a consistent solution on the basis of the unifying idea of adult development."[8]

However, upon closer scrutiny it is evident that in the use which Chickering and his associates make of the concept of development very different and partly contradictory ideas have merged. In actuality, the concept of attitude change has been revived, as has the old concept of genetically controlled maturation, such that socialization in college is sometimes regarded as nothing more than an episode in an individual life-cycle (Chickering, 1981; Chickering & Havighurst, 1981). The effect of higher education is regarded as ephemeral in comparison to the effect of genetic determination, even if the "hard realistic requirements for effective social contribution" (Chickering, 1981, p. 9) are not overlooked. It is doubtful, however, whether the university can provide, simply by imposing those hard requirements, an "increased coherence and an enhanced sense of community" (Chickering, 1981, p. 773). The development of a sense of community and the competence to cope with socio-moral conflicts will not result simply from hard requirements.

We are provided with a considerably different use of the term "development" in the work of Piaget and Kohlberg, which offers an alternative conceptual and methodological framework for the study of socialization processes in the following respects:

Individuality. The subject of the analysis of moral competence is above all the individual, as well as the structure of his behavior and judgment, and not a comparison of the isolated character variables of persons in a group. Thus the assessment methods which are based on this approach ensure that the traits of an individual are defined independently of other individuals in a group.

Manifest Judgment Behavior. The existence of moral attitudes is tested in the manifest structure of a person's judgment behavior. Competence in moral judgment is "a construct rather than an inference, and is warranted only on the grounds of 'intelligible' ordering of the manifest items" (Kohlberg, 1979, p. 14; see also Lind & Wakenhut, in this volume).

Affect and Cognition. In contrast to the classical theory of attitude and the multi-component theory of attitude, the cognitive theory of development insists that "a moral act or attitude cannot be defined either by purely 'cognitive' or by purely 'motivational' criteria" (Kohlberg, 1958, p. 16). Incomplete integration of behavior in a normative orientation and a highly differentiated value posture are not, as in the attitude paradigm, indiscriminately designated as "inconsistencies." Accordingly, we do not attribute "unreliability" to the measuring instrument. Instead we understand it to be at least partly an expression of the cognitive aspect of a judgment behavior (cf. Lind, 1985a).

Development. With the dual concept of affective-cognitive personality traits, it is possible to conceptualize socialization within the wider framework of a developmental theory. "Development" is defined as "changes in the form of reorganization of responses over time as contrasted with the change in the strength or accuracy of the responses . . . . Thus, the developmentalist focuses upon structural changes in the response" (Zigler, 1963, p. 345). In regard to the area of social-moral abilities, development means structural change in the individual's moral-cognitive system.

This wider concept of structural change allows us to present the role of the university in the educational process in a more adequate way. Socialization is not, as the theories of adaptation assume, simply a change in behavior due to altered environmental conditions, but a differentiation and integration of attitudes and norms as a consequence of the "*interaction* between the structure of the organism and the structure of environment" (Kohlberg, 1969, p. 348).

REVIEW OF EMPIRICAL FINDINGS

The two above-mentioned paradigms of simple "change" and structural "development" can be compared empirically in regard to different hypotheses about the course and result of university socialization. As we have seen, the most important difference consists in the fact that, in addition to a change in direction and intensity, development also implies a transformation of an individual's attitude system. Development is thus to be regarded as an integral, two-dimensional change that cannot be reduced to only one dimension (or to two ontologically separate dimensions) of change without the loss of essential information.

The position of development theory can be illustrated by the concept of the "conservative attitude," which as we noted above is generally viewed as a central indicator of the democratizing effect of college education. Whereas the classical attitude theory depicts socialization one-dimensionally as the acquisition and loss of "affective quantities" in time, the developmental model also takes into account the cognitive-structural dimension. In such a two-dimensional developmental model, phases of *integration* and *differentiation* can also be distinguished, as can changes in direction and intensity.

Using this conceptual framework, we may hypothesize that people's attitudes undergo a developmental process. As long as the individual has not yet (even unconsciously) developed a concept of "conservatism," he or she will not be able to respond consistently to conservative or progressive statements. The scientifically construed concept of "conservatism" is not yet "represented" in the individual and thus is not measurable by a conservatism scale. Only as the person becomes more and more acquainted with this concept will he or she respond with increasing consistency (whether positively or negatively) to conservative statements–something that we call the "phase of integration." After this takes place, the attitude of conservatism will become measurable.

In a second phase, the same statements are no longer judged solely according to this one category, but also in regard to other judgment criteria which compete with it or even cancel it. In this phase of attitude *differentiation,* we can observe an increasing preoccupation with context, which leads to a greater distrust of general statements ("slogans"). On the surface, i.e., in regard to the criteria of classical attitude testing, the attitude behavior again becomes "inconsistent" or "unreliable" and thus non-measurable. However, whereas in the beginning inconsistency means lack of judgment competence, it can later be evidence of a highly developed cognitive structure. This "two-sided" development process of integration and differentiation implied by cognitive-developmental theory is contrasted with the "one-sided" process of change included in the two-dimensional process diagram of Figure 1.

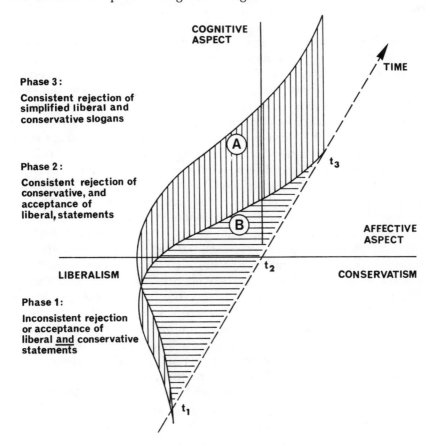

Figure 1. Change and Development: Projection of Affective-Cognitive Development onto (a) a Two-Dimensional, and (b) a Three-Dimensional Space of Change

We cannot yet present a crucial experiment which would clearly demonstrate the superiority of one paradigm over the other, but we expect to obtain firm evidence for one or the other based on findings from the longitudinal studies which we are at present carrying out in order to clarify this question. However, the research that has already been carried out offers important indications which make possible an empirical contrast of the two paradigms. Three sources are at our disposal: (1) traditional attitude studies, insofar as their results indicate that cognitive processes are involved in socialization, (2) cognitive-developmental research by Kohlberg and his collaborators, and (3) the initial findings of our own ongoing study.

The Cognitive Process of Integration

(1) Classical research on attitudes provides findings for a comparison only conditionally, as it usually treats behavior in which the cognitive developmental aspect is documented as a measurement error. Therefore, references can best be found in irregularities and "errors" insofar as they are treated at all. In this respect, two studies of university socialization are of particular interest: the well-known Bennington study by Newcomb and the large-scale longitudinal study of student teachers conducted by Dann, Cloetta, and their associates. These two studies illustrate the best use of the attitude paradigm, and also, because of their concern with the overarching democratizing effects of university education, are directly comparable in content with the cognitive-moral development model.

One of the first indications that cognitive processes played a role here was that even after very elaborate measures were taken to construct "consistent" attitude scales, it was still not possible to construct a scale in which the great majority of persons consistently answered either "liberal" or "conservative." This problem is not unusual for attitude research. However, it means that the main condition for the use of the classical notion of attitude is violated, i.e., the condition which requires that the "object of the attitude . . . in the persons questioned (1) is represented, and (2) is affectively cathected" (Cloetta, 1975, p. 38).

The problem becomes even clearer if one uses attitude scales to analyze the individual response pattern of those questioned. If one supposes that the questions on a scale are all "items in the same dimension" (Dann et al., 1978, p. 87), one should expect all items to be consistent, i.e., to be answered in accordance with the particular attitude; for example, for all the "conservative" persons, the "conservative" attitude statements are consistently answered positively and the "liberal" always negatively. The usual way to fulfill this expectation is to define attitude as the mean value and the deviation from it as "error probabilities" (see Lazarsfeld, 1959; Fischer, 1974), but this definition presupposes that "error" is precisely defined and does not render the concept of attitude vague and inaccessible.

To clarify this last point, we must consider the consistency with which subjects choose the "liberal" or the "conservative" side of the response to the items on a conservatism scale. This procedure seems legitimate if, as is ideally assumed, the items are exact replications of one another and, therefore, have identical means. We should note that the Likert method of scaling disregards this assumption, although it cannot eliminate it completely. In Figure 2, on the left, two ideal distributions of answer consistencies for the conservatism scale are shown: the theoretical distribution of complete consistent answers (1), and, for the sake of contrast, the pure chance distribution of consistency values (2). On the right is placed the distribution of actual consistency values from high school graduates *(Abiturienten),* which is taken from our own study with the Cloetta scale (3). From this we can see that before entering university the respondents were influenced to only a slight extent by the construct "conservatism" in judging the items. The assumption that this attitude is "represented" in everyone was not fulfilled. Although the judgment behavior of the subjects definitely deviated from the pure chance distribution, only a few persons were completely oriented in their response behavior toward the attitude dimension in question. Thus, most of the subjects' answers could not be understood when assessment was based on the one-dimensional attitude concept. Obviously, their response behavior was either less integrated or more strongly differentiated than was assumed. (It is important to emphasize once more that "dimension" here means an "aspect dimension" and not a separate variable, as for example in factor analysis).

The claim that unexplained differences between subjects can be attributed not only to errors in the measuring instrument but also to differences in individual cognitive structures is supported even more strongly by longitudinal studies. If the inconsistent attitude scores were really only a function of measurement error, the relationship of systematic variance to error variance would remain stable over different measuring points in time or vary only "randomly." A closer look at the findings of the "Teachers' Attitudes" research project shows that not only do the mean scores on the attitude scale change, but the reliability and consistency values change, too, following a systematic trend which runs parallel to the process of socialization. This holds true for various indicators (see Figure 3). Although the trends are not very high, due to high values at the start, the almost perfect monotonous change in every one of these (inter-individual)

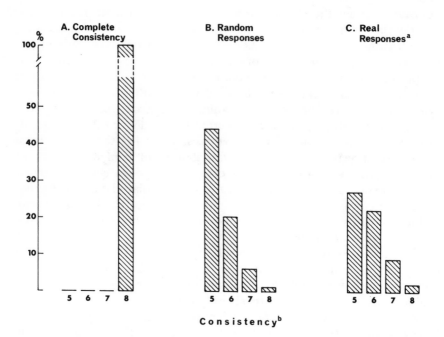

Note. High school graduates (*N* = 708). Shortened version of the MK questionnaire by Cloetta (1975). The response scales contain the category "cannot say," which was not in the original. As used here, *consistency* only refers to the number of the pure "liberal" or pure "conservative" responses.

Figure 2. Comparison of Two Theoretical Distributions of Responses (Complete Consistency, Pure Randomness) with an Empirical Response Distribution

structural values is astounding. Clearly, these findings are at odds with the classical attitude paradigm, in which these coefficients, characteristic of the measuring instrument, would be independent of whatever development tendencies were discovered. Hence, we cannot say of a test that it has "high reliability" if the concept of reliability is itself undermined by the empirical evidence. However, the cognitive-developmental theory provides us with an alternative paradigm, within which our findings can be interpreted to indicate structural changes within persons, resulting from the integration of the individual attitude systems.

(2) The findings of cognitive developmental research confirm and extend these references. In their interview study of high school and college students between the ages of 14 and 26, Kohlberg and

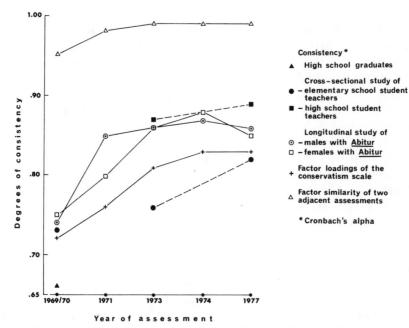

Note. The data of the high school graduates *Abitur* are from the *Forschungsgruppe Hochschulsozialisation.* All other data are from Cloetta (1975) and Hohner & Dann (1978, parts 1-3).

Figure 3. Changes in "Reliability" and Mean of Conservative Attitude Scores Before, During, and After Higher Education

Kramer (1969) established clear evidence that "there is an adult movement toward integration . . . of moral thought in its application to life" (p. 118). They observed that "the major change in moral thought past high school is a significant increase or stabilization of conventional morality of a Stage 4 variety, at the expense of preconventional stages of thought" (p. 106), and that moral development in young adults "is not only toward greater consistency of moral judgment but toward greater consistency between moral judgment and moral action" (p. 107). Hence, moral development is characterized not so much by new moral attitudes exhibited in moral discussions as by a structural process of integration of reasoning and action at new stages.

Rest (1979a, 1979b) found further evidence for this by letting subjects evaluate moral arguments in order of their importance.

Here the phenomenon of the cognitive integration of moral attitudes is shown even more clearly than in Kohlberg's interviews, in which only the frequency of reasons given is counted. Whereas at a young age the highest stages of moral judgment are already preferred, a considerable part of the integration and stabilization of this attitude does not take place until late adolescence and, in particular, during college (Rest, 1973; 1979a, pp. 133-135; 1979b, part 1, pp. 31-34). Before and during college, a relatively drastic increase takes place in the consistency of postconventional judgment preferences on different moral "issues," from 30% of postconventional answers to 50%.[9]

(3) Finally, preliminary findings from our research project on university socialization point in the same direction. To test the degree to which moral maxims were cognitively anchored, the subjects had to evaluate arguments for various decisions in moral dilemmas and were asked to address not only those arguments which supported their own opinion but also those that opposed it. By giving the subjects arguments based on opposing opinions, a cognitive threshold was created through which we could directly study the process of integrating moral attitudes during college (Lind & Wakenhut, in this volume). In an inspection of MUT data on the judgment behavior of students in professional schools, high schools, and universities, and that of scientists, a clear developmental trend could be shown (Lind, 1984a).

The Cognitive Process of Differentiation

(1) In attitude studies it is inherently difficult to find empirical evidence that this process of integrating democratic and moral attitudes really takes place, since the design of these studies and the methods of analysis dismiss signs of differentiation as signs of "unreliability." Furthermore, as I have argued above, these studies lack the methodological prerequisites necessary for investigating the cognitive-structural aspects of socialization effects. Nevertheless, some unexpected evidence that this differentiation process occurs can be found in attitude studies. For instance, Newcomb (1957) notes as a methodologically irritating effect that students in higher semesters tend more and more toward a rejection of all "conservative" and "liberal" questionnaire statements, a finding which indirectly indicates greater differentiation in their attitude structure.

(2) Direct support for this conclusion of structural differentiation can be found in the study by Fishkin et al. (1973). As these authors

show, growing rejection and critical evaluation of condensed political slogans (which are most readily associated with the dimension of "conservatism") are accompanied by a higher moral-cognitive competency. This is in line with Perry's (1970, 1981) observation that students' cognitive growth is revealed in their deviation from black and white judgments and their differentiation and reintegration of ethical reasoning (see also Murphy & Gilligan, 1980; Kitchener & King, 1981).

(3) Despite our use of different methods in the inquiry and evaluation stages, the findings from our research project and comparative research by other authors who have used the MUT or a similar instrument also support the structural differentiation thesis. Keasey's (1975) finding that differentiation of judgment behavior in relation to one's own opinion is not very advanced in young school children or in people with low general education was corroborated by Briechle (1981) and Wischka (1982). In contrast, German high school graduates *(Abiturienten)* and, in particular, university students were found to be more reflective, more critical and rational, and less bound to an opinion once held (Lind, 1984a; Schmied, 1981). However, moral-cognitive development does not stop at this point. As Figure 4 shows, scientists (in both the social and natural sciences) differentiated their judgment of arguments according to moral criteria even more than, for example, did high school graduates. This can be seen in the differences in the slope of the preference profiles of both groups.[10] However, in all the studies it was also clearly established that moral categories are not applied rigidly to all social situations without reflection, but that a differentiation is made between situations with varying moral contents (see Lind, 1985d).

CONCLUSION

The concepts of attitude and attitude change have produced in socialization research a wealth of empirical findings which cannot be neglected or regarded as irrelevant. In particular, the research project on "Teachers' Attitudes" has produced much new information which calls into question the conclusion which Newcomb has drawn from attitude research that higher education has no general effect on the development of a democratic personality. However, as I have tried to show in this chapter, students' attitudes and their development cannot be fully understood when we concentrate only on the affective aspect of attitudes, nor when we conceive their cognitive aspect as an entity that is separate from its affective

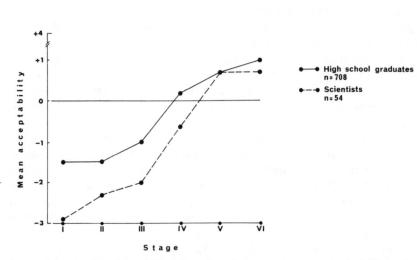

Sources: Scientists (N = 54, solid line) from Portele (personal communication). High school graduates (N = 708, dotted line), from the Forschungsgruppe Hochschulsocialisation. In both studies an older version of the MUT was used.

Figure 4. Structure of Moral Judgment of High School Graduates and Scientists

content. Hitherto supra-professional outcomes of college and university socialization—such as critical rationality, sense of responsibility, and democratic orientations—have been classified by and large as "affective" goals and contrasted with the "cognitive" goals of education, such as vocational qualifications or general belief. But, as I have argued elsewhere (see ch. 2, in this volume), we do not need to separate the two basic aspects of human behavior ontologically. So-called "affective" attitudes have their own cognitive structure, which is distinguishable but not separable from their affective contents. Thus the affective and the cognitive aspects of attitudes can be researched as a whole.

I have tried to show that this conceptual problem has significant consequences for the methods and results of socialization research. Whereas on the basis of classical attitude research—which reduces attitudes to their affective aspects—no general supra-professional outcome of higher education could be detected, the more comprehensive cognitive-structural approach makes discernible the transformation of students' personalities, as could be expected from the educational goals that the university sets for itself. The university apparently contributes its share to the evolution of the individual personality, and thus also to the evolution of social forms of existence, although this contribution may be viewed as still inadequate in view of the social problems with which the university graduates will be faced when taking over responsible positions in our society.

From this finding we can conclude that even for "initial purposes" it is not advisable to confine research to "varying degrees of favorableness and unfavorableness" and thereby disregard the structure of a person's attitudes, as certain eminent scholars have suggested (cf. Feldman & Newcomb, 1970, p. 55; Müller-Fohrbrodt & Cloetta, 1975, p. 198). We would be better advised to acknowledge the fact of structural change or development, i.e., the fact that—as Feldman and Newcomb have remarked—"there are other kinds of individual change which do not fit into [this] typology. For example, one type of change is the *reordering* by the person of value and attitude dimensions in terms of their salience or centrality to him. Also there may be other value and personality reorientations—such as the development of new frames of reference—that are not merely shifts along a given dimension" (p. 58n). Cognitive-developmental theory and research has provided methods for assessing this reordering and reorganization of individual attitude systems in the course of the socialization process, although these methods are not as clear-cut and as suitable for large scale research as are classical attitudes tests. As our own research demonstrates the assessment of structural change is not bound exclusively to interview methods but can also make use of attitude measurement, provided that it has been revised in such a way as to render the assessment of the cognitive aspect possible.

NOTES

1. Universities and other kinds of institutions of higher education (*Fachhochschulen,* etc.) are not differentiated here because in recent years they have become very much alike. For comparison, we frequently refer to college education in the United States, whose aims (general education) are more like those of German universities than are the aims of American professional schools.
2. Feldman & Newcomb, 1970, pp. 19, 99ff; see also Newcomb, 1957; Webster et al., 1962; Heist & Taylor, 1979; Trent & Medsker, 1969.
3. Müller-Fohrbrodt et al., 1978. This back-and-forth movement of attitude change has been named the *Konstanzer Wanne* (the Konstanz Dip); see Cloetta, 1975, pp. 176-177; Dann et al., 1978, pp. 37, 230; Hohner & Dann, 1978. For further studies which support these findings, see Koch, 1972, p. 135.
4. On the problem of "reliability of change" see Renn, 1973; Helmreich, 1977; Dann et al., 1978, p. 221. It seems that in the past

192   *Lind*

the psychometric and the statistical sides of the problem have not been sufficiently differentiated. "Regrettably, psychometric properties, namely reliability, have been the predominant concern in the behavioral sciences literature" (Rogosa et al., 1982, p. 726). See Möbus & Nagl, 1983, who suggest an integrated statistical model.

5. Although this affect-definition of attitudes is fundamental and accepted by most scientists, in many attitude scales we find items asking the respondent to give descriptions rather than evaluations (Cloetta, 1975, p. 43; Dann et al., 1978, pp. 368ff.). The importance of a clear distinction of Is and Ought statements in attitude research has been frequently underlined (Fishbein & Ajzen, 1975, p. 12; Triandis, 1975, pp. 4ff.; Deutscher, 1973, p. 316). Dippelhofer-Stiem (1983) has shown that this distinction is indeed of great empirical relevance when assessing the impact of the university environment on students' development.

6. For example, the committee of the American Council on Education in the Fifties explicitly stated that it was "interested only in whether or not individuals accepted or rejected items" (Dressel & Mayhew, 1971, p. 218). See also Cloetta, 1975, pp. 38f.; Müller-Fohrbrodt & Cloetta, 1975, p. 200; Dann et al., 1978, pp. 87ff.; Scott, 1968; Meinefeld, 1977, p. 190; Lippert & Wakenhut, 1978, p. 87.

7. Similarly Wilson: "Attitudes must show *variation* between individuals and between cultures, i.e., they relate to issues upon which people disagree" (1975, p. 95). This dependency of attitude or personality measurement on group or population scores is one of the main shortcomings of classical testing theory, yet most modern testing theories, have no remedy for it (Wakenhut, 1974).

8. Chickering, 1981, p. 2. For further studies on higher education in the tradition of Kohlberg and Perry, see Haan et al., 1968; Collier et al., 1974; Marton & Säljö, 1976; Parker, 1978; Rest, 1979a; Huber, 1980; Whiteley, 1980; Gilligan, 1981.

9. Rest (1979b, part 3, pp. 10, 18). These data refer to the P-score which is derived from answers to the *Defining Issues Test* (DIT). It is obtained by calculating the relative frequency of postconventional judgments (see Rest, 1979a).

10. For an interpretation of the profiles see Lind & Wakenhut (in this volume).

The research reported herein has been supported by the Deutsche Forschungsgemeinschaft as part of the ongoing longitudinal research project "University Socialization" at the University of Konstanz (see ch. 3, n. 4). I wish to thank Hanns-Dietrich Dann, Roland Wakenhut, and Thomas Wren for their comments on earlier versions of this chapter.

How Scientists Think About Science and Morality

Gerhard Portele

According to Moscovici (1973, p. xiii), *social concepts* are "cognitive systems with their own logic and language." Furthermore, they are social rather than individual concepts, in that they are determined "by a network of objective, social, and economic conditions" (Herzlich, 1975, p. 384).

For example, the social concept of "illness" is full of juridical and medical-scientific classifications (Herzlich, 1973). Since social concepts contribute to defining social groups and to rendering communication possible, they constitute the identity of the group member. Social concepts are influenced by reality; however, they are not reflections of reality but intellectual constructions, i.e., social constructions of reality. As Berger and Luckmann (1969) put it, it is through social concepts that experiences are "deciphered." To the individual the products of social concepts appear as reality, as perception-like data. "As a construction of the real the concept assumes the appearance of a perception" (Herzlich, 1975, p. 384). The research done on social concepts so far has dealt either with a scientific theory like psychoanalysis (Moscovici, 1961), or with terms like "illness" (Herzlich, 1973). These and other investigations were able to show that social concepts are specific for social groupings, that they form a coherent system, and that they are based on a "figurative scheme," all of which allows the treatment of reality in everyday life "to serve as an expression of reality and thus to shape it" (Herzlich, 1975, p. 392). The fundamental and specific function of the social concept is the regulation of behavior. "If a social representation is a 'preparation for action,' it is so because of the process of reconstruction and reconstitution of the elements in the environment" (Moscovici, 1973, xii). It is in activity that reality is constructed. It is to be assumed that scientists of different disciplines have different social concepts of science. The social concept of "science" is influenced by the subject matter of science, by the scientist's mode of activity, by the historical development of the science, and by the prevailing theory of science. It is not to be assumed that the social concept of science should be in accordance with what a theory of science reckons "science" to be. The scientists develop images of their own and other branches of science, and these images are coherent in themselves.

CONSISTENCY AND COMPLETENESS

Elsewhere (Portele, 1977, 1978) I have shown in greater detail that at least two cognitive systems are necessary for the assessment and determination of activities and their intentions. (1) The first cognitive system makes possible the decision about whether an activity is realizable, which effects it will probably have, etc. These decisions are "reality constructions" made in the course of everyday theoretical activity. (2) The second cognitive system makes possible decisions about whether an activity is permitted or even obligatory; these are moral norm systems. Like a grammar, each of the two cognitive systems has at least two necessary conditions: it must be free of contradiction, i.e., an activity may not be subjectively right and wrong (respectively permitted and forbidden) at the same time, and it must be complete, i.e., it must be possible to assess *each* appearing activity as subjectively right or wrong (respectively, as permitted or forbidden). Otherwise one cannot decide at all. A cognitive system such as a theory is free of contradiction if none of its statements can be simultaneously proven and disproven, and it is complete if, as Tarski points out, every relevant phase can be proven (Tarski, 1966, p. 144). Although it can be shown, following Gödel's theorem, that deductive systems, even non-contradictory ones, are inherently incomplete (cf. Schlegel, 1967), in practice we have to assume completeness if we want to make decisions. To return to the analogy with grammar, we may note that, even with sentences never heard before, the individual can determine whether they are right or wrong and actually produce new, correct sentences himself just because grammar is consistent and complete. This is consistent with the point I have made elsewhere (Portele, 1978), that Piaget's stages of cognitive development and Kohlberg's stages of moral development are systems of different kinds of subjective consistency and subjective completeness.

To continue this theme, we may note that Festinger's (1957) theory of dissonance is built on a notion of consistency motivation, the avoidance of psychological dissonance being nothing else but the search for psychological consistency. Similarly, White's (1959) competence motivation as well as the "intrinsic motivation" described by Portele (1975a) or Deci (1974) is best understood as motivation for completeness. The statements of the reality constructions and the statements of the moral norm system have different conceptions of psychological consistency and of psychological completeness or quasi-completeness concerning the stages of development. Hence Kohlberg has repeatedly indicated that there is a connection between cognitive development (e.g., in intelligence) and moral development in children. Regarding scientists, these considerations suggest that the different scientific disciplines will socialize them into manners of thinking specific to their discipline, creating a "habitus" specific to the discipline in the sense of Bourdieu (1979)–or, negatively expressed, a a "déformation professionelle" in the manner of thinking, e.g., "functional fixedness" (Duncker, 1935), which is again connected systematically with the moral norm system.

It is to be proposed that scientists of different disciplines have diverse *social concepts of morality* and that their conceptions of science and morality are in agreement. In an explorative study we attempted to analyze such connections by questioning scientists on their conceptions of "science" and "morality" in detailed interviews. According to Kohlberg (1976), moral systems can be analyzed as different stages of development in the way ought statements are thought to be legitimated. These statements indicate what is commanded or prohibited. The commandment or prohibition is obeyed only thanks to this "minimum of *will* for obedience, that is, *interest* (external or internal) in obedience" of which Max Weber spoke (1964, p. 157) and which comes about through the *belief in legitimation.*

The reconstruction of Kohlberg's moral stages here proposed proceeds from the assumption that different kinds of belief in legitimation underlie the moral stages. They can be reconstructed according to the following characteristics: (1) the mutual relation of the norms (addition or implication), (2) the mode of power with which the rules are enforced (coercion, legitimate power, and self-imposition), and (3) the mode of legitimation of the power (charismatic, traditional, rational).

At Stages 1 through 4 the relations between the norms are largely additions, at Stage 5 and 6 implications. "We defined a postconventional moral perspective in terms of the individual's reason, *why* something is right or wrong," wrote Kohlberg (1976, p. 37), rather than in terms of "what is right." In Stages 1 and 2 norms are enforced coercively, i.e., by punishments and rewards, since the child

Table 1

Reconstruction of Kohlberg's Moral Stages*

		Relation	Power	Legitimation
Level I	Stage 1		Coercion	
	Stage 2			
		Addition		
Level II	Stage 3		Legitimate power	Charismatic
	Stage 4			Traditional
Level III	Stage 5			Rational
		Implication		
	Stage 6		Self-imposition	

*After Kohlberg, 1976.

at this stage is not concerned about the legitimation of the power. At Stages 3 to 5 norms are enforced by "legitimate power" in Weber's sense, which is replaced at Stage 6 by the power-free disposition to "follow ethical principles." The belief in legitimation begins with exposure to charismatic authority figures and interaction with them. Thus at Stage 3 the rules are learned mainly through imitation of proximate models (Portele, 1977). At Stage 4, however, the legitimacy of the norms is founded "on the everyday life belief in the sanctity of traditions that prevailed at all times" (p. 159). The "perspective of the individual in relationships with other individuals" is not valid any longer; persons at Stage 4 take "the point of view of the system that defines roles and rules" (Kohlberg, 1976, pp. 34-35). At Stage 5 there emerges the "belief in the legitimation of codified *[gesatzter]* order" (Weber, 1964, p. 159). In short, law is fixed rationally. Finally, whereas at Stage 5 "the moral point of view is not yet something prior to the legal point of view" (Kohlberg, 1976, p. 39), Stage 6 is self-imposed and free of all coercive influence: "The perspective is that of any rational individual" (p. 35). There the judgments rest on principles rather than on social contract, with the result that ethical and other decisions are taken individually.

These criteria are sufficient to discriminate between the levels and between Stages 3 through 6. A discrimination between Stages 1 and 2 was not considered important for the purposes in question. Also, unlike Kohlberg's sequence, there is no distinction here between Type A and Type B versions of the respective stages.

DEGREE OF STANDARDIZATION IN SCIENCE

Scientific disciplines can be differentiated according to various criteria. The criterion used here refers to the activity of those who are engaged in any scientific discipline. Activities are determined by the material under investigation, and by the social organization of this activity. The *degree of standardization* is defined as the degree of predictability of the behavior (activities) of those doing research and teaching, based on the materials and the knowledge of the materials in the discipline. In contrast, the *degree of codification* is the degree of predictability of behavior based on the rules and teachings of the social organization. The degree of standardization and the degrees of codification correlate, because standardized activities are more readily codified (in the investigation of the Forschungsgruppe Hochschulkapazität: $r = .43$; see Kort, 1976, p. 53). The most standardized sciences are the natural sciences, that is to say, the sciences with a uniform, strict methodology which to all appearances can operate as an additive system of norms with traditional legitimation (Stage 4). Natural scientists regard their mode of science as exact, objective, experimental, and measurable. Applying these considerations to the moral domain, especially Stages 3 to 6, the hypothesis proposed here is as follows: *The less standardized a scientific discipline, the higher the moral level of the scientists.*

Alienation

According to Adam Schaff, alienation is the "domination of man's products over man" (1970, p. 68). Here neither man's power over other men nor the power of nature is referred to, but rather the power of the products themselves. These can be not only objects, e.g., environments, but also theories, ideas, or even moral systems. Schaff's definition is not precise enough for our purposes here. If man no longer exercises influence on his products but is instead influenced by them, he has given up the belief in his ability to alter them. The Weberian "minimum of will for obedience" in the face of the power of man's products is based on the opposite belief, viz., that human products are unchangeable. This belief need not be a conscious one, as the literature of alienation makes clear (see Geyer & Schweitzer, 1976).

Something which is "self-evident" is believed to be invariable, without one's being aware of having that belief. One of the most important processes of alienation is precisely this "deprivation of awareness" (Touraine, 1971) of the fact that man's products are man's products and thus can be changed by man. Only at the higher stages of moral development do moral rules become regarded as alterable. Thus at Stage 5 rules are seen as alterable through social contract, e.g., by majority vote, whereas from the "law and order" perspective of Stage 4 norms are accepted as traditional. At Stage 5 the norms rationally agreed to are accepted as legal and as not liable to change by individuals. Not before Stage 6 will the individual judge freely according to his own principles, regarding norms as alterable on grounds of principles. With reference to these issues, our hypothesis is as follows: *The higher the moral stage, the less the amount of alienation.* (We shall discuss the measurement of alienation below, in the section on methods.) The degree of standardization as degree of predictability on the basis of the materials and the knowledge of the materials suggests that the belief in the invariability of both the knowledge produced by man and the mode of approaching the material is higher in the more standardized disciplines. Alienation has the status here of an indicator of one's approach to reality and functions as part of a larger social concept: the higher the grade of standardization, the deeper the alienation.

SOCIAL CONCEPTS AS COHERENT SYSTEMS OF THINKING

It is to be assumed that scientists of various disciplines will also differ on other dimensions because of different moralities and different modes of alienation, and that the "social concepts" form plausible, coherent systems of thinking. The interviews with scientists, to be described in the following section, were analyzed according to different dimensions. The following dimensions refer to differences between the domains of everyday life and of science, between sciences, and between moralities or their equivalents. We examined the extent to which the interviewed person differentiated between the following:
- scientific activity and human action in general (Action Difference)
- morality in science and morality in general (Special-General Morality Difference)
- science and technology (Science-Technology Difference)
- the methodologies of science and morality (Methods Difference)
- matter and mind (Matter-Mind Difference)
- different sciences (Sciences Difference)
- different moralities (Moralities Difference)

- different extents of social responsibility of science (Social Responsibility Difference)
- the goals and accomplishments of science (Ought-Is Difference)
- morality and science (Morality-Science Difference).

In light of these considerations, then, the hypothesis here proposed is that scientists of different disciplines will differ consistently on these dimensions. More precisely, our hypothesis is: *There is a correlation between the degree of standardization of each science and these dimensions, as well as correlations between the dimensions and between moral stages and alienation.* Undoubtedly these are very undifferentiated hypotheses, which reflects the exploratory state of this project.

Methods

The subjects were 54 scientists (of whom 48 were eventually evaluated), at two universities and one research institute, ranging from scientific co-workers to full professors, randomly chosen from four disciplines, namely, political and social science, German studies, chemistry, electrical engineering. They were interviewed by other scientists in an open interview consisting of questions about:
- the aim and purpose of scientific moral action
- the causes of scientifically successful action and morally right action
- the distinctive criterion between science and morality, between science and morals
- the morality of the science
- the morality of the institution
- differences between a theory of science and of morality
- possible reasons for fundamental changes in their own science or morality.

The interviews themselves lasted for 52 minutes on the average. In addition, the scientists answered questions regarding their person (age, status, etc.). Owing to the care with which the initial contacts were made, there were only a few refusals (8), which were filled out from a replacement list.

The four disciplines mentioned have different degrees of standardization. The degree of standardization was calculated on the basis of complete comparison of pairs of 11 subjects made by scientific experts (e.g., members of the main panel of the Deutsche Forschungsgemeinschaft) in the year 1969, interviewed by the Forschungsgruppe Hochschulkapazität (1973). The order of standardization was established as (going from the lowest to the highest degrees of standardization): political and social science, German studies, chemistry, and electrical engineering.

The open interviews were classified by two persons who also scored the moral stages (individuating references to the subjects concerned were eliminated beforehand). The criteria of classification were: mode of power (coercion, legitimate power, self-imposition), mode of legitimation of power (charismatic, traditional, rational), relation of the norms to each other (additional/implication). In only two cases was there disagreement, when the raters delivered different scorings of the subject's stage (Stages 5 and 6). None of the interviewed scientists was scored as Stage 1 or 2, and three were scored as Stage 3. In the classification, inconsistency did not occur with any of the interviewed scientists (a scientist would have been judged inconsistent if, for example, his statements were classified simultaneously as "charismatic" in their mode of legitimation and as related to other norms by "implication").

The further quantitative evaluation of the interviews depended for the most part on whether a certain point was mentioned in the statements or not. From several of such categories the measurement of alienation was developed additively, by asking:
- Are changes in science possible/impossible?
- Are changes of morality possible/impossible?
- Is the selection of problems active/passive?
- Can the morality be changed by own activity (active/passive)?
- Can the science be changed by own activity (active/passive)?

Moreover, the interviews were classified according to the dimensions mentioned above, e.g., the degree of differentiation between science and technology (low, medium, strong), with care being taken to eliminate references to the specific disciplines concerned. (For more details on the methods of this research, see Portele, 1981.)

Results

Table 2 shows the numerical distribution of the scientists of different disciplines with regard to the moral stages. There it can be recognized that scientists in the fields of political and social sciences and German studies, that is, those working in disciplines with less standardization, show a greater tendency toward higher moral stages than that shown by persons in chemistry and electrical engineering, who are working in the more standardized disciplines.

The hypotheses proposed above are supported by our findings, or at least are not falsified by them (cf. Table 3). The correlation

Table 2

Distribution of the Scientists of Different Disciplines on the Moral Stages

Discipline	Moral Stage 3	4	5	6	n
Political and Social Sciences	—	1	4	5	10
German Studies	—	2	5	5	12
Chemistry	3	9	7	1	20
Electrical Engineering	—	4	2	—	6
Total	3	16	18	11	48

between degree of standardization and alienation may be a dummy correlation, occuring because of the correlation between degree of standardization and moral stage, and that between moral stage and alienation (according to the Simon-Blalock rule, $r = -.57 \times -.53 = +.3021$). This suggests that, if a dependency of moral stage and alienation on the degree of standardization is supposed, the degree of standardization does not influence alienation directly, but only indirectly through the moral stage. With its increasingly high degree of standardization (mainly among natural and technical scientists), science though not technology is regarded as a closed-end activity. Furthermore, it was claimed that one acts differently in everyday life than in science. There is only one science: diverse sciences do not exist any more than do diverse moralities. Finally, it was claimed that morality and science differ from each other, but that this does not mean that another morality prevails in science than that which operates in everyday life. As for the dimension of the social responsibility of science, it was not seen as dependent on the degree of standardization but on the degree of alienation ($r = -.41$) and on the moral stage ($r = .40$), which again are influenced by the degree of standardization.

With increasingly higher moral stages, the differences between everyday human action and scientific action are regarded as minor. Even less differentiation was made between science and technology, and between theory of science and morality. More differentiation was made concerning the social responsibility of science, as well as

Table 3

Pearson Correlations Between Degree of Standardization, Moral Stage, Alienation, and Views on Science and Morality

	1	2	3	4	5	6	7	8	9	10	11	12	13
1. Standardization	.	34	157	28	142	58	56	37	128	135	.	147	35
2. Alienation		.	153	29	137	32	45	29	.	126	141	129	.
3. Moral Stage			.	133	.	148	156	139	.	29	40	134	.
4. Action Difference				.	.	25	50	.	.	.	126	136	30
5. Special-General Morality Difference					.	.	.	140	.	.	.	20	.
6. Science-Technology Difference						.	35	25	.	21	.	149	30
7. Methods Difference							.	.	.	.	132	123	.
8. Matter-Mind Difference								.	.	.	139	24	.
9. Sciences Difference									.	33	.	37	.
10. Moralities Difference										.	.	31	.
11. Social Responsibility											.	.	.
12. Ought-Is Difference												.	.
13. Morality-Science Difference													33

Note: $n = 48$. Correlations equal to or above .20 and below 1.20 are statistically significant ($p = .05$, one-tailed test); correlations in between and decimal points are omitted.

between diverse moralities and between the goals and accomplishments of science.

If one differentiates more strongly between everyday action and scientific action—presumably in the manner of full-blooded scientists—one is also more likely to differentiate between science and technology, as well as between morality and science. Then the theory of science has very little to do with morality. Science will probably be pursued for the sake of science, providing a context in which the degree of social responsibility of science is low and the goals which this kind of science sets for itself are indeed accomplished.

SUMMARY

The scientists of different disciplines differ from one another in a large series of patterns of reasoning. The respective patterns of reasoning seem to agree with each other. Their *social concepts* seem to be coherent in themselves and with regard to each other. Our results can be summarized by the claim that for the natural and technical scientists, science is a domain secluded in itself, which is detached distinctly from other domains. Hence there exists among these scientists a tendency to separate science from everyday life. With regard to the human and social (including political) sciences, however, this tendency is not as strong. The natural and technical scientists exercise less control over their sciences, the science tending instead to control the scientist rather more than is the case with the human and social sciences. In short, alienation increases with the degree of standardization.

This alienation is probably influenced directly by the moral stage and only indirectly by the degree of standardization. Natural and technical scientists, as opposed to human and social scientists, seem inclined toward a conservative "law and order" morality with traditional legitimation, a tendency which exists interestingly enough, not only within science but also in everyday life: therefore, they are more "alienated." Their actions within and outside of science are determined by the moral norms; they are controlled by them. It certainly should be worth undertaking more precise investigations to establish what this means in respect to their activity as scientists and to their academic disciplines.

Morality and the Military Life-World

Thomas Krämer-Badoni and Roland Wakenhut

THE THEORETICAL FRAME OF REFERENCE

In the following essay we start from the basic assumption that the structure of the military "life-world" influences behavior in the sphere of moral judgment in the sense intended by Kohlberg (1976). In particular, we presume that conscripts within the military life-world judge situations which require moral judgment in a different way than do comparable groups who have not done military service. This assumption involves two concepts which need to be explained at the outset: *life-world* and *situation*. As we use them, these concepts belong to the context of a social science which is grounded, at least in part, on phenomenological philosophy.

The Concept of "Life-World"

Since we cannot undertake here a detailed account of Husserl's (1962) concept of the life-world, we shall limit ourselves to the distinction between it and a sociological concept of the life-world. "The life-world is a realm of original evidence," he wrote, explaining that

> the contrast between the subjective in the life-world and the "objective" in the "true" world lies in the fact that the latter is a theoretical-logical basis for inferring something which cannot, on principle, be perceived or, on principle, be experienced in its self-being, whereas the subjective in the life-world is characterized in each and every aspect by the fact that it can be truly experienced. (pp. 140-41)

In Husserl's view, the horizon which can be experienced subjectively and intersubjectively differs from life-world to life-world: "When we find ourselves in alien social surroundings, among the Negroes in the Congo or Chinese peasants, we realize that their truths, which are established, universally confirmed facts for them, are by no means our truths." But in spite of all their relativity, life-worlds have "a universal structure. The universal structure, to which everything relative is tied, is not itself relative. We can observe it in its universality and, with due caution, we can ascertain its existence definitively and in a way which is accessible to everyone."

Condensed to a single sentence, the life-world is for Husserl a subjectively relative, historically and situationally prescribed horizon of experience, in each case the concrete expression of a universal structure whose features are "spatial formation, motion, sensuous qualities, and the like." To characterize the transition from this phenomenological concept of the life-world to a sociological concept, we may quote Thomas Luckmann[1], who writes:

> Phenomenology describes the intentional structure of theoretical and pre-theoretical activities in human consciousness. Thus the process of phenomenological explanation begins with the most directly accessible evidence: with the examination of direct experience. For sociological, i.e., causal and functional explanation, the evidence is of a complex nature. It consists of the socially constructed historical realities of everyday life. (1979, p. 205)

These "realities of everyday life" are, to begin with, differentiations within and above the universal structure of the life-world. In our opinion, however, these differentiations are not based merely upon the necessarily different perspectives of Ego and Alter, a distinction which leads to a "multiplicity of life-worlds" with the final result that each person has his own life-world (cf. Grathoff, 1979). Nor do they rest only upon those "sub-universes of meaning" which result from the different "accentuations of role specialization" (Berger & Luckmann, 1969, p. 90). We are, rather, of the opinion that they are based upon real and normative elements and, consequently, have a decisive influence on behavior. It is immediately evident that here we are no longer dealing with individual life-worlds. For example, unemployment structures reality, its perception, and the potential plans of action for many persons at one and the same time and in a typical fashion (cf. Srubar, 1979, pp. 56-57). The same applies to the life of inmates of closed institutions, although here one must avoid the error of seeing the life-world of these people as determined by the official regulations of the institution. In this case subjective perception and structuring play just as much a part as they do in less regulated areas. We wish, then, to speak of a life-world when it can be supported that the "objective" structure of certain areas or facets of life structures the perception of reality for many in similar (typical) ways and that, in the interplay of objective and subjective moments, typical patterns of action or evaluation are produced.

The Concept of "Situation"

The concept of situation is, in the first place, a sub-category of the concept of life-world. Within a given life-world there is an abundance of different situations. These are, however, shaped by subjectively and objectively determined universal structures and do not, therefore, differ in regard to the principles of the life-world to which they belong. Seen from this angle, the situation is the concretion of a life-world. In this sense we have tried, in regard to the moral dilemmas of our research, to formulate situations which capture the principles of the military life-world as precisely as possible from a "situational" point of view (cf. Lind & Wakenhut, in this volume).

At the same time, however, the concept of situation plays a role within research strategy which we wish to explain briefly, in the light of the two following qualifications. In the social psychological research of recent years there has been growing recognition of the idea that (1) the attitudes of persons cannot be understood only as static products of their socialization (in the comprehensive sense), as the trait-concept of personological models assumes, but that (2) attitudes also depend essentially on the interaction of the person and the (social) surroundings (cf. Krämer-Badoni & Wakenhut, 1978a). In this context the concept of situation has also been taken up again. We wish to point out that the interpretation of the concept of situation in this case is different from what might be expected in view of the recent discussions of the Thomas theorem on the one hand (Ball, 1972) and of the concept of situation used in behavioristic and experimentally oriented psychology on the other.

Thomas's well-known theorem runs as follows: "If men define situations as real, they are real in their consequences" (Thomas & Thomas, 1928, p. 572). Thomas has thus postulated the significance of the situation for the real actions of men. A classic example is the burning of witches, which can only be explained in terms of belief in the existence of witches. In brief, what Thomas meant was that a situation has a real effect on human actions even when it is not real (there are no witches). We are dealing, therefore, with interpretations of certain phenomena which are socially valid precisely because they are accepted. The psychological continuation of this idea can be rediscovered in psychoanalytical theory, according to which individ-

ually inadequate behavior in certain situations can be explained by
the intrapsychic dominance of constellations stemming from early
childhood. In this case the reality which directs behavior is not the
external situation – which can only be regarded as a trigger – but the
evoked inner situation, of which the acting subject is not aware, to
say nothing of the other persons interacting with this subject in this
situation.

To the concept of situation which dominates behavioristic-
experimental psychology, the assumption of effective stimulus-
response relationships which must be controllable in experimental
situations is basic. It is evident at the outset that this is an extremely
narrow concept of situation which, furthermore, refers only to
constructed situations. (The field experiment is an exception,
although it too must submit to the same criteria of insulated
stimulus-response relationships.) For this reason we wish to dispense
with a further criticism of this concept (on this point see Bowers,
1973).

The use of the concept of situation implies for us a modification
of the assumption of the intersituational stability of attitudes or, in
the present case, of behavior involving moral judgment. There may
well be intersituational stability in such behavior, but, in all probability, it varies from life-world to life-world. In other words, the
assumption of intersituationally stable behavior involving moral
judgment has a meaning only when the concept of specific, differing
life-worlds is also taken into account.

It should not be necessary to point out explicitly that this is a
somewhat restricted concept of "situation." Nonetheless, these
remarks should suffice as a preliminary theoretical clarification of
the function which the concept has in the context of the military
life-world.

CHARACTERIZATION OF THE MILITARY
LIFE-WORLD

Although the structures which determine the external appearance of
the military life-world can be described with a high degree of inter-
subjective consistency, we must not overlook the fact that these
structures only provide the material which goes to make up the life-
world of the barracks. The decisive point is the way in which the
given structures are perceived and experienced. It is also necessary
to include the categories of perception and evaluation used to trans-
form the military surroundings into a social life-world. In what

follows, a characterization of the military life-world in the German Armed Forces will be given from the point of view of the draftee: i.e., we are not concerned with a complete description, but rather shall consider only those facts which would be subjectively relevant to a draftee.

The "Objective" Structure of the Military Life-World

The first point to mention is the sharp demarcation of the military from all non-military areas, which is expressed in the screening-off of the barracks, the wearing of uniforms, and the hierarchy of ranks according to the principle of command and obedience, of which the uniforms are a visual expression. The soldier is required to adopt new, ritualized forms of behavior such as standing to attention, saluting a superior officer, and reporting for duty. He is at the bottom of a rigid hierarchy that has a precisely defined authority and communication structure, which regulates in detail who may communicate with whom about what (on this point see Pfeiffer, 1976). On entering the armed forces the soldier is not only subject to the fundamental duty "to serve the Federal Republic faithfully and to defend bravely the rights and freedom of the German people" (*Gesetz über die Rechtsstellung des Soldaten* [Law on the Legal Position of the Soldier] Art. 7), but also has a number of his elementary basic rights restricted if not entirely suspended (cf. *Wehrpflichtgesetz* [Military Service Law] Art. 51). According to an article subsequently added to the German constitution or *Grundgesetz* (Art. 17a, Par. 1), the limitation of freedom of assembly and opinion and of the right to petition is permitted in the laws on military and civilian service. In addition, the basic rights of physical integrity (*Grundgesetz* Art. 2, Par. 2, Sent. 1; *Soldatengesetz* [Servicemen's Law] Art. 17, Par. 4), freedom of the individual (Art. 2, Par. 2, Sent. 2), freedom of movement, and the integrity of the home (*Grundgesetz*, Arts. 11, 13) are restricted for the draftee.

However, because of the emotional factors involved, the soldier is affected in a more elementary way by the reduction of opportunities to satisfy individual needs in the broader sense. It is not just that the material preconditions are lacking because pay is low in comparison to former earnings; the satisfaction of needs is also made more difficult by the physical separation from close friends and relations. Training and professional advancement are also interrupted by military service, with negative effects on future security. This legally, socially, and emotionally constricted situation of the draftee is maintained and strengthened by means of an extensive system of sanctions, which is used to punish transgressions and infringements with so-called "educational measures," disciplinary actions, and legal prosecutions. Because such "educational measures" can in practice be prescribed by all military superiors, the behavior of the soldier is constantly controlled and, if need be, sanctioned.

In contrast, the formal training activities aim not only at providing the soldier with military knowledge and skills in the narrow sense, but also at educating him for his role as a citizen. Committed as it is to promoting the principle of *Innere Führung* (inner directedness), the German Armed Forces regards itself as a democratic and constitutional military organization and as a congruent part of the basic democratic order, thus setting itself apart from earlier German military organizations. Consequently, in the context of political education, an attempt is made to develop in the soldier "the ability to act politically" and "to practice democratic procedures" as well as to teach him how "to make proper use of his rights as a citizen" (quoted from the *Zentral Dienstvorschrift* [Central Service Instructions], Dec. 1, 1973). In this training it is taken for granted that "differences of opinion are normal" and "political alternatives are useful." In order to achieve these goals, cooperative forms of instruction are to be used. The democratic format of this political education distinguishes it as a whole from the other structures of the military life-world. It is guided explicitly by the basic values of free democracy and aims to create a responsible citizen capable of political action.

The Perception and Evaluation of the "Objective" Structures

But how does the conscript entering the armed forces experience the structures we have described? One essential feature on which there is general agreement (cf. Stouffer, 1950; Treiber, 1973; Liliensiek, 1979) is that the recruit entering a military organization feels unsure of himself in his new surroundings. A series of factors and mechanisms contributes to this situation: the comprehensive regulation of behavior, with which the recruit is barely able to comply; the possibility of sanctions, mentioned earlier; and the lack of legal security, typically expressed in the cynical recommendation to carry out a command which may be illegal first and to complain about it afterwards. An important aspect is pointed out by Liliensiek (1979), who has worked out the parallels between military drills concerning cleanliness, orderliness, and military step and posture on the one hand, and the way the young child learns to control the functions of its body on the other. The regressive features of these drills remind the recruit of elementary conflicts in childhood which led him to realize "that affection can be won through obedience" (Liliensiek, 1979, p. 102). In basic training the recruit learns to overcome his insecurity by carrying out commands obediently and by endeavoring to meet the expectations of his superiors.

The consequent adaptation to the requirements of military routine does not mean that the soldier has already related his newly acquired skills to their underlying meaning as defined by the mission of the German Armed Forces. His adaptation is of a more passive kind, motivated by the desire "not to attract attention." Although he accepts the patterns of judgment and action prevailing in his surroundings, he does so because he "knows the ropes" and sees this as a way of acquiring important gratifications such as passes and weekend leave.

It is difficult to reconcile the insecurity and resultant adaptation of the soldier described above with the principles of *Innere Führung* derived from the ideal of "the citizen in uniform," on which the aim of the German Armed Forces to provide political education is based. Even if it is admitted that these are ideal aims which cannot be fully realized in practice, the soldier must become aware of the discrepancy between his own experience and the rhetoric of *Innere Führung*. How is a soldier to learn to make proper use of his legal rights as a citizen when, at the same time, several important basic rights are being restricted? How can differences of opinion be experienced as normal and political alternatives as useful when political activities in the barracks are limited? The soldier observes the extreme pressure on military superiors who try to fulfill their assigned double role as military leaders and as partners in the mediation of political education, but who fall back on military and authoritarian patterns of behavior in cases of conflict. The contradiction between the politically motivated claims or pretensions of *Innere Führung* and the restricted practice of everyday military life can be cited as an important characteristic of the military life-world. Because he experiences them so directly and intensively, the "objective" structures described above, as well as the corresponding categories of perception and evaluation which are determined by insecurity and the desire to adapt, impress on the recruit the restricted nature of the military life-world. In comparison, the educational endeavors explicitly based on the principle of *Innere Führung* recede into the background. It is not just that the time devoted to them is too brief. Because the

212   Krämer-Badoni and Wakenhut

soldier's experience of them is not personal and direct enough, they lack conviction and reality for him.

In view of the particular constitution of the military life-world in the German Armed Forces, it is questionable whether and to what extent the principles of *Innere Führung* are effective in situations of conflict in daily military routine and whether the solutions arrived at accord with those principles. For the recruit concerned, the conflict resolution strategies which are objectively prescribed in instructions, orders, and directives are not so important. What is decisive is the way he personally perceives and evaluates the actual balance of interests. Accordingly, it is particularly important to ask what motives and subjective reasons form the basis for specific patterns of action for the resolution of conflict. For example, does the conscript make use of the principles of command and obedience or of comradely feelings to justify a certain action? Do his reasons leave room for decisions of conscience, or is he simply guided by fear of punishment?

The basic assumption mentioned at the beginning, that the structure of the military life-world influences behavior in the sphere of moral judgment, can now be stated more precisely: in specifically military situations of conflict which permit or require moral evaluation, recruits will fall back on patterns of moral argumentation which reflect the restrictive structures of the military life-world. In comparable situations of conflict in civilian life, they will possibly have recourse to other patterns of argumentation independent of those used in the military situation. Furthermore, we assume that individuals who have had personal experience of the military life-world will be more strongly influenced by its restrictive nature than will those without such experience. Or to put it more generally: the greater the subject's distance from military service and the armed forces, the more their influence recedes. The distance does not have to be one of time; it can also be represented psychologically. Thus we expect that the moral behavior of conscientious objectors who find themselves in conflict situations within the military sphere will be least affected by the structures of the military life-world. Our assumptions cover differentiation in moral judgment specific to both the life-world and to the group. A differentiation specific to the life-world can count as an expression of the segmentation of moral judgment (cf. Senger, in this volume).

EMPIRICAL RESEARCH AND RESULTS

For the empirical control of our assumptions, we had access to data on a number of groups who had been examined by means of the *Moral Judgment Questionnaire* (MJQ; see Lind & Wakenhut, in this volume) which we had developed for a large-scale research project on the socialization produced by the armed forces (on this point see Wakenhut, 1979). The form of the MJQ we used contained two hypothetical situations of conflict specific to the military sphere (the dilemmas of Schneider and Neumann) and two specific to civilian life (the dilemmas of the workers and Lüddersen). The groups were questioned in the autumn of 1977 at fifty different points distributed over the entire Federal Republic of Germany. The soldiers were questioned in the barracks at ten garrisons. From the data we chose the following samples:

- Draftees in the armed forces who had just completed their basic training ($N = 367$)
- Reservists discharged from the armed forces, whose military service had finished within the previous two years ($N = 243$)
- Young male adults who had performed neither military nor alternative civilian service ($N = 274$)
- Conscientious objectors who had just completed their alternative civilian service ($N = 246$)

Those questioned differed considerably in regard to both their level of education and the extent of their religious involvement. Both of these features co-varied with the level of moral development: higher levels of education coincided with higher levels of moral development[2] and, in the case of those with religious affiliations, increased moral orientations occurred which can be assigned to Stages 3 and 4 in Kohlberg's scheme (see Siegmund, 1979; Wakenhut, 1981).

At about 55%, the high school graduates *(Abiturienten)* were overrepresented among the conscientious objectors, whereas the conscripts differed from the other groups in containing a relatively high proportion, over 70%, who described themselves as religious in some form or other. In order to exclude these influences, which were distracting from the point of view of our research interest, the four groups were set parallel to each other according to these two features. The result of this procedure was four "adjusted" samples, each containing $N = 69$ subjects.

For each sample, the mean preference was calculated in relation to the six Kohlberg stages, which were reproduced in the arguments presented (see Lind & Wakenhut, in this volume). The two military and non-military situations were also taken together in each case. From the comparison of the preference profiles in relation to the life-worlds, conclusions can be drawn about the arguments used and the extent to which they are regarded as legitimate and permissible within a specific life-world. It is precisely the relative preference for preconventional argumentation among young adults which tells us indirectly if and how far conventional argumentation has been accepted and already consolidated. Continued strong preferences for arguments of Stages 1 and 2 permit us to conclude that conventional morality is still fairly unstable. The preference profiles reflect the collective tendencies toward judgments in relation to the life-world, which are of course only indirectly connected with the individual levels of moral development. Preference profiles contain information specific to the group and the life-world, whereas the assignment of individuals to the various stages occurs independently of groups and the life-world.

The results collected in Table 1 on group-specific moralization in relation to the military life-world reveal significant differences in the preferences shown for patterns of argumentation of Stages 3 and 6. In situations of conflict in the military life-world, soldiers on active duty are least inclined to permit moral justifications guided by concrete and direct interpersonal feelings – in contrast to the conscientious objectors, who are most strongly oriented in this direction. The conscientious objectors also differ from all the other groups in showing a clear preference for justifications of actions determined by conscience and principle, whereas the other groups scarcely differ from each other, grosso modo, on this point. Finally, it is a noticeable feature of the course of the preference profiles that in the samples of young adults without experience of military or civilian service and those of conscientious objectors, the preference means increase more or less uniformly up to Stage 5. Among the soldiers and reservists, however, the preference means fall at first from Stage 1 to Stage 3 and then begin to increase again from Stage 4 onwards. This indicates the relative dominance of Stage 1 orientations over instrumental orientations and those determined by interpersonal feelings, which is obviously a characteristic of personal experience within the military life-world.

In the groups examined there is a clear agreement on the moral differentiation between the military and the non-military life-worlds, although there is evidence for some group-specific peculiarities (Tables 2 and 3). The study reveals throughout that in cases of conflict in the military life-world justifications of actions by means of postconventional morality are less often permitted. At the same time, those questioned agreed in seeing in the military life-world fewer opportunities for an instrumental, personally advantageous orientation. The reservists alone used interpersonal relations to legitimate actions in cases of conflict less in the military sphere than outside the armed forces. Finally, the soldiers showed a stronger preference for argumentation determined by avoidance of punishment when evaluating behavior in conflict situations in military life.

Table 1

Distribution of the Preference Means (x) and Standard Deviations (s) for the Military Dilemmas over the Four Groups

		Soldiers of the Armed Forces	Reservists of the Armed Forces	Without military/ civilian service	Conscientious objectors	*F*-test
Stage 1	x	2.41	2.47	2.21	2.32	1.64
	s	0.76	0.68	0.65	0.74	
Stage 2	x	2.28	2.32	2.36	2.32	0.96
	s	0.86	0.87	0.88	0.81	
Stage 3	x	2.35	2.41	2.41	2.64	5.33**
	s	0.56	0.68	0.65	0.72	
Stage 4	x	2.93	2.99	2.77	2.77	1.92
	s	0.63	0.58	0.58	0.63	
Stage 5	x	3.03	3.13	3.09	3.11	1.21
	s	0.67	0.48	0.52	0.52	
Stage 6	x	2.87	2.85	2.80	3.07	3.03*
	s	0.57	0.58	0.57	0.55	

*$p = .05$. **$p = .01$.

THE MILITARY LIFE-WORLD AND MORALITY

In the previous section we made the point that, from the preference profiles examined, it is not possible directly to infer any conclusions about individual levels of moral development. Consequently, the following interpretations do not refer directly to behavior involving moral judgment, but only to group-specific differences in the evaluation of moral argumentation. These are at best indicators for

Table 2

Distribution of the Preference Means (x) and Standard Deviations (s) for Civilian and Military Dilemmas Among Soldiers and Reservists of the Armed Forces

| | | Soldiers | | | Reservists | | |
		Civilian dilemmas	Military dilemmas	t^a	Civilian dilemmas	Military dilemmas	t^a
Stage 1	x	2.25	2.41	-2.38	2.44	2.47	-0.15
	s	0.74	0.76		0.85	0.68	
Stage 2	x	2.56	2.28	3.05**	2.71	2.32	4.47**
	s	0.78	0.86		0.76	0.87	
Stage 3	x	2.35	2.35	0.04	2.63	2.42	2.05*
	s	0.77	0.56		0.85	0.68	
Stage 4	x	2.83	2.93	-1.02	2.93	2.99	-0.90
	s	0.59	0.63		0.60	0.58	
Stage 5	x	3.50	3.03	4.86**	3.38	3.13	2.99**
	s	0.65	0.67		0.59	0.48	
Stage 6	x	3.32	2.87	4.86**	3.31	2.86	4.89**
	s	0.74	0.57		0.60	0.58	

[a]t-tests for correlated samples. $*p = .05.$ $**p = .01.$

behavior in the sphere of moral judgment, and should not be equated with that behavior itself. Our results do not, therefore, have the character of established facts; they should, rather, serve to make our assumptions more precise or to reinforce their plausiblity, so that they can serve as the basis for further research.

Our basic assumption, that the military life-world influences moral judgment, can claim a high degree of plausibility. In the preceding brief analysis of the structures of the military life-world, we have seen how extensive is the intervention in the life of the draftees. The relative dominance of the preference for arguments that are oriented toward the hard facts of punishment of bad behavior further shows the evident influence of the hierarchical organizational structure and of military practice on all those who have had personal experience in the armed forces. It should be said, however, that our results point toward a distinction, albeit a relative one, between draftees and reservists: the draftees' preference for argumentation guided by fear of sanctions is significantly higher for military dilemmas than for civilian dilemmas, whereas there is no difference in this respect among the reservists. This suggests that current mili-

Table 3

Distribution of Preference Means (x) and Standard Deviations (s) for Civilian and Military Dilemmas Among Young Adults Without Military or Civilian Service and Among Conscientious Objectors

| | | Without military or civilian service | | | Conscientious objectors | | |
		Civilian dilemmas	Military dilemmas	t^a	Civilian dilemmas	Military dilemmas	t^a
Stage 1	x	2.32	2.22	1.11	2.28	2.33	0.76
	s	0.74	0.66		0.79	0.75	
Stage 2	x	2.79	2.35	4.59**	2.68	2.32	4.54**
	s	0.69	0.88		0.74	0.82	
Stage 3	x	2.53	2.39	1.51	2.49	2.62	−1.34
	s	0.77	0.65		0.86	0.72	
Stage 4	x	2.87	2.78	1.26	2.68	2.79	−1.32
	s	0.70	0.59		0.66	0.63	
Stage 5	x	3.38	3.09	3.81**	3.41	3.11	3.89**
	s	0.62	0.52		0.59	0.53	
Stage 6	x	3.35	2.80	6.38**	3.38	3.09	3.81**
	s	0.59	0.57		0.65	0.55	

[a] t-tests for correlated samples. $*p = .05.$ $**p = .01.$

tary experience has a stronger influence on the moral thinking than past military experience does.

Important confirmation for these results can be found in empirically documented references to the fact that there are systematic relationships between the individual level of moral judgment and the military life-world. Bald et al. (1981) summarize these relationships as follows: "The affirmation of military service is accompanied by orientations which aim at the maintenance of the existing political and social order (Stage 4), while the concrete mutual interpersonal orientations (Stage 3) recede into the background. There is an increasing correspondence between rejection of military service and postconventional orientations, which are committed to the claims of constitutional principles independently of the respective concrete life-contexts."

In regard to the differences in the judgment of the military and civilian dilemmas, our comparison of the four groups does, however,

218 Krämer-Badoni and Wakenhut

show that all the groups are less inclined to accept arguments based on reasons of conscience and moral principle for the justification of actions in the military sphere than for those in the civilian sphere. This result complements and complicates our assumption about the influence of the military life-world on moral judgment. First of all, it shows that all the groups agree on legitimating behavior differently in the military and civilian spheres. It can, therefore, be assumed that a dissociation of different spheres of life is undertaken both without and in spite of personal experience. On the one hand, the groups with experience in the armed forces differ from those without such experience, but on the other hand, this difference is very greatly reduced in view of the distinction which all make between military and civilian cases of conflict. It is reduced to the greater preference shown by draftees for arguments based on avoidance of punishment in military dilemmas as opposed to civilian dilemmas.

We conclude by drawing from our results two insights which can be used to formulate hypotheses for research on moral judgment. First, Kohlberg's concept of moral judgment is universalist, not only in the sense that it has to date proved its worth at the intercultural level – a point we do not wish to discuss here – but also in the sense that it is not concerned with specific intrasocial differences affecting the choice of the dilemmas (and the arguments) – differences which we have characterized by the concept of different life-worlds. All our results indicate that these specific life-worlds exert an influence on moral reasoning. It is true that our results do not permit us to judge whether behavior in the sphere of moral judgment, the development of moral judgment, or only the preference for certain arguments is involved. In order to find this out, there should be an indispensable requirement for future research on moral judgment to include exact studies of the different life-worlds and of the individuals in them. This is not to question Kohlberg's developmental logic. The inclusion of the concept of specific life-worlds could, however, improve our understanding of the specific reasons for moral development and, as a result, permit a different social judgment of the various developmental moral stages.

The second insight is closely connected with the first. The concept of different life-worlds implies the assumption that the "objective" structure of these life-worlds is a constituent factor in the formation of consciousness, including moral consciousness. An open question remains: Does this mean that subjects whose characters have been marked and formed in various life-worlds extend to all social areas the standard of judgment they acquire in the process? Is the segmentation of moral judgment – for which, we believe, we have found pointers in our study – imposed on the subjects by the socially different life-worlds, or can it be attributed to the subjects themselves? We cannot decide this point here either. We believe, however, that the concept of the life-world, together with the situational context of the dilemmas, will permit us to clarify these problems and relationships. Within the framework of such research, it could well turn out to be the case that we are dealing not only with the conditions for the development of morality but also, and just as much, with the social conditions for the realization or repression of certain stages of morality, which is probably closely connected with the structures of the various life-worlds. This would open up research on moral development to the social sciences more than has been the case in the past and free it from the narrow confines of developmental psychology, which it appears in any case to have long outgrown.

NOTES

1. Alfred Schütz reformulated Husserl's concept of the life-world for the social sciences and gave it a new meaning (cf. Schütz, 1970). Thomas Luckmann, a student of Schütz's, has continued his work (cf. Schütz & Luckmann, 1979). Our own application of the concept of life-world not only has considerably more concrete connotations than does that of Schütz and Luckmann, but was originally formulated with a somewhat different purpose in mind. Nevertheless, we derive it partly from this tradition.
2. According to our empirical experience, there is a correlation between moral stage and the school qualification of young adults between 18 and 30, divided roughly into those completing elementary school *(Hauptschulabschluss)*, junior high school *(Mittlere Reife)*, and senior high school *(Abitur)*. It is about $r = .25$.

We would like to thank Paul Schneider and Karl Hegner for the data processing and analysis.

Segmentation of Soldiers' Moral Judgment

Rainer Senger

This essay offers some exploratory considerations of a phenomenon which, using Döbert and Nunner-Winkler's term (1975, 1978), we shall call "moral segmentation." Its characteristic feature is that people who have to solve conflicts in various social settings tend to reason at correspondingly different moral stages.

Our concept of moral segmentation is based on the assumption that the structures of various societal "life-worlds" (see Krämer-Badoni & Wakenhut, in this volume) influence the application of moral competencies, and thus that moral judgment varies systematically from one life-world to the other. The phenomenon of inconsistency due to environmental factors has not been satisfactorily accounted for in Kohlberg's theory of moral development. However, moral segmentation appears to be typical of modern industrial societies – societies whose increasing functional differentiations (political, economic, educational, and familial) may not yet be sufficiently equilibrated by integrating forces.

The following considerations originated from an investigation of the moral judgment of German officers attending military university (Senger, 1979a). To hypothesize that segmentation can be found in this military population does not assume that the German armed forces *(Bundeswehr)* are an independent, albeit relatively less democratized, segment of society. Quite apart from the controversy concerning the alleged incompatibility of the military with democracy, such an assumption would be unduly restrictive, in that it begs the question of whether "the military as part of society actually *is* society" (Wachtler, 1983).

The first part of this essay will outline the societal conditions of moral judgment within a sociological frame of reference. The second part is a brief discussion of some theoretical aspects of segmentation, which are illustrated in the third part by empirical data.

THE SOCIETAL CONDITIONS OF MORAL
SEGMENTATION

To begin, let us examine when, and in what situations, moral judgments are most likely to occur. Following Habermas (1976a; 1983), we may define the function of a moral decision as a compromise between conflicting interests, one of which is based on a generalizable perspective. In situations of conflict, moral decisions are required whenever the routine of everyday actions breaks down. The more complex societies become, the more they need principled moral structures to master the objective problem of establishing consensus. But to foster postconventional thinking is one thing, to offer possiblities for a consistent realization of these competencies is another. The experiences of everyday life suggest that moral performances are often laden with inconsistencies, frequently brought about by factors peculiar to modern industrial societies.

Society and Morality

At this point a broad outline of some socio-structural characteristics of modern society will be useful. First, groups and their normative systems have become increasingly differentiated, since the overall rationalization of almost every sector of life gives rise to specific objectives, roles, and behavior patterns. One result of this differentiation is the growing dissociation between public and private spheres, that is, between primary and secondary groups. A case in point is the economic sphere, where moral constraints have been set aside in favor of profit-maximizing strategic norms. Such an "institutionalized segmentation" (Döbert & Nunner-Winkler, 1975, p. 107) of specific sectors of life constitutes an organizational principle of industrial society. Under these circumstances it becomes difficult for the individual to integrate his various roles and to meet the competing claims of his groups.

A second structural characteristic is the preponderance of formalized, bureaucratic organizations embodying the societal requirements regulating social sub-systems. Such overwhelming processes of formalization, the effects of which Habermas (1981a) has designated as "colonizing the life-world," contribute to a spreading amorality, in that the participating actors no longer feel compelled to achieve consensus on moral contents. As Mayntz (1970) put it: "Where legal legitimacy becomes a purely formal principle, it refers only to the relations of authority but does not extend to the content of organizational goals and role duties" (p. 376). Within modern society, almost everyone acts to a certain degree as an agent of organizations, a circumstance which does not imply the abrogation of one's independent judgment, but the obligation to obey irrespective of such judgment.

Finally, a third characteristic of modern society is the high degree of instability and conflict in the socialization process. Due to the general devaluation of religion and tradition, as well as to the prevailing institutionalized morality, the cultural system provides fewer and fewer identity-forming world-views and belief patterns. With modernization the scope of absolutely binding moral regulations has been drastically reduced. Only rules covering the guarantees indispensable for peaceful social exchange are retained, such as: People should not steal, kill, or violate the personal rights of others. However, such "minimal morality" is unable to offer an overall approach to life. Consequently, it is to a large extent up to the individual himself to develop those standards and ideas which constitute identity formation.

In view of these socio-cultural conditions, it is extremely difficult for the subject consistently to realize his moral competence. He is confronted with situations of conflicting, partly incompatible goals, norms, and commitments which make inconsistencies of moral judgment nearly inevitable. Ultimately, the experience of inconsistency may result in serious stress to the personality system. Coping with inconsistencies sometimes requires new "forms of life," in which case at least two strategies are available. On the one hand, a person may try to overcome the conflicting patterns by means of a qualitatively new organization of his entire life. On the other hand, a person may try to segment moral concerns and standards according to respective sectors of life in order to preserve consistency – if only within these compartments. We suppose moral segmentation to be the more likely strategy, not only because a radical change of life is a most inconvenient affair and thus might involve some sort of life crisis, but also and more importantly because in modern society segmentations are so legitimized that the actor is provided in advance with readily acceptable justifications.

With this general outline in mind, we now turn to the military life-world. The armed forces has undergone a fundamental social change which is reflected most strongly in the soldier's professional role. The theoretical concept of role provides the starting point for our subsequent description, since the professional role is a large part of the individual and collective constructions of the military life-world. In this connection special attention must be paid to the idea of the "citizen soldier" *(Staatsbürger in Uniform)*, which is the offical educational concept of the Federal Armed Forces.

"Citizen Soldier" – An Integration Model

Within democratic societies no other profession has been more extensively examined in public discussion and controversy than the professional military. This is due to the fact that "the armed forces work in a boundary area where the democratic system becomes undemocratic for reasons of self-preservation. They operationalize and symbolize a system of authority that becomes essential when all other possibilities are exhausted" (Doorn, 1975, p. 100). The West German public was particularly concerned with this problematic issue when, during the fifties, the rise of a new German army was imminent. This historical situation, which was born not only of the memory of a disastrous war but also out of a belief in democracy, economic growth, and technological progress, called for the radical reformation of the Federal Armed Forces and their relationship to society.

The reformers, the most important of whom was Graf von Baudissin, were guided by a view of society as "living democracy." According to this view, democratization could not be accomplished merely by constitutional fiat, but required in addition the participation and engagement of citizens who were aware of the chances and risks of liberty. Consequently, the armed forces were not allowed to develop a separate way of life; rather, they had to take part in the democratic process, despite their special functional features. Thus, the central feature of the idea of the citizen soldier is "that the soldier remains committed to the civil, i.e., democratic, system of values, and dwells in the same cultural and political world as do other citizens. Being a soldier and being a civilian are two aspects of a single totality" (Baudissin, 1982, p. 166). This concept did not exclude organizational features which follow from the "combat premise," such as the hierarchical system of authority, command, and control, or forms of obedience and discipline. Rather, these features were thought to be supplemented by cooperation and initiative, due to the influences of technology and functional differentiation within the military. Hence, the tension between democratic principles and their organizational requirements was not disguised but made manifest. To come to terms with this tension and to deal with it rationally was considered the central task of the modern military profession.

Thus the traditional role of the soldier as a category sui generis had become an anachronism (see Räder & Wakenhut, 1984).

It is evident that the concept of the citizen soldier introduces a qualitatively new form of conflict resolution into the internal and external relations of the armed forces, one which corresponds to what we consider postconventional moral structures. This approach to conflict assumes a sort of "burden of proof rule" (Gessenharter, 1982, p. 86), which proceeds according to the following maxim: Allow as much personal freedom within the army as possible and require only as much restriction as is necessary for proper functioning. In other words, the actual necessity of military regulations is subject to justification in any situation of potential conflict within the ranks. This requires that officers maintain cognitive distance from their specific role norms and, if necessary, redefine them by way of more general, postconventional structures of moral reasoning.

It was this insight which in the 70's provided the basis for reforming the system of military education. The central objective was that by means of higher education the officer would acquire not only special skills but also an overall political and societal view of his profession, oriented toward liberal-democratic principles. These qualities were expected to develop when the officer actually participated in the political process on campus. This reform was a response to the modernization process at work within the army, a process which, because of its emphasis on technical and bureaucratic efficiency, threatened to undermine the ideal of the citizen soldier.

Segmentation of the Military Life-World

The military life-world will be described from the perspective of young student officers studying at a military university after three years of service in various military units and schools. Following Krämer-Badoni and Wakenhut (in this volume), we speak of a "life-world" when the objective structures of a particular sector of life define the person's general perceptions of this sector, and when specific patterns of action and evaluation result from this structuring of his perception through the objective environment. Accordingly, we begin with a description of some objective features of the military life-world.

The modern military has grown into a technical and bureaucratic super-organization in which military and civil sectors are to a large extent intertwined. However, as military combat power becomes increasingly dependent on the technology of weapons systems, the more important operational readiness becomes, and the more social interaction becomes a subordinate criterion of military performance. The linkage of bureaucracy and technology produces a high degree of centralization and formalization, which ensures adherence to controllable rules and operational procedures as they become decisive factors of military efficiency. This development is most strongly illustrated by changes in the structure of military skills. The traditionally dominating "combat roles," including that of the "heroic leader," have today been reduced to barely one-third of the military job functions, with technical and managerial roles predominating. Consequently, "civilian" job profiles and behavior patterns have to a large extent been incorporated into the daily routines of military life.

The corresponding effect on the military life-world and socialization is described clearly by Moskos through two contrasting models: "institution" and "occupation" (1981, p. 3). Their essential differences are summarized in Table 1.

Table 1

Institution versus Occupation

	Institution	Occupation
Legitimacy	service; values: duty, honor, country	marketplace economy
Role	total commitment	segmental commitment
Compensation	much in non-cash form	salary system
Residence	adjacent work and residence locations	separate work and residence locations
Spouse	integral part of military community	removed from military community
Societal	prestige based on notion of compensation	prestige based on level of sacrifice
Socialization	"vertical" — within the organization	"horizontal" — external to the organization

Adapted from Moskos (1979)

However, the trend from institution to occupation which Moskos observed has not advanced the structure of conflict-solving proposed in Baudissin's principle of the citizen soldier. Measured against this objective, both the "institution" and the "occupation" are inadequate, because neither copes in a generalizable way with the tension between democratic principles and functional military norms. An "institution" stresses corporate identity and thus tends toward isolation, whereas an "occupation" emphasizes material interests to the detriment of the moral and political aspects of the military function.

Although Moskos's two models were developed with reference to the American army, they can be regarded as "ideal types" for a framework for the description of segmentation. To a large extent these models typify the conditions of the German armed forces and are reflected in the soldier's own perceptions. An "institutional" attitude may be fostered in combat and leadership functions as a response to this type of alienation. Due to the high degree of formalization and differentiation, many soldiers experience organizational impersonality, loss of homogeneity, and extensive restrictions of their range of responsibility, constraints which they try to overcome by emphasizing the need for cooperation in their profession. This attitude may be reinforced by the fact that the legitimacy of the military and its security policy is increasingly questioned by the general public.

Such conditions may also give rise to an "occupational" attitude, or what may be conceived of as adaptations to the formalized, extrinsically motivated performance structures. In this case the officer does not experience the military role expectations and values as motivationally binding, but only as rules of a game he has chosen or is obliged to play. Such an attitude is especially likely to emerge among those charged with technical and administrative functions.

At any rate, we suppose that the armed forces are characterized by different, partially conflicting life-worlds and professional concepts which can affect the young German officer in varying degrees. Having had these previous experiences, he enters the Federal Armed Forces University where he confronts a new dissonance-producing situation. The tension is increased because of his dual legal status: that of soldier and of student. This fact introduces a role conflict between the standards of academic freedom and his commitments to the military. In this respect, military universities differ fundamentally from other universities, though the academic courses in the two types are largely comparable.

On the organizational level, this dual status takes the form of a differentiation between the academic and military sectors. During his transition phase at the university, the young officer is dramatically unsettled because competing military and scientific ideals act upon him at the same time but without being clearly formulated. Due to his former experiences of role patterns as clear, stable structures, he tends to perceive the academic sector as diffuse and threatening.

Various responses are likely to be evoked under these circumstances. In order to avoid the conflict, some officers may adopt an "institutional" orientation, submitting themselves in a merely formal way to the pursuit of academic or scientific goals, while identifying themselves in their own minds with military role norms. Other officers may stabilize the situation by strong identification with the role of the academic student. In this situation the life-world is largely structured by an "occupational" orientation, i.e., by the pursuit of qualifications for a satisfying civilian career. We assume that only a small number of students deal with the conflict by means of a "moratorium."

The military universities have not yet seized the opportunity to develop a systematic educational approach geared to the student-soldier conflict. Ideally, such an approach would make the young officer's actual situation a subject of his learning process, thereby making it possible for him to realize the educational goal of becoming a citizen soldier. Academic courses which produce "occupational" or "institutional" orientations have limited potential for social integration because they foster the segmentation of life-worlds. In what follows, this segmentation is seen as part of the developmental process, whose frame of reference is set up by correlating the three ideal types of military life-worlds to the three levels of moral development (see Table 2).

Table 2

Dimensions of Moral Segmentation

Moral Level	Perspective	Moral Concern	Life-World
Preconventional	Self vs. others	Individual self-interest	Occupational
Conventional	Primary and secondary groups	Commitment to roles and norms	Institutional
Postconventional	Ideal society	Responsibility for principles	Citizen-soldier

THEORETICAL ASPECTS OF MORAL SEGMENTATION

To summarize, our description of segmentation rests on the assumption that the contents as well as the structure of one's moral judgment may vary from one life-world to the other. This perspective suggests that segmentation is a specific form of variation – or more bluntly, *inconsistency* – regarding the cognitive stage(s) at which moral reasoning takes place. Moral development literature has documented a wealth of findings on stage variations and provided diverse explanatory schemes. Thus Kohlberg emphasizes a so-called "noncumulative sequence model" which postulates a displacement of earlier stages, whereas Levine and Van den Daele support a cumulative model. Before proceeding with a new conceptualization, it is necessary to examine these models briefly.

Cumulative and Noncumulative Models

Within the Kohlbergian model, stages are said to be hierarchically related. One of the main implications of a stage hierarchy is that a higher stage is more adequate than a lower stage, and thus is preferred by the subject: "A new stage is a new general solution to moral problems and its greater adequacy is evident on cognitive grounds. If the higher stage solution is 'seen,' it is then preferred to the lower stage solution, whatever the particular experiences with either stage solution. This is because part of seeing the higher stage is understanding why it is better than the lower stage solution" (Kohlberg, 1973, p. 194).

Investigations by Kohlberg and his colleagues have provided evidence for the hierarchical nature of the stages. They show that children, even under pressure from the experimental situation, did not tend to produce arguments proper to stages already passed through, but rejected them as "wrong thinking" (Rest, Turiel, & Kohlberg, 1969). Furthermore, Rest (1973) found that subjects' preferences concerning arguments produced by someone else tended to the highest stage they could comprehend, regardless of the subjects' own predominant stage.

Within this framework the phenomena of stage variation have been studied primarily in terms of the development of the individual. Thus the relevant studies have focused on the description of "stage mixtures" (Turiel, 1969), i.e., states of cognitive imbalance during transition to a higher stage, as well as the so-called "horizontal décalage," i.e., a delayed generalization of competences in problem areas less familiar to the subject. But by analyzing only variation due to stage acquisition, this research has largely neglected the study of those inconsistencies which are a function of different social settings and individual experiences. This type of variation, which can be considered as a case of stage use, remains undiscussed within the current formulation of Kohlberg's theory. This omission is especially glaring in his revised scoring method, which produces general maturity scores and consequently suppresses dilemma-specific stage variations.

In accord with this criticism, Levine (1979a, 1979b) has recently proposed a reformulation of the assumption of hierarchical preferences in favor of a "non-displacement perspective" or a cumulative model, respectively: "It is true that Kohlberg argues that each successive stage of reasoning in his hierarchy represents a more differentiated, universalistic orientation, and therefore, a more adaptive one. However, though this may be so on logical grounds, one cannot assume that these more adaptive structures will always be used by the respondent . . . for they may be defined as threatening or simply inapplicable by him in certain situations" (1979a, p. 148). This consideration is based on empirical findings which Levine gained by confronting young adolescents with systematically varied moral dilemmas. The subjects markedly preferred Stage 3 arguments if the hypothetical actor was a reference person (mother, friend). But in cases involving an unknown person, they selected Stage 4 arguments much more frequently.

Against this background, Levine offers a concept which should provide an explanation for stage variation due to stage acquisition, as well as stage use. With reference to Flavell's (1972) system of classifying developmental sequences, Levine specifies the "non-displacement perspective" as a mixed type of "addition" and "inclusion." In other words, lower stages are said to remain available sui generis but also to constitute elements of higher stages. Thus, transformation is defined as a process implying the manipulation of one's knowledge of earlier stages, but not the manipulation of the stages per se.

Concerning the dynamics of moral decisions, Levine assumes the existence of two processes. The first is an independent cognitive-reflexive process which scrutinizes the available structures and selects the response most suitable for the dilemma in question; the second is a cognitive strategy of "compartmentalization," which allows the coexistence of different, partly competitive modes of thinking.

Within this framework, stability and variability of moral judgment are a function of the "best fit" among moral structures, personal characteristics, and recurring patterns of environmental stimuli (Levine, 1979b, p. 156).

From this broad outline, we can see that Levine has indeed discovered some gaps in Kohlberg's theory, and has provided significant ideas for further research. However, his analysis has its own problems and gaps. First of all, Levine gives no theoretical specification of what he has designated as the "best fit." He seems to say that the solution of moral problems is at best an arbitrary matter, resting entirely on the decision of the participating actor. While this may be true for pragmatic or strategic considerations, moral judgments are supposed to be motivated by the need for achieving consensus. One cannot ignore this motivational element in a theory of morality, for without such motivation the problems of action, to which moral structures are related, cannot be solved (Döbert & Nunner-Winkler, 1978, p. 105).

Second, this impression of arbitrariness is strengthened when we take a closer look at Levine's proposal of an additive-inclusive mode of stage sequences, in which the stages lose the characteristic of "structural wholes" and are regarded as particularized response sets. This shift has far-reaching consequences for the logical status of cognitive developmental theory. Levine's approach tends toward a typology of performances rather than toward a theory of competences, and thus loses, among other things, the normative and sociocritical quality of Kohlberg's approach.

Third, we suspect Levine's approach has at least one very basic methodological problem. Owing to his assumption that the adequacy of the stages is a matter of the actor's subjective definition, his approach is radically idiographic in nature and thus must regard the data as incommensurable. However, the possibility of aggregating and comparing data is a methodological prerequisite for any empirical research concerning either individual or societal development. Cognitive-structural theories are fruitful only with the assumption that the hierarchy of stages is a psychological, motivationally significant reality, which in turn supposes that data can be collected and compared from one case to the next.

In sum, we conclude that an approach such as Levine's, which attempts to conceptualize segmentation within the framework of a cumulative model, leads to considerable difficulties. Therefore, we shall concentrate on the possibilities within Kohlberg's theory which allow a theoretical integration of the segmentation phenomenon.

Elements of a Concept of Segmentation

The foregoing considerations suggest three issues that need to be addressed: the formulation of stage sequences, the description of motivational aspects, and the analysis of the societal conditions of moral judgments. The first issue raises the basic question of whether the nature of stage development can be represented adequately by either a cumulative or a noncumulative model, taken separately. Since the models refer to different specific sequential modes, they involve different assumptions and generalizations. For instance, Kohlberg's elaboration of A- and B-substages leads to the assumption that the development within a stage produces not only greater equilibrium but also a change in the relationship between stages. What Levine has called the additive or additive-inclusive mode might apply to only the transitional phases. Lower stage principles are accepted and used for justifying action in a largely ad hoc manner (stage mixture), due to the rudimentary nature of the new organizing principle. During a later phase the stage is more equilibrated, and thus might include modes of higher stage reasoning (Flavell, 1972). Higher stage judgment includes the reasoning of lower stages and, instead of regarding each of its principles as a self-contained absolute, attends to their interrelatedness. The substitution mode favored by Kohlberg seems to characterize stages that are fully equilibrated. The dominating principle has been generalized so that earlier stages are no longer accepted. This more dynamic perspective, which has yet to be demonstrated empirically, suggests that within certain periods lower stages might remain available for use by the subject without cognitive conflict.

From another point of view, structural wholeness, i.e., truly consistent moral reasoning, may be conceived of as the aim of moral-cognitive development, an aim which is fully achieved only when the personality structure is fully equilibrated. Following Lind (see ch. 2, in this volume), we prefer to define "structural wholeness" as consistency of judgment in regard to the moral concerns characteristic for a given stage.

Both points of view, each of which seems compatible with the Kohlbergian approach, are necessary to comprehend our concept of segmentation which stands or falls with the assumption that aspects of lower stages remain available, at least temporarily, to the higher-stage subject. However, the specific feature of segmentation is that the subject may comprehend arguments that are at a structurally higher stage than the stage at which he can argue. In principle, the subject may be conscious of these higher aspects of reasoning, but his awareness will depend on the degree of structural equilibrium. For example, in the case of a fully equilibrated structure (substitution), the subject does accept his own lower stage arguments and thus strives to reduce the perceived dissonance, especially if consensus has not been reached by the participants.

The cognitive-structural description of segmentation can account for the fact that lower stages remain available; however, it cannot explain why these stages are actually used by the subject. This leads to our second point, regarding the motivational aspects of moral judgment. In Kohlberg's theory moral judgment is said to be determined by both reasoning structure and commitment for certain moral contents, i.e., by cognitive and affective aspects. The relationship between these two aspects can be seen in a study of university students (Lind, 1980d), which showed that the two components have similar developmental sequences, but that the motivational component leads the cognitive component. Subjects preferred contents typical of postconventional stages, even though their own cognitive structure was no higher than Stage 3. But the higher the development of cognitive components, the more the higher orientations were accepted, and the more the lower moral concerns were rejected.

These findings suggest that the cognitive and motivational aspects are functionally related to one another. Thus we suppose that any relevant moral concern may induce a corresponding structural aspect which in the course of the decision process may be qualified, altered, or displaced by a higher structure. However, such an alteration need not always take place. The subject may be confronted with circumstances in which the motivational aspects, i.e., his affective commitment to lower-level moral concerns, effectively inhibit the realization of higher level aspects.

At this point the concept of societal life-worlds is of crucial importance to the theorist. The life-world is mainly constituted by the fact that established rules, values, and moral standards have particular relevance for the individual, and thus are internalized to a greater or lesser extent in the course of socialization. The organizational features of the sectors of the life-world and their degree of restrictiveness are especially interesting here. A restrictive sector is, among other things, characterized by insufficient time, decision-making pressure, reduced possiblities for contacts, anonymity, and a preponderance of technically-established control. Within such a highly restrictive environment, an individual cannot usually fully manifest his judgment capabilities.

These considerations show that segmentation is a *relational* phenomenon, the existence of which can only be studied through comparisons of moral judgment within various spheres of life. In this respect we refer to the important paper by Räder and Wakenhut (1984).

In sum, we may define the process of segmentation as follows:
- The subject perceives a moral conflict, i.e., a lack of agreement among action guiding principles
- The conflict implies a moral concern which is typical or even constitutive of the respective life-world
- In this case, the subject argues using lower structural aspects than those which he uses in comparable dilemmas that do not relate to the life-world in question
- The subject either acknowledges his moral inconsistency or strives to justify the perceived dissonance.

AN EMPIRICAL STUDY OF MORAL SEGMENTATION

We investigated the phenomenon of segmentation of moral judgment at the Federal Armed Forced University in Munich in 1979. The sample consisted of 134 student officers whose average age was 25. In the first phase, data were gathered by means of a moral judgment questionnaire, the *Moralisches Urteil Fragebogen* (MUF; see Lind & Wakenhut, in this volume). The MUF is a standardized instrument for the measurement of moral competencies. It consists of four stories, which present two military conflict situations and two non-military ones. For each story, six arguments for and six arguments against the depicted behavior of a hypothetical actor are presented for evaluation. Each argument corresponds to one of Kohlberg's six stages. In the individual-oriented first step of the analysis, the dominant stages were determined from the subjects' preferences by means of the Wakenhut (1982) program MODI. In the sample-oriented second step of the analysis, average preference-profiles of the six stages were drawn up. From these we could ascertain whether typical answer patterns exist for military and non-military dilemmas. (For a more detailed description of the assignment-procedure, we refer to Lind and Wakenhut, in this volume.)

In a second phase, in order to get more information about this phenomenon, we selected 12 subjects whose preference-profiles showed distinct inconsistencies in relation to military and non-

military dilemmas. For this purpose, we constructed four additional
stories, representing everyday conflicts of the military life-world.
These stories were presented to the subjects as a mixture of story-
completion and interview techniques. This method was thought to be
especially suited to the purpose of analyzing the dynamics of moral
judgment, since the subject was supposed to construct not only the
morally correct course of action but also the most likely one, and
thereby bring to bear various motives, interests, and defense mechanisms (Döbert & Nunner-Winkler, 1978).

Preference-Profiles Specific to the Life-Worlds

Moral segmentation can be illustrated by the following results of the
MUF. Each individual subject was assigned a dominant stage on the
basis of his preferences. One of the results was that approximately
60% of the subjects preferred conventional arguments, whereas 35%
showed a preference for postconventional thinking.

To answer the basic question posed by our study, we analyzed the
preference-profiles which were separated according to military and
non-military dilemmas. The results are shown in Figure 1.

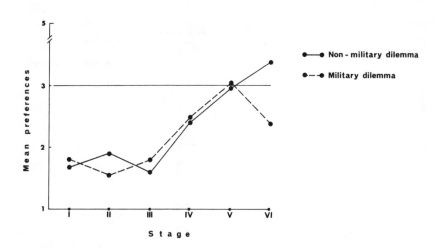

Figure 1. Mean Stage Preferences in Military and Non-Military Dilemmas

It is obvious that instrumental and postconventional arguments are used less for dilemmas in the military environment than for those in the non-military environment, while comradely orientations are increasingly apparent in these situations as stage scores increase. The crucial point is that some of these officers, according to our assignment of dominant stages, are capable of Stage 5 reasoning but use the arguments appropriate to that stage less for military than for non-military dilemmas.

To get a more differentiated evaluation, we analyzed the separate moral dilemmas according to the profiles of pro and con arguments. Figure 2 shows results with the military dilemma of "Private Neumann," who has to decide whether to report to his superior that one of his comrades has tried to persuade the other privates to become conscientious objectors. The figure shows that pro arguments of Stages 5 and 6, supporting the conventional, i.e., traditional military, solution to this dilemma are most preferred, whereas the structurally equivalent contrary arguments at these stages are preferred far less. What seems to be dominating the judgment processes are the moral concerns of Stages 3 and 4, i.e., ésprit de

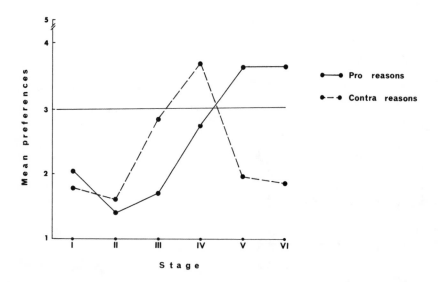

Figure 2. Mean Stage Preferences for Pro and Con Reasons

corps and military order, which constitute a large part of the military' life-world.

On the Dynamics of Moral Segmentation

Further information on the dynamics of moral segmentation can be found in case studies using interviews and story-completions. To begin, we may consider the respective problem solutions offered by two Stage 5 officers, which contrast a case of moral segmentation with a case of judgment that fully realizes the available competence. The officers were confronted with the following conflict situation, which they had to resolve by completing the story with themselves in the role of commander.

Story 1: SERVICE PREPARATION

In the course of basic training, three draftee privates report to the company commander and propose that they prepare for duty every morning (i.e., rising, cleaning their quarters, having breakfast) on their own responsibility. To be supervised in such matters by their superiors is not, they feel, to be treated as adults.

One of the subjects completed the story with the company commander rejecting the proposal on the basis of army regulations. Significantly, the subject also gave the impression that he himself would not have been very happy with such a decision. The following exchange then ensued between the interviewer (I) and the subject (S):

I: What is going on in your mind when you reject the draftees' proposal?
S: In this situation, I don't understand the necessity of supervision. All the same, I have to comply with the regulation. How should I put it? – I would have to do something which I do not necessarily understand. This would make me uneasy.
I: Why, in this case, is the regulation more important to you than the request of the privates?
S: Because the regulation represents an order or rule. Our living together – the military life – is controlled by such rules and regulations. Their necessity can be illustrated and justified, on the one hand, by our special type of organization and, on the other hand, by special situations in case of war.
I: Does this also apply during peacetime?
S: (hesitating) If we do not comply with the regulation in this individual case, the functioning of the military would not be jeopardized for the time being. But if we ignore the regulation in this individual case, all the

regulations can be ignored. And thus, in effect an example is set for similar situations which might perhaps be more serious. It is a question of order.

The determining feature for this segmentation at Stage 4 is the fact that the subject argues in accordance with formalized expectations which he supposes to exist; however, he regards his decision cognitively and emotionally as inadequate in terms of legitimate human requirements. The rigid adherence to regulations involves the legitimizing belief that characterizes bureaucratic thinking: the regulation is justified not by its content, but by its formal existence. Thus, the subject fails to relativize the regulations, in the sense of relating them to the particular situation.

In contrast, the other subject was able to reach a decision which corresponded to his competence. In his story, the company commander had accepted the proposal of the privates.

> S: Well, first of all, I found it very positive that the soldiers came to me with this proposal. This is evidence of the fact that they have thought about the matter and of their concern about it . . . After all, this is precisely the kind of soldier who is sought after: one who has ideas, who acts cooperatively, and who contributes to my decisions. In addition, I would like to remove restrictions which I did not like during my basic training either. These restrictions were not just unpleasant for me; rather, I simply could not understand their necessity. I mean, at home I get up quite on my own. Why shouldn't I get up on my own here too?

Through unadulterated postconventional reasoning, this officer is able to reconstruct adequately the concept of the "citizen soldier" and to define the relevant situations of conflict according to this principle. Military regulations are not conceived of as unalterable facts but as matters for interpretation. On this basis, the officer can meet the privates' demand for responsibility because he concludes that such a decision will not be detrimental to military functioning.

The second case is one of a segmentation at the preconventional level. The subject, who was otherwise identified as being at Stage 4, deals with the following story.

Story 2: A TRIP HOME

After a maneuver of 14 days duration, the company returns to the barracks late in the evening. The company commander has received the order not to let the soldiers go on leave until after they have had a night's sleep. Private Hoffmann asks the commander to let him drive home (300 kilometers away), because his girlfriend has had a serious accident.

The subject refused this request on the basis of his responsibility for the soldier's welfare. However, subsequent questions revealed that the subject was motivated primarily by his fear of consequences.

> S: Nevertheless, I am quite sure if something were to happen, I would be held responsible . . . I mean, the order given by the commander is obligatory. If I give the soldier permission to drive home – regardless what means of transport he will use – and for some reason something were to happen, the commander could hold me responsible.

The dominating motive of avoiding punishment is further evidenced in other parts of the interview:

> I: Would you allow him to drive home the next morning? – You can't be sure whether or not he had slept.
> S: Yes, in my opinion, this is now a purely legal problem. The order was to drive home not earlier than the next day, after bed rest. Whether the soldier concerned can sleep at night is not my problem at that point in time. But I have complied with my obligation in that I did not allow the soldier to drive home immediately after the maneuver . . . Well, if he did not go to sleep – I would not be allowed to let him drive home, any more than on the previous day. But he had the opportunity. Whether he slept or not . . . does not interest me any more.

The following reasoning reveals additional characteristics of segmentation: the realization of an inadequate solution and, at the same time, the justification of the perceived dissonance:

> I: What is going on in your mind, when you tell the soldier that he is not allowed to drive home?
> S: Well, it could be that I . . . (hesitating) well, I can imagine that I would think: Damn it, old buddy . . . I perhaps feel for him, I feel sorry for him or something like that. It is very hard for him to stay here. But, on the other hand, I would think, I am justified by the order given by the commander and by my obligation of providing for the soldier's welfare.

This interview sequence illustrates that a subject's highest cognitive-structural capacities (here Stage 4) will remain unrealized if the corresponding motivation is not actualized at the same time. Although conventional moral structure is typically characterized by justifying one's actions on the basis of legal rules and orders, this subject's reasoning is almost exclusively controlled by the anticipation of negative consequences. While the decision is based on these lower motivational concerns, the higher Stage 4 structure is still present for reflection, as is manifested in the effort to reduce cognitive dissonance.

At the end of this brief empirical illustration, we may recall once again the operational and theoretical presuppositions of our approach. In addition to the obvious fact that the data available to us is not from typical *Bundeswehr* officers, the fact that we have used standardized questionnaires to gain access to their moral judgments must be kept in mind. Without weighing the advantages and disadvantages of this method, it must be noted that sample *preference* profiles lead only to very tentative conclusions about individual *judgment processes*. In the final analysis, we must recognize the exploratory character of our study, which is based on the assumption that moral segmentations are determined by social differentiation. Thus, our still very selective and hypothetical statements about the military life-world touch on only *one* of the many social areas in which this phenomenon is manifested. This consideration puts our previous considerations concerning the phenomenon of segmentation into a larger social-theoretical context.

CONCLUSION: A RELATED APPROACH

Our view receives additional support from social theory and the theory of social evolution, in particular Jürgen Habermas's (1981) theory of communicative action. In this theory a two-step concept of society is suggested. Society as a "life-world" refers to the area of cultural reproduction, socialization, and social integration. In this life-world the coordination of actions is secured by acts of communicatively achieved consensus, which Habermas refers to as "communicative rationality." Society as a "system" includes the areas of rational economic and administrative action, which are systematically integrated via control media such as money and power ("instrumental rationality").

According to Habermas, the development of modern societies reveals a paradox, since there are two historical processes moving in opposite directions. The one process is the increase of communicative rationality, which paves the way for an expanding rationality of the system. The other process is the penetration of the life-world by the demands of the system, viz., monetarization and bureaucratization, thus forcing communicative actions to adjust to these formally organized subsystems. Under normal conditions, the life-world proves resistant to this pressure. However, matters are different when the society's very forms of system integration are changing:

> The routine awareness is deprived of its synthesizing power; it is fragmented.... Only with these prerequisites are the conditions for colonizing the life-world met: the imperatives of the subsystems, which have become independent, penetrate into the life-world from outside – like colonial masters into a tribal society – and force assimilation. (Habermas, 1981a, p. 43)

This description by Habermas is close to what we have called moral segmentation. In other words, in Habermas's social theory moral segmentations are represented as a product of social evolution in modern industrial societies. The paradox which he describes is a paradox of modern times in general and, when related to the German military, accounts for an inescapable tension in the above-mentioned concept of "citizen soldier." Inasmuch as this reform-minded concept postulates the identity of the civilian and military values or value references, it opens up the possibility, on the one hand, for the social and political integration of the armed forces, and, on the other hand, the introduction of technological and economic developments into the armed forces.

However, here as elsewhere the problems created at the junction between a rational (i.e., technically efficient) system and a life-world are considerable. Because of the special importance in the armed forces of symbolic communication, these problems are essentially legitimation problems, which demand innovative management by military leaders and politicians. Our discussion in this essay of the Federal Armed Forces educational reform program in Germany during the 70s is a particular instance of this larger point.

In this respect, we must acknowledge that the "citizen soldier" concept has its limitations, notwithstanding its considerable normative, critical, and innovative force. The idea that the armed forces might establish a "postconventional island" in a society characterized by its preoccupation with technological-economic progress is unrealistic.

However, for the purpose of moral research, we would like to propose the following conclusion: perhaps it is not only the conditions of moral development which are important, but also the social conditions for the application of moral principles. If so, then moral research should assume the task of examining the political and pedagogical practice of society with the particular aim of exploring the chances for reflection and experimentation necessary to actualize moral principles.

Our optimistic belief in the possibility of social rationality is, of course, an assumption, one which is based on Lawrence Kohlberg's own assumption "that a higher stage is a better stage." Without these assumptions, the concept of moral segmentation as described in the present context would be irrelevant.

Single-Issue Movements

Political Commitment and Moral Judgment

Michael Schenk and Gerhard Bohm

As a new form of organized political activity, single-issue movements
(Bürgerinitiativen) have become a social phenomenon that is no longer
a negligible political and social factor in society. The quantitative
significance of this phenomenon is undeniable, since it now includes
more citizens than the membership of all the political parties
combined.[1] In addition, it can be expected to have considerable
qualitative effects in the sphere of political culture and eventually, in
the medium- and the long-term, to lead to behaviorally significant
changes in attitudes toward basic political axioms which have to date
been unquestioned.[2] The new participatory structures which have
developed out of the single-issue movements have greater potential
for political socialization than do those associated with such traditional contexts of political education as the schools.[3] Learning in
situations, which is associated with the commitment to single-issue
movements, is believed to lead to an extension of the relationships
between thought and action.[4]

The higher development of moral judgment in stimulating
surroundings postulated in the theory of cognitive development (in
the sense of Piaget and Kohlberg) can be regarded as a model of
situational learning. According to this theory, human beings are
inclined by nature to develop democratic forms of behavior, and this
development is favored and fostered by the model of a democratic
environment.[5] It is asserted that single-issue movements endeavor to
realize the following elements of democratic environments to a
particular degree (Zillessen, 1974): mutual recognition and respectful
treatment of one another, the desire to achieve justice among individuals on the basis of equality and reciprocity, cooperation among
individuals, and the search for competent control of the environment, particularly in situations in which cognitive dissonance or dise-

quilibrium is perceived between the real social conditions and the stated ideal principles. In this case political commitment within such single-issue movements is presumably related to the development of the moral judgment of those active within the movements.

Two general sets of research questions can be formulated in regard to the level of moral judgment of the members of single-issue movements. First, do single-issue movements constitute specific life-worlds that foster the development of moral judgment (Kohlberg, 1969, p. 399), and how are they constituted? Do they permit the participants to take on active roles and to acquire the experience in dealing with conflicts that promotes the further development of moral cognition by creating disequilibrium? (See Kohlberg, 1969, pp. 397ff.) Second, how far does the stage of moral judgment reached by a subject influence his or her political commitment, choice of political activities, and forms of political protest?

THEORETICAL BACKGROUND

The Single-Issue Movements

Although the term "single-issue movements" *(Bürgerinitiativen)* is new, citizen's initiatives have always existed in all times and places, from the *secessio plebis* in ancient Rome to the rise of parties and unions in nineteenth century Europe and America. However, the growing sensitivity and self-awareness of wide circles of the population was first promoted by the student movement and the extra-parliamentary opposition, which brought to public consciousness both critical reflection on conditions and concrete action. Whereas the extra-parliamentary opposition concentrated on questions of national and international relevance, the subsequent single-issue movements, as they are understood today, were primarily interested in regional and communal questions, and were only secondarily concerned with national problems.[6] In contrast to a critique of the entire social system, the single-issue movements shifted the emphasis of argumentation to problems which could be directly experienced at the regional and local levels: the lack of nursery schools, overcrowded classrooms, the spoiling of the countryside through the construction of roads and houses, air and water pollution, the destruction of housing estates through speculation, marginal groups such as immigrant workers and drug addicts, and nuclear disarmament.

The central point of political commitment is the context of civic needs, the humane quality of life. Consequently, the legitimacy of the political order is no longer measured exclusively in terms of the fundamental values of the liberal tradition – freedom, human dignity, and equality – but also in terms of the actual overall human way of living and the psycho-social and physio-material (environmental) conditions for a humane existence (Guggenberger, 1978, p. 21). The single-issue movements concentrate, therefore, quite decisively on the sphere of social reproduction, on the conditions of political and institutional life, and on reproduction for the labor force (Offe, 1973): living conditions, environment, traffic, transport, upbringing, education, communication, etc.[7] Although there was originally a marginal tendency to relate the problems of reproduction to capitalist structures, the movement has in the meantime clearly developed beyond the lines of politico-economic conflict.[8] The ideology of the single-issue movements is reform, which has both priority over the critique of capitalism and ideas for transcending the whole system (Lange et al., 1973). As a result, functional disturbances are attributed not so much to the structure of the political system as to the inadequate exploitation by those living within it of the possibilities it provides.

Although single-issue movements are in principle open to every citizen regardless of his or her political and social provenance, political participation is effectively restricted to members of the middle and upper-middle class (Infas, 1973). These are the so-called social activists – citizens whose origins, education, and social circumstance have provided them with the ability and the willingness to assert themselves effectively in social and political life (Mayer-Tasch, 1977, p. 84). For this reason the single-issue movements have not yet succeeded in developing a "democracy from below"; they tend, rather, to practice "democracy from above" (Fuhrmann, 1976, p. 138).

Aims of the Movements and Individual Motivation for Participation

Single-issue movements are concerned with problems that range across a heterogeneous spectrum. This makes it difficult to pin them down to some particular form, e.g., by way of definition, which would squarely contradict the two driving forces of the movement: spontaneity and flexibility.[9] However, empirical findings suggest that the majority of the movements are single-issue movements, while the remainder concentrate on more general goals.[10] Single-issue movements of a reactive kind (preventive actions) and those which are genuine initiatives (e.g., self-help organizations) roughly balance each other. There are as many initiatives to prevent projects (e.g., in the fields of industry, environment, and traffic) as there are to start them (e.g., in the areas of education and social facilities; cf. Borsdorf-Ruhl, 1973).

The demands which single-issue movements make on their social surroundings, and particularly on the political system, differ considerably. There are movements which either straightforwardly assert purely egoistic interests, reflecting the "I'm all right, Jack" mentality of "Don't build here; go somewhere else," or else do so under the guise of more general interests.[11] Other sorts of movements present an extreme challenge to the legal order in their rhetoric (e.g., concerning ecological issues) and breach it in their actions, appealing to the German constitution (Art. 20, Par. 4) on the grounds that their basic rights to life and personal integrity are fundamentally threatened by a (political) decision of the majority.[12]

As the various movements differ according to the catalogue of their goals, demands, and ideas, so also do the citizens active within them reveal a differentiated motivational structure. The many and varied motives for participation in a single-issue movement include those based on "direct material or immaterial interest" – ambitions for a political career, financial advantage, the fascination of the political game, group pressures, self-fulfillment, etc. (Knöpfle, 1974, p. 712; Schenk, 1982). The individual motivation for participation in single-issue movements ranges from the extremely egoistic to the extremely altruistic. Not all the initiators and members of a movement are directly affected in a matter of existential concern. In about 15% of the cases, the founders can be characterized as advocates (Davidoff, 1972) of those personally affected (e.g., marginal groups). Furthermore, a set of concepts relating to the whole of society influences the single-issue movements (particularly in regard to ecology) which are directed against, among other things, the criterion of progress through technical and economic growth, and which raise questions about the survival of present and future generations.

From this general analysis of the goals of the movements and the motivation of their members, it is clear that no sweeping "judgments" can be made about the moral judgment of members of single-issue movements. On the contrary, a differentiated analysis of the various movements with their varying membership, structure, and goals is necessary. Nevertheless, earlier theoretical and empirical work on moral judgment provides a series of theoretical expectations of the relationship between political commitment within single-issue movements and the moral judgment of their members.[13]

Commitment to Single-Issue Movements and Moral Judgment

Hypothesis I: The activists in left-wing protest groups are at either the preconventional or the postconventional stage, but not the conventional stage (Fishkin et al., 1973; Haan, 1975; Haan et al., 1977). The following hypothesis is complementary to this one.

Hypothesis II: Most members of conservatively-oriented groups are at a conventional level, manifesting a "law and order" mentality (Fishkin et al., 1973; Haan et al., 1977; Ijzendoorn, 1978). Hypotheses I and II can be derived from Kohlberg's definition of stages and have already been confirmed by the empirical studies quoted above, in particular those on American college populations and on activists in the "Free Speech Movement," one of the early single-issue movements.

Hypothesis III: Individuals with varying levels of moral judgment differ in regard to the way they argue. Those at conventional levels (Stages 3 and 4) maintain that public authorities and their representatives do not properly implement laws that are in themselves good. In contrast, persons at postconventional levels (Stages 5 and 6) advocate an improvement of laws and conditions (Haan et al., 1977; Merelman, 1969).

Hypothesis IV: Members of movements with democratic forms of internal organization reach a higher level of moral judgment than do members of groups with hierarchical and authoritarian structures, because the experience of democratic conflicts fosters the development of judgment (Döbert & Nunner-Winkler, 1975; Ijzendoorn, 1978, p. 87). A democratic attitude corresponds to the two highest stages of moral judgment on Kohlberg's scale (Lind, Sandberger, & Bargel, in this volume).

Hypothesis V: Central figures reveal a higher (postconventional) stage of moral judgment than do less central figures, because their central position exposes them to numerous behavioral expectations and requires them to take on a variety of roles (see Ijzendoorn, 1978, pp. 88f.). The integration of different behavioral expectations, which follows necessarily from this situation, finally leads to a higher development of moral judgment in the sense intended by Piaget.

Hypothesis VI: Individuals with postconventional structures of moral judgment deviate from the average of the population in, among other things, their attitudes toward family conventions, organized religion, and social norms (Haan et al., 1977). This fits the evidence that citizens with emancipatory aims clearly prefer unconventional life-styles, e.g., living in communal flats or participating in alternative projects (Infratest, 1978).

THE METHODS OF THE STUDY

Selection of the Groups

For our study we selected two single-issue movements, hereafter called Movement I and Movement II, which are at opposite ends of the spectrum of movements as presented in Mayer-Tasch (1977, pp. 104-122). Movement I is a long-term or permanent movement, and Movement II is a short-term or ad hoc initiative.[14] Whereas the former expressly aims to influence existing or emerging political, economic, social, or cultural conditions and developments, the latter reacts under pressure to a situation (usually created by actions of the authorities) which the group members regard as deplorable.

The first movement we have examined corresponds roughly to the first type mentioned above. The primary goal of Movement I is the establishment of a social facility, the necessity for which has been demonstrated by a needs analysis carried out by the movement itself. The movement consists of about fifty members. After the achievement of the first goal, many members of the movement, especially those in leading positions, wish to set new goals in the social sphere as a concrete means of realizing an exemplary, emancipatory form of organization, an alternative to conventional political organizations. They also aspire to realize this in their dealings with one another. The executive committee consists of twelve persons who – by their own account – were elected only in order to satisfy the requirements of the law on societies and associations. Decisions are made at meetings held at regular intervals, with all the members present having equal rights. According to our observations, after some confusion this egalitarian procedure generally leads a consensus supported by all the participants. However, this is true only of an active core of about 25 persons, whereas many other members, especially those who joined the movement later, feel that they either have not been accepted or have actually been excluded from a circle characterized by a variety of close informal and private relationships. Although most of the founding members have known each other from their previous work for the Social Democratic Party, the movement deliberately maintains independence from the political parties in order to avoid the restrictions involved in party political work and to realize a different model of political organization. Nonetheless, the party members continue to be active in their party, and preference for the Social Democrats and the Green Party clearly predominates among members of the movement.

Movement II consists of 19 members. It is more loosely structured than Movement I, and contains a core of six persons, of whom one is dominant while the rest form an almost completely passive following. Most relationships converge radially upon the dominant leading personality, who coordinates the work and delegates it when necessary. The movement arises from the integration of a number of unsuccessful individual projects directed against worsening living conditions for a middle-class population in an area close to the town center. The town council was held primarily responsible for the worsening of conditions, because it had permitted the establishment of a noisy firm in an area already overburdened with traffic and activity. The aims of the movement are restricted entirely to the residential area, so the movement is to be dissolved when concrete improvements have been achieved. In contrast to the aims of Movement I, those of Movement II are confined to the interests and personal advantage of its members. Compared to the members of Movement I, the members of Movement II manifest a clearly conservative political preference, namely, for the Christian Democratic Union and the Christian Socialist Union. Movement II is involved in a head-on confrontation with the town council, pursuing its goals through large expenditures for publicity and legal advice.

The members of the two movements differ considerably in regard to their attitudes and values. Whereas Movement I can be identified with the "new progressive values" expressed, for example, in the rejection of "technical and economic growth in favor of more humane and co-operative forms of living," Movement II can be described as "in conformity with the system." The different political party inclinations emphasize this. For the purpose of comparison, Table 1 summarizes some socio-demographic data on the two single-issue movements, including references to the population structure of the town in which they operate.

Collection of Data

After being asked questions about the single-issue movements, all the interviewed members of the movements under study were given an

Table 1

Socio-Demographic Data on the Two Single-Issue Movements and on the Town in Which They Operate (Percentages)

		Movement I	Movement I'	Town
Religion	Catholic	44.7	72.2	72.6
	Protestant	29.8	22.2	20.4
	None	25.5	5.6	2.2
Schooling	Elementary (Volksschule)	17.0	16.7	73.0
	Junior High (Mittelschule)	31.9	33.3	24.0[a]
	Senior High (Gymnasium)	19.1	5.6	
	University	31.9	44.4	3.0
Age	20-25	10.6	5.6	8.6
	26-29	25.5	5.6	5.2
	30-35	31.9	11.1	7.6
	36-45	23.4	38.9	13.6
	46-59	6.4	22.2	17.6
	60 and older	2.1	16.7	22.2
Political Party[b]	CDU/CSU	4.3	61.1	50.4
	SPD	59.6	22.2	39.6
	FDP	8.5	5.6	7.9
	Greens	25.5	0.0	1.5
	Others	2.1	11.1	0.6

Note: The sample size for Movement I was 50, for Movement II it was 19, and for the Town it was 250,000.

[a]Town = Junior High Schools, Senior High Schools, and Vocational Schools are taken together.

[b]Single-issue movements: stated preference. Town: votes in the general election, 1980.

additional questionnaire on moral judgment containing the Lüddersen dilemma from Wakenhut's (1982) *Moralisches Urteil Fragbogen* (MUF; Moral Judgment Questionnaire) and the Magazine dilemma developed by Lind and adapted to the format of the MUF (see Lind & Wakenhut, in this volume). Our own questionnaire was designed according to the Experimental Questionnaire conception which has been explained elsewhere in detail (Lind, 1982b). It was left to the subjects to decide whether to fill in the questionnaire immediately in the presence of the interviewer or, if they lacked the time, to fill it in later and return it in a reply-paid envelope. To achieve higher return rates, two follow-up actions were carried out. From the 47 members of Movement I who were questioned, we received 22 analyzable standardized tests, or questionnaires on moral judgment; from the 18 members of Movement II questioned we received 12.

In order to validate the results of the standardized tests, we followed the research strategies of the interpretative paradigm in the social sciences (Wilson, 1971; Hoffmann-Riem, 1980) and invited those who had filled out the questionnaire to take part in both a group discussion of the results of the study to date and an oral presentation of two further dilemmas taken from Kohlberg's standard interview on moral judgment (Eckensberger et al., 1976). Four members of Movement I came to this session.

As can be expected from experiences with written interviews, not all the questionnaires were returned. Apart from the usual reasons for refusal, manifest fears and objections to contributing to a further "report on the state of national sentiment" (Heinrich Böll) apparently played a considerable role in the present case. This was revealed primarily by members of the more left-wing Movement I, who asked sarcastically if the questionnaires came from the security forces, returned incomplete and crossed-out questionnaires, and in two cases provided detailed justifications for their refusal to answer these questions. One person argued the need to prevent investigation of private personal judgments and, by implication, of psychological conditions; another spoke against the frightening practice, growing in the country at the moment, of prying into the ideas and opinions of citizens and then using the information against them if they deviate from the norms "set by the authorities." This often-mentioned, disquieting sense of official observation and control even of thoughts and opinions made the field-work considerably more difficult. The fear that, for instance, measurements of "attitudes toward property" could be misused by employers in selecting applicants for jobs is part of the same general concern. The importance of these two arguments in the failure to complete the questionnaires cannot be assessed. Furthermore, there were also reports of difficulties in dealing with the moral dilemmas used in our questionaire and in our interviews. (On the problem of the "ecological validity" of the dilemmas see Ijzendoorn, 1978, p. 19; Lind & Wakenhut, in this volume).

FINDINGS

Because of the loss of data mentioned above and the narrow range of the samples, only a few of our results can be validated statistically. They serve, however, as stimuli to further research. The assessment of the hypotheses is based mainly on the answers to the questionnaire on moral judgment. The moral judgment of the persons interviewed was substantially guided throughout by moral categories as established in an intra-individual, three-factor analysis of variance (Dilemma x Stage x Pro-Con). Supplementary analyses were carried out with the answers given in the Kohlberg interview.

Hypotheses I and II. We found members of the politically left-wing Movement I to be either at a preconventional or postconventional level of moral judgment, whereas the members of Movement II operate at preconventional, conventional, and postconventional levels of judgment. This corresponds with our first hypothesis. It does not, however, support the second hypothesis (see Table 2). Both single-issue movements contain some members who do not actually seem to operate at higher stages, and who should be considered as belonging to Stage 2. They indulge in opportunistic or "fair weather" argumentation *(Schönwetterargumentation)*, i.e., they argue at the higher level only when the direction of the argument fits their attitude. In the judgment of arguments contrary to their attitudes, however, they remain at a low level. They cannot put themselves in the shoes of someone whose opinion differs from their own.[15] This stance is also characteristic of the actions of Movement II, which can fight a businessman accused of noise disturbance to the point where he is financially ruined, for the sole reason that it cannot tolerate violation of its own legal claims. (The central, leading personality of Movement II described above is one of the untypical representatives of Stage 5.)

Table 2

Distribution of the Subjects with Different Levels of Moral Judgment in the Single Issue Movement Groups I and II

Judgment Stage:	1	2	3	4	5	6
Movement I (n = 21)	—	6	—	—	14	1
Movement II (n = 12)	—	1	—	4	7	—

Hypothesis III. The Lüddersen dilemma, in particular, reveals that, on the question of participation in a demonstration, members of Movement II manifest a stronger preference than that shown by members of Movement I for arguments at Stages 1 to 3 – for instance, feelings of security in the mass of demonstrators, loss of values, and the firm belief that its actions are in order as long as all the neighbors take part (Figure 1). On the other hand, members of Movement I have a significantly stronger preference for the post-conventional arguments that unauthorized demonstrations are justifiable if the authorities and the courts turn a deaf ear, and that health and life have a higher value than that of formal legal provisions. In contrast, the members of Movement II clearly prefer counter-arguments, particularly the preconventional Stage 1 argument that demonstrations should be avoided because of the penalties to be incurred, the postconventional argument of Stage 5 which gives priority to the utilization of all legal means, and the Stage 6 argument rejecting force as a means of political dispute (see Figure 1).[16] In the Magazine dilemma, members of Movement I, with the exception of those at Stage 6, have a stronger preference than do members of Movement II for arguments in favor of publicizing unconstitutional practices of the security forces, whereas members of Movement II, with the exception of those at Stage 2, prefer arguments against publicizing such practices. A sifting of the correspondence and publications (press releases, fliers, and pamphlets) of the two movements reveals that the first group draws its arguments from humanitarian considerations and social and human obligations, and that it wants an improvement of social conditions, whereas the second group demands the enforcement of norms and laws which, in its opinion, are supported imperfectly, or not at all, by the authorities. This result corresponds to our third hypothesis. It also fits the assumption, formulated in the second hypothesis, of a "law and order" attitude among members of conservative groups.

Hypothesis IV. The different distribution of the levels of judgment in both movements (see Table 2) suggests our fourth hypothesis, that a higher level of moral judgment can be found in democratically organized groups. However, this finding has not been validated statistically.

Hypothesis V. The objects chosen for research have different communication structures. Whereas Movement I possesses a dense communication network in which the members of the inner circle have especially close relationships with one another, the interpersonal relationships in the communication network of Movement II

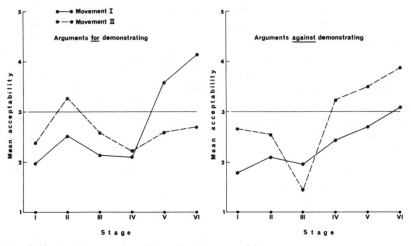

Note. Scale: 1 = "not good at all," to 5 = "very good."

Figure 1. Evaluation of the Arguments on the Lüddersen Dilemma by the Members of the Two Movements

are incompletely developed and are mainly built around a single person. In both movements differing central positions can be discerned. However, a relationship between the characteristic values of the individual positions in the movements' communication or occupational networks (e.g., Bavela's index of centrality; cf. Schenk, 1981; 1982) and the level of moral judgment could not be established, so it was not possible to confirm our fifth hypothesis.

Hypothesis VI. In Movement I we found a negative correlation between the "attitude toward marriage" and the level of moral judgments: the higher the level of judgment, the more negative the attitude toward marriage. In both movements there was a positive correlation between the level of moral judgment and attitudes toward living in communal flats: the higher the level of judgment, the more communal flats were valued (for Movement I, p = .01). We interpret this as support for our sixth hypothesis, according to which individuals with the capacity for postconventional moral judgment deviate from conventional attitudes toward social norms. The large percentage of persons with the capacity for a high level of moral judgment questioned in Movement I who had left the church points in the same direction.

DISCUSSION

Since their inception at the end of the sixties, the single-issue movements have come to include a variety of civic initiatives which differ in regard to their aims as well as the composition of their membership. Some of the movements react to the pressure of situations that are usually created by the actions of public authorities and, because they are directly affected, work for improvements and advantages for themselves within the existing conditions. But there are other movements which endeavor to achieve essential changes and improvements in conditions, e.g., in the social, educational, and ecological spheres, although many of their members are not directly affected *themselves. Per definitionem,* it is usually possible to attribute different levels of moral argumentation to these two contrasting types of movement. For the first type, the reference to social norms is characteristic, corresponding to Kohlberg's conventional level (Stages 3 and 4), whereas the second type is assigned to a postconventional level (Stages 5 and 6) with its emphasis on ethical principles, etc. (Merelman, 1969).

In the present investigation of two types of movement which differ in aims and form, the clear attribution to different stages could not be confirmed statistically, in spite of a tendency in this direction (see Table 2). The distribution of the levels of judgment in the left-wing progressive Movement I indicates a high share of preference for preconventional arguments, a finding already established by Haan and her colleagues (1968). Following a proposal by Döbert and Nunner-Winkler (1975), this can be interpreted as "protest-instrumentalism." It is remarkable, however, that this group, in contrast to others, is generally consistent in its rejection of preconventional arguments – even when these arguments favored a demonstration that the group supported against a nuclear reactor (Figure 1). According to the present state of our knowledge, this is rated as a sign of a higher degree of competence in moral judgment (Lind & Wakenhut, in this volume).

NOTES

1. The *Frankfurter Allgemeine Zeitung* (Sept. 7, 1976), for example, writes that the single-issue movements have become a "plague." [Editor's note: The German political situation described here has changed little since this chapter was first written, except that the political party of the Greens *(die Grünen),* which grew out of single-issue movements concerned with protecting the environment and abandoning the arms race, has in the meantime become the third strongest party in the parliaments of most of the German states.]

2. Almond and Verba (1963) define culture as "the specifically political orientations and attitudes toward the political system and its various sectors and the attitudes toward the role of the citizen within this system" (p. 33). For a review of single-issue movements, see also Guggenberger (1980), Butz et al. (1974), Grossmann (1973), Armbruster and Leisner (1975).

3. See Mayer-Tasch (1977, p. 160), Dienel (1978), and especially Gronemeyer (1973).

4. Out of the dialectic of action and learning, all the initially separate aspects *can* grow together and become a genuine oppositional power: needs, experience, knowledge, ideas, abilities, and interpersonal communication. See particularly Gronemeyer (1977, p. 92).

5. The determination of the elements of democratic environments which promote moral development stems from Friedman (1977, pp. 338f.). Kohlberg himself (1977) emphasizes the beneficial effects of democratic environments on moral development.

6. On this and the following point cf. Mayer-Tasch (1977, pp. 10ff.), Guggenberger (1978, pp. 19f.), and Mez (1977). Whereas the basic conflict of the late sixties and early seventies referred to the opposition between socialism and capitalism, the conflict today is one of economic and technical growth versus humane quality of life.

7. The public dispute provoked by the single-issue movements is, according to Bahr (1977), concerned with the "life and death" of our society. This is especially true for the ecological sphere. On this point Mayer-Tasch has spoken of an "ecological civil war."

8. The earlier empirical findings support this very clearly. Cf. the works of Lange et al. (1973), Borsdorf-Ruhl (1973), and Kodolitsch (1975, 1978).

9. On this point see Mez (1977, p. 101). Mayer-Tasch's (1977) definition seems the most suitable: "In the attempt to acquire a concept of them, one can refer to single-issue movements as spontaneously created and more or less loosely organized groups of citizens who, for a specific reason or in pursuit of a general goal, undertake actions of self-help or attempt to win influence over the processes by which political objectives are formulated at the communal, regional, and supra-regional levels" (p. 14).

10. See n. 7.
11. For the intensive interviews carried out with representatives of the single-issue movements, cf. research report on the project by the Deutsche Forschungs-Gemeinschaft (DFG; the German Research Association) on "Communication structures in single-issue movements" (Schenk, 1981).
12. According to the motto: "Better active today than radioactive tomorrow" (Guggenberger, 1978, p. 38, n. 34).
13. Friedman (1977) and Ijzendoorn (1978) contain summary accounts of the relationship between moral judgment and political activity. For recent German work, see the papers of the work group "Attitudes and Moral Judgment in Research on Socialization," presented at the 31st Congress of the Deutsche Gesellschaft für Psychologie (Eckensberger, 1979).
14. In the framework of a DFG project (see n. 11), social and communicative networks were analyzed and, in addition, a series of sociographic data, attitudes, and forms of behavior were elicited, using as examples the movements mentioned here. A detailed account of the methods and results of the project can be found in the final report (Schenk, 1981, 1982).
15. For the separation of the answer matrices in the MUF into those which conform to and those which are contrary to opinion, and for the calculation of the stage scores, see Lind and Wakenhut, in this volume.
16. For Movement I and Movement II, respectively, the mean preferability of moral reasoning (and, in parentheses, the related significance) for Pro- and Con-Arguments was as follows. Pro-Argument, Stage 5: 3.6 and 2.6 (n.s.); Pro-Argument, Stage 6: 4.1 and 2.1 ($p < .05$, two-tailed). Con-Argument, Stage 1: 1.9 and 2.7 ($p < .05$, two-tailed); Con-Argument, Stage 5: 2.8 and 3.7 (n.s.); Con-Argument, Stage 6: 3.1 and 4.0 (n.s.).

Moral Judgment Competence and Political Learning

Horst Heidbrink

HOW POLITICAL ARE MORAL DILEMMAS?

A fascinating question: If Lawrence Kohlberg's stage theory of the development of moral judgment were applied to political judgments, could politically controversial questions be morally decided in an "objective" manner? To establish the underlying moral stage, one would only need to analyze the arguments actually given – e.g., for and against squatting, nuclear power plants, deployment of medium-range missiles. The morally right side of the debate would then be the one whose proponents' arguments corresponded to the higher stage of moral development.

Such a procedure would have to assume that Kohlberg's stage theory applies to political judgments as well as to moral ones. However, difficulties arise at this point, since we lack a precise differentiation between moral and political judgments. For instance, Lockwood (1976, p. 317) limits his discussion to features which have the same impact on political questions as on moral ones. Kohlberg himself (1977, p. 16) is obviously of the opinion that the development of political judgment – seen from a psychologist's point of view – represents a part of moral development. His view apparently is that political and moral education are largely identical. If common points and overlappings are emphasized in this way, there is, indeed, the danger that differences will be lost sight of.

The structural differences between real political problems and moral dilemmas, which are of crucial importance for Kohlberg's approach, are essential to the question of the transferability of the theory.

In Europe, a woman was near death from a rare form of cancer. There was one drug that the doctors thought might save her, a form of radium that a druggist in the same town had recently discovered. The druggist was charging $2,000, ten times what the drug cost him to make. The sick woman's husband, Heinz, went to everyone he knew to borrow the money, but he could get together only about half of what the drug cost. He told the druggist that his wife was dying and asked him to sell it cheaper or to let him pay later. But the druggist said, "No." So Heinz got desperate and broke into the man's store to steal the drug for his wife. (Kohlberg, 1976, p. 41)

The fictitious setting of the story (somewhere "in Europe") makes it pointless to ask questions about the social causes of the precarious position of the husband – just as it would be pointless to propose specific political solutions, such as introducing legislation for health insurance. The Heinz story is a dilemma precisely because all alternatives are blocked. There is only one choice left to the husband: the death of his wife or theft.

Are moral dilemmas therefore of an apolitical nature, since they refer to fictitious situations which have little to do with reality? For purposes of comparison, let us consider a real problem situation, as reported in the German news magazine *Der Spiegel* (No. 23, 1981):

Every month for two and a half years the compulsory health insurance provider AOK in Euskirchen receives a reminder. The sender is the Institute for Experimental Hematology and Blood Transfusion Services of Bonn University, which is insisting on the refund of the treatment costs for a single patient. During the last thirty months, a debt of 23,949,263 DM has accumulated for the man. The health insurers from the Rhine Area keep refusing to pay.

So even the German health insurance system does not totally prevent the kind of problems contained in Heinz's dilemma. Contrary to the Heinz story, however, the situation in the case of the hemophiliac blood recipient remains ambiguous. The *Spiegel* article raises factual questions, whereas in the Heinz dilemma clear factual statements are made. As a consequence of its involvement in a barely understandable health system, the hemophiliac case shows high complexity and little transparency. To make it structurally comparable to the Heinz story, all unclear aspects would have to be clarified through additional information or additional assumptions, and the possible actions would have to be reduced to a set of clear-cut alternatives.

So the peculiarity of a moral dilemma lies less in its content than in its structure. Therefore, the fact that dilemmas with political contents can be constructed without special difficulties is in no way sufficient as a condition for the applicability of moral judgment theory to the political sphere. One of the most important structural particularities of moral dilemmas consists in the fact that they are in principle not optimally solvable: there is no possible action which does not produce some undesirable consequences. In the Heinz story, the husband has no chance to rescue his wife and also to satisfy the druggist. He has only two very imperfect options: to rob the pharmacist and so rescue his wife, or to refrain from stealing and thus let his wife die. Whatever alternative the subject chooses, the consequences are comparably unfortunate. For this reason Kohlberg ascribes little significance to the subject's actual choice. Pro- and con-decisions are of the same value at each stage, in that a dilemma is treated as though it were completely symmetrical. Information about someone's stage is, therefore, to be taken from his reasons, not from his chosen course of action.

In practice, however, it is often rather difficult for the subject to understand a dilemma's socio-moral structure, since this becomes obvious only in the course of a confrontation with arguments belonging to the next higher stage.

From the point of view of the next stage, pro and con reasons seem equally inadequate. From the point of view of one's own stage, the chosen option is, however, sufficiently legitimated. The cognitive conflict which may arise when one is confronted with arguments of the next higher stage would, therefore, conform to the insight that one has been led into the dilemma by one's own reasoning. For a person to face this conflict directly, and not try to avoid it by mobilizing defense or repression mechanisms (cf. Döbert & Nunner-Winkler, 1978) may indicate that he or she is already in transition from one stage to the next (cf. Kohlberg, 1969, p. 403). Presumably, the more determined and assertive one's arguments for or against an option in a symmetrical dilemma are, the more firmly one is bound to the stage one has attained. This "assertiveness of opinion" might be an important indicator for predicting the behavior that will manifest itself in the face of new information. It may be that persons showing little assertiveness are often in the middle of a reorientation process and hence more ready to accept new information. On the other hand, persons who usually judge in an extreme manner regard new information as a threat to whatever equilibrium has been achieved between their cognitive structure and their social environment.

This admittedly very speculative interpretation of the feature here called "assertiveness of opinion" refers to the symmetrical structure of moral dilemmas. However, political problems very seldom exhibit such symmetry. Consequently, in the absence of special information, we cannot assume that the decision and the stage of reasoning are independent of each other. A further essential difference has already been mentioned: the structure of a moral dilemma is set up by the person making the judgment, unlike that of political problems, in which, to a large extent, the specific situations are formulated in advance, or "preconstructed." This preconstruction can determine the stage up to which a problem is symmetrical, or the stage from which an asymmetry is found, such that reasons for certain decisions can no longer be given. Therefore, it is difficult to assess political arguments in an "objective" manner. Since a classification according to Kohlberg's stage system is neutral regarding the validity of the assumptions underlying the given arguments, the quality of political judgments does not depend only on their moral stage, but also, and equally, on its congruence with reality (cf. Schneider, 1982).

Political learning constitutes an interactive process between the individual and his environment. When regarding identical aspects of reality, individuals may develop quite different internal representations. Recognition is determined not only by the objective structure of the "outside world" but also by the individually formed cognitive structure, i.e., the "inside world." For interaction with the political or social environment, the individual's stage of moral judgment is especially important. It may be assumed that, according to the level of moral development, political problem situations can be interpreted in various ways. New information is understood in a manner which allows it to be easily assimilated at the level of insight appropriate to one's stage of moral reasoning. The purpose of this procedure is to keep intact the balance between the individual and his environment once that balance is reached. We are more inclined to regard the environment in terms of our former experience than to keep changing ourselves to keep pace with the changing demands of the environment. The accommodation processes which are necessary for the further development of the moral judgment structure affect one's own self-interpretation and, hence, are risky (cf. Heidbrink, 1979, p. 18). The more strongly one is bound to an already-attained stage of moral judgment, the less able one will be to alter the quality of his or her political awareness. If this thesis holds, the ability for political learning closely depends on the process of moral judgment development.

COGNITIVE COMPLEXITY

Formally, the transformation of real political problems into moral dilemmas constitutes a reduction of complexity. By means of additional hypothetical assumptions, complex political circumstances can be brought to a "moral crux." At the same time, this transformation evens out inter-individual differences in the subjective judgment scopes. In the extreme case, political circumstances can be thought of in complete abstraction from the network of concrete social relationships, thereby eliminating all opportunities to interpret situations in a subjective manner. Problems are depoliticized, but at the cost of letting all the morally "nonproblematic" options fall victim to complexity reduction.

From a psychologist's point of view there are, according to Dörner (1976, p. 18), three main kinds of complexity reduction that are possible when solving problems: (1) abstraction, (2) formation of complexes, and (3) reduction. By means of abstraction, unessential variables are eliminated from the problem area, which result in a restriction of focus to those properties which are essential for the solution. Formation of complexes is, according to Dörner, the grouping of single properties into an integral whole. Reduction is carried out by considering a common basic property, which has as its consequences or symptoms other single properties, instead of considering all the single properties as a set.

When dealing with political circumstances, the appropriateness of the performed complexity reductions is often a matter of controversy. If, for instance, you do not distinguish between different reactor types when discussing nuclear power plants, one person may accept the omission as a reasonable abstraction, but another may seize on it as a generalization that negates your argument. The formation of complexes can be even more explosive when applied to political circumstances, for it determines the consideration's "degree of resolution." The stronger the formation of complexes, the lower the degree of resolution. A very high degree of resolution leads to a "microscopic" view of the problem, whereas a low degree of resolution creates distance and allows the overall design to come into view. Different kinds of complex forming may lead to problem definitions which may have almost nothing to do with each other. Then the problem solutions will look correspondingly different. In the nuclear power debate, some demand a "general change of view" and trust in alternative forms of energy, economy, and lifestyle, while others counter that security systems in nuclear power plants are becoming more and more sophisticated. The most rigorous, and at the same time politically most risky, of these three ways of reducing complexity is the one which Dörner simply calls "reduction." In the extreme case, all political problems can be reduced to a single common "basic evil." As an example, Dörner mentions the reduction of all economic and political difficulties in the twenties and thirties to a "conspiracy of Zionism."

In politics, reductions of complexity may be seen only partially as individual processes, because given reductions are often adopted unreflectively. Individual persons seldom have either the opportunity or the ability to see political circumstances in their full complexity. For example, whatever is presented in the media as "politics" is necessarily more or less reduced in advance. If somebody is unable to recognize such reductions for what they are, he is helpless and has to take them at face value.

The ability to deal with complex information in a complex manner is treated in the theory of cognitive complexity (Harvey et al., 1961; Schroder et al., 1975; Mandl & Huber, 1978; Streufert & Streufert, 1978). Huber (1982) gives a comprehensive treatment of the importance of this approach for political learning processes. As in the theory of moral judgment, learning is seen as an interaction between the individual and his environment. The actual information-processing capacity results from interactions between the individual cognitive structure and certain properties of the situation. In the present context, the most important property is the complexity of information, for example, the complexity of a political message. In empirical investigations, an optimal learning environment has proved to be one which is moderately complex with respect to the degree of cognitive structuredness. This relationship corresponds to a U-curve: either too much or too little complexity in the environment leads to a decrease in the actual information-processing capacity.

In contrast to real political problems, moral dilemmas show little information complexity and therefore require only a relatively modest processing capacity. Of course, they can (and should) evoke very differentiated moral considerations, but these are processes which should be distinguished from direct information processing. If students are confronted with moral dilemmas in a politics course, their moral judgment can be improved (Blatt & Kohlberg, 1975), but their ability to cope with complex political circumstances remains largely unaffected.

According to our theoretical opinion, three "levels of understanding," marked by specific difficulties or learning impediments, can be analytically distinguished in political learning processes. The first level pertains to the form of presenting political circumstances, i.e., their surface structure. On this level, difficulties of understanding may be avoided through the choice of a different form of presentation which is more suitable for the learner. The concept of understandability developed by Langer et al. (1974) refers to this level. Learning impediments on the second or third level are more serious, because they are caused by the detail structure and thus do not depend on the way the facts are presented. On the second level, the understanding does not fail because of an unnecessarily complicated description, but because of the actual complexity of the facts. Merely simplifying the form of presentation will not be sufficient here; the complexity of the facts themselves must be reduced. The third level pertains mainly to the arguments given for possible problem solutions or the justifications of the consequences of actions, and is therefore associated with the stage of moral judgment. If the moral stage of the learner lies more than one stage below the stage of reasoning presented, an adequate understanding is impossible (Kohlberg & Turiel, 1971, p. 450).

With respect to the learner, these three levels can be considered a chain of barriers or filters. The first filter reduces descriptions which are too complicated, the second reduces factual complexity which is too high, and the third reduces moral arguments which are too pretentious. We have tried to show that moral dilemmas are so constructed that they usually pass smoothly through the first and second filters. Indeed, they require as direct a passage as possible to the third filter, i.e., to the person's moral judgment stage. With political problems this does not happen, because the first two filters are sensitive to real political circumstances producing partial or even complete blockage well before moral judgment is involved.

It should now be clear why political education cannot be reduced to moral education. Moral judgment is a necessary but insufficient condition for the development of political judgment. It is important that students experience complexity as a constitutive property of political relations and of political thinking, and that they learn to cope properly with this complexity.

MORAL JUDGMENT, COGNITIVE
COMPLEXITY, AND POLITICAL LEARNING

The present investigation has been performed as a pilot study preceding a more extensive project dealing with questions of the use of media in political classes at vocational schools. It was designed to test instruments for measuring the stage of moral judgment and the degree of cognitive structuredness, and to assess the importance of both properties for political learning processes.

Both properties are treated as independent variables, while the learning performance and the learning progress serve as dependent variables. Therefore the goal of this investigation was not to verify instructional possibilities for promoting cognitive and moral development, but to prove that both dimensions of development influence the gathering and processing of political information.

The investigation was performed in the winter of 1979 in 12 classes of vocational schools with a total of 294 students. In order to provide a comparable learning situation for all students, an educational television film from the series *Politik Aktuell* (Current Politics) of the German broadcasting company WDR was used. The film is entitled *Organe aus zweiter Hand* (Secondhand Organs) and discusses a controversial legislative proposal concerning organ donations.

Lind's *Moralische Urteil Test* (MUT; see Lind, 1978a; Lind & Wakenhut, in this volume) was employed to determine the moral judgment competence of the students. Two stories from the MUT were used, that of the workers and that of the physician. The degree of cognitive structuredness was determined through two incomplete sentences taken from *The Paragraph Completion Test* (PTC; Schroder et al., 1975), namely, "When I am criticized . . . " and "When I am in doubt . . . " The teaching goals of the educational television film were pinpointed by means of a related analysis (cf. Heidbrink, 1978). A teaching-goal-oriented test, LOT, based on these teaching goals, was devised specifically for this study to measure prior knowledge and learning progress. The test consisted of 15 multiple choice problems, which were given as a pretest to the experimental group and as a posttest to all students. In order to examine a possible sensitizing influence, the control group's pretest did not contain any questions related to the film.

Findings on Moral Judgment Competence

Further details of the investigation design and other procedures will not be discussed, since this would be of no direct relevance to the results described here.[3] However, a more detailed look at the *findings* from the study will allow us to compare our results with those of the other studies described elsewhere in the present volume. Table 1 shows median and standard deviations for the stage preferences. For our purposes all four stage-specific items of the stories of the workers and the physician were averaged.[4]

Table 1

Medians and Standard Deviations of Stage Preferences (MUT)[4]

	Medians	Standard deviations	*n*
Stage 1	1.6	0.74	273
Stage 2	1.5	0.75	274
Stage 3	2.0	0.72	269
Stage 4	2.1	0.63	276
Stage 5	2.6	0.63	271
Stage 6	2.6	0.64	265

As expected, the medians depend on the theoretical order of stages. A clear increase in the values can be noticed as subjects advance to the next moral level, that is, at Stage 3 (conventional level) and at Stage 5 (postconventional level). For the analysis of the cognitive aspect of moral development, two measures were computed. At first, the degree of moral differentiation (the so-called "Stage factor") was determined by Lind's (1978a, 1985d) method of the intra-individual decomposition of variance components (see also Lind & Wakenhut, in this volume). Additionally, intra-individual rank correlations (Kendall's *tau*) between the stage preferences and the theoretical order of stages were computed (Heidbrink, 1982, p. 86).

The analysis of variance shows that the Stage factor explains on average the highest proportion of the response variance, whereas the Story factor, i.e., differential acceptability due to the dilemma context, explains the lowest. Hence, when assigning preference values, the students orient themselves more according to the stage-specific quality of the given reasons than to the congruity of the reasons with the direction of their decision (the Pro-Con factor). Systematic differences in the responses to both stories seldom occur.

Table 2

Means and Standard Deviations of the Individual Structure of Moral Judgment (MUT)

	Means	Standard deviations
Stage factor	0.27	0.17
Pro-Con factor	0.17	0.20
Story factor	0.05	0.07
Rank correlation *tau*	0.26	0.20

Despite the nearly identical numerical values for the Stage factor and the rank correlation *tau*, it should be emphasized that two clearly different operational realizations of moral judgment are involved. The Stage factor constitutes an intra-individual measure of variance which responds in the same manner to each kind of consistent distinction among arguments assigned to different stages. Because six stages allow $7! = 720$ different sequences, the maximum value 1 may be achieved theoretically by the same number of sequences. The rank correlation, instead, yields the optimal value $+1.0$ only if the empirical rank order of preference values is exactly equal to the theoretical order of stages. The correlation of these two measures was $r (tau) = .73$ $(N = 256)$. The correlation value allows the conclusion that the variance, which is explained by the Stage factor, may indeed reflect Kohlberg's stage hierarchy. A model data analysis, which included the calculation of *tau*-values for each possible sequence of stages, also revealed a very good congruity of the empirical response structures to a theoretical ideal structure (cf. Heidbrink, 1984). After all, these findings may be considered a strong substantiation of both the validity of the MUT and the correctness of the moral judgment theory. This also follows from the close resemblance of our results to those of others using the MUT (cf. Lind, 1985d).

Correlations between All Three Variables

Before examining the influence of moral judgment and cognitive structuredness on the learning processes initiated by the television film, it was necessary to determine whether the students had made any measurable learning progress. Indeed, in the experimental group a highly significant difference between pretest and posttest values of the learning-goal-oriented test was obtained. A comparison with the control-group's posttest values revealed that the sensitizing influence of the pretesting could be statistically identified, but only within an order of magnitude which was negligible compared to that of the learning progress caused by the television film alone. Table 3 contains the correlations of the MUT and the PCT with the learning-goal-oriented learning achievements.[5]

Table 3

Correlations Between MUT, PCT, and Learning Achievement[5]

Learning Achievement:	Pretest	Posttest	Progress (diff.)
MUT			
Stage factor	0.25**	0.32**	0.22**
Rank correlation *tau*	0.29**	0.41**	0.28**
Extremity of opinion	−0.03	−0.29**	−0.31**
PCT	0.41**	0.45**	0.26**

**p = .01; *n* = 140.

The correlations in Table 3 fully support our hypotheses. Both moral judgment measures show a highly significant correlation with all three learning-goal-oriented achievement measures. As expected, the students' degree of cognitive structuredness also correlates positively with learning achievements. Remarkably, the empirical results are compatible with the rather speculative thesis that extremity of opinion in the MUT can be considered an indicator of one's fixation at a certain stage and, therefore, as a measure of one's openness to new information. The insignificant correlation with the pretest achievements may be explained as a consequence of the time lag between the pretested learning processes, which of course must have been performed before the investigation started, and the determination of the extremity. This supports the opinion that extremity is a property which depends on the actual level of development.

PEDAGOGICAL IMPLICATIONS

The results of our study suggest that, corresponding to our theoretical considerations, cognitive complexity and moral judgment constitute important preconditions of political learning processes. Although the empirical evidence covers only a small section of the theoretically postulated relationships, it nevertheless suggests the notion that the chosen approach opens a promising path which may lead to a better understanding of political learning processes.

Pedagogically, it is important to take into consideration the students' actual cognitive and moral development stages. Of course this does not mean that teachers need to determine each student's development level by means of extravagant testing procedures before teaching about political issues. In our opinion, "indirect" methods of taking the students' learning readiness into account seem less costly and at the same time more appropriate to the goals of political education. Teachers need lesson plans and other teaching materials designed to offset whatever difficulties might arise from the students' developmental differences.

Such lessons could be based upon moral dilemmas which, because of their above-mentioned lack of complexity, involve special cognitive preconditions. But the lessons must not be restricted to fictitious situations nor to the level of "private" morals. Hence, moral dilemmas must eventually be "politicized." This should be done by the students themselves in the course of a discursive process. In small heterogeneous groups it might be equally important to stimulate moral judgment through arguments from the next higher stage, and to create complexity by discussing the conditions which have been introduced in the situation of the story. This type of procedure closely resembles that of political games, although the goal of describing reality as well as possible should never be forgotten.[8]

Taking complexity into account offers the opportunity to utilize Kohlberg's approach for the purpose of political education without falling victim to the danger of "depoliticization." The more the student realizes that complexity is a constitutive property of politics, the less he or she risks mistaking reductions for reality itself. Making this awareness vivid is especially important for the development of political judgment, because otherwise reductions could lead to a rigid conception of the world, a conception that is politically dangerous as well as naive and undifferentiated. In contrast, the knowledge that unsubstantiated assumptions about reality may lie beneath one's view of political problems seems a promising precondition for openness to other lines of argument.

NOTES

1. For the measure "extremity of opinion" *(Bilanzextremität)* in the MUT, see Lind (1978a, p. 196).
2. We refer to the project Politische Bildung und Schulfernsehen in der Berufsschule (political education and educational television in vocational schools), carried out at the FEoLL-Institut für Medienverbund und Mediendidaktik by W. Hagemann, M. Schneider, and the author.
3. For a comprehensive description of the results, see Heidbrink (1982).
4. For vocational students the response scale was divided into five options instead of the original nine. For the evaluative calculations the raw values were transformed into values ranging from 0 to 4. For the sake of better comparability, the median in each case is given instead of the arithmetic mean. The two measures differ only slightly here.
5. The given correlations refer to the experimental group. Due to missing data, some correlations are based on fewer cases (minimum: 110).
6. The learning progress was determined by means of the regression differences.
7. For a description of these multivariate relationships, see Heidbrink (1982, p. 101).
8. On the basis of the procedure which is only roughly described here, a curriculum covering human rights education was realized in cooperation with the German broadcasting company WDR. These activities were financially supported by the Ministry of Culture of the German federal state of Nordrhein-Westfalen.

PART THREE

Philosophical Epilogue: Phylogeny and Ontogeny

What is Social about Morality?
Morals, Morality, and Ethics in Social Science Perspectives

Hans A. Hartmann

KANT AND HIS COMMENTATORS

Two things inspire the soul with ever new and increasing wonder and awe, no matter how often and sustainedly the thoughts are concerned with them: the star-bedecked heavens over me and the moral law within me.

This is perhaps the best-known and most personal statement by Immanuel Kant (1724-1804), found both in the conclusion of his *Critique of Practical Reason* (1788) and on his tombstone at the Cathedral of Königsberg. Kant was a Critical Idealist, however, because of the emphatic context in which it stands ("Duty! Thou sublime, grand word . . . ") and because of its poetic formulation (unusual for Kant's Prussian Protestantism), the sentence sounds more "idealistic" than "critical." It would perhaps be more fitting for the idealism of a philosopher like Schelling or a poet like Schiller, but no matter. The sentence has a convincing ring to it, and the person reading it today cannot help being moved by its earnestness and simplicity. At the same time, however, he will not be able to suppress a certain uneasiness. Two hundred years after the Age of Enlightenment, the "star-bedecked heavens" have spread themselves cold and eternal over Katyn, Auschwitz, and My Lai, and persons who felt the moral law within themselves when it counted died as martyrs, emigrated, or – more conveniently – simply held their peace.

When he named the heavens and morality in a single breath, Kant was expressing two ideas. The first is that the categorical imperative as an eternal law of morality ("Act in such a way that the maxim underlying your will at all times could be considered as a principle of a universal law!") lays claim to the same binding authority as do the celestial mechanics of natural laws. The second is that the binding force behind responsible action is the awe one feels before this law of morality – comparable to the awe one feels before cosmic eternity. Man's "intelligent freedom" is to recognize as necessary that which in moral and natural terms does not allow itself to be thought of in any other way. These assumptions – reasonable as they may sound – have aroused not a little controversy in the intervening years.

Kant's statement is often misinterpreted or misunderstood. Indeed, the sentence quoted above seems better to fit the capacities and inclinations of a self-satisfied bourgeoisie than the rigorous formalism demanded by the categorical imperative or by Kant's injunction, "Have the courage to use your own intellect!" The vulgar interpretation of Kant's "star-bedecked heavens" and "moral law" may well be expressed in this fashion: "That which is good (true, valuable) is written in the stars and in man's genes." And worse yet: "One person has it, and the other doesn't." Here, cosmology is transformed into magic and mythology, humanism into biologistic determinism, and critical idealism into mindless conservatism: the individual equipped with "intelligent freedom" is left to dangle in a moral and empirical vacuum between heredity and cosmic destiny. Could it be that the combination of these two assumptions (which can be found even in the thinking of a modern preceptor of psychology like Hans Jürgen Eysenck) represents a vestigial form of German idealism that has been distorted beyond recognition?

Be that as it may, Kant's ethics – understood, misunderstood, or unheeded by the educated public, and regarded by scholars as either unquestionable or out of the question – placed such a burden on the shoulders of moral philosophy that its further development concentrated primarily on a critical discussion of his ideas. As Kant's contemporary Friedrich Schiller noted in his epigram "Kant and His Commentators":

> How doth a single rich man feed so many beggars!
> When kings build, there is always plenty for carters to haul.

The categorical imperative could be met with imperative expressions of agreement, as in such neo-Kantian slogans as "Back to Kant" (Liebmann) or even "Onwards to Kant" (Kremer), or one could chafe at it, as did most other moral philosophers (more on that later). However, in the final analysis no one was able to ignore it.

COMTE AND SOCIAL PHILOSOPHY

In the meantime, however, transcendental idealism had gained a competitor in modern social philosophy. Founded by the French Positivist Auguste Comte (1798-1857), social philosophy formed the basis for the empirical social sciences which were to develop at the turn of the twentieth century. For social philosophy, morality neither fell from heaven nor was based in feeling, as suggested by the philosopher Nicolai Hartmann (1882-1950), who developed a non-formal ethics of values and who postulated an objective "realm of values" wherein values enter into consciousness through an act of "value feeling" (N. Hartmann, 1935, p. 105). For social philosophy, morality (and not only morality) was "something in the air" – a social phenomenon or a formal socio-historical process. According to Comte, human reason – which as we shall see later is a necessary precondition for morality – develops in three stages: theological, metaphysical, and positivistic-empirical.

Comte's countryman and colleague Emile Durkheim (1858-1917) turned directly to the question of the social development of ethics by distinguishing two ideal types of social and ethical systems. The first, traditional society, is characterized by a small population, historically stable living conditions, little social differentiation or developmental dynamic, an effective system of social sanctions, and relative isolation from the outside world. According to Durkheim, these societies develop a "mechanical solidarity" founded on an almost perfect socialization process based on cultural tradition. The second type of social system, industrial society, is characterized by increasing population density, territorial expansion, developmental dynamics, an expanded communication network, differentiated living conditions, greater behavioral freedom, and decreasing influence of social sanctions. In industrial societies the relative unity of traditional society erodes, and with it goes the ethos of mechanical solidarity. The conflicts which develop in industrial societies through the diversity of opposing interests, demands, behavior expectations, and intentions can be dealt with only when individuals integrate heterogeneous value orientations and modes of behavior. Durkheim called this individually achieved synthesis "organic solidarity" (cf. Bertram, 1980).

These were strong claims. The voice of practical reason – whether mechanically followed or organically integrated – was reduced to a system of social rules derived from the exigencies of human coexistence, adapted to changing social conditions, and subject to modification through these conditions. In Durkheim's typology, it would seem that the moral subject becomes a mere function of the social system in which he lives and that he can do no more than make the best of an externally imposed situation.

The idea that morality and ethics are embedded in or even justified by particular socio-historical contexts would have been categorically rejected by both Kant and Nicolai Hartmann, each of whose systems of ethics was based on a priori assumptions. Kant's formalistic ethics was rooted in human reason, Hartmann's ethics of value in "value feeling," which – being a good Kantian – he considered "no less objective than mathematical insight" (1935, p. 141). The description and analysis of actual moral judgments and behavior were of little or no interest to Kant or Hartmann, nor were prescriptions for acting morally in concrete situations. Anyone who asked them, "What should I do?" would have either been considered "amoral" or else been told "Go ask your reason!" or "Go ask your (value) feelings!" The true interest of these two philosophers is expressed in Hartmann's assertion: "Ethics does not teach directly what ought to be here and now in a given situation, but rather the nature of what should happen in general" (1935, p. 3). Even a compromise proposal based on assumptions of social science – that reason and feeling in human history and in individual development need a certain period of time to articulate things whose "absolute" and "ideal" form can be dormant – would not have been accepted by either Kant or Hartmann. Hartmann, for example, commenting on the meaning of psychology for ethics, stated that "psychology can provide only a certain preparatory analysis. Within certain limits it can doubtlessly shed light on the empirical structures of feelings, convictions, passions, or volitional phenomena. However, as an empirical science, the ideal content comprising ethical reality remains foreign to it" (1935, p. 62).

PIAGET AND DURKHEIM

We already know how the categorical imperative was supposed to have been instantiated in "individual reason" and Hartmann's absolute value hierarchy in feeling: they were there to begin with as a priori states. But how does the thing that Durkheim called solidarity make its way into the hearts and minds of people?

Durkheim's answer is unambiguous: it comes about through education and – historically and biographically rather late – through a little down-to-earth reflection. The "self-evident character" of mechanical solidarity in traditional societies is transmitted through an almost perfect socialization process in which social mechanisms (role models, threats of sanction, promises of gratification) and – in psychoanalytical terms – unconscious functions of adaptation (imitation, identification) and internalization interact dynamically. According to Durkheim, the acquisition of organic solidarity in industrial societies is based on a somewhat more differentiated, and in part more explicit, process which consists of three phases guided by three hierarchical principles: the principle of discipline (i.e., following rules without direct threat of sanctions), the principle of group cohesiveness (supportive and altruistic group behavior), and the principle of autonomy (critical reflection and the universalization of social rules). In order to effectively promote and shape this process, which is ultimately directed at creating a common social consciousness and a feeling of cohesive community, a carefully directed, energetic educational intervention was needed, one whose drill field and parade ground is the school.

Durkheim's contribution was exceedingly ambitious. Following in the footsteps of Comte, he plucked morality from the theological firmament and from the crystal mountain of metaphysics, placing it squarely on the ground of social development. Instead of an "eternal moral law," he spoke unceremoniously and quite pragmatically of historically based systems of social rules and forms of solidarity, while at the same time emphasizing their historical origins, their concrete justification and application, their historical phases, and the parallel nature of social and individual development. To top this off, Durkheim (1956, 1961) formulated a moral pedagogy to which he sought to apply his sociological theories.

Nevertheless, Durkheim drew upon himself not only the disdain of those committed to metaphysical ethics, but also criticism from his own camp (cf. König, 1978; Bertram, 1980). The co-founder of sociology was indeed rather heavy-handed in many of his methods. His dichotomous ideal typology was too simple, his concept of history too undifferentiated and deterministic, and his assumption of a simple isomorphism between social ethics and individual morality too mechanistic and reductionist. Above all, since his theory did not contain a model of social conflict, it could not differentiate between the different types of learning involved in mechanical and organic solidarity, and it treated the relationship between social macrostructure and individual microstructure in industrial society much as it treated that relationship in traditional society. Thus Durkheim's theory is better described as an undifferentiated model of the internalization of social rules than as a model of autonomous moral development. In view of the conflicts and contradictions inherent in industrial society, his concept of "organic solidarity" remains a euphemism, his moral pedagogy having been accused of being both doctrinaire and indoctrinating, anticipating the theory and practice of totalitarian collective education (Kohlberg, 1971a, p. 61; Kohlberg & Turiel, 1971).

One of Durkheim's critics, the Franco-Swiss psychologist Jean Piaget (1896-1980), took him seriously enough to take the trouble to stand his entire approach squarely on its head. While appreciative of Durkheim's "strong positivistic spirit," Piaget was unwilling to accept Durkheim's notion that the individual development of moral consciousness is only an epiphenomenon of social development, and that the moral subject is only a passive organism shaped by his social environment and indoctrination. In *The Moral Judgment of the Child* (1977/1932), Piaget replaced Durkheim's normative sociological model with a structural-developmental one and defined moral social-ization as a highly spontaneous process of interaction between indi-vidual cognitive development and social communication. On the basis of his empirical analysis of children's progressively advancing ability to understand rules, Piaget distinguished between two stages of moral judgment: (1) the stage of obligatory conformism or hetero-nomous, authority-oriented morality, which (after an intermediate period of cooperation with a peer group) is replaced by (2) the second stage of rationally founded moral autonomy. There are obvious parallels between the two models (for instance, Durkheim's concept of development also progresses from externally imposed morality to social cooperation to moral autonomy). However, it should not be forgotten that the switch from a sociological paradigm to one of developmental psychology also involves a change in the empirical object of study: Durkheim was interested in social actions, Piaget in individual cognition.

This is surely a major reason that Piaget, ever the culturally opti-mistic psychologist, drew a sharp boundary line between his work and the cultural pessimism of Durkheim the pedagogue: Piaget trusted in the power of autonomous moral development and rejected the pedagogical interventionism espoused by Durkheim. In Piaget's view, the necessary and sufficient conditions for developing moral autonomy are children's trust in authority figures (in addition to cognitive development), a differentiated social environment, and the individual's experience of equality and reciprocity. The task of educators is to lay the groundwork for these things – and nothing more. Piaget was singularly humorless on this point: "It is, as we said in connection with Durkheim, absurd and even immoral to wish to impose upon the child a fully worked-out system of discipline, when the social life of children among themselves is sufficiently developed to give rise to a discipline infinitely nearer to that inner submission which is the mark of adult morality" (Piaget 1977, p. 392).

This assertion sounds almost Kantian; however here, too, Piaget draws a strict line of demarcation: "One may say, to begin with, that in a certain sense neither logical nor moral norms are innate in the individual mind . . . . This does not mean that everything in the a priori view is to be rejected. Of course, the a priori never manifests itself in the form of ready-made innate mechanisms. The a priori is the obligatory element, and the necessary connections impose themselves only little by little, as evolution proceeds. It is at the end of knowledge and not in its beginnings that the mind becomes conscious of the laws immanent to it . . . . Such is the a priori: it is neither a principle from which concrete actions can be deduced nor a structure of which the mind can become conscious, but a sum-total of functional relations implying the distinction between the existing states of disequilibrium and an ideal equilibrium yet to be realized" (Piaget 1977, pp. 386f.).

Here Piaget is referring to a basic principle of his developmental epistemology, one that – insofar as it is "idealistic" – is much closer to the aesthetic idealism of Goethe (development is progression, the individual being a "previously molded form developing dynamically") than to the transcendental idealism of Kant or N. Hartmann. Both Goethe and Piaget were "idealistic" epistemologists, although they were influenced by the natural sciences.

KOHLBERG AND THE RENAISSANCE OF MORAL PSYCHOLOGY

As Piaget built on Durkheim, so the American psychologist Lawrence Kohlberg (born, 1927) has built on Piaget. For more than a quarter century now, Kohlberg has devoted his life to the study of moral judgment and moral pedagogy, producing some of the most stimulating – and most widely criticized – work in the field of psychology (cf. Bertram, 1980; Oser, 1981a). Since the articles contained in this volume are intimately concerned with Kohlberg's theory, which was treated at length in Chapter 2, we shall consider only those aspects directly related to the social aspects of moral development.

In spite of its thematic concentration, Kohlberg's work is many-sided and characterized by conflicting elements. In both its theoretical and practical consequences, it is provocative and difficult to grasp; politically, it is not only topical but also critical of contemporary society. This has to do not only with the subject matter of Kohlberg's work, but also with the personality of its author, who unites the most heterogeneous cultural, scientific, and political influences. Kohlberg's intellectual background is American, strongly influenced by the philosophy of pragmatism and the moral pedagogy of John Dewey (1916; cf. Kohlberg & Turiel, 1971). At the same time, he is also European, showing marked affinities with German idealism and the formalistic a priori ethics of Kant. Finally, like Freud he is something of a Jewish visionary, embodying the severity and messianic hopefulness of the Old Testament. Kohlberg's professional interests are also threefold. As a moral philosopher, his thinking is speculative and normative; as a psychologist, he conducts basic empirical research (bowing to professional pressure, he has also increasingly used statistical methods, with mixed results); and as a pedagogue he seeks to give his theoretical insights and empirical findings a practical form. Politically, Kohlberg considers himself a radical democrat who speaks out for the basic values of freedom, equality, and justice (which makes him suspect to the political right), but at the same time he has been criticized from religious corners (cf. Sullivan, 1977a, 1977b) and from the political left as being a liberal whose reserved formalism lacks fraternal élan and ultimately works to stabilize the system. Similar arguments can be heard from those who maintain that his theory has a patriarchical bias (cf. Gilligan, 1977; Schreiner, 1979). The man and his work are not homogeneous entities, easy to pigeonhole in terms of a particular "school" or ideological direction.

Unlike Piaget's concept of moral judgment, Kohlberg's theses have generated considerable publicity and controversy. There are a number of reasons for this. Piaget's book, since it was one of many within the framework of his *oeuvre*, was easy to overlook. In addition, it appeared between the two world wars, on the eve of Hitler's seizure of power, when the world had every reason – but apparently too little time – to reflect on questions of morality and ethics. Written in French, Piaget's monograph remained almost completely unknown to the Anglo-Saxon (and the German-speaking) world, and was rediscovered by Kohlberg only later. Also, Piaget's theory was without direct conceptual equivalents and was politically innocuous, in that for the most part it was not bound to any particular sociopolitical concept and lacked explicit implications for educational practice. It was only later that the relevance of his theory for social criticism and education was discovered (cf. Harten, 1977a, 1977b). By contrast, Kohlberg was both a psychologist researching morals and a moralist, someone who had taken it upon himself not only to justify a normative ethics with empirical methods, but also to speak out for its application in education and society. Scientifically, Kohlberg's studies coincided with psychology's more acute awareness of its methodological and epistemological problems. Since his papers were published concurrently with the "cognitive paradigm change" of the psychology of the 1960's, they received not only wide attention and acceptance, but also intensified scrutiny and criticism. Politically, Kohlberg managed to get caught in the crossfire of a socio-political debate that had become increasingly concerned with problems of legitimacy and theoretical approaches to political action.

KOHLBERG'S MODEL OF MORAL DEVELOPMENT

The core of Kohlberg's theory of the cognitive development of moral judgment is a model consisting of six – and later, though provisionally, seven (see Kohlberg & Kramer, 1969) – stages situated on three levels as follows:

PRECONVENTIONAL LEVEL
Stage 1. Orientation toward punishment and obedience. (Maxim: What does not harm me is permitted.)
Stage 2. Hedonistic, instrumental-relativistic orientation. (Maxim: What is useful to me and does not necessarily harm others is permitted.)

CONVENTIONAL LEVEL
Stage 3. Good-boy-nice-girl orientation. (Maxim: The approval of people whose opinion I value determines what is permitted.)
Stage 4. Law-and-order orientation. (Maxim: What is expected of a good citizen determines what is permitted.)

TRANSITIONAL STAGE TO THE POSTCONVENTIONAL LEVEL
Stage 4½. Orientation toward collective utility. (Maxim: What brings the greatest happiness for the greatest number is permitted or even imperative.)

POSTCONVENTIONAL LEVEL

Stage 5. Orientation toward legalistic social contracts. (Maxim: It is imperative to hold to agreements which protect individual rights and which serve the common good.)

Stage 6. Orientation toward universal ethical principles. (Maxim: It is imperative to work for freedom, equality, and justice and to preserve respect for man's dignity as an individual. A conscience trained in such principles stands above existing laws.)

Elaborated descriptions of the stages can be found in most of Kohlberg's works, as well as in those of his followers and critics (cf. Lind, ch. 2 in this volume). Of particular importance are studies that do not take a merely descriptive approach to these stages but also treat them in terms of structural development (i.e., development of identity, acquisition of competence), in terms of communication theory (Döbert & Nunner-Winkler, 1975, pp. 106ff.; Habermas, 1976a, pp. 63ff.), or in terms of behavioral theory (Eckensberger & Reinshagen, 1980, pp. 115ff.).

Kohlberg (1969) assumes that the development of moral judgment constitutes an invariant, universally valid structural sequence composed of the above-mentioned stages. The necessary conditions for this process are the development of intelligence (in Piaget's sense, 1976; cf. Kuhn et al., 1977) and the acquisition of social roles (role-taking in Selman's sense, 1971; cf. also Eckensberger & Reinshagen, 1980, p. 93); sufficient conditions are the development of empathy and sympathy (cf. Hoffman, 1975; Lind, Sandberger, & Bargel, in this volume). The goal of Kohlberg's moral pedagogy is to help individuals achieve the highest possible stage of morality.

Habermas, who was strongly influenced by cognitive theories of the development of moral judgment, has derived from his own theory the necessity of a seventh stage to supersede Kohlberg's Stage 6 (the idea of moral freedom, a formalistic ethics). This seventh stage (the idea of moral and political freedom, universal speech ethics, communicative ethics) is not founded in a priori fashion, but must be produced through communicative competence (cf. Habermas, 1976, as well as ch. 1 of this volume). Habermas's approach also implies a more critical attitude toward the existing socio-political order. What would an ethic accomplish if the person who takes the ethic seriously and exercises his moral freedom to the full were to find himself on the very fringes of society – or even in jail?

MORAL JUDGMENT AND SOCIAL
ENVIRONMENT

The individual development of moral judgment has up until now been described as a socio-cognitive or a socio-communicative process. Now, however, it is time to expand its social perspective, for this developmental process takes place not in a social vacuum, nor even in a socially neutral space, but in typical and specific social environments. Typical environments are defined as those which are valid for particular cross-sections of the population, for example in regard to cultural, national, and class origin, race, religion, political affiliation, profession, language, familial structure, etc.; specific environments are those in which concrete individuals live (family, circle of friends, school class, parish, club, work place, etc.). According to Kohlberg's developmental logic, which defines the stages of his model as an invariant sequence valid for every culture, each individual development of moral judgment under all possible constellations of typical and specific social environments must take on the same structural pattern and form; according to a rigorous but in itself problematical viewpoint, a single exception would force Kohlberg at least to limit his theory's field of application. By contrast, socio-cultural differences in the rate of individual or group moral development and in the attainability of modal and maximal judgment stages are not only compatible with Kohlberg's theory, but are derivable from it. These differences depend on the kind and extent of typical and specific conditions which either stimulate or hinder development within particular social environments. For Piaget, social stimulation (atmosphere of trust, differentiated social structure, principles of equality and behavioral reciprocity) is decisive for moral development; Kohlberg may place even more importance on it. He goes so far as to bind the success of his moral pedagogy to the institution of a "just community," that is, one marked by justice, fairness, and strictly democratic rules. Here, Kohlberg seeks to realize in "pedagogical niches" what would be utopian for society as a whole.

In order to test adequately Kohlberg's model with all its implications it is not enough to conduct longitudinal analyses of arbitrarily selected samples. Rather, such analyses must be systematically applied to the most heterogeneous social environments and supplemented by intracultural and intercultural cross-sectional analyses aimed at identifying and differentiating conditions stimulating or disruptive to moral development. The research carried out by Kohlberg and his colleagues, which ranges from studies of children "in the backwoods of Turkey" to those of kibbutzim and upper-middle class American academics, has been collected, organized, and commented on by C. P. Edwards (1984) in regard to problems of cultural comparison and stimulating conditions. The scope of these studies has been limited, and differentiation of stimulating conditions is still little more than a crude sociological classification. Research here has just begun and much remains to be done. The articles in the second part of the present volume analyze the discrete aspects of the development of moral judgment and also in part the stimulating conditions required for it in various social environments.

HISTORY AND SOCIO-CULTURAL
EVOLUTION OF MORAL CONSCIOUSNESS

It is time to extend the social perspective of moral development to include a dimension that was ignored or forgotten in (moral) psychology since Piaget turned Durkheim on his head: namely, that of history or social evolution. Durkheim's hypothesis that social morals and individual morality develop parallel to one another generated more doubts than agreements. However, in spite of justified criticism of its weaknesses, his theory does contain a central point that has recently received increased attention in the social science debate on morality, all of which has led to attempts to stand Piaget and Kohlberg right-side-up again.

The still speculative preoccupation with the development of macrostructures goes back as far as the pre-Socratics; in the second half of the 18th century, it had a resurgence, then reached a new zenith in the 19th century in the theories of Laplace, Hegel, Comte, Darwin, and Spencer. Of particular interest for the further course of this discussion is the tying together of ontogenesis and phylogenesis. In 1866 the German zoologist and Darwinist Ernst Haeckel (1834-1919) formulated his "basic law of biogenetics," according to which the individual development of a species (ontogenesis) represented a condensed repetition of the entire development of the species (phylogenesis). Strictly speaking, the "basic law of biogenetics" was not a law but a rule, since this type of repetition can be shown to occur in many areas of development without necessarily having to do so in each and every one of them. As an analogy to Haeckel's "law" and under the influence of Spencer, who (with Lamarck) claimed that different forms of human knowledge are hereditary experiences acquired by the human species, the American psychologist Stanley G. Hall (1846-1924) formulated in his *Adolescence* (1904) a "basic law of psychogenetics," which claims that man's psychological ontogenesis is a repetition of his socio-cultural phylogenesis. (In 1895 James M. Baldwin had already published a book with the title *Mental Development in the Child and the Race.*) By contrast to Haeckel's "biogenetic law," Hall's psychogenetic one is considered purely speculative and has up until now remained empirically unfounded (it is interesting to note that before formulating his "law" Hall had been involved in the study of how children's ideas of God and morality develop). In any event, these attempts to describe human development are heuristically provocative and can be rephrased for our context by asking the following questions: Is there a social evolution of moral consciousness? Can it be reconstructed as a universally valid sequence of stages? Are there homologies between social evolution and ego development, i.e., between the historical constitution of collective identities and the development that Kohlberg conceptualized for individual moral judgment?

Kohlberg himself (Kohlberg & Elfenbein, 1975), Habermas's pupils Döbert and Eder (Eder, 1973a, 1973b; 1976; Döbert, 1973a, 1973b; 1974), Habermas (1973; 1976b, 1976c), Harten (1977a), and Schluchter (1979) have all dealt with these and related problems. The starting point of their research is, however, no longer a biological theory of evolution or Hall's "basic law of psychogenetics," but sociologically expanded theories based on structural developmental psychology (Kohlberg, Harten), Hegel's philosophy of history (Döbert, Eder, Habermas), and Max Weber's history of society (Schluchter). Habermas, who has integrated Eder's and Döbert's studies into his own work, attempts to relate his reconstruction of the phylogenetic stages of moral consciousness to Kohlberg's onto-   . genetic model. In an early article (1973, pp. 195ff.), Habermas notes that his assumptions were "very audacious and uncertain"; in his later works such explicit qualifiers are absent. However, it is still necessary to stress that the following schema (Table 1), which summarizes (and in part supplements and modifies) Habermas's ideas, must, because of its even more rigorous classificatory system, be viewed as a speculative reconstruction.

The schema is for the most part self-explanatory (particularly columns 1-3) and therefore requires only a few supplementary remarks. Column 1 contains a widely used scheme of historical periodization, wherein the first and last stages are obscured by the mists of the prehistoric past and the utopian future. The year 1130 B.C. is proposed as an approximate historical marker and refers to Biblical Israel, which is generally regarded as the first developed

Table 1

**Reconstruction of the Socio-Cultural Evolution of Morality
(The Phylogeny of Moral Consciousness)**

Historical Stage	Case Model	Form of Social Organization	Interpretatory System	Conflict Resolution, Morality, Law, Ethics	Ontogenetic Stage of Morality
Prehistoric social groups (from 1 million years B.C.)	Primal hordes (hunters and gatherers)	Small groups, absolute patriarchy	Natural myth	Rule of the strong; subjugation, submission, obedience	1
	Totemic brotherhoods	Small groups of competing equals		Rule of the capable; exchange of equivalents; naive hedonism	2
Archaic (neolithic) communities (from 8000 B.C.)	Tribal communities (agriculture, stock farming)	Family, kinship relations	Mythical views of life and the world	Restoration of the status quo ante, vengeance, family and tribe morality, moral realism, ethics of success	3
Early developed cultures (from 4000 B.C.)	Greek city-state (from 750 B.C.)	City-states, kingdoms, slave-owner societies	Polytheism	Conventional, person-oriented morality, individual responsibility, punishment instead of vengeance, kinship vs. state morality, ethics of virtue	3 ↓ 4
Developed cultures (from 1130 B.C.)	Early Christian Middle Ages (from 590 A.D.)	Class societies with extreme inequalities	Monotheism	Developed conventional morality, differentiation between law and ethics, traditional natural law, punishment for transgression of norms, ethics of belief	4
Early modernity (from the end of the 15th century A.D.)	Reformation (from 1517)	Developed class societies tending towards the national state and transition from competitive to monopoly capitalism	Denominalization	Rationally based natural law, ethics of personal conviction *(Gesinnungsethik)*	4 ↓
Modernity (from the 2nd half of the 18th century)	Age of Enlightenment, industrial revolution		Secularization	Rationally (utility) based formal law, ethics of personal conviction →ethics of responsibility *(Verantwortungsethik)*	4½
Present (20th century)	Modern industrial society	Modern constitutional state → egalitarian society	Pluralism	Rationally based formal law, private vs. state morality, (idea of moral freedom, formalistic ethics)	5 (6)
Future (utopian)	Postindustrial society	Internationalism → universal self-government	Universalism	Universalized interpretation of needs, universal political morality, idea of moral and political freedom, universal ethic of speech, communicative ethics	7

culture. In column 2, these stages are correlated with different case
models, whose prehistoric variants ("primal horde" and "totemic
brotherhoods") are problematical not only in terminological regard
but also vis à vis the implicit Freudian concepts, which do not have a
firm ethnological foundation. The "beginning" of the Christian
Middle Ages is usually marked by the papacy of Gregory I (590-604).
The arrows in column 3 refer to hypothetical, ideal states of social
organization. The as-yet hypothetical evolutionary development of
these organizational forms could be studied to discover whether and
to what extent they represent a phylogenetic parallel to the ontogenetic role-taking. However, I have chosen to treat the development of what I have called the "interpretatory systems," which is
more amenable to the short discussion that this space permits.

"Interpretatory systems" (column 4) are defined here as generalized, socially based approaches to interpreting the "world" and "life."
In the first stage, that of natural myth, there has not yet developed a
subject-object differentiation and there is no polarity between nature
and society or between the real and the supernatural; nature is
interpreted in social terms and the social community is experienced
as something natural. At the same time, the individual who has "no
knowledge of others" within his culture is passively subjugated to
natural myth. This type of myth lays claim to a universally valid
interpretation of the world, but is at the same time internally inconsistent. It is contradictory and applies to specific situations, since its
main function is to allay man's primal fears.

Natural myth then splits up and forms competing, group-specific
mythical views of life and the world, with each raising a dogmatic
claim to consistency. These mythical world views overcome the isolation of the individual in the stage of natural myth by developing
social consciousness (knowledge of others, ingroup-outgroup differentiation), and by differentiating between society and nature and, at
least in part, between the real world and the supernatural, which
interpenetrate each other. With the growing "individualization"
accompanying the transition from archaic tribal cultures to early
developed cultures, the socialized subjects recognize that the individual as a social actor plays a much greater role than was originally
assumed. Since people in this third stage are not yet able and willing
to accept the responsibility implied by this insight, they transfer
these qualities to anthropomorphic, personalized gods who can err
just as they themselves do and whose deficiencies they must endure.
In the step upward to polytheistic religion, further distinctions are
made between a real and a supernatural order, which are for the
most part independent. The gods intervene at random in human
lives without at the same time taking great interest in them; individual families and persons are protected by particular gods and
must be on guard against others. According to this thinking, both
mortals and immortals are subject to a transcendental fate which in
the final analysis rules out true personal responsibility. However, in
spite of this relativization of power relationships and responsibility,
both gods and people must bear personal responsibility for the
consequences of false or illicit behavior.

With the transition from early to developed cultures, this relativizing system of interpretation becomes increasingly inadequate for
integrating the already quite heterogeneous social groups within a
central state, whose claim to absolute authority demands a commen-

surate world view. In the canonistic act involved in founding a
monotheistic religion, a single, personal, and at the same time
abstract God replaces the anthropomorphic, personalized gods of
old. The monotheistic God is ever-present, omniscient, omnipotent,
and raises absolute claims to be revered and to punish. God directs
the destiny of man (who is also answerable to Him) from the realm
of the supernatural. With increased social differentiation,
monotheism still remains the valid interpretatory system for society
as a whole, although it is diffused by dogmatic and polarizing
denominational conflicts. Social and personal identity thus become
firmly bound to a specific religious denomination; dissidents and
heretics are at best but tolerated and are excluded from the privileges enjoyed by true believers and from the certainty of salvation.
With the advent of secularization, individual responsibility in the face
of the claims of religious and denominational dogmatism starts to
play an increasingly important role; and finally in pluralistic society,
the individual must come to accept even the contradictions between
the various metaphysical systems of thought and to give up ideological distinctions between friend and foe. In Habermas's utopian
conception, this attitude is universalized in regard to all possible
systems of interpretation and all members of a fictional world
society.

MORALITY AS A SPIRAL STAIRCASE?

This rather narrative depiction of a hypothetical evolutionary development of socio-cultural systems and their world views can be rephrased in
conceptually abstract terms and – analogous to the reinterpretation of
Kohlberg's ontogenetic theory by Eckensberger and Reinshagen (1980,
pp. 109, 129) – can be transformed into a spiral-shaped structural model.
The first cycle in this spiral is composed of natural myth, mythical world
views, and polytheism, the second of monotheism, denominalization,
and secularization. The stages of the first cycle correspond in position
and structure to those of the second; in both cycles structural development proceeds from unity and totality (natural myth, monotheism) to
polarity and dogmatism (mythical world views, denominalization), and
finally to diversity and relativization (polytheism, secularization). In regard to legitimization, unity and totality need no justification and come
about "naturally"; dogmatism requires only a justification of the ruler's
prerogative, whereas the final, relativizing type of thought requires logically founded justifications. With the stage of pluralism, there begins a

third cycle, in which the structural variants of unity, polarity, and diversity permanently interact and renew themselves. The idea of unity in diversity and diversity in unity, formulated by Heraclitus (544-483 B.C.) in his 8th Fragment, becomes the guiding principle of social consensus, which is based on the solution of potentially polarizing conflicts through compromise or consensus. The pluralistic system is not "natural," nor can it be dogmatically founded; it can develop only through the free association of autonomous individuals who have recourse to accumulated historical knowledge and dynamic processes of normative value formation. In all three cases, evolutionary impulses originate in both the individual and the socio-political sphere. In the first cycle, man is defined "symbiotically" by something that lies outside his self ("natural" identity); in political terms this corresponds to a desire for preserving the status quo. In the second cycle, man defines himself "egocentrically," in contrast to others, be it as a creation of God (in terms of religious faith,) or as a private person (role identity); politically, the dominant motive is the imperial expansion of influence zones. Finally, in the third cycle, man defines himself in terms of others through dialogue with them (ego-identity); the political expression of this is a democratic ideology which requires the universalization of democratic values.

Just as individual socio-cognitive development can be considered a necessary condition for the ontogenesis of moral judgment, so can the development of different types of social organization and interpretatory systems be considered the necessary condition for the phylogenesis of conflict-solving models, morals, legal systems, and philosophical systems of ethics, as depicted in column 5 of Table 1. The reconstruction of these different stages requires us to derive specific rule systems from the corresponding forms of social organization and interpretatory systems, a process which cannot be undertaken here. In column 6, the phylogenetic "moral stages" have been tentatively correlated with Kohlberg's ontogenetic stages. The first three relationships between columns 5 and 6 do not need further comment. The conflict between tribal and civic ethics in early developed cultures corresponds to the ontogenetic transition from good-boy-nice-girl orientation (Stage 3) to law-and-order orientation (Stage 4) in Kohlberg's model. The ethics of government rule, which in pure form determines collective thought in developed cultures, is broken up in early modernity through the appearance of interdenominational schisms. In modernity, governmental ethics are reinterpreted in utilitarian terms; in the present, as a consequence of the increased influence of individual ethics, they are replaced by legalistic contracts which correspond to the constitutional basis of modern states. The idea of moral freedom which Kant articulated in his formalistic ethics remained a philosophical construction without a basis in reality (as is Kohlberg's Stage 6). This of course applies even more to the postulate of moral and political freedom formulated by Habermas in his theory of communicative ethics. According to Habermas, the autonomous individual is no longer obliged to follow an a priori "moral law" but must instead construct such a law himself, not only by tolerating dissenting modes of thought (as Kant demanded), but by entering into a process of permanent dialogue with dissenters and supporting them – even at the tragic cost of entering into conflict with society as a whole. Incidentally, in his evolutionary theory Habermas assumes that the evolutionary process is driven forward by the discrepancy between social processes of policy formulation and policy implementation (and the conflicts that result therefrom), and suggests in addition that "ontogenetic learning processes are well ahead of the evolutionary impulses in society. Thus as soon as the structurally limited steering capacities of society are overwhelmed by unavoidable problems, society can, under certain circumstances, have recourse to individual learning capacities (which are also accessible to others through world views) and use these to institutionalize new learning levels" (1976c, p. 136).

It should be clear how speculative these theories are. Rather than criticize their respective assumptions, models, and conclusions, we here engage in a critical, and self-critical, review of the intellectual tradition shared by these theories.

The type of thought outlined above – from Hegel to Habermas – rests on an unshakeable faith in the continuity of history and the evolution of reason as the basic conditions for developing identity, a faith in the presence of regularities, and a faith in the power of rationality and the possibility of planning and guiding future development. The idea that identity might also originate in "chaos" through the power of emotions, or in a discontinuous process, is rejected or avoided. One need only recall how discomfitted Kohlberg was by his pupil Kramer's discovery of apparent regressions in the ontogenetic development of moral judgment (Kohlberg & Kramer, 1969) and his subsequent efforts to reintegrate this *faux pas* into the lockstep of his theory (Kohlberg, 1973). Kohlberg's and Piaget's theories of moral and cognitive development and Habermas's theory of history are excellent examples of a tradition in Western philosophy which has dominated both the natural sciences and the humanities since the time of Aristotle (384-322

B.C.). The basic heuristic concepts of this tradition bear the names of entelechy, teleonomy, meaning, regularity, order, organization, continuity (stages and phases), structure (differentiation and integration), harmony, aesthetics, balance, and symmetry (cf. Feyerabend, 1976; Bischof, 1981). The costs incurred by the exclusion of other intellectual traditions from this line of thought are as yet unforeseeable.

FROM ABRAHAM TO HABERMAS?

It has been a long way from Abraham's act of obedience to Kant's vision *On Eternal Peace* (published in 1795) and to Habermas's universalistic ethics. Man whiled away approximately a million years on the preconventional level, then almost ten thousand on the conventional one. With the arrival of modernity, philosophy propounded a conventional "law-and-order ethic" (Stage 4), not least because of a deep-seated anthropological pessimism – as expressed, for example, by the chief ideologue of feudalism, Machiavelli (1469-1527), in *The Prince* (1514) or by the absolute monarchist Hobbes (1588-1679) in *Leviathan* (1651). It was only in the second half of the 18th century that the major works of postconventional ethics appeared, under peculiar social conditions and developments. In imperial, economically expansionistic England, David Hume (1711-1776) with his *Treatise on Human Nature* (1739) and *Enquiry Concerning the Principles of Morals* (1751) founded utilitarianism, which later reached its apogée in the works of Adam Smith (1723-1790), Jeremy Bentham (1748-1832), and John Stuart Mill (1806-1873). In centralistic France, influenced as it was by the early awakening of feelings of national identity and class structure, there developed a philosophy of government whose best-known representatives, Montesquieu (1689-1755) in *The Spirit of the Laws* (1748) and Rousseau (1712-1778) in *The Social Contract* (1762), formulated the concept named in the latter title (Stage 5). And in politically divided and economically still backward Germany there developed, as compensation, so to speak, the philosophy of idealism, whose founder Kant, under the influence of Hume and Rousseau, developed a formalistic ethics oriented toward moral principles which (because it lacks all communicative elements) does not quite fit Kohlberg's Stage 6.

The further development of philosophical ethics in the 19th century, which for the most part remained in critical dialogue with Kant's momentous work, led (at least when forced into the framework of Kohlberg's model) to what would seem to be philosophical "regressions." Hegel (1770-1831), the philosopher of the Prussian state's ideology, argued in his *Basic Principles of Legal Philosophy* (1821) for the central role of the state (Stage 5, with a tendency toward Stage 4 for popular use) but regained the socio-historical perspective neglected by Kant. Hegel's rival Schopenhauer (1788-1860), who was particularly incensed by Kant's "tasteless" doctrine that the moral subject must be insensitive to the suffering of others (cf. in this regard Nietzsche's comment in *The Dawn*, 1881, no. 132), argued in his treatise *On the Foundation of Morality* (1840) for an ethics of compassion and identification with others, indeed with all living things; however, similarities with Kohlberg's Stage 3 are rendered void by Schopenhauer's proposal to universalize empathy. Schopenhauer not only unleashed the emotional dimensions of ethics, which had been hemmed in by Hume's utilitarian followers, but in his treatise *On the Freedom of Human Will* (1839) he also criticized from a voluntaristic point of view Kant's idealistic doctrine that the driving force behind human actions is respect for moral law. Schopenhauer's pupil and Kant's bitter foe, Friedrich Nietzsche (1844-1900) ultimately turned to a philosophy of "hammer-like blows" (*Twilight of the Idols*, 1889). This philosophy, which is characterized by empathy as well as aggressive voluntarism and a hedonistic, affirmative view of life, can be said to have returned to Kohlberg's Stage 2 (if one reduces Nietzsche's thought to the dimensions of cognitive theory). Whatever else one might think about Nietzsche and his ethics, which evoked a catastrophic echo in National Socialism and a constructive one in existentialism (cf. Camus, 1951-52), he helped attune our ears to all tones of false moralizing. "Friedrich Nietzsche is . . . a terrible question mark on the road that European man has traveled up to now . . . . Nietzsche [embodies] the suspicion that this road has been a false one" (Fink, 1960, p. 7). It is questionable whether the discussion of morality in contemporary social science has succeeded in allaying this suspicion, and it is worth reflecting on whether its deliberate avoidance of this topic should be regarded as something positive.

In the course of the 20th century there have developed quite heterogeneous schools of philosophical ethics and empirical research on morality: Dewey's moral pragmatism, the non-formal ethics of values of Scheler (1973) and N. Hartmann, the anti-normative hermeneutic psychology and sociology of Dilthey, Weber, Jaspers, and Spranger, the empirical research on values in psychology (cf. Dukes, 1955) and cultural anthropology (cf. Rudolph, 1959), existential ethics, moral psychology, equity theory, analytical speech ethics, the normative Kantian ethics of John Rawls and Robert Nozick, and the communicative ethics of Habermas. Together with theological views of moral philosophy, these heterogeneous theories comprise a polyphonic and dissonant choir which we should welcome as the music of the future. In a pluralistic society, ethical discourse should be controversial in all its arguments, for all realms of life, and for all social environments, but should also be founded on an honest dialogue respecting other points of view. The central role that Lawrence Kohlberg has played in this discussion should be a point of pride for the discipline of psychology.

Contributors

Tino Bargel, Research Sociologist, Forschungsgruppe Hochschule of the Social Science Faculty, University of Konstanz. Major fields of research and publications are education and socialization, social ecology and regional development, politics and social change. Address: Sozialwissenschaftliche Fakultät, Universität Konstanz, Postfach 5560, D-7750 Konstanz.

Hans Bertram, Professor of Sociology and the Director of the Deutsches Jugendinstitut. Main fields of research and publications are society and the family, cognitive and moral development, and methods of socio-ecological analysis. Address: Deutsches Jugendinstitut, Saarstr. 7, D-8000 München 40.

Gerhard Bohm, Clinical Psychologist, specializing in working with handicapped persons and disturbed families. Fields of research and publications are political participation and moral reasoning. Address: Landsbergerstr. 7, D-8900 Augsburg.

Rainer Döbert, Research Sociologist at the Institute for Sociology, Free University of Berlin. Major fields of research and publications are identity formation during adolescence, development of moral consciousness, and the social history of religion. Address: Institut für Soziologie, Freie Universität Berlin, D-1000 Berlin.

Jürgen Habermas, Professor of Philosophy, Goethe University of Frankfurt. Major fields of research and publications are philosophy and the social sciences, with special interest in the theory of communicative behavior, including issues in moral psychology. Address: Fachbereich Philosophie, Johann-Wolfgang Goethe Universität, Postfach 1119-32, D-6000 Frankfurt/M. 11.

Hans A. Hartmann, Professor of Psychology in the Department of Economic and Social Sciences, University of Augsburg. Major fields of research and publications are economic psychology, social psychology, and psychodiagnostics, with special interests in ethics and its application to psychology. Address: Wirtschafts- und Sozialwissenschaftliche Fakultät, Universität Augsburg, D-8900 Augsburg.

Horst Heidbrink, Psychologist and Lecturer at the Fernuniversität in Hagen. Major field of research and publications is educational psychology, with special interests in the psychology of social interaction, cognitive-moral development, and educational psychology. Address: Fernuniversität Hagen, Fachbereich Erziehungs- und Sozialwissenschaften, Postfach 940, D-5800 Hagen.

Thomas Krämer-Badoni, Professor of Sociology at the University of Bremen. Major fields of research and publications are urban and regional planning. Address: Universität Bremen, Fachbereich 9, Postfach 330 440, D-2800 Bremen 33.

Georg Lind, Research Psychologist at the Forschungsgruppe Hochschulsozialisation, University of Konstanz. Major fields of research and publications are social and educational psychology, with special interests in cognitive-moral and ego development, and psychometric and experimental methods. Address: Sozialwissenschaftliche Fakultät, Universität Konstanz, Postfach 5560, D-7750 Konstanz.

Gertrud Nunner-Winkler, Research Sociologist at the Max-Planck-Institut für Psychologische Forschung in Munich. Major field of research is the socio-moral development of adolescents. Address: Max-Planck-Institut für Psychologische Forschung, Leopoldstr. 24, D-8000 München.

Fritz Oser, Professor of Education, University of Fribourg, Switzerland. Major fields of research and publications are moral education and religious development, with special interests in moral discourse pedagogy and the impact of teachers' moral competence on their professional performance. Address: Institut für Pädagogik, Rue St.-Pierre-Canisius 19, CH-1700 Fribourg, Switzerland.

Gerhard Portele, Professor of Higher Education, University of Hamburg. Main fields of research and publications are socialization in higher education and the social psychology of science. Address: Interdisziplinäres Zentrum für Hochschuldidaktik, Universität Hamburg, Sedanstr. 19, D-2000 Hamburg 13.

Johann-Ulrich Sandberger, Research Sociologist at the Forschungsgruppe Hochschule, University of Konstanz. Major fields of research and publications are social inequality and political ideology. Address: Sozialwissenschaftliche Fakultät, Universität Konstanz, Postfach 5560, D-7750 Konstanz.

Rainer Senger, Educational Sciences Researcher and Major i.G. of the Federal Armed Forces Command and General Staff College at Hamburg. Main fields of research and publications are military sociology and security policy. Address: Gustav-Schwabstr. 1, D-2000 Hamburg 52.

Michael Schenk, Professor at the Institut für Publizistik at the University of Mainz. Major field of research and publication is communication theory, with special interests in moral judgment and political participation. Address: Institut für Publizistik, Universität Mainz, Postfach 3980, D-6500 Mainz.

André Schläfli, Psychologist in the Neurological Clinic of the University of Zürich. Major fields of research and publications are moral education, neuropsychology, and the psychology of emotions. Address: Neurologische Klinik USZ, Neuropsychol. Abteilung, Frauenklinikstr. 26, Postfach, CH-8091 Zürich, Switzerland.

Roland Wakenhut, Professor of Applied Psychology, University of Augsburg. Major fields of research and publications are political psychology, military psychology, and Statistics. Address: Wirtschafts- und Sozialwissenschaftliche Fakultät, Universität Augsburg, Memminger Str. 14, D-8900 Augsburg.

References

Adelson, J., & O'Neill, R. P. (1966). Growth of political ideas. The sense of community. *Journal of Personality and Social Psychology 4*, 295-306.

Adorno, T. W. (1980). *Minima Moralia*. Frankfurt: Suhrkamp (orig. publ. 1951).

Adorno, T. W., Frenkel-Brunswik, E., Levinson, D. J., & Sanford, N. (1969). *The authoritarian personality*. New York: Harper (orig. publ. 1950).

Aldous, J. A., Osmond, M. W., & Hicks, M. W. (1979). Men's work and men's families. In W. R. Burr & R. Hill (Eds.), *Contemporary theories about the family: Vol. 1. Research-based theories.* New York: Free Press, pp. 227-259.

Alker, H. A., & Poppen, P. J. (1973). Personality and ideology in university students. *Journal of Personality 41*, 653-671.

Allport, G. W. (1929-30). The composition of political attitudes. *American Journal of Sociology 35*, 220-238.

Allport, G. W. (1961). *Pattern and growth in personality.* New York: Holt, Rinehart and Winston.

Almond, G. A., & Verba, S. (1963). *The civic culture. Political attitudes and democracy in five nations.* Princeton, NJ: Princeton University Press.

Armbruster, B., & Leisner, R. (1975). *Bürgerbeteiligung in der Bundesrepublik.* Göttingen: Schwartz.

Asch, S. E. (1952). *Social psychology.* Englewood Cliffs, NJ: Prentice Hall.

Bahr, H. E. (1977). Neue Friedensbewegung in der Provinz? Initiativen gegen lokale Strukturgewalt. *Frankfurter Hefte 32*, 19-25.

Bald, D., Krämer-Badoni, T., & Wakenhut, R. (1981). Innere Führung und Sozialisation. Ein Beitrag zur Sozio-Psychologie des Militärs. In *Unsere Bundeswehr? Zum 25 jährigen Bestehen einer umstrittenen Institution.* Frankfurt: Suhrkamp, pp. 134-166.

Ball, D. W. (1972). "The definition of situation": Some theoretical and methodological consequences of taking W. I. Thomas seriously. *Journal for the Theory of Social Behavior 2*, 61-82.

Bargel, T. (1973). Probleme der Rezeption empirischer Sozialforschung. In H. Walter (Ed.), *Sozialisationsforschung* (Vol. 1). Stuttgart: Frommann, pp. 119-238.

Baudissin, W. Graf v. (1982). Staatsbürger in Uniform und Innere Führung: Zwei Principien zur Demokratisierung des Militärs am Beispiel der Bundeswehr. In C. Hürle &. C. v. Rosen (Eds.), *Nie wieder Sieg!* Munich: Piper.

Beilin, H. (1971). Developmental stages and developmental processes. In M. Green, D. Ross, P. Ford, & G. Flamer (Eds.), *Measurement and Piaget.* New York: McGraw-Hill, pp. 172-189.

Belenky, M., & Gilligan, C. (1983). Der Einfluss einer Abtreibungskrise auf die Moralentwicklung. In G. Lind, H. Hartmann, & R. Wakenhut (Eds.), *Moralisches Urteilen und soziale Umwelt.* Weinheim: Beltz, pp. 211-222.

Bem, D. J., & Allen, A. (1974). On predicting some of the people some of the time. *Psychological Review 81*, 506-520.

Bennett, L. W. (1975). *The political mind and the political environment.* Lexington: Heath.

Bereiter, C. (1963). Some persisting dilemmas in the measurement of change. In C. Harris (Ed.), *Problems in measuring change.* Madison: University of Wisconsin Press, pp. 3-20.

Berger, P., & Luckmann, T. (1969). *Die gesellschaftliche Konstruktion der Wirklichkeit.* Frankfurt: Suhrkamp.

Bergling, K. (1981). *Moral development. The validity of Kohlberg's theory.* Stockholm: Almqvist and Wiksell International.

Berkowitz, M. W. (1981). Moral peers to the rescue. A critical appraisal of the "+1" convention in moral education. *Phi Delta Kappan 62*, 488-489.

Bertram, B. (1976). *Typen moralischen Urteilens.* Unpubl. dissertation, University of Düsseldorf.

Bertram, H. (1978). *Gesellschaft, Familie und moralisches Urteil. Analysen kognitiver, familialer und sozialstruktureller Bedingungszusammenhänge moralischer Entwicklung.* Weinheim: Beltz.

Bertram, H. (1980). Moralische Sozialisation. In K. Hurrelmann & D. Ulich (Eds.), *Handbuch der Sozialisationsforschung.* Weinheim: Beltz, pp. 717-744.

Bertram, H. (1981). *Sozialstruktur und Sozialisation.* Neuwied: Luchterhand.

Binford, M. B. (1983). The democratic political personality: Functions of attitudes and styles of reasoning. *Political Psychology 4*, 663-684.

Bischof, N. (1981). Aristoteles, Galilei, Kurt Lewin – und die Folgen. In W. Michaelis (Ed.), *Bericht über den 32. Kongress der Deutschen Gesellschaft für Psychologie in Zürich 1980.* Göttingen: Hogrefe, pp. 17-39.

Blasi, A. (1980). Bridging moral cognition and moral action: A critical review of the literature. *Psychological Bulletin 88*, 1-45.

Blasi, A. (1983). Moral cognition and moral action: A theoretical perspective. *Developmental Review 3*, 178-210.

Blass, W. (1982). *Jugendkriminalität und Moralentwicklung: Theoretische Analysen und empirische Forschung.* Unpubl. ms., Freiburg.

Blatt, M., & Kohlberg, L. (1975). The effects of classroom moral discussion upon children's level of moral judgment. *Journal of Moral Education 4*, 129-161.

Blauner, R. (1966). *Alienation and freedom: The factory worker and his industry.* Chicago: University of Chicago Press.

Block, J. (1977). Advancing the psychology of personality. In D. Magnusson & N. Endler (Eds.), *Personality at the crossroads.* Hillsdale, NJ: Erlbaum, pp. 37-63.

Bloomberg, M. (1974). On the relationship between internal-external control and morality. *Psychological Reports 35*, 1077-1078.

BMJFG [Bundesministerium für Jugend, Familie und Gesundheit]. (1981a). *Psycho-soziale Entstehungsbedingungen unerwünschter Schwangerschaften.* Stuttgart: Kohlhammer.

BMJFG [Bundesministerium für Jugend, Familie und Gesundheit]. (1981b). *Materialien zum Bericht der Kommission zur Auswertung der Erfahrungen mit dem reformierten Art. 218 StGB.* Stuttgart: Kohlhammer.

Bock, R. D. (1975). *Multivariate statistical methods in behavioral research.* New York: McGraw-Hill.

Böll, H. (1975). *Berichte zur Gesinnungslage der Nation.* Cologne: Kiepenheuer & Witsch.

Boesch, E. E. (1984). The development of affective schemata. *Human Development 27*, 173-183.

Borsdorf-Ruhl, B. (1973). *Bürgerinitiativen im Ruhrgebiet.* Essen: Schriftenreihe Siedlungsverband Ruhrkohlenbezirk, Nr. 35.

Bourdieu, P. (1979). *Entwurf einer Theorie der Praxis.* Frankfurt: Suhrkamp.

Bowers, K. S. (1973). Situationism in psychology: An analysis and a critique. *Psychological Review 80*, 307-336.

Breslin, A. (1981). Tolerance and moral reasoning among adolescents in Ireland. *Journal of Moral Education 11*, 112-127.

Briechle, R. (1981). *Die Messung der moralischen Urteilsfähigkeit im MUP und MUT.* Zwei geschlossene Instrumente für Jugendliche. Arbeitsbericht 1/81, Projekt Entwicklung im Jugendalter. Mimeo, University of Konstanz.

Bronfenbrenner, U. (1973). *Zwei Welten. Kinder in USA und USSR.* Munich: Deutscher Taschenbuchverlag.

Broughton, J. M. (1978). Criticism and the developmental approach to morality. *SAS Catalog of Selected Documents in Psychology 8*(4), 82, Ms. 176.

Broughton, J. M. (1981). Piaget's structural developmental psychology. *Human Development 24*, 78-109, 195-224 and 257-285.

Brown, S. R. (1970). Consistency and the persistence of ideology: Some experimental results. *Public Opinion Quarterly 34*, 60-68.

Budner, S. (1962). Intolerance of ambiguity as a personality variable. *Journal of Personality 30*, 29-50.

Bull, N. J. (1969). *Moral judgment from childhood to adolescence.* London: Routledge & Kegan Paul.

Burton, R. (1963). Generality of honesty reconsidered. *Psychological Review 70*, 481-499.

Burton, R. (1978). Interface between the behavioral and the cognitive-developmental approaches to research in morality. In B. Z. Preisseisen, D. Goldstein, & M. H. Appel (Eds.), *Topics in cognitive development* (Vol. 2). New York: Plenum, pp. 115-123.

Butz, W. H., Dzuck, K., Haffner, S. Harrach, S., Hegı, F., Metzger, H. D., Noack, H. J., Oeser, K., Parow, E., & Rickers, P. (1974). *Bürger initiativ* Stuttgart: Deutsche Verlags-Anstalt.

Ceasar, B. (1972). *Autorität in der Familie: Ein Beitrag zum Problem schichtspezifischer Sozialisation.* Reinbeck b. Hamburg: Rowohlt.

Campbell, A., Converse, P. E., Miller, W. E., & Stokes, D. E. (1960). *The American voter.* New York: Wiley.

Camus, A. (1951-52). Nietzsche und der Nihilismus. *Der Monat 4*, 227-236.

Chickering, A. W. (Ed.). (1981). *The modern American college.* San Francisco: Jossey-Bass.

Chickering, A. W., & Havighurst, R. (1981). The life cycle. In A. W. Chickering (Ed.), *The modern American college.* San Francisco: Jossey-Bass, pp. 16-50.

Cloetta, B. (1975). *Einstellungsänderung durch die Hochschule. Konservatismus – Machiavellismus – Demokratisierung. Eine empirische Untersuchung über angehende Lehrer.* Stuttgart: Klett.

Cohen, R. (1984). Verhaltenstherapie zu Beginn der achtziger Jahre. *Psychologische Rundschau 35*, 1-9.

Colby, A. (1978). Evolution of a moral-developmental theory. In W. Damon (Ed.), *Moral development.* San Francisco: Jossey-Bass, pp. 89-104.

Colby, A., Gibbs, J., Kohlberg, L., & Speicher-Dubin, B. (1978). *Standard form scoring manual, Part II.* Mimeo, Center for Moral Education, Harvard University.

Colby, A., & Kohlberg, L. (in press). *The measurement of moral judgment.* 2 vols. New York: Cambridge University Press.

Colby, A., Kohlberg, L., Gibbs, J. C., & Lieberman, M. (1983). A longitudinal study of moral development. *Monographs of the Society for Research in Child Development, 48*(1-2, Serial No. 200), 1-96.

Collier, G., Wilson, J., & Tomlinson, P. (Eds.). (1974). *Values and moral development in higher education.* London: Croom-Helm.

Converse, P. (1964). The nature of belief systems in mass publics. In D. E. Apter (Ed.), *Ideology and discontent.* Glencoe, IL: Free Press, pp. 206-261.

Converse, P. (1970). Attitudes and non-attitudes: Continuation of a dialogue. In E. Tufte (Ed.), *The quantitative analysis of social problems.* Reading, MA: Addison-Wesley, pp. 168-189.

Coombs, C. H., Dawes, R. M., & Tversky, A. (1970). *Mathematical psychology. An elementary introduction.* Englewood Cliffs, NJ: Prentice Hall.

Dahl, R. A. (1961). *Who governs? Democracy and power in an American city.* New Haven: Yale University Press.

Damon, W. (1977). *The social world of the child.* San Francisco: Jossey-Bass.

Dann, H.-D., Cloetta, B., Müller-Fohrbrodt, G., & Helmreich, R. (1978). *Umweltbedingungen innovativer Kompetenz. Eine Längsschnittuntersuchung zur Sozialisation von Lehrern in Ausbildung und Beruf.* Stuttgart: Klett.

Davidoff, P. (1972). Anwaltsprinzip und Pluralismus in der Planung. In L. Lauritzen (Ed.), *Mehr Demokratie im Städtebau.* Hannover: Fackelträger Verlag, pp. 149-173.

Dawes, R. M. (1972). *Fundamentals of attitude measurement.* New York: Wiley.

Deci, E.L. (1974). *Intrinsic motivation.* New York: Plenum Press.

Deutscher, I. (1973). *What we say/what we do.* Glenview, IL: Scott, Foreman.

Devereux, E. C. (1977). *Psychological ecology.* Unpubl. ms., Cornell University.

Dewey, J. (1916). *Democracy and education.* New York: Free Press.

Dienel, P. C. (1978). Zur Stabilisierung funktionaler Sozialisation. In B. Guggenberger & U. Kempf (Eds.), *Bürgerinitiativen und repräsentatives System.* Opladen: Westdeutscher Verlag, pp. 198-308.

Dippelhofer-Stiem, B. (1983). Hochschule als Umwelt. Probleme der Konzeptualisierung, Komponenten des methodischen Zugangs und ausgewählte empirische Befunde. *Blickpunkt Hochschuldidaktik 74.* Weinheim: Beltz.

Döbert, R. (1973a). Zur Logik des Übergangs von archaischen zu hochkulturellen Religionssystemen. In K. Eder (Ed.), *Entstehung von Klassengesellschaften.* Frankfurt: Suhrkamp, pp. 330-363.

Döbert, R. (1973b). *Systemtheorie und die Entwicklung religiöser Deutungssysteme.* Frankfurt: Suhrkamp.

Döbert, R. (1974). Die evolutionäre Bedeutung der Reformation. In C. Seyfarth & W. M. Sprondel (Eds.), *Religion und gesellschaftliche Entwicklung.* Frankfurt: Suhrkamp, pp. 303-312.

Döbert, R., Habermas, J., & Nunner-Winkler, G. (Eds.). (1977). *Entwicklung des Ichs.* Cologne: Kiepenhauer & Witsch.

Döbert, R., & Nunner-Winkler, G. (1975). *Adoleszenzkrise und Identitätsbildung.* Frankfurt: Suhrkamp.

Döbert, R., & Nunner-Winkeler, G. (1978). Performanzbestimmende Aspekte des moralischen Bewusstseins. In G. Portele (Ed.), *Sozialisation und Moral.* Weinheim: Beltz, pp. 101-121.

Döbert, R., & Nunner-Winkler, G. (1983). *Abwehr und Bewältigungsprozesse in normalen und kritischen Lebensprozessen.* Unpubl. ms., Max-Planck-Institut für psychologische Forschung, Munich.

Döbert, R., & Nunner-Winkler, G. (1985). Moral development and personal reliability: The impact of the family on two aspects of moral consciousness in adolescence. In M. W. Berkowitz & F. Oser (Eds.), *Moral Education: Theory and application.* Hillsdale, NJ: Erlbaum, pp. 147-173.

Dörner, D. (1976). *Problemlösen als Informationsverarbeitung.* Stuttgart: Kohlhammer.

Doorn, J. van (1975). *The soldier and social change.* Beverly Hills: Sage.

Dressel, P. L., & Mayhew, L. B. (1971). *General education: Explorations in evaluation.* Westport, CN: Greenwood Press (orig. publ. 1954).

Drucksache des Deutschen Bundestages 8/3630 (1980). *Bericht der "Kommission zur Auswertung der Erfahrungen mit dem reformierten Art. 218 des StGB,"* Stellungnahme der Bundesregierung, Jan. 31, 1980.

Dukes, W. F. (1955). Psychological studies of values. *Psychological Bulletin 52,* 24-50.

Duncker, K. (1935). *Zur Psychologie des produktiven Denkens.* Berlin: Springer.

Durio, H. F. (1976). A taxonomy of democratic development. A theoretical interpretation of the internalizing of democratic principles. *Human Development 19,* 197-218.

Durkheim, E. (1956). *Education and sociology.* Glencoe, IL: Free Press.

Durkheim, E. (1961). *Moral education: A study in theory and application of the sociology of education.* New York: Free Press (orig. publ. 1922).

Durkheim, E. (1976). *Soziologie und Philosophie.* Frankfurt: Suhrkamp (orig. publ. 1898-1911).

Eckensberger, L. H. (Ed.). (1979). *Bericht über den 31. Kongress der Deutsche Gesellschaft für Psychologie in Mannheim 1978: Grundlagen und Methoden der Psychologie.* Göttingen: Hogrefe.

Eckensberger, L. H. (1983). Research on moral development in Germany. *The German Journal of Psychology 7,* 195-244.

Eckensberger, L. H. (1984). *On structure and content in moral development.* Paper prepared for the Second Ringberg Conference on moral judgment, July 22-29, 1984. Mimeo, University of Saarbrücken.

Eckensberger, L. H., & Reinshagen, H. (1980). Kohlbergs Stufentheorie der Entwicklung des Moralischen Urteils: Ein Versuch ihrer Reinterpretation im Bezugsrahmen handlungstheoretischer Konzepte. In L. H. Eckensberger & R. K. Silbereisen (Eds.), *Entwicklung sozialer Kognitionen.* Stuttgart: Klett, pp. 65-131.

Eckensberger, L. H., Villenave-Cremer, S., & Reinshagen, H. (1980). Kritische Darstellung von Methoden zur Erfassung des Moralischen Urteils. In L. H. Eckensberger & R. K. Silbereisen (Eds.), *Entwicklung sozialer Kognitionen.* Stuttgart: Klett, pp. 335-377.

Edelstein, W., & Keller, M. (1982a). *Perspektivität und Interpretation.* Frankfurt: Suhrkamp.

Edelstein, W., & Keller, M. (1982b). Perspektivität und Interpretation. Zur Entwicklung des sozialen Verstehens. In W. Edelstein & M. Keller (Eds.), *Perspektivität und Interpretation.* Frankfurt: Suhrkamp, pp. 9-43.

Edelstein, W., Keller, M., & Wahlen, K. (1980). Kognition und soziale Kognition: Eine Analyse von Beziehungsmustern. In M. Keller, P. Roeders, & R. K. Silbereisen (Eds.), *Newsletter Soziale Kognition 3.* Berlin: Technische Hochschule, pp. 39-52.

Eder, K. (1973a). Komplexität, Evolution, Geschichte. In F. Maciejewski (Ed.), *Theorie der Gesellschaft oder Sozialtechnologie. Supplement 1.* Frankfurt: Suhrkamp, pp. 9-42.

Eder, K. (1973b). Die Reorganisation der Legitimationsform in Klassengesellschaften. In K. Eder (Ed.), *Entstehung von Klassengesellschaften.* Frankfurt: Suhrkamp, pp. 288-299.

Eder, K. (1976). *Zur Entstehung staatlich organisierter Gesellschaften.* Frankfurt: Suhrkamp.

Edwards, C. P. (1984). Cross-cultural research on Kohlberg's stages: The basis for consensus. In S. Modgil & C. Modgil (Eds.), *Lawrence Kohlberg: Consensus and controversy.* London: Fahner Press.

Entwistle, N. (1979). Stages, levels, styles or strategies: Dilemmas in the description of thinking. *Educational Review 31,* 123-132.

Erlanger, J.H. (1974). Social class and corporal punishment in child rearing. *American Sociological Review 39,* 68-85.

Etheredge, L. (1979) Hardball politics: A model. *Political Psychology 1,* 3-26.

Eysenck, H. J. (1980). *Intelligenz, Struktur und Messung.* Berlin: Springer.

Feldman, K., & Newcomb, T. (1970). *The impact of college on students.* San Francisco: Jossey-Bass.

Fend, H. (1971). *Konformität und Selbstbestimmung.* Weinheim: Beltz.

Fend, H. (1984). *Die Pädagogik des Neokonservatismus.* Frankfurt: Suhrkamp.

Fend, H., Knörzer, W., Nagl, W., Väth-Szusdziara, R., & Specht, W. (1974). *Forschungsprojekt Sozialisationseffekte unterschiedlicher Schulformen: Schüler-, Lehrer- und Elternfragebogen.* Mimeo, University of Konstanz.

Fenton, E. (1978). Moral education: The research findings. In P. Scharf (Ed.), *Readings in moral education.* Minneapolis: Winston Press, pp. 250-263.

Festinger, L. (1957). *Theory of cognitive dissonance.* Evanston: Row & Peterson.

Feyerabend, P. (1975). *Against method. Outline of an anarchistic theory of knowledge.* London: Verso.

Fink, E. (1960). *Nietzsches Philosophie.* Stuttgart: Kohlhammer.

Fischer, G. H. (1974). *Einführung in die Theorie psychologischer Tests.* Bern: Huber.

Fishbein, M., & Ajzen, I. (1975). *Attitudes, beliefs, intentions, and behavior.* New York: Addison-Wesley.

Fishkin, J., Keniston, K., & Mackinnon, C. (1973). Moral reasoning and political ideology. *Journal of Personality and Social Psychology 27,* 109-119.

Flavell, J. H. (1972). An analysis of cognitive-developmental sequences. *General Psychological Monographs 86*, 279-350.

Ford, M. E., & Tisak, M. S. (1983). A further search for social intelligence. *Journal of Educational Psychology 75*, 196-206.

Forschungsgruppe Hochschulkapazität (1973). *Organisation der Hochschule und des Studiums. HIS-Brief 36.* Munich: Verlag Dokumentation.

Frankena, W. K. (1973). *Ethics* (2nd ed.). Englewood Cliffs, NJ: Prentice-Hall.

Friedman, D. A. (1977). Political socialization and models of moral development. In S. A. Renshon (Ed.), *Handbook of political socialization: Theory and research.* New York: Free Press, pp. 329-361.

Fuhrmann, H. (1976). Politik zu Fuss oder Demokratie von oben: Bürgerinitiativen. *Transfer 2*, 133-139.

Gadamer, H. G. (1960). *Wahrheit und Methode.* Tübingen: Mohr.

Gessenharter, W. (1982). Hochschulen der Bundeswehr – Probleme und Perspektiven. In K.-E. Schulz (Ed.), *Die Neuordnung von Bildung und Ausbildung in der Bundeswehr.* Baden-Baden: Nomos, pp. 81-98.

Geulen, D. (1975). Konzeptuelle Probleme der Erfassung von Sozialisationsprozessen im Hochschulbereich. In T. Bargel, G. Framhein, L. Huber, & G. Portele (Eds.), *Sozialisation in der Hochschule.* Hamburg: Arbeitsgemeinschaft für Hochschuldidaktik, pp. 83.-95.

Geyer, R. F., & Schweitzer, D. R. (1976). *Theories of alienation. Critical perspectives in philosophy and social science.* Leiden: Nijhoff.

Gibbs, J. C. (1977). Kohlberg's stages of moral judgment: A constructive critique. *Harvard Educational Review 47*, 43-61.

Gilligan, C. (1977). In a different voice: Women's conception of the self and morality. *Harvard Educational Review 47*, 481-517.

Gilligan, C. (1980). *Do the social sciences have an adequate theory of moral development?* Unpubl. ms., Harvard University.

Gilligan, C. (1981). Moral development. In A. W. Chickering (Ed.), *The modern American college.* San Francisco: Jossey-Bass, pp. 139-157.

Gilligan, C. (1982). *In a different voice: Psychological theory and women's development.* Cambridge, MA: Harvard University Press.

Gilligan, C., & Murphy, J. M. (1979). Development from adolescence to adulthood: The philosopher and the dilemma of the fact. In D. Kuhn (Ed.), *Intellectual development beyond childhood. New directions for child development 5.* San Francisco: Jossey-Bass, pp. 85-99.

Gilligan, J. (1976). Beyond morality: Psychoanalytical reflections on shame, guilt, and love. In T. Lickona (Ed.), *Moral development and behavior.* New York: Holt, Rinehart and Winston, pp. 144-158.

Glaserfield, E., & Kelley, M. (1982). On the concepts of period, phase, and level. *Human Development 25*, 152-160.

Gold, A. R., Christie, R., & Friedman, L. N. (1976). *Fists and flowers: A social psychological interpretation of student dissent.* New York: Academic Press.

Gootnick, A. T. (1974). Locus of control and political participation of college students: A comparison of unidimensional and multidimensional approaches. *Journal of Consulting and Clinical Psychology 42*, 54-58.

Grathoff, R. (1979). Über Typik und Normalität im alltäglichen Milieu. In W. M. Sprondel & R. Grathoff (Eds.), *Alfred Schütz und die Idee des Alltags in den Sozialwissenschaften.* Stuttgart: Enke, pp. 89-107.

Greenberg, E. S. (Ed.). (1970). *Political socialization.* New York: Atherton.

Greenstein, F. (1968). Harold Lasswell's concept of democratic personality. *The Journal of Politics 30*, 696-709.

Gronemeyer, R. (1973). *Integration durch Partizipation.* Frankfurt: Fischer.

Gronemeyer, M. (1977). Aufgewacht aus dem Tiefschlaf. Von der Unzufriedenheit zum Protest. *Kursbuch 50*, 81-100.

Grossmann, H. (1973). *Bürgerinitiativen.* Frankfurt: Fischer.

Guggenberger, B. (1978). Krise der repräsentativen Demokratie. In B. Guggenberger & U. Kempf (Eds.), *Bürgerinitiativen und repräsentatives System*. Opladen: Westdeutscher Verlag, pp. 18-48.

Guggenberger, B. (1980). *Bürgerinitiativen in der Parteiendemokratie*. Stuttgart: Kohlhammer.

Gurin, P., Gurin, G., Lao, R., & Beattie, M. (1969). Internal-external control in the motivational dynamics of Negro youth. *Journal of Social Issues 25*, 29-53.

Haan, N. (1969). A tripartite model of ego functioning. *Journal of Neural and Mental Disease 148*, 14-29.

Haan, N. (1975). Hypothetical and actual moral reasoning in a situation of civil disobedience. *Journal of Personality and Social Psychology 32*, 255-270.

Haan, N. (1977). *Coping and defending: Process of self-environment organizations*. New York: Academic Press.

Haan, N. (1978). Two moralities in action contexts: Relationships to thought, ego relation, and development. *Journal of Personality and Social Psychology 36*, 286-305.

Haan, N., Smith, H. B., & Block, J. H. (1977). Moral reasoning of young adults: Political-social behavior, family background, and personality correlates. *Journal of Personality and Social Psychology 10*, 183-201.

Haan, N. (1977). *Coping and defending: Processes of self-environment organizations*. New York: Academic Press.

Habermas, J. (1973). Notizen zum Begriff der Rollenkompetenz. In J. Habermas (Ed.), *Kritik und Kultur*. Frankfurt: Suhrkamp, pp. 195-231.

Habermas, J. (1976a). Moralentwicklung und Ich-Identität. In J. Habermas, *Zur Rekonstruktion des historischen Materialismus*. Frankfurt: Suhrkamp, pp. 63-91.

Habermas, J. (1976b). Können komplexe Gesellschaften eine vernünftige Identität ausbilden? In J. Habermas, *Zur Rekonstruktion des historischen Materialismus*. Frankfurt: Suhrkamp, pp. 92-126.

Habermas, J. (1976c). Zum Theorienvergleich in der Soziologie: Am Beispiel der Evolutionstheorie. In J. Habermas, *Zur Rekonstruktion des historischen Materialismus*. Frankfurt: Suhrkamp, pp. 129-243.

Habermas, J. (1981a). *Theorie des kommunikativen Handelns* (Vols. 1-2). Frankfurt: Suhrkamp.

Habermas, J. (1981b). Responsibility and its role in the relationship between moral judgment and action. Unpubl. ms.

Habermas, J. (1982). A reply to my critics. In J. B. Thompson, D. Held, & J. Habermas (Eds.), *Critical debates*. Cambridge, MA: MIT-Press, pp. 219-283.

Habermas, J. (1983). *Moralbewusstsein und kommunikatives Handeln*. Frankfurt: Suhrkamp.

Hare, R. M. (1963). *Freedom and reason*. Oxford: Clarendon Press.

Harten, H.-C. (1977a). *Der vernünftige Organismus oder gesellschaftliche Evolution der Vernunft. Zur Gesellschaftstheorie des genetischen Strukturalismus von Piaget*. Frankfurt: Syndikat.

Harten, H.-C. (1977b). *Kognitive Sozialisation und politische Erkenntnis. Piagets Entwicklungspsychologie als Grundlage einer Theorie der politischen Bildung*. Weinheim: Beltz.

Hartmann, N. (1935). *Ethik* (2nd ed.). Berlin: de Gruyter.

Hartnack, J. (1962). *Wittgenstein und die moderne Philosophie*. Stuttgart: Kohlhammer.

Hartshorne, H., & May, M. A. (1928-30). *Studies in the nature of character. Vol. I: Studies in deceit. Vol. 2: Studies in service and self-control. Vol. 3: Studies in organization of character*. New York: Macmillan.

Harvey, O. J., Hunt, D. E., & Schroder, H. M. (1961). *Conceptual systems and personality organization*. New York: Wiley.

Hecker, K., & Schusser, H. (1980). *Bundeswehr und Zivildienst. Aspekte der Ausbildung und Sozialisation*. Munich: Deutsches Jugendinstitut.

Heidbrink, H. (1978). Verfahren zur Analyse der Sach- und Lernstruktur von Schulfernsehendungen. In G. Brodke-Reich (Ed.), *Soziales Lernen und Medien im Primarbereich.* Paderborn/Hannover: Schrödel/Schöningh, pp. 219-236.

Heidbrink, H. (1979). *Kognitive Voraussetzungen politischen Lernens. Theoretische Grundlagen und Messmethoden.* Mimeo FEoLL, Paderborn.

Heidbrink, H. (1982). Zur Bedeutung kognitiver Komplexität und moralischer Urteilsfähigkeit für politische Lernprozesse. In W. Hagemann, H. Heidbrink, & M. Schneider (Eds.), *Kognition und Moralität in politischen Lernprozessen.* Opladen: Leske, pp. 73-107.

Heidbrink, H. (1984). Zur Validität der moralischen Urteilstheorie von L. Kohlberg. In K. Ingenkamp (Ed.), *Sozial-emotionales Verhalten in Lehr- und Lernsituationen.* Landau: Erziehungswissenschaftliche Hochschule Rheinland-Pfalz, pp. 323-338.

Heist, P., & Taylor, M. (1979). *The Block plan. A preliminary report on a ten-year evaluation of the Colorado College Block Plan format for intensive study.* Colorado Springs, CO: The Colorado College.

Helmreich, R. (1977). *Strategien zur Auswertung von Längsschnittdaten.* Stuttgart: Klett.

Herzlich, C. (1973). *Health and illness. A social psychological analysis.* London: Academic Press.

Herzlich, C. (1975). Die Soziale Vorstellung. In S. Moscovici (Ed.), *Forschungsgebiete der Sozialpsychologie* (Vol. 1). Frankfurt: Athenäum, pp. 381-406.

Hess, R. D., & Torney, J. V. (1967). *The development of political attitude in children.* Chicago: Aldine.

Hetzer, H. (1931). Die Entwicklung zur sittlichen Persönlichkeit. In J. Neumann (Ed.), *Die Entwicklung zur sittlichen Persönlichkeit.* Gütersloh: Bertelsmann, pp. 257-281.

Higgins, A. (1980). Research and measurement issues in moral education interventions. In R. Mosher (Ed.), *Moral education.* New York: Praeger, pp. 92-107.

Hinder, E., & Kanig, G. (1981). Zur Messung des sozial-moralischen Urteils. Neue methodische Entwicklungen. University of Fribourg, Switzerland, *HASMU-Bulletin 1,* 20-39.

Hochheimer, W. (1963). Sexualstrafrecht in psychologisch-anthropologischer Sicht. In F. Bauer et al. (Eds.), *Sexualität und Verbrechen.* Frankfurt: Fischer, pp. 84-117.

Hoffman, M. (1970). Conscience, personality and socialization techniques. *Human Development 13,* 90-126.

Hoffman, M. (1975). Developmental synthesis of affect and cognition and its implications for altruistic motivation. *Developmental Psychology 11,* 623-627.

Hoffmann-Riem, C. (1980). Die Sozialforschung einer interpretativen Soziologie. *Kölner Zeitschrift für Soziologie und Sozialpsychologie 32,* 339-372.

Hohner, H.-U., & Dann, H.-D. (1978). *Der Oberprimanerlängsschnitt – Teil I: Die Stichprobe. Teil II: Die Instrumente. Teil III: Zur externen und internen Validität der Studie.* Mimeo, Projekt Lehrereinstellungen, University of Konstanz.

Holstein, C. (1976). Irreversible stepwise sequence in the development of moral judgment. *Child Development 47,* 51-61.

Holzkamp, K. (1972). *Kritische Psychologie.* Frankfurt: Fischer.

Huber, G. L. (1982). Kognitive Komplexität als Bedingung politischen Lernens. In W. Hagemann, H. Heidbrink, & M. Schneider (Eds.), *Kognition und Moralität in politischen Lernprozessen.* Opladen: Leske, pp. 15-33.

Huber, L. (1980). Sozialisation in der Hochschule. In K. Hurrelmann & D. Ulich (Eds.), *Handbuch der Sozialisationsforschung.* Weinheim: Beltz, pp. 521-550.

Huber, L., & Vogel, U. (1984). Studentenforschung und Hochschulsozialisation. In D. Goldschmidt, U. Teichler, & W.-D. Webler (Eds.), *Forschungsgegenstand Hochschule.* Frankfurt: Campus, pp. 107-153.

Husserl, E. (1962). *Die Krisis der europäischen Wissenschaften und die transzendentale Phänomenologie.* (Husserliana Vol. 6). The Hague: Nijhoff

IfD [Institut für Demoskopie] (1973). *Allensbacher Berichte* (Vol. 20). Mimeo, Allensbach.

Ijzendoorn, M. H. v. (1979). Moralität, Kognition und politisches Bewusstsein. *Zeitschrift für Pädagogik 25*, 547-567.

Ijzendoorn, M. H. v. (1980). *Moralität, Kognition und politisches Bewusstsein.* Weinheim: Beltz.

Infas [Institut für angewandte Sozialwissenschaft]. (1983). *Junge Männer '82.* Bericht, Bonn-Godesberg.

Infratest (1978). *Politischer Protest in der Bundesrepublik.* Munich.

Inglehart, R. (1977). *The silent revolution.* Princeton, NJ: Princeton University Press.

Jacob, P. (1957). *Changing values in college. An exploratory study of the impact of college teaching.* New York: Harper & Row.

Jencks, C., Bartlett, S., Corcoran, M., Crause, J., Eaglesfield, D., Jackson, G., McClelland, K., Mueser, P., Olneck, M., Schwartz, J., Ward, S., & Williams, J. (1979). *Who gets ahead? The determinants of economic success in America.* New York: Basic Books.

Johnson, D. W., & Johnson, R. T. (1979). Conflict in the classroom. Controversy and learning. *Review of Educational Research 49*, 51-70.

Kärn, M. (1978). Vorsicht Stufe! Ein Kommentar zur Stufentheorie der moralischen Entwicklung. In G. Portele (Ed.), *Sozialisation und Moral.* Weinheim: Beltz, pp. 81-100.

Kant, I. (1949). *Critique of practical reason and other writings in moral philosophy* (L. W. Beck, Ed. and Trans.). Chicago, IL: University of Chicago Press (orig. publ. 1788).

Karlen, K. (1981). Kursbericht eines Gruppenleiters. University of Fribourg, Switzerland, *HASMU-Bulletin 2*, 14-15.

Keasey, C. B. (1971). Social participation as a factor in the moral development of preadolescents. *Developmental Psychology 5*, 216-220.

Keasey, C. B. (1974). The influence of opinion-agreement and quality of supportive reasoning in the evaluation of moral judgments. *Journal of Personality and Social Psychology 30*, 477-482.

Keasey, C. B. (1975). Implicators of cognitive development for moral reasoning, In D. DePalma & J. Foley (Eds.), *Moral development.* New York: Wiley, pp. 39-56.

Keating, D. P. (1978). A search for social intelligence. *Journal of Educational Psychology 70*, 218-233.

Kegan, R., & Noam, G. (1982). Soziale Kognition und Psychodynamik: Auf dem Wege zu einer Klinischen Entwicklungspsychologie. In W. Edelstein & M. Keller (Eds.), *Perspektivität und Interpretation.* Frankfurt: Suhrkamp, pp. 422-460.

Kelman, H. C. (1974). Attitudes are alive and well and gainfully employed in the sphere of action. *American Psychologist 11*, 310-324.

Kempf, W. (1978). *Kritische Bemerkungen zu impliziten Voraussetzungen psychologischer Testtheorie und -praxis.* Mimeo, University of Konstanz.

Kitchener, K. S., & King, P. M. (1981). Reflective judgment: Concepts of justification and their relation to age and education *Journal of Applied Development Psychology 2*, 89-116.

Klages, H., & Kmieciak, P. (Eds.). (1979). *Wertwandel und gesellschaftlicher Wandel.* Frankfurt: Campus.

Knöpfle, F. (1974). Organisierte Einwirkungen auf die Verwaltung. *Deutsches Verwaltungsblatt 89*, 707-716.

Koch, J. (1972). *Lehrer-Studium und Beruf.* Ulm: Süddeutsche Verlagsgesellschaft.

Kodolitsch, P. v. (1975). Gemeindeverwaltungen und Bürgerinitiativen. *Archiv für Kommunalwissenschaften 14*, 264-278.

Kodolitsch, P. v. (1978). Effizienzsteigerung oder Systemüberwindung. In B. Guggenberger & U. Kempf (Eds.), *Bürgerinitiativen und repräsentatives System.* Opladen: Westdeutscher Verlag, pp. 337-357.

Köckeis-Stangl, E. (1980). Methoden der Sozialisationsforschung. In K. Hurrelmann & D. Ulich (Eds.), *Handbuch der Sozialisationsforschung.* Weinheim: Beltz, pp. 321-370.

Kohlberg, L. (1958). *The development of modes of moral thinking and choice in the years ten to sixteen.* Unpubl. Ph.D. dissertation, University of Chicago.

Kohlberg, L. (1964). Development of moral character and moral ideology. In M. Hoffman & L. Hoffman (Eds.), *Review of child development research* (Vol. I). New York: Russel Sage Foundation, pp. 383-431.

Kohlberg, L. (1969). Stage and sequence. The cognitive developmental approach to socialization. In D. Goslin (Ed.), *Handbook of socialization theory and research.* Chicago: Rand McNally, pp. 347-480.

Kohlberg, L. (1971a). Stages of moral development as a basis for moral education. In C. M. Beck, B. S. Crittenden, & E. Sullivan (Eds.), *Moral education: Interdisciplinary approaches.* Toronto: University of Toronto Press, pp. 23-92.

Kohlberg, L. (1971b). From is to ought: How to commit the naturalistic fallacy and get away with it in the study of moral development. In T. Mischel (Ed.), *Cognitive development and epistemology.* New York: Academic Press, pp. 151-235.

Kohlberg, L. (1973a). Continuities in childhood and adult moral development revisited. In P. B. Baltes & K. W. Schaie (Eds.), *Life-span developmental psychology: Personality and socialization.* New York: Academic Press, pp. 179-204.

Kohlberg, L. (1973b). *Standard scoring manual: Moral judgment interview.* Mimeo, Center for Moral Education, Harvard University.

Kohlberg, L. (1975). The cognitive-developmental approach to moral education. *Phi Delta Kappan 56*, 670-677.

Kohlberg, L. (1976). Moral stages and moralization: The cognitive-developmental approach. In T. Lickona (Ed.), *Moral development and behavior.* New York: Holt, Rinehart and Winston, pp. 31-53.

Kohlberg, L. (1979). *The meaning and measurement of moral development.* Heinz Werner Memorial Lecture. Worcester, MA: Clark University Press.

Kohlberg, L. (1980). *Philosophic issues in the study of moral development.* Center for Moral Education, Harvard University.

Kohlberg, L. (1981). *Essays on moral development: Vol. 1. The philosophy of moral development.* San Francisco: Harper & Row.

Kohlberg, L. (1982). A reply to Owen Flanagan and some comments on the Puka-Goodpaster exchange. *Ethics 92*, 518-528.

Kohlberg, L. (1984). *Essays on moral development: Vol. 2. The psychology of moral development.* San Francisco: Harper and Row.

Kohlberg, L. (1985). The status of the theory. In S. Modgil & C. Modgil (Eds.), *Lawrence Kohlberg: Consensus and controversy.* London: Falsici.

Kohlberg, L., & Candee, D. (1984). The relationship of moral judgment to moral action. In W. M. Kurtines & J. L. Gewirtz (Eds.), *Morality, moral behavior and moral development.* New York: Wiley, pp. 52-73.

Kohlberg, L., & Candee, D. (Eds.). (In press). *Research in moral development.* Cambridge, MA: Harvard University Press.

Kohlberg, L., Colby, A., Gibbs, J., & Speicher-Dubin, B. (1978). *Standard form scoring manual* (mimeo, 4 vols.). Center of Moral Development and Education, Harvard University.

Kohlberg, L., & D. Elfenbein (1975). The development of moral judgments concerning capital punishment. *American Journal of Orthopsychiatry 45*, 614-640.

Kohlberg, L., & Kramer, R. (1969). Continuities and discontinuities in childhood and adult moral development. *Human Development 12*, 93-120.

Kohlberg, L., Levine, C., & Hewer, A. (1983). Moral stages: A current formulation and a response to critics. In J. A. Meacham (Ed.), *Contributions to human development* (Vol. 10). Basel: Karger.

Kohlberg, L., & Turiel, E. (1971). Moral development and moral education. In G. S. Lesser (Ed.), *Psychology and educational practice.* Glenview, IL: Scott, Foresman, pp. 410-465.

König, R. (1978). *Emile Durkheim zur Diskussion.* Munich. Hanser.

Kohn, M. (1969). *Class and conformity. A study in values.* Homewood: Dorsey.

Kohn, M. (1973). Occupational experience and psychological functioning: An assessment of reciprocal effects. *American Journal of Sociology 38*, 97-118.

Kohn, M. (1977). *The reciprocal effects of the substantive complexity of work and intellectual flexibility: A longitudinal assessment.* Unpubl. ms., NIMH Bethesda, Maryland.

Kohn, M. (1981). *Persönlichkeit, Beruf und Soziale Schichtung.* Stuttgart: Klett.

Kohn, M. (1982). *On the transmission of values in the family.* Unpubl. ms., Washington.

Kort, U. (1976). *Akademische Bürokratie: Eine empirische Untersuchung über den Einfluss von Organisationsstrukturen auf Konflikte an westdeutschen Hochschulen.* Munich: Verlag Dokumentation.

Krämer-Badoni, T., & Wakenhut, R. (1978a). Theorie der Entwicklungsstufen des moralischen Bewusstseins und interaktionistische Einstellungsforschung: Versuch einer Integration. In L. H. Eckensberger (Ed.), *Entwicklung des moralischen Urteilens.* Saarbrücken: Universitätsdruck, pp. 211-251.

Krämer-Badoni, T., & Wakenhut, R. (1978b). Möglichkeiten der Skalierung von moralischem Urteilsverhalten. In L. H. Eckensberger (Ed.), *Entwicklung des moralischen Urteilens.* Saarbrücken: Universitätsdruck, pp. 379-391.

Krämer-Badoni, T., & Wakenhut, R. (1979). Moralisches Urteil und politische Einstellungen bei unterschiedlichen sozialen Gruppen. In L. H. Eckensberger (Ed.), *Bericht über den 31. Kongress der Deutschen Gesellschaft für Psychologie in Mannheim 1978: Grundlagen und Methoden der Psychologie.* Göttingen: Hogrefe, pp. 313-315.

Krathwohl, D., Bloom, B., & Masia, B. (1964). *Taxonomy of educational objectives. Handbook II: Affective Domain.* New York: McKay Company.

Kudera, S. (1982). *Das Bewusstsein der Deutschen. Empirische Ergebnisse und arbeitssoziologische Argumente zu einigen Interpretationsklischees der Meinungs- und Werteforschung.* Forschungsbericht 82.03, Hochschule der Bundeswehr, Munich.

Kuhlmann, W. (1975). *Reflexion und kommunikative Erfahrung.* Frankfurt: Suhrkamp.

Kuhmerker, L., Mentkowski, M., & Erickson, L. (1981). *Evaluating moral development.* New York: Character Research Press.

Kuhn, D. (1978). Mechanisms of cognitive and social development: One psychology or two? *Human Development 21,* 92-118.

Kuhn, D., Langer, J., Kohlberg, L., & Haan, N. (1977). The development of formal operations in logical and moral judgment. *Genetic Psychology Monographs 95,* 97-188.

Kurtines, W. M., & Greif, E. B. (1974). The development of moral thought: Review and evaluation of Kohlberg's approach. *Psychological Bulletin 81,* 453-470.

Lakatos, I. (1978). *The methodology of scientific research programmes: Vols. 1-2. Philosophical papers* (J. Worwall & G. Currie, Eds.). London: Cambridge University Press.

Lane, R. E. (1962). *Political ideology: Why the American common man believes what he does.* New York: Free Press.

Lane, R. E. (1973). Patterns of political belief. In J. N. Knutson (Ed.), *Handbook of political psychology.* San Francisco: Jossey-Bass, pp. 83-116.

Lange, R. P., et al. (1973). Zur Rolle und Funktion von Bürgerinitiativen in der Bundesrepublik und Westberlin. *Zeitschrift für Parlamentsfragen 4,* 247-286.

Langer, J., Schultz v. Thun, F., & Tausch, R. (1974). *Verständlichkeit in Schule, Verwaltung, Politik, Wissenschaft – mit einem Selbsttrainingsprogramm zur Darstellung von Lehr- und Informationstexten.* Munich: Reinhardt.

Lapsley, D. K., & Serlin, R. C. (1984). On the alleged degeneration on the Kohlbergian research program. *Educational Theory 34,* 157-169.

Lasswell, H. (1951). *The political writings of Harold D. Lasswell.* New York: Free Press.

Lavoie, D., & Culbert (1978). Stages of organization and development. *Human Relations 31,* 417-438.

Lazarsfeld, P. (1959). Latent structure analysis. In S. Koch (Ed.), *Psychology: A study of science* (Vol. 3). New York: McGraw-Hill, pp. 476-543.

Lee, L. C. (1971). The concomitant development of cognitive and moral modes of thought: A test of selected deductions from Piaget's theory. *Genetic Psychology Monographs 83,* 93-146.

Lefcourt, H. (Ed.). (1981). *Research with the locus of control constructs: Vol. 1. Assessment methods.* New York: Academic Press.

Leming, J. (1981). Curricular effectiveness in moral value education. A review of research. *Journal of Moral Education 10*, 147-164.

Lempert, W. (1982). Moralische Urteilsfähigkeit: Ebenen und Stufen, Anwendungsbereiche und Anwendungsbedingungen, Entwicklungspfade und Entwicklungskontexte. *Zeitschrift für Sozialisationsforschung und Erziehungssoziologie 2*, 113-126.

Lenning, O. T., Munday, L. A., Johnson, O. B., Well, A. R., & Brue, E. J. (1974). *The many faces of college success and their nonintellective correlates: The published literature through the decade of the sixties.* (Monograph 14). Iowa City, IA: American College Testing Program.

Lepsius, M. R. (1979). Soziale Ungleichheit und Klassenstrukturen in der Bundesrepublik Deutschland. In H. U. Wehler (Ed.), *Klassen in der europäischen Sozialgeschichte.* Göttingen: Vandenhoeck & Ruprecht, pp. 166-209.

Levine, C. (1979a). The form-content distinction in moral development research. *Human Development 22*, 225-234.

Levine, C. (1979b). Stage acquisition and stage use. An appraisal of stage displacement. *Human Development 22*, 145-164.

Levy-Suhl, M. (1912). Die Prüfung der sittlichen Reife jugendlicher Angeklagter und die Reformvorschläge zum Par. 56 des deutschen Strafgesetzbuches. *Zeitschrift für Psychotherapie*, 146-161 and 232-254.

Lickona, T. (1976). Critical issues in the study of moral development and behavior. In T. Lickona (Ed.), *Moral development and behavior.* New York: Holt, Rinehart and Winston, pp. 3-27.

Liliensiek, P. (1979). *Bedingungen und Dimensionen militärischer Sozialisation.* Frankfurt: Lang.

Lind, G. (1976). Überlegungen und Hinweise zur Auswertung des "Moralisches-Urteil-Tests" (m-u-t). In G. Lind, A. Nielsen, & U. Schmidt (Eds.), *Moralisches Urteil und Hochschulsozialisation: Materialien, Beiträge.* Arbeitsunterlage 40, Projekt Hochschulsozialisation. Mimeo, University of Konstanz, pp. 119-146.

Lind, G. (1978a). Wie misst man moralisches Urteil? Probleme und Möglichkeiten der Messung eines komplexen Konstrukts. In G. Portele (Ed.), *Sozialisation und Moral.* Weinheim: Beltz, pp. 171-201.

Lind, G. (1978b). Der "Moralisches-Urteil-Test" (MUT). Anleitung zur Anwendung und Weiterentwicklung des Tests. In L. H. Eckensberger (Ed.), *Entwicklung des moralischen Urteilens.* Saarbrücken: Universitätsdruck, pp. 359-378.

Lind, G. (1979). Sozialisation versus Selektion: Empirische Nachlese zum Zusammenhang zwischen Moral und Standardisierungsgrad der Umwelt. In G. Lind (Ed.), *Moralische Entwicklung und soziale Umwelt. Bericht des Projekts Hochschulsozialisation.* Mimeo, University of Konstanz, pp. 88-95.

Lind, G. (1980a). Zur Bestimmung des Entwicklungsstandes der moralischen Urteilskompetenz beim Übergang vom Gymnasium auf die Universität. In J. Domnick (Ed.), *Aspekte grundlagenorientierter Bildungsforschung.* Forschungsberichte 18, University of Konstanz, pp. 151-164.

Lind, G. (1980b). *Intraindividuelle Varianzkomponentenzerlegung der Antwortmuster des "Moralisches-Urteil-Tests" (Algorithmus für das Programmsystem KOSTAS).* Arbeitsunterlage 65, Projekt Hochschulsozialisation. Mimeo, University of Konstanz.

Lind, G. (1980c). *Zur Evaluation des Einflusses der politischen Bildung auf den Inhalt und die Struktur moralisch-politischer Orientierungen.* Mimeo, FEoLL, Paderborn.

Lind, G. (1982a). Das Konzept des Experimentellen Fragebogens: Eine Methode zur Erfassung von "subjektiven Theorien"? In H.-D. Dann, W. Humbert, F. Krauser, & K.-C. Tennstädt (Eds.), *Analyse und Modifikation subjektiver Theorien von Lehrern.* Forschungsbericht 43, University of Konstanz, pp. 144-158.

Lind, G. (1982b). Experimentál questionnaires: A new approach to personality research. In A. Kossakowski & K. Obuchowski (Eds.), *Progress in psychology of personality.* Amsterdam: North-Holland, pp. 132-144.

Lind, G. (1984a). Theorie und Validität des "Moralisches-Urteil-Tests." Zur Erfassung kognitiv-struktureller Effekte der Sozialisation. In G. Framhein & J. Langer (Eds.), *Student und Studium im internationalen Vergleich.* Klagenfurt: Kärntner Druck- und Verlagsgesellschaft, pp. 166-187.

Lind, G. (1984b). *Dynamic-structural attitude unit: Concept and measurement.* Paper prepared for the European Symposium on Concept Formation and Measurement, Rome, Sept. 25-29, 1984. Unpubl. ms., University of Konstanz.

Lind, G. (1985a). Growth and regression in cognitive-moral development of young university students. In C. Harding (Ed.), *Moral dilemmas: Philosophical and psychological issues in the development of moral reasoning.* Chicago: Precedent, pp. 99-114.

Lind, G. (1985b). Moral judgment competency and education in democratic society. In P. Weingartner & G. Zecha (Eds.), *Conscience: An interdisciplinary view.* Dordrecht: Reidel.

Lind, G. (1985c). *Moralische Urteilskompetenz und berufliche Ausbildung* (2nd ed.). Arbeitsunterlage 77, Projekt Hochschulsozialisation. Mimeo, University of Konstanz.

Lind, G. (1985d). *Inhalt und Struktur des moralischen Urteilens. Theoretische, methodologische und empirische Untersuchungen zum Urteils- und Demokratieverhalten bei Studierenden.* Bericht des Projekts Hochschulsozialisation. Mimeo, University of Konstanz.

Lind, G. (1985e). Parallelität von Affekt und Kognition in der moralischen Entwicklung. In F. Oser, W. Althof, & D. Garz (Eds.), *Entstehung moralischer Identität, Soziogenese, moralisches Handeln und Schuld.* Munich: Peter Kindt.

Lind, G., Nielsen, A., & Schmidt, U. (1976). *Moralisches Urteil und Hochschulsozialisation: Materialien, Beiträge.* Arbeitsunterlage 40, Projekt Hochschulsozialisation. Mimeo, University of Konstanz.

Lind, G., Sandberger, J.-U., & Bargel, T. (1981-82). Moral judgment, ego-strength and democratic orientations: Some theoretical contiguities and empirical findings. *Political Psychology 3/4,* 70-110.

Lind, G., & Wakenhut, R. (1980). Erfassung von moralischem Urteil mit standardisierten Fragebogen. *Diagnostica 26,* 312-334.

Lippert, E. (1981). Die Ableistung des Wehrdienstes als moralische Entscheidung. In H.-P. Klingemann & M. Kaase (Eds.), *Politische Psychologie. Politische Vierteljahresschrift, Sonderheft 12,* pp. 93-100.

Lippert, E., & Wakenhut, R. (1978). Zur Zentralität von Einstellungen. *Zeitschrift für Soziologie 7,* 87-96.

Lipset, S. M. (1965). University student politics. In S. M. Lipset & S. S. Wohlin (Eds.), *The Berkeley student revolt.* New York: Doubleday, pp. 1-35.

Locke, D. (1983a). Moral reasons and moral action. In H. Weinreich-Haste & D. Locke (Eds.), *Morality in the making.* London: Wiley, pp. 111-124.

Locke, D. (1983b). Theory and practice in thought and action. In H. Weinreich-Haste & D. Locke (Eds.), *Morality in the making.* London: Wiley, pp. 157-170.

Locke, D. (1983c). Doing what comes morally. The relation between behavior and stages of moral reasoning. *Human Development 26,* 11-25.

Lockwood, A. L. (1976). Moral reasoning and public policy debate. In T. Lickona (Ed.), *Moral development and behavior.* New York: Holt, Rinehart and Winston, pp. 317-325.

Loevinger, J. (1957). Objective tests as instruments of psychological theory. *Psychological Reports 9,* 635-694.

Loevinger, J. (1976). *Ego development.* San Francisco: Jossey-Bass.

Löw-Beer, M. (1982). *Selbsttäuschung.* Unpubl. dissertation. University of Frankfurt.

Luckmann, Th. (1979). Phänomenologie und Soziologie. In W. M. Sprondel, & R. Grathoff (Eds.), *Alfred Schütz und die Idee des Alltags in den Sozialwissenschaften.* Stuttgart: Enke, pp. 196-206.

Lumsden, J. (1976). Test theory. *Annual Review of Psychology 27*, 251-280.
Mandl, H., & Huber, G. (Eds.). (1978). *Kognitive Komplexität*. Göttingen: Hogrefe.
Marton, F., & Säljö, R. (1976). On qualitative differences in learning. *British Journal of Educational Psychology 46*, 4-11 and 115-127.
Mayer-Tasch, P. C. (1977). *Die Bürgerinitiativbewegung*. Reinbeck b. Hamburg: Rowohlt.
Mayntz, R. (1970). Role distance, role identification and amoral role behavior. *Archives Européennes de Sociologie 11*, 379-386.
McCarthy, T. A. (1982). Rationality and relativism. In J. B. Thompson, D. Held, & J. Habermas (Eds.), *Critical debates*. Cambridge, MA: MIT Press, pp. 57-78.
McClosky, H. (1964). Consensus and ideology in American politics. *American Political Science Review 58*, 361-382.
Mead, G. H. (1967). *Mind, self and society*. Chicago: University of Chicago Press (orig. publ. 1934).
Meehl, P. E. (1978). Theoretical risks and tabular asterisks: Sir Karl, Sir Ronald, and the slow progress of soft psychology. *Journal of Consulting and Clinical Psychology 46*, 806-834.
Meinefeld, W. (1977). *Einstellung und soziales Handeln*. Reinbeck b. Hamburg: Rowohlt.
Merelman, R. (1969). The development of political ideology: A framework for the analysis of political socialization. *American Political Science Review 63*, 750-767.
Meulemann, H. (1981). Wertwandel, kulturelle Teilhabe und sozialer Wandel. Eine Synopse der Wertewandlungen in der BRD zwischen 1949 und 1980 und ein Ansatz zu ihrer sozialstrukturellen Erklärung. Unpubl. ms., University of Cologne.
Mez, L. (1977). Bürgerprotest und Theorie. *Kursbuch 50*, 101-112.
Miller, G. A., Galanter, E., & Pribram, K. H. (1960). *Plans and the structure of behavior*. New York: Holt, Rinehart and Winston.
Miller, R., & Swanson, G. (1958). *The changing American parent*. New York: Wiley.
Mirels, H. (1970). Dimensions of internal vs. external control. *Journal of Consulting and Clinical Psychology 34*, 226-228.
Mischel, W. (1968). *Personality and assessment*. New York: Wiley.
Möbus, C., & Nagl, W. (1983). Messen, Analyse und Prognose von Veränderungen. In J. Bredenkamp & H. Feger (Eds.), *Hypothesenprüfung*. Göttingen: Hogrefe, pp. 239-470.
Moers, M. (1930). Zur Prüfung des sittlichen Verständnisses Jugendlicher. *Zeitschrift für angewandte Psychologie 34*, 431-511.
Montada, L. (1983). Moralisches Urteil und moralisches Handeln. Gutachten über die Fruchtbarkeit des Kohlberg-Ansatzes. *Wehrpsychologische Untersuchungen* (Vol. 2/83). Bundesministerium der Verteidigung.
Morrison, D. F. (1976). *Multivariate statistical methods* (2nd ed.). New York: McGraw-Hill.
Moscovici, S. (1961). *La psychoanalyse, son image et son publie*. Paris: Presses Universitaires de France.
Moscovici, S. (1973). Foreword. In C. Herzlich (Ed.), *Health and illness. A social psychological analysis*. London: Academic Press, pp. ix-xiv.
Moskos, C. (1981). *Institution versus occupation: Contrasting models of military socialization*. Unpubl. ms.
Mowrer, O. H. (1972). Conscience and unconscious. In R. C. Johnson, P. R. Dodecki & O. H. Mowrer (Eds.), *Conscience, contract, and social reality*. New York: Holt, Rinehart and Winston, pp. 349-371.
Müller-Fohrbrodt, G., & Cloetta, B. (1975). Zur Bedeutung von Einstellungsforschungen für die Sozialisationsforschung im Bereich der Hochschule. In T. Bargel, G. Framhein, L. Huber, & G. Portele (Eds.), *Sozialisation in der Hochschule*. Hamburg: Arbeitsgemeinschaft für Hochschuldidaktik, pp. 196-205.

Müller-Fohrbrodt, G., Cloetta, B., & Dann, H.-D. (1978). *Der Praxisschock bei jungen Lehrern. Formen – Ursachen – Folgerungen. Eine zusammenfassende Bewertung der theoretischen und empirischen Erkenntnisse.* Stuttgart: Klett.

Murphy, J., & Gilligan, C. (1980). Moral development in late adolescence and adulthood: A critique and reconstruction of Kohlberg's theory. *Human Development 23,* 77-104. 23, 77-104.

Neumann, J. (Ed.). (1931). *Die Entwicklung zur sittlichen Persönlichkeit.* Gütersloh: Bertelsmann.

Newcomb, T. (1957). *The personality and social change: Attitude formation in a student community.* New York: Holt, Rinehart and Winston (orig. publ. 1943).

Newcomb, T. (1974). What does college do for a person? Frankly very little. *Psychology Today 8,* 72-80.

Nisan, M. (1984). Content and structure in moral judgment: An integrative view. In W. M. Kurtines & J. L. Gewirtz (Eds.), *Morality, moral behavior and moral development.* New York: Wiley, pp. 208-226.

Noack, R. W. M., & Silbereisen, R. K. (1982). *Jugendsituation. Theoretischer Ansatz zur Analyse jugendspezifischer Umwelten, methodische Zugänge und erste Ergebnisse.* Mimeo, Free University of Berlin.

Nunner-Winkler, G. (1978). Probleme bei der Messung des moralischen Urteils mit standardisierten Verfahren. In L. H. Eckensberger (Ed.), *Entwicklung des moralischen Urteilens.* Saarbrücken: Universitätsdruck, pp. 337-358.

Nunner-Winkler, G. (1980). Struktur und Inhalt politischer Orientierungen. In G. Schmitt (Ed.), *Politische Bildungsprozesse – Ergebnisse der Forschung als Kritik der Praxis?* Tutzing: Akademie für politische Bildung, pp. 221-241.

Nunner-Winkler, G. (1984). Two moralities? A critical discussion of an ethic of care and responsibility versus an ethic of rights and justice. In W. M. Kurtines & J. L. Gewirtz (Eds.), *Morality, moral behavior and moral development.* New York: Wiley, pp. 348-361.

Oerter, R. (1985). *Lebensbewältigung im Jugendalter.* Weinheim: Chemie Verlag.

Offe, C. (1973). Bürgerinitiativen und Reproduktion der Arbeitskraft im Spätkapitalismus. In H. Grossmann (Ed.), *Bürgerinitiativen.* Frankfurt: Fischer, pp. 152 -165.

Olweus, D. (1976). Der moderne Interaktionismus von Person und Situation und seine varianzanalytische Sackgasse. *Zeitschrift für Entwicklungspsychologie und Pädagogische Psychologie 8,* 171-185.

Oser, F. (1981a). *Moralisches Urteil in Gruppen. Soziales Handeln. Verteilungsgerechtigkeit.* Frankfurt: Suhrkamp.

Oser, F. (1981b). Moralische Erziehung als Intervention. *Unterrichtswissenschaft 3,* 207-224.

Oser, F. (1984). Cognitive stages of interaction in moral discourse. In W. M. Kurtines & J. L. Gewirtz (Eds.), *Morality, moral behavior and moral development.* New York: Wiley, pp. 159-174.

Oser, F., & Schläfli, A. (1985). But it does move: The difficulty of gradual change in moral development. In M. Berkowitz & F. Oser (Eds.), *Moral education: Theory and application.* Hillsdale, NJ: Erlbaum, pp. 269-296.

Parker, C. A. (Ed.). (1978). *Encouraging development in college students.* Minneapolis: University of Minnesota.

Pawlik, K. (1976). Ökologische Validität: Ein Beispiel aus der Kulturvergleichsforschung. In G. Kaminski (Ed.), *Umweltpsychologie.* Stuttgart: Klett, pp. 59-72.

Peck, R. F., & Havighurst, R. J. (1962). *The psychology of character development.* New York: Wiley.

Perry, W. (1970). *Forms of intellectual and ethical development in the college years.* New York: Holt, Rinehart and Winston.

Perry, W. (1981). Cognitive and ethical growth: The making of meaning. In A. W. Chickering (Ed.), *The modern American college*. San Francisco: Jossey-Bass, pp. 76-116.

Pfeiffer, D. (1976). *Organisationssoziologie*. Munich: Juventa.

Phillips, D., & Nicolayev, J. (1978). Kohlbergian moral development. A progressing or degenerating research program? *Educational Theory 28*, 286-301.

Piaget, J. (1973). *Erkenntnistheorie der Wissenschaften vom Menschen*. Frankfurt: Ullstein (orig. publ. 1970).

Piaget, J. (1976). *Psychologie der Intelligenz*. Munich: Kindler.

Piaget, J. (1977). *The moral judgment of the child*. Harmondsworth: Penguin (orig. publ. 1932).

Pittel, S. M., & Mendelsohn, G. A. (1966). Measurement of moral values: A review and critique. *Psychological Bulletin 66*, 22-35.

Popper, K. (1968). *The logic of scientific discovery*. London: Hutchinson (orig. publ. 1934).

Portele, G. (1975a). *Lernen und Motivation. Ansätze zu einer Theorie intrinsisch motivierten Lernens*. Weinheim: Beltz.

Portele, G. (1975b). Sozialisation in der Hochschule: Vorschläge für ein Forschungsprogramm und einige fachspezifische Ergebnisse. In T. Bargel, G. Framhein, L. Huber, & G. Portele (Eds.), *Sozialisation in der Hochschule*. Hamburg: Arbeitsgemeinschaft für Hochschuldidaktik, pp. 96-110.

Portele, G. (1978). "Du sollst das wollen!" Zum Paradox der Sozialisation. In G. Portele (Ed.), *Sozialisation und Moral*. Weinheim: Beltz, pp. 147-168.

Portele, G. (1979). Widerspruchsfreiheit und Vollständigkeit als Eigenschaften kognitiver Systeme. In H. Ückert & D. Rhenius (Eds.), *Komplexe menschliche Informationsverarbeitung*. Bern: Huber, pp. 71-79.

Portele, G. (1981). *Entfremdung bei Wissenschaftlern: Soziale Vorstellungen von Wissenschaftlern verschiedener Disziplinen über "Wissenschaft" und "Moral."* Frankfurt: Campus.

Power, C., Higgins, A., Kohlberg, L., & Reimer, J. (In press). *Democracy and schooling: The moral cultures of three democratic schools*. New York: Columbia University Press.

Räder, G., & Wakenhut, R. (1984). *Morality and the military organization*. Paper presented at University College, University of Toronto, June, 1984.

Rawls, J. (1971). *A theory of justice*. Cambridge, MA: Belknap Press.

Reese, H. W., & Overton, W. F. (1970). Models of development and theories of development. In L. R. Goulet & P. B. Baltes (Eds.), *Life-span developmental psychology: Theory and research*. New York: Academic Press, pp. 115-145.

Reinshagen, H. (1978). Forderungen für die Messung des moralischen Urteils mit standardisierten Verfahren. *Diagnostica 24*, 137-145.

Renn, H. (1973). *Die Messung von Sozialisierungswirkungen*. Munich: Oldenbourg.

Rest, J. (1973). The hierarchical pattern of moral judgment: A study of patterns of comprehension and preference of moral stages. *Journal of Personality 41*, 86-109.

Rest, J. (1975). The validity of tests of moral judgment. In J. R. Meyer, B. Burnham, & J. Chovlat (Eds.), *Values education: Theory, practice, problems, prospects*. Waterloo, Ontario: Laurier, pp. 103-116.

Rest, J. (1979a). *Development in judging moral issues*. Minneapolis: University of Minnesota.

Rest, J. (1979b). *The impact of higher education on moral judgment development*. Technical Report, Minnesota Moral Research Project. Mimeo, University of Minnesota.

Rest, J. (1983). Morality. In P. H. Mussen (Ed.), *Handbook of Child Psychology* (Vol. 3). New York: Wiley, pp. 556-629.

Rest, J., Turiel, E., & Kohlberg, L. (1969). Level of moral development as a determinant of preference and comprehension of moral judgment made by others. *Journal of Personality 37*, 225-252.

Riegel, K. (1973). Dialectical operations. *Human Development 16*, 346-370.

Robinson, J. O., & Shaver, P. R. (1973). *Measures of social-psychological attitudes.* Ann-Arbor, Michigan: Survey Research Center.

Rogosa, D., Brandt, D., & Zimowski, M. (1982). A growth curve approach to the measurement of change. *Psychological Bulletin 92*, 726-748.

Rohrmann, B. (1978). Empirische Studien zur Entwicklung von Antwortskalen für die sozialwissenschaftliche Forschung. *Zeitschrift für Sozialpsychologie 9*, 222-245.

Rokeach, M. (1973). *The nature of human values.* London: Free Press.

Rosenberg, M. J., & Hovland, C. I. (1963). Cogitive, affective, and behavioral components of attitudes. In M. J. Rosenberg, C. I. Hovland, W. J. McGuire, & J. W. Brehm (Eds.), *Attitude organization and change: Analysis of consistency among attitude components.* New Haven: Yale University Press, pp. 1-14.

Rotter, J. B. (1966). Generalized expectancies for internal versus external control of reinforcement. *Psychological Monographs 30*, 1-26.

Rudolph, W. (1959). *Die amerikanische "Cultural Anthropology" und das Wertproblem.* Berlin: Duncker & Humboldt.

Sandberger, J.-U. (1979). Zu Struktur und Relevanz von soziopolitischen Grundwerten: Am Beispiel von Abiturienten. In H. Klages & P. Kmieciak (Eds.), *Wertwandel und gesellschaftlicher Wandel.* Frankfurt: Campus, pp. 381-415.

Sandberger, J.-U. (1983). Zwischen Legitimation und Kritik. Vorstellungen von Akademikern, Studenten und Bevölkerung zur sozialen Ungleichheit. *Zeitschrift für Soziologie 12*, 181-202.

Sanford, N. (1962). *The American college.* A psychological and social interpretation of the higher learning. New York: Wiley.

Sanford, N. (1973). Authoritarian personality in contemporary perspective. In J. N. Knutson (Ed.), *Handbook of Political Psychology.* San Francisco: Jossey-Bass, pp. 139-170.

Schaff, A. (1970). *Marxismus und das menschliche Individuum.* Reinbeck bei Hamburg: Rowohlt.

Scharf, P. (1978). *Readings in moral education.* Minneapolis: Winston Press.

Scheler, M. (1973). *Formalism in ethics and non-formal ethics of values* (5th ed.). Translated by M. S. Frings & R. L. Funk. Evanston, IL: Northwestern University Press.

Schenk, M. (1981). *Kommunikationsstrukturen in Bürgerinitiativen.* DFG Projektabschlussbericht. Mimeo, University of Augsburg.

Schenk, M. (1982). *Kommunikationsstrukturen in Bürgerinitiativen. Empirische Untersuchungen zur interpersonellen Kommunikation und politischen Meinungsbildung.* Tübingen: Mohr.

Schlegel, R. (1967). *Completeness in science.* New York: Appleton Century & Crofts.

Schluchter, W. (1979). *Die Entwicklung des okzidentalen Rationalismus. Eine Analyse von Max Webers Gesellschaftsgeschichte.* Tübingen: Mohr.

Schmidt, M. (1981). *Veränderung des moralischen Urteils bei Adoleszenten.* Unpubl. Lizentiatsarbeit, University of Fribourg, Switzerland.

Schmied, D. (1981). Standardisierte Fragebogen zur Erfassung des Entwicklungsstandes der moralischen Urteilskompetenz. *Diagnostica 27*, 51-65.

Schmitt, M. (1982). *Zur Erfassung des moralischen Urteils: Zwei standardisierte objektive Verfahren im Vergleich.* Bericht aus der Arbeitsgruppe "Verantwortung, Gerechtigkeit, Moral," Fachbereich Psychologie. Mimeo, University of Trier.

Schneider, M. (1982). Moralisches Urteil und politisches Argument im Unterricht. In W. Hagemann, H. Heidbrink, & M. Schneider (Eds.), *Kognition und Moralität in politischen Lernprozessen.* Opladen: Leske, pp. 165-186.

Schreiner, G. (1979). Gerechtigkeit ohne Liebe: Autonomie ohne Solidarität? *Zeitschrift für Pädagogik 25*, 505-528.

Schroder, H. M., Driver, M. J., & Streufert, S. (1975). *Menschliche Informationsverarbeitung.* Weinheim: Beltz.

Schütz, A. (1970). Über die mannigfaltigen Wirklichkeiten. In A. Schütz, *Das Problem der sozialen Wirklichkeit: Vol. 1. Gesammelte Aufsätze.* The Hague: Nijhoff.

Schütz, A., & Luckmann, T. (1979). *Strukturen der Lebenswelt* (Vol. 1). Frankfurt: Suhrkamp.

Schuhler, P. (1978). Probleme bei der Erfassung des moralischen Urteils mit offenen und geschlossenen Verfahren. In R. K. Silbereisen (Ed.), *Newsletter Soziale Kognition 2*, 162-168.

Scott, W. A. (1968). Attitude measurement. In G. Lindsey & E. Aronson (Eds.), *Handbook of Social Psychology* (Vol. 2). Reading, MA: Addison-Wesley, pp. 204-273.

Selman, R. L. (1971). The relation of role-taking to moral judgment in children. *Child Development 42*, 79-92.

Selman, R. L. (1976). Social-cognitive understanding: A guide to educational and clinical behavior. In T. Lickona (Ed.), *Moral development and behavior*. New York: Holt, Rinehart and Winston, pp. 299-316.

Selznick, G. J., & Steinberg, S. (1969). *The tenacity of prejudice: Anti-Semitism in contemporary America*. New York: Harper.

Senger, R. (1979). *Die moralische Entwicklung von Offizieren während des Studiums an der Hochschule der Bundeswehr sowie Formen moralischer Segmentierung*. Unpubl. Diplomarbeit, Hochschule der Bundeswehr, Munich.

Shaw, M., & Wright, J. (1967). *Scales for the measurement of attitudes*. New York: McGraw-Hill.

Shweder, R. (1975). How relevant is an individual difference theory of personality? *Journal of Personality 43*, 455-484.

Siegmund, U. (1979). Das moralische Urteilsniveau von religiösen Studentengruppen. In G. Lind (Ed.), *Moralische Entwicklung und soziale Umwelt*. Zentrum I Bildungsforschung. Mimeo, University of Konstanz, pp. 13-21.

Simpson, E. (1976). A holistic approach to moral development and behavior. In T. Lickona (Ed.), *Moral development and behavior*. New York: Holt, Rinehart and Winston, pp. 159-170.

Simpson, E. (1983). Émil's moral development. A Rousseauean perspective on Kohlberg. *Human Development 26*, 198-212.

Spence, L. D. (1981). Moral judgment and bureaucracy. In R. Wilson & G. Schochet (Eds.), *Moral development and politics*. New York: Praeger, 137-171.

Srubar, I. (1979). Die Theorie der Typenbildung bei Alfred Schütz. Ihre Bedeutung und ihre Grenzen. In W. Sprondel & R. Grathoff (Eds.), *Alfred Schütz und die Idee des Alltags in den Sozialwissenschaften*. Stuttgart: Enke, pp. 43-64.

Steinkamp, G. (1980). Klassen- und schichtspezifische Ansätze in der Sozialisationsforschung. In K. Hurrelmann & D. Ulich (Eds.), *Handbuch der Sozialisationsforschung*. Weinheim: Beltz, pp. 253-284.

Stouffer, S. A. (1950). Adjustment during army life. In S. A. Stouffer (Ed.), *Measurement for prediction: Studies in social psychology in World War II* (Vol. 1). Princeton, NJ: Princeton University Press, pp. 155-229.

Streufert, S., & Streufert, S. C. (1978). *Behavior in the complex environment*. Washington: Winston.

Sullivan, E. (1977a). *Kohlberg's structuralism. A critical appraisal*. Monograph Series 15. Toronto: The Ontario Institute for Studies in Education

Sullivan, E. (1977b). A study of Kohlberg's structural theory of moral development: A critique of liberal social science ideology. *Human Development 20*, 352 -376.

Sullivan, E., & Quarter, J. (1972). Psychological correlates of certain postconventional moral types: A perspective on hybride types. *Journal of Personality 40*, 149-161.

Tarski, A. (1966). *Einführung in die mathematische Logik*. Göttingen: Vandenhoek & Ruprecht.

Thomas, W. I., & Thomas, D. S. (1928). *The child in America*. New York: Knopf.

Thurstone, L. L. (1931). The measurement of social attitudes. *Journal of Abnormal and Social Psychology 26*, 249-269.

Tomkins, S. (1965). Affect and the psychology of knowledge. In S. S. Tomkins & C. Izard (Eds.), *Affect, cognition and personality: Empirical studies*. New York: Springer, pp. 72-97.

Touraine, A. (1971). *Die postindustrielle Gesellschaft.* Frankfurt: Suhrkamp.
Treiber, H. (1973). *Wie man Soldaten macht.* Düsseldorf: Bertelsmann.
Trent, J., & Medsker, L. (1968). *Beyond high school: A psychological study of 10,000 high school graduates.* San Francisco: Jossey-Bass.
Triandis, H. C. (1975). *Einstellungen und Einstellungsänderungen.* Weinheim: Beltz.
Turiel, E. (1969). Developmental processes in the child's moral thinking. In P. H. Mussen, J. Langer, & M. Covington (Eds.), *Trends and issues on developmental psychology.* New York: Holt, Rinehart and Winston, pp. 92-133.
Turner, S. (1980). Modelling and evaluating theories involving sequences: Description of a formal method. *Quality and Quantity 14,* 511-518.
Wachtler, G. (1983). Struktur- und Funktionswandel der Streitkräfte. Eine gesellschafts-theoretische Neuorientierung der Militärsoziologie. In W. R. Vogt (Ed.), *Sicherheitspolitik und Streitkräfte in der Legitimitätskrise.* Baden-Baden: Nomos, pp. 59-78.
Wakenhut, R. (1974). *Messung gesellschaftlich-politischer Einstellungen mit Hilfe der Rasch-Skalierung.* Bern: Huber.
Wakenhut, R. (1979). Effects of military service on political socialization of draftees. *Armed Forces and Society 5,* 626-641.
Wakenhut, R. (1981). Sozialisationsforschung und Lebenskundlicher Unterricht. *Dokumentation zur katholischen Militärseelsorge 8,* 48-71.
Wakenhut, R. (1982). *Der Moralisches-Urteil-Fragebogen (M-U-F). Vorläufiges Manual für die Arbeit mit dem M-U-F* (revised ed.). Mimeo, University of Augsburg.
Walker, L. J. (1983). Sources of cognitive conflict for stage transition in moral development. *Developmental Psychology 19,* 103-110.
Walker, L. J. (In press). The hierarchical nature of moral stages. In L. Kohlberg & D. Candee (Eds.), *Research in Moral Development.* Cambridge, MA: Harvard University Press.
Weber, M. (1964). *Wirtschaft und Gesellschaft. Studienausgabe* (Vols. 1-2). Cologne: Kiepenheuer & Witsch.
Weber, M. (1968). *Methodologische Schriften* (J. Winkelmann, Ed.). Frankfurt: Fischer.
Webster, H., Freedman, M., & Heist, P. (1962). Personality changes in college students. In N. Sanford (Ed.), *The American college.* New York: Wiley, pp. 811-846.
Weinreich, H. (1975). Kohlberg and Piaget: Aspects of their relationship in the field of moral development. *Journal of Moral Education 4,* 201-213.
Weinreich-Haste, H., & Locke, D. (Eds.). (1983). *Morality in the making.* London: Wiley.
Werner, H. (1957). The concept of development from a comparative and organismic point of view. In D. B. Harris (Ed.), *The concept of development.* Minneapolis: University of Minnesota Press, pp. 125-148.
White, R. W. (1959). Motivation reconsidered. The concept of competence. *Psychological Review, 66,* 297-333.
Whiteley, J. M. (1980). Extracurricular influences on the moral development of college students. *New Directions for Higher Education 31,* 45-50.
Williams, B. (1985). *Ethics and the limits of philosophy.* Cambridge, MA: Harvard University Press.
Wilson, G. (1975). Attitude. In *Encyclopedia of Psychology* (Vol. 1). London: Fontana, pp. 95-97.
Wilson, T. (1971). Normative and interpretative paradigms in sociology. In J. Douglas (Ed.), *Understanding everyday life.* London: Routledge and Kegan Paul, pp. 57-79.
Wischka, B. (1982). *Moralisches Bewusstsein und Empathie bei Straftätern.* Unpubl. Diplomarbeit, University of Marburg.
Zängle, W. (1978). *Einführung in die politische Sozialisationsforschung.* Paderborn: Schöningh.
Zentrale Dienstvorschrift 12/1. (1973). Politische Bildung. Bonn: Bundesminister der Verteidigung.

Zentrum I Bildungsforschung an der University of Konstanz (1973). Sozialisation in Bildungsinstitutionen. *Zeitschrift für Pädagogik 6,* 849-855.

Zigler, E. (1963). Metatheoretical issues in developmental psychology. In M. Marx (Ed.), *Theories in contemporary psychology.* New York: Macmillan, pp. 341-369.

Zilessen, H. (1974). Bürgerinitiativen im repräsentativen Regierungssystem. In *Beilage zur Wochenzeitung "Das Parlament,"* March 23, 3-22.

Index of Names

Index of Subjects